MEXICO
Adventures in Nature

Brad Wetzler

Text and Photography
by Ron Mader

JOHN MUIR PUBLICATIONS
SANTA FE, NEW MEXICO

John Muir Publications, P.O. Box 613, Santa Fe, New Mexico 87504

Printed in Canada.
First edition. First printing September 1998.

Library of Congress Cataloging-in Publication Data
Mader, Ron, 1963–
    Mexico : adventures in nature / Ron Mader.
        p.   cm.
    Includes index.
    ISBN 1-56261-340-5
    1. Mexico—Guidebooks. 2. Natural history—Mexico—Guidebooks.
    3. Outdoor recreation—Mexico—Guidebooks. I. Title.
    F1209.M25   1998
    917.204'836—DC21   98-6815
                                        CIP

Editors: Dianna Delling, Elizabeth Wolf, Chris Hayhurst
Graphics Editor: Tom Gaukel
Production: Janine Lehmann
Design: Janine Lehmann
Cover Design: Janine Lehmann
Typesetting: Kathleen Sparkes
Maps: Kathleen Sparkes, White Hart Design—Albuquerque, NM USA
Printer: Transcontinental, Inc., Quebec, Canada
Cover Photos:
    Front cover, large: © Fridmar Damm/Leo de Wys Inc. (Sierra de Miahuatlan)
    Front cover, small: © Dede Gilman/Photo Network
    Back cover, large: © Grace Davies/Photo Network (Mayan Ruins at Tulum)
    Back cover, small: © Mark Newman/Photo Network
Title page photo: Mission church, Satevó, Chihuahua—Brad Wetzler
All interior photos by Ron Mader except where noted.

Distributed to the book trade by
Publishers Group West
Berkeley, California

ACKNOWLEDGMENTS

Perhaps the greatest pleasure in writing a book is the time in which one pauses and reflects on the encouragement and advice of others which have made such an effort possible. I would like to thank my parents, John and Barbara Mader, whose love of travel and education was contagious. Tom Buckley offered a place to stay in the Centro Histórico of D.F. during my visits and was instrumental in helping me understand Mexican history.

Via the Eco Travels in Latin America website, I've met a number of souls who I look forward to meeting in real life. A number of academics have shared a great deal of info, including Bob Healy, Roger Steeb, Molly Molloy, Dean Hendrickson, Axel Kersten, David Bray, and Scott Walker. Thanks also to Josue Ybarra Rossow and Leo Medellin, who host their own exceptional websites from northern Mexico. Special kudos to Andrea Kaus, whose interest in local participation made me reevaluate what "participation" means. Finally, it wouldn't have been possible to create these linkages without the help of my Austin friend Bill Christensen, who maintains these electronic labyrinths as an authentic "green builder."

This book wouldn't have come about if it weren't for a friendship with Richard Mahler. I reviewed his book *Guatemala: A Natural Destination* (now published as *Guatemala: Adventures in Nature*) in November of 1995. At that time, I was pleased to discover a nature-friendly travel guide, and I'm pleased to contribute to this series. Meanwhile, I also struck up a conversation with the venerable Carl Franz and Lorena Havens of *The People's Guide to Mexico*. Many thanks to these new friends.

Many thanks to the writers of previous Mexico books that have inspired me—notably Herb and Carla Felsted, Joe Cummings, Mike Nelson, T.P. Ramamoorthy, Tim Burford, and Lane Simonian. In assisting with travels in Mexico, I want to thank the now defunct Miami office of the Mexican Tourism Bureau, notably Cidlali Treviño and Benito Echeveria. For other travel assistance, thanks to Bobby and David Settles and Arturo Gonzalez.

I have a number of Mexican friends, most of whom are committed to conservation and love exploring their own country: Rogelio Ballesteros, Jorge Chavez de la Peña, Hector Ceballos, Raul Marco del Pont, Enrique Beltran Gutierrez, Hugo Guillen, Febo Suarez, and Marcos Lazcano.

These individuals give me great hope that true cross-border dialogues are being formed that will foster successful conservation efforts.

Special kudos to Jorge and Johannes Werner, Paul Sherman, and Les Beletsky in initial editing, and to Deborah McLaren, Maria Araujo, Ian and Margo Baldwin, Tim Dunn, Phil Crossley, Melissa Biggs, Anthony Wright, Blanca Robleda, Ronald Nigh, and Mark Stevenson for insightful comments. I would be terribly inconsiderate if I didn't mention my gratitude for the advice and editing skills of Dianna Delling at John Muir Publications in Santa Fe, New Mexico.

CONTENTS

CONTENTS

CONTENTS

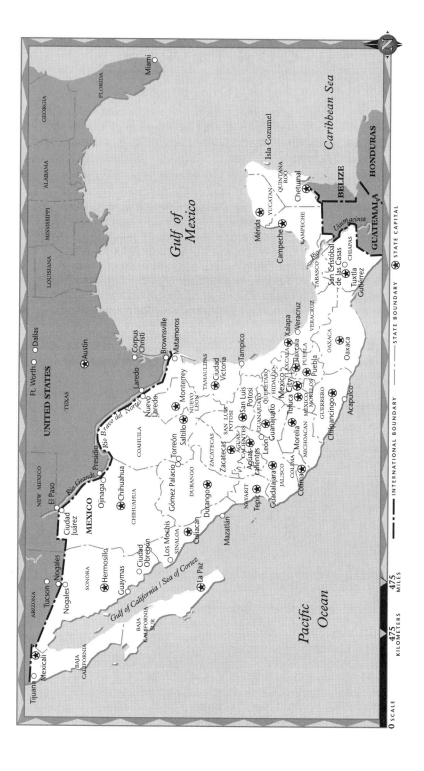

N

Miami

GEORGIA

FLORIDA

Caribbean Sea

ALABAMA

Gulf of Mexico

HONDURAS

MISSISSIPPI

Isla Cozumel

BELIZE

QUINTANA ROO

Chetumal

LOUISIANA

YUCATÁN

Mérida

CAMPECHE

Campeche

GUATEMALA

Usumacinta

Río

TABASCO

CHIAPAS

San Cristóbal de las Casas

Ft. Worth

Dallas

Corpus Christi

Brownsville

Tuxtla Gutiérrez

UNITED STATES

Austin

Matamoros

Tampico

Xalapa

Tlaxcala

Veracruz

TEXAS

Laredo

Ciudad Victoria

Puebla

VERACRUZ

OAXACA

Nuevo Laredo

Monterrey

TAMAULIPAS

México City

PUEBLA

MORELOS

Oaxaca

Río Bravo del Norte

NEW MEXICO

Presidio

NUEVO LEÓN

San Luis Potosí

QUERÉTARO

Toluca

HIDALGO

GUERRERO

Acapulco

El Paso

Ojinaga

Chihuahua

COAHUILA

Saltillo

SAN LUIS POTOSÍ

GUANAJUATO

MÉXICO

Chilpancingo

Rio Grande

Ciudad Juárez

MEXICO

CHIHUAHUA

Gómez Palacio

Torreón

ZACATECAS

Zacatecas

AGUAS-CALIENTES

León

Guanajuato

Morelia

MICHOACÁN

ARIZONA

Tucson

Nogales

Hermosillo

DURANGO

Durango

Aguas-calientes

JALISCO

COLIMA

Nogales

SONORA

Guaymas

Los Mochis

SINALOA

Culiacán

NAYARIT

Tepic

Guadalajara

Colima

Mexicali

Ciudad Obregón

Mazatlán

BAJA CALIFORNIA

Tijuana

Gulf of California / Sea of Cortez

La Paz

BAJA CALIFORNIA SUR

Pacific Ocean

0 SCALE

475 KILOMETERS

475 MILES

INTERNATIONAL BOUNDARY

STATE BOUNDARY

★ STATE CAPITAL

WHY MEXICO?

Perhaps no other country in the world is as tourist-friendly as Mexico. The country has an excellent system of ground-, air-, and sea-based transportation, tens of thousands of hotel rooms, and cuisine that is world-famous for its flavor and diversity. Biologists call Mexico a "megadiversity country" because of its incredible variety and abundance of flora and fauna. The country is home to almost every kind of ecological habitat on Earth, making it the perfect destination for travelers interested in nature and the environment.

Environmental awareness and tourism, however, have yet to tread the same path. Environmental tourism in Mexico is like the famed Copper Canyon, a gorge in Chihuahua deeper than the Grand Canyon in the United States, with conservation marooned on one side and tourism on the other. Sometimes it appears that there's no bridge across the abyss.

Perhaps it's the hybrid origin of "ecotourism" that makes each side distrust the concept. Conservationists shudder when tourism leaders brand amusement parks as ecotourism destinations. Likewise, when environmentalists devise complicated eco-trips that tour operators can't book, the operators see ecotourism as nothing more than utopian whimsy.

Until recently, most of Mexico's protected areas and biosphere reserves were simply off-limits to tourism. Either the government tried to keep areas "tourist-free" because of the lack of park guides, or the

*Charreadas, Mexico's own brand of rodeo, is also the
national sport according to a 1933 presidential decree.*

areas themselves were too remote to attract visitors. But in the early
1990s organized tours and individual travelers discovered and raved
about the natural wonders of Mexico. Whether to watch birds or whales,
people began visiting the great outdoors to experience the diversity and
beauty of nature. Tourism providers discovered the accompanying economic benefits of offering natural-history tours, and communities began
to see that ecotourism offered the potential to expand their income base.

Given the diversity of Mexico's wildlife and natural attractions, a
broader approach to tourism in the country makes sense. Although
Mexico has enjoyed great success as a tourism market, the majority of
the country's promotions highlight mass tourism, which generally has
been environmentally and culturally insensitive. Estuaries and mangroves have been filled in for golf courses. Forests have been cut down
without the benefit of reforestation programs. "Non-governmental"
organizations run by former or current government officials have taken
money for the administration of the programs and invested very little of
the capital in rural areas.

No one can deny that, in terms of tourism, Mexico is the most successful country in Latin America. Its coastal megaresorts receive the

lion's share of visitors. Cancún receives close to 3 million visitors each year; Puerto Vallarta sees another 2 million. According to the government's secretariat of tourism, SECTUR, tourism is the Mexico's third-largest industry. It generates roughly $7 billion a year, third-highest behind only the petroleum industry and the border industrial plants known as *maquiladoras*. In 1996 Mexico received nearly 22 million visitors, making the country seventh in the world for in-bound tourism.

The current flood of visitors is a far cry from 1929, when just 20,000 tourists visited Mexico. Tourism became fashionable in the late 1940s, then again in the 1960s and 1970s. Whether the country was popularized by classic Gene Autry movies or *The People's Guide to Mexico* (Carl Franz, John Muir Publications), Mexico seemed to offer something for everyone.

In 1974 the government set up FONATUR (the National Fund for Tourism Development), which has since become synonymous with Mexico's megaprojects. By 1989 FONATUR had financed 128,000 new hotel rooms and had an annual advertising budget of $30 million. What did it advertise? Its new rooms! Discount airfares from major U.S. cities often make flights to Cancún less expensive than those to Miami. But until recently, FONATUR has focused exclusively on catering to the masses. Today, state and local government offices are promoting lesser-known destinations with a newfound environmental sensitivity. Recent arrangements between the nation's ecology secretariat (SEMARNAP) and SECTUR also promote responsible ecotourism.

Mexican people are learning that tourism can be developed in ways that help rather than hurt their communities. The town of Cuatro Ciénegas, for example, is located near a reserve filled with beautiful, rare, and endangered white gypsum dunes. It is one of only three places in the world with such a landscape, yet until last year the dunes were being mined for industrial use. With help from the state environmental department, Cuatro Ciénegas mayor Susan Moncada closed the dunes to further excavation, but the town needs an alternative revenue-producing business. Your visit will help convince the townspeople their leaders made the right decision.

Cuatro Ciénegas is just one town among many ecologically important areas in Mexico. As the strength of the nation's ecotourism industry grows, such areas will stand a better chance of survival. Of course, for ecotourism in Mexico to become a reality, travelers must know what the country has to offer. This book is the first and most comprehensive guide for the independent traveler who wishes to explore the natural diversity found in Mexico.

A BRIEF HISTORY OF MEXICO

THE OLMEC, MAYA, AND AZTEC CIVILIZATIONS

Thousands of year ago there were no people in the Americas. So the native flora and fauna were in for a shock when wandering humans crossed the Bering Strait on a land bridge now submerged under Arctic waters. This event took place more than 20,000 years ago and forever changed the face of a continent that native peoples throughout history have named "Turtle Island."

The landscape in what is present-day Mexico underwent another radical change when native people domesticated maize around 9,000 B.C. and established subsistence agriculture about 2,000 years later. Small villages soon emerged along Mexico's southern shores in areas now known as Veracruz, Tabasco, and the Yucatán; and, by 1500 to 1000 B.C., the Olmecs had established the cradle of Mesoamerican civilization, based in San Lorenzo on the Gulf of Mexico.

Who were the Olmecs? While scholars debate the history of a people without a written language, the archaeological record places the Olmec heartland around the Bay of Campeche. But the Olmec art style is found throughout Mesoamerica, demonstrating the widespread dissemination of their culture. The Olmecs greatly influenced contemporary as well as successive Mesoamerican civilizations. Subsequent civilizations subscribed in particular to the Olmecs' belief that a king's power derived from and was legitimized by his access to supernatural deities.

The Maya were influenced by their Olmec predecessors and maintained that culture's philosophy of kingship. Although the Maya never built an empire—in fact, the autonomous city-states often feuded—they established cosmopolitan centers in the Yucatán and Chiapas around 800 B.C. Their civilization was one of the few in the world that had developed a system of writing, with which they recorded battles and successions of power. Although their cities collapsed—due in part to ecological deterioration—the Maya deserve respect for developing the tools that permitted these cities to flourish for a thousand years.

Around 300 B.C. an indigenous group migrated to the Valley of Mexico, north of present-day Mexico City. Within a few centuries they constructed the metropolis and the giant pyramids of Teotihuacán. Who they were remains a mystery, while some experts suggest they were Otomis. By A.D. 350 the population numbered 200,000, making Teotihuacán the largest city in the world at the time. From A.D. 650 to 850 the city declined and was finally sacked and burned. At the same time, other great centers collapsed—all in some part because of environmental destruction.

In the 14th and 15th centuries the Aztecs created a vast empire whose boundaries stretched north to the region controlled by the Huastecs (present-day San Luis Potosí and Veracruz) and south to the land ruled by the Mixtecs (present-day Oaxaca).

The Aztec god Huitzilopochtli, whose name means "hummingbird on the left," was said to have been born at Coatepec (Serpent Hill) near Tula. Legend says that Coatlicue was sweeping the temple when she discovered a ball of feathers. She placed it in her dress and it disappeared. She then discovered that she had become pregnant. When Coatlicue's daughter Coyolxauhqui discovered this, she conspired with her 400 brothers to kill her mother. When Coatlicue was slain, Huitzilopochtli emerged, fully armed. He immolated his sister Coyolxauhqui and slew his 400 brothers. Huitzilopochtli became the sun god, his sister the moon goddess, and his 400 brothers the stars, which disappear every morning in the bright sunlight.

The Aztecs thus identified with the sun, which had to defeat the powers of darkness in the underworld each night before it could rise again. The Aztecs believed in sacrifice and warfare—both were means of shedding blood to ensure the sun's return. Consequently, the ruler was obliged to spill a requisite amount of human blood to propitiate the gods. Instead of killing their enemies, Aztec warriors brought their victims home alive, where they were then sacrificed in ritual ceremonies.

In only two centuries, the Aztecs rose from a wandering tribe to the rulers of an enormous empire. Throughout their history they believed their destiny to be one of cosmic significance. When they arrived in the Valley of Mexico, the Aztecs moved from place to place until they came upon a series of promising omens: a juniper tree with a spring gushing underneath it, a group of white willows without a single green leaf, and white water snakes. The priests believed that they had discovered the promised land and founded the city of Tenochtitlán.

During the reign of the first Aztec rulers, the city paid tribute to the wealthier nearby cities. But soon the Aztecs' vision of cosmic superiority led to the expansion of the empire. One of the earliest towns it conquered was Xochimilco, a place renowned for its architects. The Aztecs ordered these architects to construct a causeway between Tenochtitlán and the mainland. Xochimilco's causeways, or raised gardens, provided the food for the fast-growing empire. Meanwhile, the humble temple was expanded time after time in order to honor the gods.

THE ENCOUNTER

In the late 1400s Christopher Columbus initiated his journey in search of valuable spices in India. Only the Spanish persist in calling the 1492 arrival in the New World the "Discovery." In Mexico, the event is more appropriately referred to as the "Encounter." Regardless of the semantics, two worlds collided, and Mexico was at the center of global change.

Twenty-seven years after Columbus made the initial European contact with the New World, in 1519, Spanish conquistadors led by Hernán Cortés arrived on a Veracruz beach. After a bloody war, Cortés and an army of Indian allies conquered the Aztec empire and imprisoned the Aztec king, Moctezuma. Within a decade the Spaniards had carried out some of their most violent acts in the subjugation of the Aztec empire, later killing Moctezuma himself. Today the conquest (1519–1521) is depicted in the Diego Rivera murals at the National Palace in Mexico City.

The Spanish took the Aztec Templo Mayor apart piece by piece and constructed their center of government in its place. This fateful decision to build what would become the world's largest city in a valley prone to earthquakes would have dire environmental consequences in years to come. The Spanish began to drain the lagoons and canals surrounding the city, destroying the majority of the raised gardens that provided the empire with its crops. They ruled Mexico until the early 1800s, when revolutionary fever stirred throughout the country. In 1810 the priest of Dolores issued El Grito (The Cry), which even now is reenacted every year on September 16. In 1821 Mexico declared its independence, and Spain's viceroy agreed to the terms.

MEXICAN INDEPENDENCE

The next century spun out a series of presidents and rebellions, invasions by France and the United States, and the beginning of Mexico's Revolution. France's Emperor Maximilian, who arrived in Mexico City in 1864, ruled the nation for three years from Chapultepec Castle. But Maximilian's reign was short-lived, for when Napoleon II withdrew the French troops, he was executed by the Mexicans.

In 1876 General Porfirio Díaz was elected president. He learned how to manipulate the ballot box well enough to be reelected again and again until finally, in 1911, he was ousted from power. The presidency of Porfirio Díaz was a period of authoritarian rule. Marked by significant architectural and engineering advancements, much of it funded by foreign treasuries, the period is referred to as the "Porfiriato." Díaz's iron-fisted control, the expansion of large rural estates encroaching on communal lands, and limited access to political participation for the burgeoning middle class all contributed to the 1910–1920 Mexican Revolution.

While politically this was a period of corruption and tyranny, Díaz' reign was not without its merits, some environmental in nature. He supported the work and followed the recommendations of forestry expert

Miguel Angel de Quevedo, who campaigned to create more public parks in Mexico City. He also promoted the use of reforestation and forest protection to safeguard Mexico's scarce water resources. In his work, Quevedo noted a major difference between Mexico and its North American neighbors. Unlike Canada and the United States, which enjoyed rainfall on a regular basis, Mexico's link to tropical systems resulted in cycles of dry spells and heavy rains. Forests were a remedy to prevent both flooding and droughts.

Mexico City was at particular risk. During the summer rains the valley often flooded. There are markers on the older buildings in the Centro Histórico of Mexico City which indicate that floodwater levels reached up to 10 meters (33 feet) high. To prevent such floods, Porfirio initiated the gigantic *desagüe* project, which drained the majority of the former lakes in the Valley of Mexico so that when the heavier rains did fall, water was diverted from the city center.

CONSERVATION IN THE 20TH CENTURY

President Lázaro Cárdenas (1934–1940) implemented Mexico's most progressive program, the *ejido* system of communal farming communities, and expropriated the oil industry from U.S. and European companies. Like Díaz did before him, Cárdenas asked conservationist Miguel Angel de Quevedo for help on the environmental front. Cárdenas was no saint and admitted to Quevedo that as governor of Michoacán he had been inattentive to environmental issues. The forests had been denuded and springs had dried up. Quevedo wasn't discouraged. As the new head of the country's environmental department and with more political power than ever, he made forest conservation and reforestation his top priorities. Because of Quevedo's recommendations, the government created 40 national parks and seven reserves.

Conservation took a back seat from the 1940s to the 1960s as Mexico made industrialization its top priority. In contrast to the actions of Cárdenas, presidents during this period created a total of only seven national parks. Fortunately, in this period environmentalists did work toward creating a number of world-famous institutions. In 1952 Enrique Beltrán created the Mexican Institute of Renewable Natural Resources (IMERNAR), which analyzes environmental problems.

In the late 1960s and early 1970s environmental awareness grew at a tremendous pace throughout the world. Mexican environmentalists created environmental centers, several which exist to this day. They include

7

the Center for Ecodevelopment (1972), now the Center for Environment and Development, or CECODES; and Veracruz' Institute of Ecology (1974).

In the late 1980s the terrible contamination of Mexico City could no longer be ignored. Protests against pollution and government inaction engaged a diverse section of the population. There were street protests, angry letters to the editors of the city's largest papers, and an intellectual backlash. One of Mexico's most famous environmental groups, Grupo de Cien (1985), led by novelist and poet Homero Aridjis, was created at this time, precisely to speak out against the development-at-all-costs policy—particularly at the cost of environmental well-being. This group, now whittled down to Homero and his wife Betty—perhaps Grupo de los Dos would be a more accurate name—continues to be an influential voice of environmental conscience.

Also in the 1980s, during the De la Madrid administration, Mexico created its first national environmental department (SEDUE). In 1988, at the end of De la Madrid's term, the country passed the watershed General Law of Ecological Equilibrium. That same year, in a contested presidential election, Carlos Salinas was elected president.

Salinas has a poor—and deservedly so—reputation in Mexico. But during his tenure Salinas transformed the Secretariat of Urban Development and Ecology (SEDUE) into the Secretariat of the Environment (SEDESOL) and gave the agency greater responsibilities.

The Mexico City government implemented the "One Day without a Car" program in 1989 that first requested, then ordered, every automobile owner in Mexico City to desist from driving for one working day a week. The program has been a mixed success. Automobile sales set records in 1991 and 1992; some speculate that wealthier residents simply purchased a second car to circumvent the law. (To avoid fines in Mexico City, see the chart of no-driving days in Chapter 5.)

In 1990 Salinas banned commercial harvesting of sea turtles. A year later Mexico signed onto the Convention on International Trade in Endangered Species (CITES), which monitors trade and declares which species are threatened or in danger of extinction. Before Salinas left office, Conservation International presented him with an "Environmentalist of the Year" award.

In retrospect, one might question the long-term damage Salinas' economic policies caused the environment. Within days after he left office in 1994, the peso was devalued, falling to less than half its original value in just a few weeks.

Mexico's current president, first elected in 1994, is Ernesto Zedillo. Like his predecessor, he transformed the country's environmental agency. SEDESOL became SEMARNAP, a full-fledged Secretariat for

An outdoor market in the city of Tequila

the Environment, Natural Resources, and Fisheries. The major change
in this most recent restructuring was that all of the natural resource
ministries were merged into one organization, and the budget of the
National Ecology Institute (Instituto Nacional de Ecologia, or INE)
was doubled. Mexico's General Law for Ecological Equilibrium was
revised in 1997. The objectives of the legislation are to turn the focus
toward "sustainable development," promote decentralization of environmental responsibilities from federal to state governments, and open
the door for citizen participation. Under this new law, SEMARNAP is
charged with creating a public information system with inventories of
natural resources, atmospheric emissions, and environmental permits.
While this is an improvement over the 1988 law, it still allows the government various means to deny citizens access to information.

The 1990s will also be remembered as a time of continuing citizen
involvement in environmental and societal changes. On Columbus Day in
1992, a day that marked 500 years since the Encounter, protesters marched
to the statue of Columbus (known in Spanish as Cristóbal Colón) across
from the Holiday Inn and splashed paint on the great "discoverer's" face.
Then they dug up the flowers planted in the garden surrounding the statue
and ceremoniously carried them west to the next monument on Paseo de la

9

Reforma, one honoring Moctezuma, the last Aztec king. Performers who ordinarily banged on drums, or *tambores*, for tourists strode down the street, reclaiming the day for the indigenous population of the Americas.

ENVIRONMENTAL TEAMWORK

In 1996 President Ernesto Zedillo announced that SEMARNAP's portion of the budget for protected areas would increase from 8 million to 21 million pesos (almost $3 million). With commitments from the World Bank and non-governmental organizations (NGOs), the total budget for operation of national parks, biosphere reserves, and areas set aside for the protection of flora and fauna was 50 million pesos a year for 1997–98.

Unfortunately, the large multinational institutions involved in the funding have a mixed reputation in Mexico. The World Bank has had more projects collapse in Mexico than in any other country, although both government and non-governmental organizations are reluctant ever to admit failure. Top-down environmental strategies have unwittingly displaced local peoples and concentrated power within the elite.

Success will be measured by the ability of Mexico's poor to succeed in a changing marketplace without destroying the environment. Economist David Barkin notes that the *campesino* farmers, judged to be inefficient by the standards of a modern economy, have developed the technology to provide basic goods and services. "It is extraordinary to learn about the vast variety of products that are produced in a typical Mexican cornfield," he writes. "There are more than 50 useful products which people use in their daily existence harvested from the *milpa*. In a modern cornfield, only one product is produced: corn to be consumed by animals and, incidentally, by Mexicans."

DECENTRALIZATION: MEXICO'S FEDERALISM

One of the major building blocks of President Zedillo's political platform is the decentralization of the federal government. This "new federalism" transfers powers and authorities from the federal government to the states and municipalities. Although the concept is enshrined in the Mexican Constitution, previous presidents have paid little more than lip service to it. Mexico City and the presidency have long been the hub of power, finance, and authority in the country—and therefore the targets of widespread suspicion among Mexicans. If the transfer of responsibility and funding to the states takes place, it will be one of the most significant events in Mexican history.

SEMARNAP has repeatedly pressed for the decentralization of the management of protected areas. Often state and local governments have complained to the federal government that the centralized approach did not take into account regional issues and needs.

In 1995, SEMARNAP signed an agreement declaring that six national parks in the State of Mexico would be decentralized, citing the lack of financial resources and the necessity for local administration of more natural areas. All of the parks were less than 600 hectares (1,482 acres) in area, except Parque Nacional Nevado de Toluca, which has 51,000 hectares (126,000 acres).

In December 1996, SEMARNAP announced that another 14 national parks would be decentralized and that the states would have authority. This is in line with the strategy of the secretariat's 1995–2000 Action Plan. Parks included Baja California's Sierra de San Pedro Mártir and Nayarit's Isla Isabel. In another move to decentralize, control of the huge Calakmul International Biosphere Reserve in the state of Campeche was turned over to a management team consisting of state and local governments and representatives from Pronatura, an environmental group.

It's too early to gauge the direction or success of such decentralization programs, but indigenous groups in Mexico now have a greater voice in the protection of their traditional lands. Furthermore, the belief that local communities know best how to manage protected areas such as biosphere reserves is gaining acceptance worldwide. The present-day Maya were involved in the creation of the Yum Balam Reserve, the Huicholes at Wirikuta in San Luis Potosí, the Papagos in the expanded biosphere reserve of El Pinacate y Gran Desierto de Altar in Sonora, and the Seris in managing Isla Tiburón.

However, decentralization still has a long way to go. The demand for greater local authority was a root cause of the Zapatista insurrection in 1994. Mestizo and indigenous peoples alike continue to complain that decisions affecting their environment are still being made in Mexico City rather than in their own communities.

THE MEXICAN ECONOMY

Mexico has a population of 95 million people and an average annual income of $4,000 (compared with $25,800 in the United States). There are grave disparities between Mexico's richest and poorest citizens. According to a 1991 United Nations Development Program report, the life expectancy for the poorest Mexicans is 53 years—20 years less than the average for the richest Mexicans.

The 1994 financial crisis that devalued the Mexican peso by more than half continues to have severe repercussions on the country's economy. The government initially believed that the slowing of capital inflows and the rising pressure on the peso that started in 1994 was a temporary phenomenon. The Mexican Treasury Department (Hacienda) reassured foreign investors that they would be able to maintain the exchange rate within their pre-determined level of exchange and raised interest rates to attract inflows. The authorities also shifted the composition of domestic public debt from peso-denominated securities (*cetes*) to dollar-indexed securities (*tesobonos*), which transferred the exchange rate risk from investors to the government. The government hoped that, in time, structural reforms would lead to stronger productivity and enable the economy to grow out of the account imbalance. But the recession has been much more severe than initially expected.

The banking system continues to be a source of concern. While bank restructuring has kept the system from going under, portfolios continue to deteriorate. By the end of 1995 past-due amounts had risen to about 18 percent of bank loans. By United States accounting standards, overdue loans rose to almost one-third of total bank loans. Debtors have formed associations to protest the increase in the interest on their loans.

"La Crisis," as it is known in Mexico, has prompted numerous protest marches as well as a comic book of the same name. Predicting the future is a risky endeavor, but every Mexican president's *sexenio* (six-year term) enjoys a rosier middle period, and the final years of President Zedillo's term in office should be much more stable than the beginning. Also, banks have accepted international accounting standards and will have to be more honest about loan approval procedures and property assessments. If one of the reasons for Mexico's economic problems was the lack of open records, this has been corrected.

With its course charted, the government continues to focus on liberalizing the trade and financial sector as well as promoting privatization, deregulation, and tax reform.

ENVIRONMENTAL BUSINESS

Environmental business is a fast-growing industry in Mexico. Twenty years ago it was assumed that the government or the development banks would fund water treatment plants, but Mexico is turning toward private business and investment, offering concessions to companies that invest in Mexico. New wastewater treatment plants, filters for polluting smokestacks, and facilities to dispose of hazardous waste are being constructed throughout the country.

Business consortiums and institutions with vested interests tout the billion-dollar potential of this market. For example, in 1996 Mexico City Mayor Oscar Espinosa announced a $1.5-billion plan to improve air quality in the nation's metropolis. The plan promotes economic incentives, new

The Ejido System

One of the factors that fueled the Mexican Revolution was that concentrated land ownership left most farmers without their own land. President Lázaro Cárdenas (1934-1940) created the ejido system by turning over large estates to communities of peasant farmers. Today collectively owned ejidos comprise 60 percent of Mexico's territory. Even more stunning, the ejidos form the basis of 90 percent of the country's parks and reserves. Farming may still take place in the ejidos, so don't be surprised to find corn growing or cattle ranching in a national park. It may be hard to tell if you're in an ejido—the areas are notoriously poorly marked.

Despite the fact that ejidos own much of the land in protected areas, the government has been slow to promote local conservation control within the ejidos, choosing instead to fund more glamorous international efforts. Needless to say, it can be disconcerting to ejido residents when international environmental groups come flying or driving expensive four-wheel-drive vehicles into the "parks"—their homes—when they can't get any form of rural development assistance. New government strategies seek to give more control to the local farmers, but so far technical assistance and financial credit still have to find their way into rural Mexico.

In many of the parks, the local farmers (ejidarios) control access to protected areas. You may be asked to pay a small admission fee. In San Nicolás Park in Mexico City, the ejido is counting on ecotourism to pay for some of its conservation efforts. Likewise, Cenote Cristal is run by the ejido outside of the Tulum ruins in the Yucatán. The Mexican government is now entrusting these communities with implementing conservation strategies.

If your interests lean toward medicinal plants or agroecology, you couldn't ask for better tour guides than these farmers. Many of these projects are new, so be patient as the ejidarios are just learning the ropes of the tourism business.

technologies, and environmental education. Over the next four years an additional $10-billion investment will be required. Stay tuned to find out if Mexico finds the necessary investment sources to achieve its goals. Previous results have fallen short of initial projections.

The truth is that while green investments and environmental efficiency may be cost-effective in the long run, environmental businesses stumble over short-term financing problems and inadequate information concerning green technologies.

The opportunities are endless and stretch from high-tech to low-tech. The first paper recycling plant in Mexico was built in 1954 in San Luis Potosí. There are now 60 such plants operating in Mexico and, according to the National

Brad Wetzler

Cross outside the mission church in Satevó, Chihuahua

Institute of Recycling (Inare), the country recycles 170,000 tons of paper and cardboard each month. About 43 percent of all paper is recollected. The institute estimates that Mexico City reuses only 10 percent of recyclable materials.

MEXICAN CULTURE

Answer quickly: Is Mexico part of North America or Latin America? The answer is both, and Mexicans pride themselves on their links to both North and South. The country entered into the historic NAFTA trade agreement with the United States and Canada while simultaneously pursuing relations with other Latin countries to the south. In the 1980s and 1990s Mexico attempted (as official policy) to be the poorest of the rich instead of the richest of the poor.

Other examples stem from Mexico's mestizo history: The country is a mix of European and indigenous races. Look at the European influence—particularly French—of Paseo de la Reforma, the avenue built by order of Emperor Maximilian and Empress Carlota in the late 1800s.

Of Mexico's 95 million people, 15 percent are Caucasian, 60 percent mestizo (of mixed European and Indian ancestry), and 25 percent

Oil Production in Mexico

Mexico ranks eighth among the world's crude oil–producing nations. The vast majority of Mexico's oil is produced in Campeche Bay; onshore drilling in Tabasco and Campeche provides the rest.

Mexico's wells are producing at their maximum level, and earnings have gone to pay off Mexico's loan from the United States after the collapse of the peso. Analysts are concerned that Mexico has not developed new areas of oil deposits for more than a decade. Crude oil production peaked in 1982 and has leveled off in the last decade. In 1996 Mexico earned more than $10 billion from the oil industry, the leading source of income for the country.

Mexico's national oil company, Pemex, says it has invested $2 billion in the past decade in fuel improvement programs. It remains under pressure to clean up its emissions and operations, particularly in Tabasco.

indigenous. There are also descendants of the Africans who were brought to the country as slaves. Government policy has encouraged a lower birth rate, so the current population increase is 2.2 percent a year, but even at this modest rate of growth there will be 137.5 million Mexicans by the year 2025. This population pressure will greatly impact wilderness areas, so leaders now are urging the creation of programs that will conserve the natural patrimony while still providing for Mexico's poor.

Spanish is the official language of Mexico, but there are 50 indigenous languages that are still spoken. In the cities, the traveler's broken Spanish or English will not be an impediment to successful interaction.

Architecture reflects the melding of indigenous art and structure, European influence and 20th-century modernism. But nearly all Mexican towns are built around a central meeting place, a plaza called a *zócalo*. The original and most inspiring zócalo is in the heart of Mexico City, but every town center is unique.

Mangrove trees

RESPONSIBLE TOURISM IN MEXICO

2

After successfully pioneering such large-scale, megatourism destinations as Acapulco, Puerto Vallarta, and Cancún, Mexico is now attempting to promote small-is-beautiful ecotourism. Local nature guides are being trained throughout the country while state tourism offices such as those in Oaxaca and Veracruz lead the way in marketing Mexico's natural destinations.

In the global tourism industry, nature-based travel services and destinations are the market's hottest niches. For developing countries with limited financial resources, nature-based tourism promotes both environmental conservation and local economic development. That's the idea, anyway. For it to become a reality, much depends on you, the traveler.

LINKING NATURE AND TRAVEL

Like most buzzwords that pop in and out of our language, "ecotourism" is a confusing term used by different people to mean different things. Without a standard definition, anything involving tourism and the environment may be referred to as ecotourism. This is true even if the act of tourism diminishes or destroys that environment, lacks an educational component, and involves no respect for indigenous peoples of the area. At its best, ecotourism is a tool to channel the energies of the tourism market toward building sustainable economies. At its worst, it is a marketing tool that sells environmentally destructive activities under nature's banner.

This book, in addition to providing useful information about hotels, restaurants, and destinations, will help readers refine their travel sensibilities by shedding light on issues that are sometimes hidden beneath the lure of the luxuriant rain forests.

There are real campesinos attempting to feed their children by burning the forest and planting corn; there are real environmentalists who sometimes give their lives in service to their beliefs; and there are real decisions that caring and educated travelers can make either to improve or degrade the delicate environments through which they pass.

As you travel through Mexico and through other countries, including your own, ask yourself the following questions:

1. To what degree does the introduction of tourism encourage members of the local community to preserve and protect their natural surroundings?

2. Are poor local people being displaced to make way for a resort that will profit a wealthy owner? You might not want to see a milpa, a campesino's cornfield, in the buffer zone of a national park, but remember that he and his family were probably born here and you are a guest who is just passing through. In the best circumstances, locals are hired as guards and guides and let their fields go fallow.

3. Who owns the resort or hotel? How does the travel agent you're paying support local conservation efforts? Ask around. Community-owned hotels and tourism services do the most good to support the goals of ecotourism.

4. Where does the food that is served come from, and does the demand for that food hasten environmental degradation? Some hotels serve iguana meat, or lobster out of season. The food might be tasty but the consequences of eating it are bitter.

5. Where does the sewage that you flush from your hotel bathroom go? If human waste washes out onto a coral reef, causing an algae bloom that strangles the ecosystem, how good do you feel about the waterfront location of your hotel?

Exploring Ecotourism

While there is no single strict definition, this book embraces the most common tenets of ecotourism, which hold that it is a form of tourism that assists local environmental conservation efforts, includes the active participation of local communities, and can pay for itself (is sustainable over the long run).

By definition, ecotourism assures the traveler—and local leaders—that a portion of the financial resources spent on a vacation remains in the area to protect the environment and bolster the local economy. Eco-travelers don't necessarily expect air-conditioned suites; they want to immerse themselves in the adventure of getting to know a particular place.

Ecotourism serves as a catalyst to stimulate other services and practices important to sustainable development, such as environment-friendly lodging, organic agriculture, the promotion of local handicrafts, and environmental education. In Spanish, this is called *un ciclo virtuoso* (a virtuous cycle). One of the advantages of ecotourism is that it has the potential to offer both large and small trips for travelers of all incomes. There are ecotourists who take educational cruises and those who backpack throughout the rural countryside. There is shoestring ecotourism and gold-card ecotourism. It is not about money. It is about intention and the effects of one's actions.

An ecotourism boom is just around the corner, travel agents say, although numbers are difficult to estimate. In 1989 the World Tourism Organization (WTO) found that nature travel represented 7 percent of all travel. If, according to the WTO, the 1994 tourism market was worth $3.4 trillion . . . well, you can do the math yourself. Nature tourism is expected to grow much faster than tourism as a whole, which is forecast to grow by an average of 3.7 percent a year during the 1990s. These studies are subject to debate and standard criteria are lacking. But tourism industry leaders acknowledge a growing demand among their clients to search out environment-friendly destinations and are now catering to this growing market.

Even if those involved in the activity don't consider themselves eco-tourists, nature-based tourism is becoming increasingly popular in Mexico. Nature tourists range from divers who plumb the reefs along the coast of Quintana Roo to rafters running the rapids in Veracruz. So far, the ecotourism organizations that do exist either approach the subject on a purely academic basis or a commercial basis (including the nonprofits and universities). Environmental tourism is not about building exclusive hotels in the wilderness; it's about learning how to minimize and even counteract destructive habits.

The Ecotourism Rating Scale

Since ecotourism is difficult to define, John Shores, a grassroots environmental consultant and head of the U.S. Peace Corps division of ecotourism, has proposed a system that would rate operations on a 0 to 5 scale. His system classifies the levels of ecotourism, much like the difficulty scale used to classify white-water rafting or technical climbing. Shores' proposed levels follow.

Level 0: The entry level of ecotourism requires that the travelers be exposed to or made aware of the fragility of the ecosystems they have come to enjoy. This is the lowest "awareness" threshold. Incidental nature travel would usually qualify at this level.

19

Level 1: Level 1 ecotourism requires that a net positive flow of monetary support occur between the traveling ecotourist and the ecosystems visited. Financial earmarks, whether airport departure taxes or designations of a portion of land-travel costs, would qualify at this level.

Level 2: Level 2 requires that the ecotourist engage in a personal way in supporting the environment. Some ecotourists have planted trees, others have participated in litter cleanups.

Level 3: Level 3 requires certifying that the specific tour system is benign to the environment. The system should include the international air travel as well as on-site transportation and accommodations. This level requires demonstrating that the net effect of the traveler's presence is neutral or positive.

Level 4: Level 4 requires demonstrating that the net effect of the traveler is positive. Eco-friendly actions such as using appropriate technology, low energy consumption, recycling, organic agriculture, sustainable harvesting methods, and personal contributions to ecosystem restoration can balance less environmentally benign aspects of the larger tour system, such as air travel, stays in luxury hotels, and excessive energy consumption.

Level 5: This level should be the ultimate goal for ecotourism supporters, whether they are tour operators, travelers, or resource management agencies. A perfect "5" in ecotourism is a trip in which the entire system operates in an environmentally sound way. Advertising, transportation, accommodations, treatment of residual products—all are considered. No deluge of third-class mail solicitations, no advertising in non-recyclable magazines. Transportation is environmentally benign (no Concordes, limited use of petroleum products—in fact, maybe only solar and animal transport, walking, biking, and swimming qualify). On-site accommodations and all visitor and staff activities are benign to the environment. Heating and air conditioning are solar and low-impact. Foods and souvenirs are produced in sustainable ways. All residual products are handled in a benign way, and sewage containment and treatment is carefully monitored. Used products are recycled, soaps and cleaning solutions are biodegradable, and non-degradation of the environment is the standard.

Shores' 0–5 scale offers a great deal to the dialogue and debate about ecotourism. It also requires a council that can offer accreditation. Perhaps by the time the next edition of this book appears, I will be able to offer a case-by-case evaluation of tourism destinations in Mexico. As it stands currently, most of the destinations would rank between Levels 0 and 3.

RESPONSIBLE TOURISM

Mexico: Adventures in Nature will help travelers understand the nature of development/conservation compromises and, in so doing, guide them toward the environmental destinations in which their visit is a vote for conservation and local economic well-being. When travelers support tours and destinations that play an active role in environmental protection and local development, tour operators and resort owners come to see that there is a significant new niche in the tourism market comprised of travelers who are more interested in the local environment than in duplicating their home environment with First-World comforts.

Responsible tourism is mindful and meaningful travel. If you want to experience a new culture, learn a new language, or come to understand the challenges of environmental policy and conservation, unlimited options await you in Mexico. Both the tourism sector and environmental groups in Mexico are actively developing ideas and infrastructure to better present the nation's wilderness to foreign visitors and nationals alike.

As you pass through the wilderness, take only pictures and leave only footprints—but don't leave footprints on the coral. And don't purchase souvenirs made from threatened resources such as black coral or any endangered species. Instead, support the work of local artisans whenever possible, and let them know how much you appreciate their skills.

Although I am serious about conservation and ecotourism, I am not implying that responsible travel has to be hard work and no fun. Far from it! I believe that if you are interested in finding the answers to the questions above, and if you find yourself asking other questions as you travel through the country, your experience in Mexico will be greatly enhanced. The process is one of adding meaning and knowledge to your adventure. By educating yourself about the complex interactions between natural systems and the human economy, you will magnify what you gain from your travel experience. Too often travelers build walls around themselves. The purpose of travel is to break out of the cubbyholes we've constructed for ourselves and break through the wall that separates us from the world around us.

Be as inquisitive and diligent as seems appropriate to your own level of interest. And don't be surprised if many of your questions can't be answered immediately. But by asking yourself as well as local residents the type of questions listed above, you'll arouse an interest in the issues, which will determine whether or not nature-based travel is indeed sustainable. Asking questions about the natural world places a tangible value on resources that have too often been neglected or exploited. Initial inquiries often result in further exploration by the locals. If they can't answer your question, or that of the next traveler, they'll probably find out the answer before the third person asks the same question. If Mexicans don't like what they find out, they might well attempt to change things. Your curiosity can help change things for the better.

BRIDGING THE GAP

The two components of ecotourism—economic development and environmental conservation—are often at odds. Many tourism agencies and officials do not place a high value on environmental protection. Their focus is on the utilization of resources for profit, not on conservation. Conservationists, on the other hand, often hold the attitude that environmental problems are caused by people, and so people, including tourists, should go away. Those who respect both tourism and conservation are in fact few and far between. The challenge is to find a bridge across this gap. Who can argue against development that is sustainable, or against income that provides locals with a financial incentive to protect their resources?

Instead of creating cities from villages, as was done with the Mexican megaresorts of Cancún or Huatulco, ecotourism highlights the local biological diversity and the surrounding towns and villages. This approach spreads the economic benefits throughout the countryside instead of hoarding them in an urban center.

Ecotourism succeeds when it not only benefits a local community but involves it from start to finish. On the northern border, linkages between Tamaulipas and Texas promote tourism to both the El Cielo Biosphere Reserve and Cuatro Ciénegas Protected Area. Research has shown that the poor are more likely than any other group to protect and improve their environment—if given the opportunity and resources. Ecotourism must have a strong local component if the promoters want the tourism to be sustainable.

"Ecotourism efforts must be kept in local hands to be successful," says Maria Araujo, international affairs director for Texas Parks and Wildlife Department, which promotes ecotourism projects both in Texas and in its neighboring Mexican states. "Money that comes into the area must remain there. On a simple level, this means not bringing in box lunches."

Keeping the financial revenues in a rural setting and in local hands remains a challenge to the traditional manner of developing tourism, Araujo says. But it will be the only way to assure the local community of the value of preserving the habitat the tourists have come to see.

In 1995 Mexico's Tourism Secretariat (SECTUR) and the National Institute of Ecology (INE) signed an agreement to collaborate on ecotourism development. Efforts are underway to coordinate and prioritize projects that link tourism and conservation. The two institutions even collaborated on a color map of protected areas. The campaign slogan "*¡Déjate conquistar por nuestros Parques Nacionales!*" ("Let our national parks win you over!") is creative. But how do you get to where the wild things are?

WHERE ARE THE WILD THINGS?

Mexico boasts the Copper Canyon and the lion's share of the Mundo Maya. The nation is known scientifically as a megadiversity country. Only Colombia, Peru, Brazil, and Indonesia are home to a greater number of plant and animal species. Mexican tour operators, long accustomed to promoting megaprojects, are now discovering profit potential in Mexico's lush natural resources, such as the Sea of Cortez and the white gypsum dunes of Cuatro Ciénegas, Coahuila, recently featured in an issue of *National Geographic.* The only obstacle to enjoying these places that travelers face is poor publicity. The tourist kiosks offer plenty of materials on jet skis and underwater submarines, but scant information on the world-famous Sian Ka'an Biosphere Reserve and none on Yum Balam or El Edén Reserves.

While government tourism offices of other countries, such as Belize, Costa Rica, and Ecuador, provide a smorgasbord of information on environmental highlights—including the names and histories of national parks, reserves, and environmental groups, and, most important, maps—SECTUR has only recently developed its information infrastructure to inform travelers of the environmental highlights Mexico has to offer.

Until 1995 it was virtually impossible to get a map of Mexico's national parks and biosphere reserves. Previously, these places were charted only in official papers and scientific literature. Unfortunately, the same year the map of protected areas appeared, it went out of print.

In October 1996 I was invited to give a presentation on information distribution for the International Colloquium on Protected Areas and Ecotourism in Mexico and Central America. The biggest obstacle, I argued, is that people will not go to parks if they don't know they exist. And they won't get to the parks if they don't have directions.

If this sounds too simplistic, consider that the best source I've found for environmental tourism destinations is not SECTUR, but reliable word-of-mouth from fellow travelers and from lesser known scientific journals. Green resorts and tourism providers are also using the Internet as a cost-effective way to attract visitors. I shouldn't criticize SECTUR too harshly—the situation in Costa Rica is a good example of how eco-tourism surged from grassroots efforts, and only when it was maturing did the government's Institute of Tourism jump on the bandwagon.

At the international colloquium several important points were made and echoed by participants: (1) conservation shouldn't have to prove itself worthwhile solely on economic criteria; (2) environmental tourism should not be the exclusive domain of international visitors; and (3) the need for management plans and carrying capacity studies is greater now than ever.

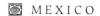

Practical ecotourism needs a bigger boost from both tourism and environmental leaders. It's not enough to offer training and build lodges; it's now high time to promote the type of ecotourism that actually protects the environment and empowers local communities.

Community-based environmental tourism generally does not generate enough profits for expensive ads or coverage in the leading travel magazines. These local projects rarely have the budget for advertisements or for commissions to travel operators who might book a trip. A 500-room hotel has a budget for magazine advertisements and perhaps even TV infomercials. A five-cabin eco-lodge, in contrast, puts a sign in a window and hopes to attract people who pass by.

MEXICO'S PARKS AND RESERVES

What makes a national park a national park and a biosphere reserve a biosphere reserve? There is a big difference between parks and reserves in Mexico, and it is important to understand Mexico's system of classification of these protected areas. In Mexico there are 93 protected areas covering 11.7 million hectares (29 million acres) or 6 percent of the national territory.

There are nine different types of natural protected areas in the System

Sierra de los Organos National Park

of Natural Protected Areas in Mexico (El Sistema Nacional de Areas Naturales Protegidas, or SINAP): biosphere reserves, special biosphere reserves, national parks, natural monuments, national marine parks, natural resource protected areas (which include forestry reserves), flora and fauna protected areas, urban parks, and ecological conservation zones. The federal government has jurisdiction over the first seven types of parks, while the urban parks and ecological conservation zones are managed by state and municipal governments. National parks, biosphere reserves, ecological reserves, and marine parks are part of SINAP. These areas are managed by the INE.

National parks are often not the most biologically diverse areas in Mexico, but they are noteworthy for historical or aesthetic reasons. For example, Mexico's volcanoes are national parks. So are many of the archaeological ruins. National parks may be created because of their scientific or historical value, or simply because they are considered appropriate for tourism development.

The majority of Mexico's national parks were created in the 1930s under the administration of Lázaro Cárdenas. He created the Department of Forestry, Fish and Game, which supervised the designation of 40 parks chosen for their scenic beauty, recreational potential, and ecological value. Designed by Miguel Angel de Quevedo, the park system emphasized Mexico's highland forests.

In contrast, the **biosphere reserves** are areas of genuine biological diversity. Most are more isolated than the national parks. To qualify, the reserves must have an area greater than 10,000 hectares (24,700 acres) with at least one ecosystem not significantly altered by human activity. These parks are also inhabited by species that are considered to be endemic, threatened, or in danger of extinction. **Special biosphere reserves** are almost identical, except they do not have to be as large. All biosphere reserves have a nucleus zone as well as a managed-use (or buffer) zone around the periphery. New population centers in the biosphere and special biosphere reserves are strictly prohibited.

In the beginning of the century, De Quevedo argued that tourism in the national parks was beneficial to both rural Mexicans and international visitors. He believed that international tourism could promote cooperation among Mexico and other countries and argued that by creating the national parks Mexico was becoming "a civilized country."

Mexico also has almost a dozen reserves with special designation from the Man and the Biosphere Program (MAB) network. The program was created in 1970 by the United Nations Educational, Scientific, and Cultural Organization (UNESCO) to unite national and international research, conservation, and training activities. Not all of Mexico's biosphere reserves are part of this network. Those that are included are Calakmul, El Cielo, El Pinacate y Gran Desierto de Altar, El Triunfo, El Vizcaíno, Mapimí, Michilía, Montes Azules, Sian Ka'an, and Sierra de Manantlán.

Regardless of their designation, parks are not always protected. Nearly half of the forests in the Chacagua lagoons have been cut down. Likewise, the ice-capped volcano of El Nevado de Toluca National Park is now 75-percent deforested. Mexico often lacks the levels of security and environmental education needed to keep these areas green.

Biosphere reserves have three goals: conservation, training, and sustainable human development compatible with conservation. Unlike national parks, biosphere reserves allow people to continue to live in protected natural areas. In addition to biological surveys and ecological studies, research is encouraged on sustainable resource use in order to encourage the local community to participate in the protection of wildlife. Residents hope to benefit from sustainable development, including ecotourism.

In the biosphere reserves, Mexico has pioneered the use of a zoning system that allows use of parks for tourism and economic productivity and declares other areas off-limits except for scientific study. The idea was proposed by Mexican scientist Enrique Beltrán at the First World Conference on National Parks held in Seattle in 1962.

Under SEMARNAP's 1995–2000 Environmental Program, conservation will receive more funds for protection. The government is also calling for economic subsidization of protected areas, including the promotion of ecotourism. Discussions about privatization and park concessions continue, but ownership is a sticky issue. Of the 732,000 hectares of national parks, only 15 percent is owned by the federal government. The owners of most of the land within the parks are private individuals, ejidos, or cities.

Mexico also negotiated a grant with the Global Environmental Facility (GEF)—part of the World Bank—which from 1992 to 1995 assigned $25 million to ten of Mexico's 18 biosphere reserves. Unfortunately, only $4 million was allocated to projects. A redesigned $20-million World Bank/GEF project will structure a private trust fund for ten of Mexico's high-priority protected areas, including El Triunfo, Mariposa Monarca, Calakmul, Sian Ka'an, Ría Lagartos, Montes Azules, El Vizcaíno, Islas del Golfo, Sierra de Manantlán, and Isla Contoy. Details, however, are hard to find.

Parks are continuously being created. In 1996 SEMARNAP announced four additions to its Protected Natural Areas program: Bahía de Loreto in Baja California, dry subtropical forest in the Sierra de los Alamos in Sonora, and two areas of coral reefs in Quintana Roo. Another area under consideration for park status is Barrancas del Cobre (Copper Canyon).

Also in 1996, Mexico passed three major decrees to protect the Great Maya Reef. In March of that year, Mexico declared 8,500 hectares (21,000 acres) of coral reef and marine habitat offshore of Cancún and Isla Mujeres a national marine park. In June two other decrees were made. The first protects 11,750 hectares (29,000 acres) of Cozumel's reef system as a national marine park, and the second designates the 14,175 hectares (350,000 acres) of Banco Chincorro's reef and marine system a biosphere reserve. All of these areas are within the state of Quintana Roo, which depends heavily on tourism revenues.

PARKS, RESERVES, AND PROTECTED AREAS IN MEXICO
National Parks

Baja California	Constitución del 1857
	Sierra de San Pedro Mártir
Chiapas	Cañón del Sumidero
	Lagunas de Montebello
	Palenque
Chihuahua	Cascada de Basaséachi
	Cumbres de Majalca
Coahuila	Balneario de los Novillos
Colima	Nevado de Colima
Guerrero	El Veladero
Hidalgo	El Chico
	Los Mármoles
Federal District	Cerro de la Estrella
	Cumbres del Ajusco
	Desierto de los Leones
	El Tepeyac
Michoacán	Cerro de Garnica
	Insurgente José María Morelos y Pavón
	Lago de Camécuaro
	Pico de Tancítaro
	Rayón
Morelos	Cacahuamilpa Caverns
	El Tepozteco
	Lagunas de Zempoala
Nayarit	Isla Isabel
Nuevo León	Cumbres de Monterrey
	El Sabinal
Oaxaca	Benito Juárez
	Lagunas de Chacagua

Querétaro	El Cimatario
Quintana Roo	Xel-Ha
San Luis Potosí	El Gogorrón
	El Potosí
State of Mexico	Bosencheve
	Desierto del Carmen
	Insurgente Miguel Hidalgo y Costilla
	Iztaccíhuatl–Popocatépetl
	Los Remedios
	Molino de Flores
	Nevado de Toluca
	Sacromonte
	Zoquiapan
Tlaxcala	La Malinche Matlalcueyatl
Veracruz	Cañón del Río Blanco
	Cofre del Perote
	Pico de Orizaba
Zacatecas	Sierra de los Organos

National Marine Parks

Quintana Roo	Cozumel
	Puerto Morelos
Veracruz	Reefs of Veracruz
Yucatán	Alacranes Reef

National Historic Parks

Chiapas	Palenque
Hidalgo	Tula
Quintana Roo	Tulum
Yucatán	Dzibilchaltum

Biosphere Reserves

Baja California South	El Vizcaíno Sierra de La Laguna
Campeche	Calakmul
Chiapas	El Triunfo
	El Encrucijada
	Lacantún
	Montes Azules
Durango	La Michilía
	Mapimí
Jalisco	Chamela-Cuixmala
Nayarit	Archipiélago de Revillagigedo

Querétaro	Sierra Gorda
Quintana Roo	Banco Chinchorro
	Sian Ka'an
Sonora	Alto Golfo de California y Delta del Río Colorado
	El Pinacate y Gran Desierto de Altar
	El Vizcaíno
Tamaulipas	El Cielo
Tabasco	Pantanos de Centla

Special Biosphere Reserves

Baja California South and Sonora	Islas del Golfo de California
Chiapas	Agua Azul Waterfall
Coahuila	Sierra de Santa Marta
Michoacán and State of Mexico	Mariposa Monarca
Oaxaca	El Ocote Forest
Quintana Roo	Isla Contoy
	Ría Celestún
	Ría Lagartos
	Sonora Cajón del Diablo
	Isla Rasa
	Isla Tiburón
	Isla Guadalupe
Veracruz	Volcán de San Martín

Natural Monuments

Chiapas	Bonampak
	Yaxchilán
Nuevo León	Cerro de la Silla

Areas of Protection for Flora and Fauna

Campeche	Laguna de Términos
Coahuila	Cuatro Ciénegas
Mexico City	Chichinautzin Biological Corridor
Quintana Roo	Chan-Kin
	Yum-Balam

29

Seals in the Sea of Cortez

3

FLORA AND FAUNA OF MEXICO

Mexico's indisputable wealth lies in its biological diversity. The country boasts a cornucopia of ecosystems, including dryland vegetation, tropical dry forests, tropical evergreen forests, coniferous forests, grasslands, and aquatic systems.

In total number of species, Mexico ranks fifth in the world, just after Peru, Indonesia, Brazil, and Colombia. It ranks first in the number of reptiles species and it boasts the majority of the world's pine and cacti species. Mexico is home to more than 1,000 bird species, 450 mammals (142 found nowhere else on the planet), 640 reptiles, and 330 amphibians. Insect species number in the hundreds of thousands. It has the second-greatest mammal diversity of any nation. It is also among the top ten countries in the world for the number of restricted-range bird species and endemic bird areas it supports.

Why such diversity? Most of Mexico lies within the intersection of North and South America. These continents were separated for millions of years and each developed its own unique species. This changed when a land bridge emerged, connecting the Americas. The biological richness results from great habitat variation and diverse ecological regions, complex topography, climate, geology, and geographical location.

Mexico also has the most endangered and now extinct freshwater fish in the world. According to biologist Salvador Contreras, there are 20 fish species now known to be extinct, and out of 480 species scientists have identified in Mexico, 160 are at risk—and most of them are found nowhere else on earth. Eight new species have been discovered in the last three years; at the same time many are going extinct while they are being studied. The chief culprit is the depletion of freshwater springs and underground aquifers for residential and industrial use. "You might be able to protect a tree by putting a fence around it," says Contreras, "but an underground spring? If it's out of sight, it's out of mind."

According to the 1994 INEGI Environmental Review, there are at least 242 species in danger of extinction, 435 considered threatened, 244 considered rare, and 84 subject to special protection. Of all of these species, 411 are native to Mexico, and of these 124 are in danger of extinction.

Mexico is taking a number of steps to protect its wildlife. In 1991 it joined the Convention on International Trade in Endangered Species (CITES), a global organization that four years earlier declared Mexico to be one of the most notable traffickers of wildlife in the world. More than 6 million animals were sold in a legal manner to the United States alone in 1991 and 1992, with an importation value of $19 million. Veracruz, Tamaulipas, Chiapas, Quintana Roo, and Oaxaca are the states most affected by the legal and illegal traffic in animals. Although there are laws against illegal trafficking, the capacity for enforcing them is low. More shocking, in a study of the black market, CITES estimated that 85 percent of the animals that were captured died before they could be sold.

TOPOGRAPHY

MOUNTAINS

More than half of Mexico's mountainous surface area is higher than 1,000 meters (3,280 feet) above sea level, and only one-third has an elevation of less than 500 meters (1,640 feet). Perhaps the most confusing aspect of travel in Mexico is that all of the major mountain ranges are called the Sierra Madre (Mother Range). However, there are actually three separate mountain ranges, in the east, west, and south.

The Western Sierra Madre is the main mountain chain (1,400 kilometers or 868 miles), running parallel to the Pacific coast and interspersed with some small mountains. The Eastern Sierra Madre (600 kilometers or 372 miles) runs northwest to southeast down the Gulf coast. Between these two cordilleras is the Altiplano, a high plateau, interspersed with some small mountains, at an altitude of 3,000 meters (9,843 feet). The 950-kilometer (589-mile) Eje Neovolcánico is a chain of volcanoes and mountains that runs east to west across the country and includes Mexico's highest peak, Pico de Orizaba (5,675 meters). In the southern half of the country, the 1,100-kilometer (682-mile) Southern Sierra Madre stretches across the states of Guerrero and Oaxaca to the Pacific Ocean.

FORESTS

Mexico supports a variety of different trees ranging from more than 50 species of pine to mahogany, zapote, ceiba (the holy tree of the Maya), oak, and cypress. The national tree is the cypress, or *ahuehuete*, which thrives along rivers and creeks in the semi-arid regions. Near Oaxaca, in the town of Tula, is the famed giant cypress (42 meters wide), now more than 2,000 years old.

The country is rich in temperate and tropical forests. Mexico possesses 1.3 percent of the world's total forest resources, with one-quarter of the country's total land area classified as forest lands, according to the World Forestry Institute. Most of Mexico's forest is found in the temperate-cold coniferous and broad-leafed forests in the states of Chihuahua, Durango, Jalisco, Michoacán, Oaxaca, Chiapas, and Guerrero. The tropical and subtropical forests are comparable in size, but they account for only 10 percent of Mexican forest production. Tropical forests are located in the states of Chiapas, Quintana Roo, Yucatán, Campeche, Tabasco, and Oaxaca.

Central Mexico is covered with pine and oak forests, along with a diverse undergrowth and strands of liquidambar, the genus of sweetgum, used throughout the Americas. In Southern Mexico, the forests are low jungles or tall deciduous forests, combined with mangroves, marshes, and savannas.

Commercial forestry has encountered numerous obstacles, including the fact that wood production costs are currently 35 to 40 percent higher than the world average. Importation of cheaper softwoods from the United States is expected to further reduce Mexico's lumber production. Mexico's lumber output in 1994 was 5.9 million cubic meters, its lowest production in 22 years. Many communities that have depended on forestry are diversifying their income with tourism. It's best not to be a purist and demand that towns near nature treks completely abandon commercial logging. Until environmental tourism can prove its mettle, logging— even if unsustainable—will continue.

Deforestation

Before the Spanish conquest, about two-thirds of the country was forested. Not all was virgin forest and, in fact, evidence links deforestation to the downfall of several Mayan cities and the great Aztec city of Teotihuacán. Today, only one-fifth of the country remains verdant, mainly in the south and east. According to INEGI, deforestation in

Mexico is estimated at more than 500,000 hectares (1.2 million acres) per year, one of the worst rates in the world. Unofficial estimates suggest a greater amount, from 600,000 to 1 million hectares (1.5 to 2.5 million acres) per year. Why are the forests cut down? Not for need of trees.

Cattle ranching has destroyed more than three-quarters of the high forests that covered Mexico at the turn of the century. Subsidies given to ranchers in the past few decades have made this industry profitable. In the Lacandón rain forest, which originally occupied 15 million hectares (37 million acres) in the state of Chiapas, 90 percent of the land has been converted to grazing pastures. Along with the trees, numerous animal and plant species have perished due to the loss of their related habitats.

Deforestation remains a large problem in the tropics because it is often viewed as a measure of progress. It is also a means for the poorest segment of Mexico's rural population to gain unclaimed land. Fifty percent of Mexican farmers now live off subsistence wages, meaning they simply do not grow enough food to support their families. Either they move further into the forests, thereby increasing deforestation, or migrate to the cities.

Erosion

Among the most serious environmental threats in Mexico is soil erosion and the resulting conversion of productive lands into sterile wastelands. According to the World Watch Institute, at least 70 percent of agricultural land is affected by soil erosion. In the arid regions of Mexico, the worst cases of erosion have taken place in Sonora, Baja California Sur, and Chihuahua. In the temperate areas, erosion has affected Oaxaca, Tlaxcala, and Guanajuato. Furthermore, according to INEGI, in seven of the 31 states of Mexico erosion has affected almost 40 percent of the total land area.

As Mexico's most fertile soils are eroded, agricultural production will be diminished. This is perhaps one of the most unglamorous environmental stories, with some of the most potent consequences.

CORAL REEFS

The United Nations declared 1997 the Year of the Reef, and Mexico has much to celebrate. The Yucatán Peninsula is the northernmost boundary of the Great Maya Reef, the longest reef in the Northern Hemisphere. In the Mexican Caribbean, it stretches from Isla Contoy to the Belizean border. Other reefs are found off the coast of Veracruz.

Coral reefs are the marine equivalent to tropical rain forests and are restricted to a tropical belt around the world between 30 degrees north and south latitudes. These living colonies of marine animals are under tremendous pressure. According to Sea Grant College, 10 percent of the earth's reefs have collapsed, and more are at risk of destruction in the next 20 years.

If you want to visit the reefs, remember that you are a guest in a very fragile environment. Avoid using suntan lotion and make sure to stay clear of the coral. To keep from getting burned, take a hat if you're going out for an extended boat trip and wear a long sleeved shirt. If you're tired, float; don't try to stand on the reef.

FAUNA

MAMMALS

Of the 4,500 terrestrial and marine mammals in the world, Mexico has more than 500. That's more than 10 percent—another reason why Mexico is called a megadiversity country. The tropics are home to marsupials, primates, and the tapir. The spider monkey can be found in the south from Jalisco to the Yucatán Peninsula. Howler monkeys are also found in the tropics. Tourists often mistake their frightening roars—hence their name—for those of jaguars. The tropics are home to collared peccary and white-lipped peccary, fierce relatives of the hog. These animals are omnivorous in the wild, though they can be tamed.

Roger Steeb

Desert Bighorn

35

The majority of Mexico's mammals live in more temperate zones. The most widely distributed are deer (white-tailed deer, mule deer, and tiny brocket deer). Desert bighorn sheep live in the northern deserts, though hunting and competition with livestock diminished their numbers earlier this century. They are found in Baja California's San Pedro Mártir and Sierra de Juárez Mountains and in Sonora's El Pinacate.

In the seas are almost 30 species of cetaceans, ranging from the blue whale, the largest mammal on earth, to the 50-kilogram (110-pound) vaquita, the smallest porpoise. Manatees (also called sea cows, an apt though less poetic name) frequent the warm coastal waters and can be found in lagoons and estuaries.

Mexico is a cat lover's paradise. There are jaguars, bobcats, ocelots, margay, jaguarundi, and mountain lions. The jaguar is the third-largest feline in the world and was greatly respected in Mesoamerican religions. Today the species is threatened by hunters and habitat loss.

BIRDS

Because Mexico's geographic terrain soars from coastal lagoons and low-lying deserts to the incredible heights of the Sierra Madres, the country has natural barriers that provide an incredible number of microclimates for an array of bird species.

Birds in Mexico are a mix of North American species such as geese and cranes and South American species such as quetzals and toucans. Out of some 9,000 species in the world, 769 breed in Mexico; an additional 257 species migrate—or are blown off course—to Mexico. With only 11 percent of the land area contained in Canada and the United States, Mexico supports more bird species than the combined number of species—less than 800—of its northern neighbors.

Migratory birds take advantage of a more reliable food source in the tropics. Scientists theorize that tropical migration began 10 to 30 million years ago when a colder, seasonal climate replaced a subtropical climate in North America. Tropical migrants will spend up to a third of each year migrating. But what has evolved over millions of years is threatened by the destruction of tropical forests. The Food and Agriculture Organization (FAO) of the United Nations estimates that 17 million hectares (42 million acres) of tropical forest are destroyed each year.

The highest number of species is found in southeastern Mexico. More than 70 percent are found in the tropics. If you want to go where the birds are, head to Calakmul Biosphere Reserve in Campeche or the Selva Lacandona rain forest in Chiapas. To stay closer to the U.S. border, visit the Sierra Gorda Biosphere Reserve in Querétaro or my favorite cabin in the mountains, Renacer de la Sierra outside of Monterrey.

REPTILES

More than 1,000 reptile species live in Mexico, including turtles, lizards, iguanas, Gila monsters, American and Morelet crocodiles, and rattlesnakes. Many of the reptiles are enjoyed in Mexico as a main course or a tasty treat. Once, at a roadside diner on the Pacific coast, I purchased what I thought were corn tamales. To my surprise, I found I was eating iguana, with much of the skin left intact. While life may be full of tasty surprises, I wish I had been better prepared for this one. It's been ten years since I've been able to eat tamales.

There are no alligators in Mexico. Instead, Mexico has one species of caiman and two species of crocodiles. "In many areas, local people call crocodiles *lagartos* and consider them different from crocodiles," says Marcos Lazcano, biologist and owner of El Edén reserve, outside of Cancún. "The name *lagarto* originated when the Spaniards conquered Mexico and called the various species *lagartos*, a name used for a large lizard (El Lagarto) in Spain."

Turtles

Mexico is home to seven of the eight species of sea turtles in the world; all are threatened or endangered. Sea turtles spend almost all their lives at sea, but like all reptiles the females must lay their eggs on land. Turtles can live to be 100 years old, and the female can lay as many as 200 eggs in her nest, or "clutch." The survival of the turtles depends as much on finding alternate livelihoods for turtle poachers as on establishing laws and fines. The responsible traveler declines to purchase sea turtle products.

The **Kemp's ridley**, the smallest of sea turtles, is also the most endangered. It was named for Richard Kemp, a fisherman who shipped specimens to Harvard University from Key West, Florida, in the late 1800s. Kemp's ridley turtles, which live in the Gulf of Mexico and the Atlantic Ocean, lay 95 percent of their eggs on a beach at Playa Rancho Nuevo, in Tamaulipas, Mexico.

The **leatherback** is the largest of the sea turtles, and can be found in the Atlantic, Pacific, and Indian Oceans. An individual can weigh more than a ton. **Green** turtles inhabit tropical and subtropical seas and nest on the southern beaches. The **black turtle**, medium sized and found in the Pacific, is primarily herbivorous but sometimes eats mollusks and crustaceans. **Hawksbill** turtles prefer the coral reefs and rocky areas in tropical seas. **Loggerheads** are also hearty turtles, weighing more than 400 pounds when they are adults. The **olive ridley** is a small turtle, weighing between 70 and 80 pounds, and is found in the Pacific.

FLORA

Nearly one in ten of the earth's plant species is found in Mexico, and almost half of the plants in Mexico are found nowhere else. Plants are not only beautiful, they have practical and medicinal applications, a truth known to every group who has ever lived in Mexico. Mexico's botanical gardens date back to the Aztec kings. The country's important gardens are featured in this book's destination chapters.

Mexico's array of ecosystems allows for this staggering diversity of plant life. Tropical rain forests along the Gulf Coast and in Southern Mexico boast tall trees, 30 to 50 meters (98–165 feet) in height, such as the ceiba. The understory consists of palms and ferns. Tropical dry forests, located on the Pacific coast, have much shorter trees, 15 meters (49 feet) tall. These trees often have lichens attached to their trunks. The cloud forests of Mexico are found on the Gulf slopes of mountains found in Tamaulipas, Veracruz, and Oaxaca. Mexican deserts in the northern borderlands have a profusion of cacti. Desert grasslands extend as far south as northeastern Oaxaca.

NATIVE PLANTS

Botanical knowledge of native plants is used throughout Mexico for both culinary and medicinal purposes. *Epizote*, or wormseed, is used for its distinctive flavor in preparing the traditional dish of pinto or black beans. It is

Saguaro cactus

also used to eliminate parasitic worms. Aloe's cool gel can relieve burns. If mixed with water and lemon juice, it can be used as a tonic that improves digestion. Red hibiscus, high in vitamin C, can produce a tea or tonic that helps fight colds. Papaya is high in vitamins A and C and lysine. It's used for digestive "cleansing" and can be an effective remedy for stomach problems. The flowers from banana plants are used to alleviate symptoms of bronchitis and dysentery. The forests and gardens are pharmacies and markets—if you know where to look. If you're not sure, don't experiment—many plants can also pose grave health risks.

Agroecology

The emerging movement of agroecology links agriculture and environmental issues.

Promoted by activist academics such as Ronald Nigh and David Barkin, the concept is embraced by Mexico's Secretariat of the Environment as a needed bridge between environmental conservation and rural development.

"It is in peasant and indigenous agricultural communities that the most innovative experimentation toward sustainability is being carried out, supported by environmental and grassroots support groups," writes David Carruthers, a California-based scholar. The shift to organic agriculture, such as in coffee production, is just one example of agroecology in action. There are also programs that incorporate holistic range management for beef production.

Perhaps a threat greater even than industrial agrochemicals to the ecosystem is the notion that all food should be hoarded for human consumption—what novelist Daniel Quinn calls "totalitarian agriculture" in his book The Teachings of B. *"We hunt down our competitors, we destroy their food, and we deny them access to food," writes Quinn. "Totalitarian agriculture is based on the premise that all the food in the world belongs to us, and there is no limit whatever to what we may take for ourselves and deny to others."*

As certain species of freshwater fish disappear forever in the northern borderlands, and tropical mammals and birds find their habitats sacrificed for the production of cattle, we might ask at what point we will intervene and put brakes on the productive yet hazardous agriculture that makes our world a poorer place every day.

FOOD AND CASH CROPS

Mexico's native plants can now be found throughout the world. Its flora include the holy trinity of Mesoamerican agri-religion—maize, beans, and gourds. Many garden flowers, such as zinnias, cosmos, marigolds, and dahlias, first took root here. There are more than 20,000 flowering plants in Mexico.

Scientists have mapped out the "gene belt" that circles the world between the Tropics of Cancer and Capricorn. The majority of agricultural centers have their origin in this region, and Mexico is unique because of its megadiversity and its location within the belt. Unfortunately, many of Mexico's plant species are going extinct. The site of the discovery of *teosinte*, a grass closely related to maize, is now protected in the Sierra de Manantlán Biosphere Reserve. *Zea diploperennis*, another relative of domesticated corn, is endemic to the state of Jalisco and is known by agricultural scientists as *la madre de maíz* ("the mother of maize"). This plant contains genes resistant to seven diseases that afflict cultivated corn. Its extinction would be the harbinger of other grave problems.

Maize

According to the Mayan book of creation, the Popul Vuh, in the first world gods made people out of wood. But there were complications and the gods destroyed that race of humans. What worked? After the initial four creations, the gods formed people out of maize dough.

What is the difference between maize and corn? "Corn" is a term used for a grain regardless of variety. "Maize" is the homegrown word for the most familiar plant, *Zea mays*. This is the third most important crop in the world, following wheat and rice.

Originally, maize may have been domesticated in the Tehuacán valley of southern Puebla and northern Oaxaca around 5,000 B.C. Researchers debate whether the ancestor of maize was teosinte; however, that plant appears to be almost inedible, and it's hard to prove that early farmers would have spent much time developing it as a food crop.

In the next few thousand years, farmers cultivated maize throughout the Americas, and eventually the hearty crop supplanted other grains. Following Columbus' first voyage to the Americas, maize was introduced to the Old World. By 1498 it was being harvested in Spain and soon it spread across the rest of the world. Once domesticated, nothing was wasted of this plant. The husks are used for tamales. The corn silk can be made into a tea (reportedly good for the kidneys), and the ears of corn can be left to dry and then stored for later consumption. It is also prepared as a sweet, called *elote*. Maize may be served in both cooked and uncooked forms, as corn tortillas or a delicious hot drink called *atole*.

Avocado

Avocados are indigenous to Mexico and have medicinal properties. According to some reports, daily consumption can lower high blood pressure. Early botanists prescribed them for dysentery and to stop hair from falling out. A ripe avocado should be tender but not mushy. Usually arriving in markets very green and very tough, they should be left to mature and darken before using. They can then be mashed to make guacamole or sliced for toppings and fillings. Avocado leaves, either whole or ground, are also used in Mexican dishes.

Coffee

Coffee is not native to the Americas. It was introduced to the highlands of Mexico and Central America in the late 1800s. There are two varieties of coffee trees, arabica and robusta. Arabica is more flavorful and contains less caffeine than robusta. The best-flavored arabica beans come from the highest altitudes (1,000 meters up to the frost zone at 1,700 meters).

Unlike most other coffee-producing nations, Mexico, the world's fourth-largest producer of coffee, relies primarily on small growers rather than large plantations. More than 750,000 hectares (1.9 million acres) are cultivated by some 280,000 coffee producers, the majority farming fewer than 5 hectares each. Farmers are discovering the growing market for organic and specialty coffees, which brings higher returns. The gourmet coffee market could become a $5-billion industry by the end of the century, according to the Specialty Coffee Association of America.

Mexico is the leading producer of organic coffee, almost all of which is farmed by indigenous groups. Fields are concentrated in Chiapas and Oaxaca, and are also found in Guerrero, Veracruz, Puebla, and San Luis Potosí. Traditional coffee farms are being converted and farms certified for international exports.

According to the National Coordinator of Coffee Producing Organizations (CNOC), Mexico is the world leader in the export of organic coffee and the pioneer in developing organic coffee cultivation techniques. CNOC comprises 65,000 producers from 85 regional organizations in eight states.

But being a major leader in coffee production does not necessarily translate into being a good provider of high-quality java. Don't expect to find in Mexico the type of coffeeshops you find in the United States and Europe. Most Mexican restaurants offer hot water and dried coffee, usually Nescafé, which is the brunt of coffee snobs' ubiquitous joke, "*Nescafé no es café.*" However, in homes the best coffee is served as *café de olla*, prepared by putting coffee into a pot of boiling water.

Cocoa

According to scholars, cocoa beans once served as currency in the Maya world. Counterfeiting was a common crime. Vendors would fill the bean husks with sand and blend the fake beans with the real ones. The cacao tree was considered an incarnation of the tree of life. The beans were ground and mixed with water to form a drink that is said to have symbolized blood and was called "the drink of the gods."

Today cocoa is an important cash crop in southern Mexico, and many cocoa plantations can be found in the state of Tabasco near Villahermosa.

Tomatoes

Although the tomato originated in Peru, it was traded and grown in Mexico during pre-Columbian times. The Náhuatl named it *Xicotamatl*, and it is known in Mexico as *jitomate*. The Spanish sent samples back from Peru, but most Europeans considered it poisonous (because other members of the nightshade family are poisonous). Although it took a few centuries, this New World plant returned to conquer the global diet. According to Maya scholar Sophie Coe, the tomato is the second-most studied (and genetically altered) plant after maize. Botanists classify this plant as a fruit, not a vegetable.

Magueys and Agaves

Agaves are not cacti! The common name for the genus *agave* is maguey, referred to in the United States as the "century plant." There are 136 species, 26 subspecies, and 29 varieties of the genus *agave*; all are from the Americas and most are found in Mexico. Their leaves are long and spiky, and while resistant to drought and extreme temperatures, they take time to mature. Agaves bloom at between eight and 25 years of age. The pulque agave takes ten to 12 years to flower, while the agave that produces tequila and the less-refined mezcal requires eight to 12 years to flower. The sisal agave, native to the Yucatán, produced the henequen (twine) boom in the early 1900s.

The agave that is used to prepare pulque grows in the dry

Agave

central highlands and farther south along the Western Sierra Madre. The drink, served as a ritual beverage and intoxicant, was a favorite of Toltec and Aztec leaders. But after the conquest its ritual importance was downplayed. When the Spanish conquistadors arrived, they referred to the plant as "maguey" because they believed it to be identical to a plant they had encountered in the Caribbean.

Magueys thrive where other plants don't fare so well. They reproduce by sending out offshoots. Farmers transplant the offspring and, after ten to 12 years, the plant sends up a great flower stalk. Pulque production, however, requires cutting off this central spike.

Blue mezcal is the common name for *agave tequilana* or the tequila agave. Although the plant can be grown in many places, the resulting drink lacks the characteristic flavor of that produced at its namesake town of Tequila, in Jalisco. The *agave tequilana* is smaller than the maguey that produces pulque and has straight, narrow spikes.

In the processing, the spikes are removed to expose the plant's heart, which is then chopped into pieces and roasted. When the cooked heart is shredded, the juice streams out. Sugar is added and the mixture ferments for four days and is distilled several times. The tequila is then aged for anywhere from several months to seven years. As it ages, the colorless tequila turns a golden hue.

Surveying the Oaxaca Valley

4

EXPLORING
MEXICO

The active traveler will find that exploring Mexico through nature- and culture-based activities is easy and rewarding. This chapter reviews some of Mexico's most popular activities, from whale-watching to mountain biking, and presents a list of recommended outfitters for each. Additional outfitter and tour guide information (along with specifics about where to enjoy these types of activities) can be found throughout this book.

WILDLIFE VIEWING

BIRD-WATCHING

Because Mexico is located in the transition zone between North and South America, the country has a mixture of the avian species typical to each continent. Out of some 9,000 species in the world, 769 breed in Mexico, and an additional 257 are found as migrants or accidentals. Compare this to the combined number of species—less than 800—in the much larger land area shared by Canada and the United States.

Mexico is habitat to hummingbirds, woodpeckers, macaws, parrots, vultures, toucans, and quetzals. Few places in Mexico are without our feathered friends, though some places are particularly good for bird-watching, such as southern Mexico (El Triunfo in Chiapas, Calakmul in

Campeche and Celestún, and Ría Lagartos and the Sian Ka'an in Quintana Roo).

The northern borderlands support more than half of Mexico's 1,026 bird species. Many state and city chapters of the Sierra Club or National Audubon Society schedule regular trips to the border.

Within Mexico, your best bet for bird-watching is to check with the Mexican chapter of the **Audubon Society** in San Miguel de Allende. The chapter organizes monthly trips. Consult the newspapers in town, or call Fin Taylor at (415) 20254. The San Miguel chapter works closely with other groups in Central Mexico and sometimes offers trips to the Sierra Gordo in Queretaro. In Guanajuato, monthly trips are organized by **Secretos del Bosque**. Call the group at (47) 17-20-98 or (47) 17-01-11.

Among the bird-identification books available are the *Peterson Field Guide to Mexican Birds* and, in Spanish, *Aves de Nuevo León* (Birds of Nuevo Leon), published in 1996 and available at Monterrey bookstores.

Birding Tour Operators

Ecoturismo Yucatán, Calle 3 #235 between 32-A and 34 in Colonia Pensiones, (99) 25-21-87 or 20-27-72, e-mail ecoyuc@minter.cieamer .conacyt.mx. One of the few companies in Mexico that deserves to be singled out for its natural history tours. The company is run by Alfonso Escobedo, a professional guide, and his wife, Roberta Graham de Escobedo. They take groups on bird-watching trips to the Celestún Biosphere Reserve and Río Lagartos.

Victor Emmanuel Tours, P.O. Box 33008, Austin, TX 78764, (512) 328-5221 or (800) 328-8368. This company offers high quality, expensive birding and natural history tours. One of its specialties is touring the El Triunfo Biosphere Reserve in Chiapas.

WHALE-WATCHING

Whale-watching is pursued in waters around the globe. As a commercial tourism niche, it's a relative newcomer compared to bird-watching. Trips can last from an hour to a week. Its supporters praise this type of tourism as a "non-consumptive" use of whales with recreational, educational, and scientific dimensions. Local communities also benefit economically from the tourism revenues.

Mexico offers several places to observe whales. In the winter months the animals migrate from chilly Arctic waters to the Baja Peninsula. The Pacific Ocean and the Sea of Cortez are home to blue whales, the largest living creatures on earth, as well as to humpback, sperm, finback, minke, gray, and killer whales. La Paz and Loreto, excellent travel hubs, offer whale-watching trips. Whales are the star attraction at the San Ignacio and Scammon's Lagoons, accessible from San Ignacio or Guerro Negro, Baja California. Whales also swim in the bays off the coast of Nayarit and Jalisco, and regular tours are offered in Puerto Vallarta.

Whale-Watching Tour Operators

Baja Discovery, P.O. Box 152527, San Diego, CA 92195, (800) 829-2252, e-mail BajaDis@aol.com, Web site http://www.bajadiscovery.com/. With more than 20 years experience in the region, this company offers luxury nature-tourism, including "safari-style" camping in San Ignacio.

Baja Expeditions, 2625 Garnet Ave., San Diego, CA 92109, (800) 843-6967, fax (619) 581-6542, e-mail travel@bajaex.com, Web site http://www.bajaex.com/. Just a few years older than Baja Discovery, this company offers a variety of nature-based trips in the region. Seven-day trips cost around $1,100.

Ecotourism Kuyima, on Plaza San Ignacio in San Ignacio, (115) 4-00-26, fax (115) 4-0070. Located across from the mission, this agency is run by the local ejido and a fishing cooperative. While these people are not long-term locals, they have a good reputation in the community, and this is a well-respected travel provider.

Expediciones Ecotur, kilometer 16 on the highway to Ensenada, (66) 36-11-83, U.S. fax (619) 662-1720. There are a number of travel packages available from this reputable company. A five-day hiking trip to the Sierra de San Francisco costs $295. The trip can be combined with whale-watching. This Tijuana-based company works very closely with the guides at Ecotourism Kuyima.

Malarrimo Eco-Tours, 1.4 kilometers (1 mile) west of Highway 1 on the edge of Guerrero Negro, (115) 70-1-00. Offers two trips a day to Laguna Ojo de Liebre, leaving at 8 a.m. and noon. The cost is about $40 and includes a box lunch and beverage.

Open Air Excursions, Guerrero #339, in the center of town, (322) 2-33-10, e-mail openair@vallarta.zonavirtual.com.mx. This highly recommended small company offers a variety of environmental trips including sea kayaking, hiking, bird-watching, and whale-watching. Their trips combine environmental education, scientific research, and tourism. The company is owned and operated by two oceanologists and professional adventure tourism guides, Oscar Frey and Isabel Cardenas. The business supports several conservation projects, including a scientific camp that studies sea turtles, a program of the Mexico's National Fisheries Institute; and the photography of humpback whales that return to Banderas Bay each year. The photos document the relationships within whale families and help researchers understand migratory habits and territorial patterns.

TURTLE-WATCHING

Seven of the world's eight species of sea turtles live in Mexico; all are threatened or endangered. An interesting private project, **Custodio de los Tortugas**, in the state of Nayarit, works with local ejidos as well as the government's environmental secretariat to these turtles.

In the United States, the San Francisco–based **Earth Island Institute** sponsors a Sea Turtle Restoration Project active in Mexico and, primarily, in Central America. Earth Island Institute, along with Mexico's Grupo de los 100, has actively lobbied for improved legislation and increased security measures to protect the turtles. For information on these projects, contact EII, 300 Broadway, Ste. 28, San Francisco, CA 94133, (800) 859-7283.

The most famous turtle camp is located in the state of Oaxaca in the town of **Mazunte**. Although this used to be a famous "killing beach" where the local economy was based on the slaughter of turtles, the town has made a dramatic U-turn. The new outlook? Tourism and naturally produced cosmetics. Time will tell if Mazunte's ecotourism project is sustainable, but you can help make the difference by visiting. (See Chapter 12 for more information.)

Earthwatch sponsors scientific trips that document turtle nesting and migratory habits out of Bahia de Los Angeles, Baja California. (See "Natural History," below, for details.)

Turtle-Watching Tour Operators

Custodio de los Tortugas, Platanitas, Nayarit, (329) 22954 or, in the U.S., (509) 996-3356; e-mail custodio@methow.com, Web site http://balsam.methow.com/~custodio/. The week-long research expedition program is $850. Staying at the lodge costs $75 per day.

Mazunte, Mazunte, Oaxaca, (958) 406-22. Contact Ecosolar, 543-4431 or 543-7398, e-mail ecosolar@laneta.apc.org, Web site http://www.laneta.apc/mazunte. Ecosolar, a environmental consultation group in Mexico City, can help make reservations for work on this community project for turtle conservation on Oaxaca's Pacific Coast.

Protecting the Turtles:
El Custodio de las Tortugas

El Custodio de las Tortugas is a Mexican corporation "dedicated to resource conservation management and development planning." A private business, El Custodio is deeply committed to protecting the largest sea turtle nesting beach in the state of Nayarit, about 97 kilometers (60 miles) north of Puerto Vallarta.

El Custodio has permission to assist in patrolling the beach from the Secretariat of Environment, Natural Resources, and Fisheries (SEMARNAP) and from a group called CEREP (Cooperativa Ejidal de la Reserva Ecológica de Platanitos), made up of representatives of local communities that own the land near El Custodio, in a 45,000-hectare (111,150-acre) reserve called Platanitos.

The project is growing exponentially. The owners are purchasing more land for turtle protection and have a written agreement with the local farming community Ejido El Espino that designates the estuaries behind the turtle camp as an ecological zone.

The state of Nayarit has funded one turtle camp which protected and released more than 50,000 hatchlings of several endangered sea turtle species last season. Custodio has been authorized to assist in building and maintaining an additional camp which will at least double these results.

The project has various options for travelers, including a sea-kayak trip that spends several nights at El Custodio before continuing along the coast for another three nights.

Kayak trips cost $150 to $200 per day per person; the week-long research expedition program costs $850. Staying at the lodge costs $75 per day. For more information call (329) 2-29-54 or, in the U.S., (509) 996-3356; e-mail custodio @methow.com, Web site http://balsam.methow.com/~custodio/.

ADVENTURE SPORTS

BACKPACKING AND DAY HIKING

Mexico has numerous hikes for day-trippers as well as more dedicated backpackers. An excellent guidebook is *Backpacking in Mexico* by Tim Burford (Globe Pequot Press, 1997). Hiking in Mexico is enjoyed by nationals and foreigners alike. If you have a good guide or map, you'll enjoy Mexico from the ground up. Take your time.

As Mexican terrain varies from deserts to mountains to wetlands, choose your shoes carefully. A good pair of hiking boots may be perfect if you're climbing mountains, but sport sandals will be better for the beach or kayaking. If you have large feet like the author, you should know that even getting flip-flops may be impossible in Mexico.

Hiking and Backpacking Outfitters

Al Aire Libre, Centro Comercial Interlomas, Local 2122 Lomas Anahuac, 52760 Huixquilucan, Edo de Mexico, (5) 291-9217, e-mail RCHRISTY@compuserve.com. Offers hiking and rock climbing trips throughout Cental Mexico.

Expediciones Ecotur, Km. 16 on the highway to Ensenada, Baja California, (66) 36-11-83, U.S. fax (619) 662-1720. This reputable company offers a number of travel packages. A five-day hiking trip to the Sierra de San Francisco costs $295.

View of the Sierra Madre Occidental, State of Durango

RIVER TRIPS

Veracruz has seen a boom in companies taking people down the Pescados-Antigua. In addition, the Filobobos boasts the Toltec-Husasteco archaeological zone El Cuajilote, best visited via river. Rafting is also becoming big business in Morelos and Chiapas. On the Guatemalan border, the Río Usumacinta is recommended for rafting during the winter dry season.

River-Trip Operators

Far Flung Adventures, Terilingua, Texas, (800) 359-4138. Operates river-rafting trips in the Santa Elena Canyon on the Rio Grande in Big Bend National Park on the Texas border. Also runs trips into Mariscal Canyon and Boquillas Canyon, and seasonal excursions to Veracruz and Chiapas.

Mexico Verde, José María Vigil No. 2406, Col. Italia Providencia, 44620 Guadalajara, Jalisco, (3) 641-5598, fax (3) 641-1005. Offers rafting trips throughout Mexico. For the past several years they have specialized in Veracruz.

Río y Montaña, Prado Norte 450-T, Lomas de Chapultepec, 11000 Mexico, D.F., 520-2041, fax 540-7870, e-mail rioymontana @compuserve.com.mx. Another well-respected adventure tourism company which specializes in Veracruz. Most of the Veracruz trips leave on the weekends and feature two descents for $250.

Veraventuras, Santos Degollado No. 81-8, 91000 Xalapa, Veracruz, (28) 18-95-79 or 18-97-79, fax (28) 18-96-80. This local company tailors specialized tours throughout Veracruz, and offers single-day, three-day, and week-long trips. Three-day tours on the Pescados-Antigua and Actopan Rivers cost $125 to $225 depending on accommodations.

Villa Calmecac, Zacatecas 114, Cuernavaca, (73) 132-146, e-mail meliton@mail.giga.com. One of Mexico's few truly eco-friendly hotels is run by Meliton Cross, one of the founding members of AMTAVE, Mexico's ecotourism promotion association. The small hotel ($20 per night) offers various workshops as well as full-day rafting, canoeing, and kayak trips ($40) on the Amacuzac River in southern Morelos from June through October.

DIVING AND SNORKELING

Mexico's coral reefs offer spectacular diving. Divers come from around the world to visit the Yucatán. Cozumel, too, is an important mecca for divers, who have long fought the development of a controversial pier. Another popular spot, Akumal, also boasts great diving and snorkeling. Near the Sian Ka'an Biosphere Reserve, offshore of Xcalak, is the Chinchorro Reef. The entire Maya Reef that extends along the coast of Quintana Roo was declared a protected area in 1997.

Inland diving can be exciting as well. The two lakes on top of the Nevado de Toluca (an extinct volcano west of Mexico City), at 4,500 meters (14,764 feet), are among the world's highest places for diving. A warmer option is the Laguna de Media Luna in the state of San Luis Potosí.

Diving-Trip Operators

Aqua Safari, on Cozumel Island between Calles 5 and 7, on the waterfront, 2-01-01 or 2-31-01, e-mail dive@aquasafari.com. The PADI certification course costs $350, and a two-tank dive trip costs $50. The shop rents diving gear and cameras. The operation also has a small inn with 12 rooms ($35 per double).

Asociación Nacional de Operatores de Actividades Acuaticas y Turisticas, 15 Avenida Norte No. 299-B, Cozumel, Quintana Roo, e-mail annoat@cozunet.finred.com.mx, Web site http://www.cozumel.net /diving/anoaat. This is the national association of water-based tour operators and a terrific source of information.

Buceo Total, Xicotencatl 186, Col. del Carmen Coyoacan, 04100 Mexico, D.F., (5) 688-3736, fax 604-2869. Offers diving trips to the craters of extinct volcanoes, such as Nevado de Toluca, as well as coastal reef diving. The cost is $100 per day.

Nautilus Dive Shop, Costera Miguel Aleman #450, Acapulco, (74) 83-11-08. Provides NAUI certification courses, and rents and services equipment. The owners have 20 years of experience and provide bilingual guides.

Subaquatec, Andrea de Casdagno 57, Col. Mixcoac, 03700 Mexico, D.F., (5) 611-3517, fax 598-4300, e-mail subaqua@inetcorp.net.mx. Arranges diving trips on the Pacific and in the Yucatán. A four-night trip to the Veracruz reefs costs $180.

MOUNTAIN BIKING

Rental bikes are available at many of the resorts. In the Yucatán, the frequent use of *topes* (speed bumps) slows down the automobile traffic and makes bicycling safer than in the big cities.

If you take your own bike, pick up a sturdy crate from a bicycle store. Or buy an inexpensive bike in Mexico and sell it before you leave.

Biking-Trip Operators

Bike Mex, Guerrero 361 in the Colonia Centro, Puerto Vallarta, tel./fax (322) 3-1680, e-mail bikemex@vallarta.zonavirtual.com.mx. Offers a variety of one- and multi-day bike trips in the region. For the advanced cyclist, they offer the "Killer Doney Trail," which climbs high into the Sierra Madre. Less-taxing trips stay closer to sea level.

B-B-Bobby's Bikes, Miramar 399, (322) 3-00-08, e-mail bbikespv @acnet.net, Web site http://www.cupertinobike.com/bobby.htm. Offers a variety of options including both professionally guided and self-guided circuits ranging from $20 to $50. All mountain bike rentals and self-guided tours include a map and instructions, cycle computer, helmet, gloves, two large water bottles, a mini-pump, and a fanny pack. The most frequently requested routes, Playa Grande and Río Cuale/Vallejo pass through cobbled streets of Vallarta's picturesque outlying villages. The rides cost $35 each and are about 20 kilometers (12 miles) long.

Grupo Advent, Fresno 293-A, Santa María de la Rivera, (5) 547-0649, e-mail advent@ienlaces.com.mx. Mexico City–based guided trips go to Teotihuacán, Ajusco, Tepotzlán, and Valle de Bravo. Day trips cost $50 plus rental. Inquire about multi-day trips throughout the country.

EXPLORING HISTORY AND CULTURE

ARCHAEOLOGICAL AND NATURAL HISTORY EXPEDITIONS

Archaeological travel in Mexico has always been linked with nature-based tourism. Most of the ruins are in rural areas. Bird-watchers will have a field day at Palenque or Yaxchilán, in Chiapas. In turn, those fascinated by the history of the ancient Maya or Toltecs will learn a great deal from the environment. You can book a trip in advance or after you arrive in Mexico; ask your hotel clerk about the regional ruins or parks.

Archaeological and Natural History Tour Operators

Far Horizons, P.O. Box 91900, Albuquerque, NM 87199-1900, (505) 343-9400, e-mail 75473.3100@compuserve.com. Offers archaeological and cultural tours led by talented scholars.

International Expeditions, One Environs Park, Helena, AL 35080, (800) 633-4734, Web site http://www.ietravel.com. Offers a variety of archaeological and nature-based trips.

Earthwatch, Box 9104, Watertown, MA 02272, (800) 776-0188. International nonprofit volunteer organization, founded in 1972, whose purpose is to give top scientists, humanists, and other scholars the money and people-power to carry out their fieldwork. Those who participate in programs donate their time, money, and labor to field expeditions.

University Research Expeditions, University of California, Berkeley, CA 94720-7050, (510) 642-6586, fax (510) 642-6791. This program builds partnerships between scientists and the public. Participants are expected to share the costs of the expedition and lend a helping hand. The program is coordinated by the University of California, and part of the fee is considered a contribution to the university and therefore tax-deductible. Academic credit can be arranged for students participating in this field research, and some partial scholarships are available. Topics change depending on the current research, but recent expeditions have included archaeology of Maya farmers in the Yucatán and prehistoric

Land's End, Cabo San Lucas

hunters of Baja California. Spanish is helpful but not mandatory. The cost for the two-week program runs from $1,200 to $1,500.

EcoGrupos Vallarta, Ignaciono L Vallarta 243, Puerto Vallarta, (322) 2-6606, e-mail 74174.2424@compuserve.com. Tours include whale-watching from Punta Mita beach and an all-day tour to **Isla Isabel**, a marine-bird sanctuary. The island formed from a volcano on the bottom of the Pacific Ocean more than 2 million years ago. EcoGrupos was one of the first travel providers in Mexico to offer natural history tours.

SOCIAL TOURISM
Various groups in the United States and Mexico offer "social tours" which aim to give travelers an accurate idea of what life is really like in another place. Often churches and progressive groups pull together informal tours. Ask around in your community if this is of interest to you. More organized events are offered by the groups below.

Social Tourism Operators
Global Exchange, 2017 Mission St., Ste. 303, San Francisco, CA 94110, (415) 255-7296, e-mail globalexch@igc.org. This group, one of the best-known in the United States, offers "Reality Tours" that "explore the other face of Mexico." Visitors interact with indigenous communities to learn about their history, culture, and present-day struggles. Trips include visits to Oaxaca for the Day of the Dead, coffee tours of Chiapas, and specialized outings focusing on women's issues.

Casa de los Amigos, Calle Ignacio Mariscal 132, 06030 Mexico, D.F., (52) 5 705-0646, fax (52) 5 705-0771, e-mail amigos@laneta.apc.org, Web site http://www.laneta.apc.org/amigos. This Mexico City Quaker house sponsors a series of week-long seminars on such topics as the environment, poverty, and women. An annual conference and grassroots tour entitled the "Urban Megalopolis and Environmental Impact on Mexico City" reviews infrastructure and social themes at play in the world's largest city. Spanish is not required for these programs, but participants must be at least 17 years old. The cost is $200.

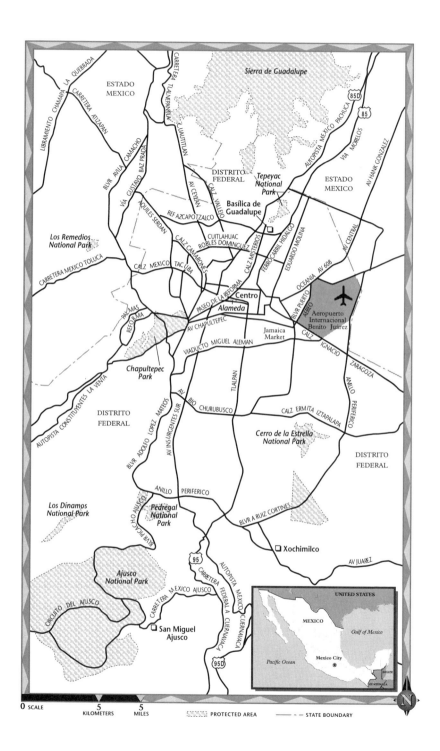

ESTADO MEXICO

Sierra de Guadalupe

LIBRAMIENTO CHAMAPA LA QUEBRADA

CARRETERA ATIZAPAN

CARRETERA TLALNEPANTLA CUAUTITLAN

AUTOPISTA MEXICO PACHUCA

85D

85

VIA MORELOS

AV HANK GONZALEZ

DISTRITO FEDERAL

ESTADO MEXICO

Tepeyac National Park

BLVR AVILA CAMACHO

VIA GUSTAVO BAZ PRADA

AQUILES SERDAN

AV CEYLAN

CALZ VALLEJO

REF AZCAPOTZALCO

Basílica de Guadalupe

Los Remedios National Park

CALZ CAMARONES

CUITLAHUAC ROBLES DOMINGUEZ

CALZ MISTERIOS

FERROCARRIL HIDALGO

EDUARDO MOLINA

AV CENTRAL

CARRETERA MEXICO TOLUCA

CALZ MEXICO TACUBA

AV 608

OCEANIA

PALMAS

REFORMA

PASEO DE LA REFORMA

Centro

Alameda

BLVR PUERTO AEREO

Aeropuerto Internacional Benito Juárez

AV CHAPULTEPEC

Jamaica Market

CALZ IGNACIO ZARAGOZA

ANILLO PERIFERICO

Chapultepec Park

VIADUCTO MIGUEL ALEMAN

TLALPAN

AV RIO CHURUBUSCO

CALZ ERMITA IZTAPALAPA

AUTOPISTA CONSTITUENTES LA VENTA

DISTRITO FEDERAL

BLVD ADOLFO LOPEZ MATEOS

AV INSURGENTES SUR

Cerro de la Estrella National Park

DISTRITO FEDERAL

Los Dínamos National Park

ANILLO PERIFERICO

BLVR PICACHO AJUSCO

Pedregal National Park

BLVR A RUIZ CORTINES

Xochimilco

AV JUAREZ

Ajusco National Park

95

CARRETERA MEXICO AJUSCO

AUTOPISTA MEXICO A CUERNAVACA

CIRCUITO DEL AJUSCO

CARRETERA FEDERAL A CUERNAVACA

San Miguel Ajusco

95D

UNITED STATES

MEXICO

Gulf of Mexico

Pacific Ocean

Mexico City

BELIZE

GUATEMALA

0 SCALE

5 KILOMETERS

5 MILES

PROTECTED AREA

STATE BOUNDARY

N

5

MEXICO CITY AND VICINITY

Most people don't think of Mexico City, with a population of 20 million people, as an environmental destination. But keep an eye on the world's largest metropolis—instead of being behind the curve, the Federal District (known as "D.F." in Spanish) may be leading the pack. The city is actually quite green with its numerous open spaces, including Alameda and Chapultepec Parks.

Mexico City is situated in the southern part of the Valley of Mexico and lies about 2,200 meters (7,326 feet) above sea level. The sprawling metropolis is surrounded by mountains and volcanoes that reach altitudes of more than 5,000 meters (16,400 feet). The snowcapped volcanoes Popocatépetl and Ixtaccíhuatl tower over the Valley of Mexico, just 45 kilometers (28 miles) to the southeast, but are rarely visible from the city itself because of the air pollution. When the sky is clear and they are visible, they provide a spectacular sight, especially at sunrise and sunset when the clouds over the valley turn violet, orange, and blood-red.

In many ways, it's easy to dismiss the idea that this city could ever successfully live within its means. Mexico City and its surrounding metropolitan area is the most populated urban area the world has ever known. The city's world-infamous smog inflicts grave health problems on its residents.

To make matters worse, the metropolis is built on a saline lake bed (basically, compacted mud). Earthquakes regularly shake the city, sometimes, as in 1985, with tragic consequences. The catastrophe, which

Mexico City, with Alameda Park on the left

claimed the lives of more than 9,000 people, was the result of the collision of the Cocos Plate with the lighter American Plate, some 350 kilometers (217 miles) west of the capital. The earthquake sent seismic waves racing inland, and in the sediment-filled bowl of bedrock underneath Mexico City, the waves were amplified. A 1986 *National Geographic* article stated that at the height of the quake "twenty seismic waves swelled at 20-second intervals below the city, making its lake-bed foundations wobble like jelly."

While the danger of earthquakes is always present, measures have been taken to alert the *Chilangos* (common slang for the residents of Mexico City) of impending danger. An alarm system installed on the Pacific coast gives a 30-second warning—provided the earthquake tremors hail from that direction. Meanwhile, since the 1985 disaster, officials have taken the opportunity to convert many of the lots where buildings toppled into public parks.

When I made my first trip to Mexico City, I expected the worst, so I was entirely surprised to find out that not only was the city not as bleak as it had been painted in newspaper reports, it was actually quite friendly. Like many travelers, I intended to race through Mexico City, but there were too many attractions to pass up. If you travel in Mexico, plan on spending some leisurely time in the capital.

The city's parks carve out numerous green spaces, the largest of which are the 850-hectare (2,100-acre) Chapultepec Park and the cozy

Alameda Park, immortalized in Diego Rivera's mural *Dream of a Sunday Afternoon in the Alameda*. I still remember lying down under the trees of the Alameda and realizing that the only thing I didn't like was the wheezing drone of the organ grinders.

I returned to Mexico City several times and eventually accepted a position at *The News*, Mexico's oldest English-language newspaper. During 1992 and 1993 I worked in the finance section and as the newspaper's environmental correspondent. I took a careful look at the city's environmental movers and shakers to see what roles they were playing in the quality of life in Mexico City. It was also my job to find all the wonderful places that exist in Mexico, including museums, parks, nature reserves, archaeological ruins, environmental education centers—anything that was related to the country's natural environment. The best surprise of all was that I found many places to commune with nature in the very heart of Mexico.

WATER

A pressing environmental problem is Mexico City's seemingly unquenchable thirst for water. The city consumes 3.5 million cubic meters (125 million cubic feet) of water every day, twice the level of many industrialized countries. This is because much of the water is lost through leaky pipes before it reaches household taps.

Business concessions have been granted to companies in Mexico City that are building water-supply and treatment plants. Although the investment potential looks great, many enterprises have been frustrated by citizens' unwillingness to pay for their water. In addition, the country's recent economic crisis brought many of these projects to a standstill.

Most of the urban water supply is pumped from aquifers beneath the city. The removal of the groundwater has caused some of the buildings to sink more rapidly than usual. The water table has dropped by 32 meters (105 feet), and the city itself has sunk by 7 meters (23 feet) since 1940. Efforts are underway to construct physical supports for buildings such as Bellas Artes and the cathedral.

About 20 to 30 percent of the city's water is pumped uphill 1,000 meters (3,280 feet) from the Lerma and Cutzamala Rivers, 100 kilometers (62 miles) to the west. The rest is pumped from underground aquifers. Sewage is disposed of out of town, much to the frustration of outlying communities. Built in 1900, the Great Sewage Canal (Gran Canal de Desagüe) megaproject drove a pipeline through the northern hills to carry human waste and garbage outside the valley. At the beginning of the century, gravity was sufficient to pull the putrid black waters out of town. But as the city began to sink,

59

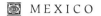

11 pumping stations had to be constructed. Today, yet another deep drainage system is being built.

AIR QUALITY

Mexico City measures its air quality every hour of every day. Pollution is usually worse on the southern edge of town because the prevailing winds are from the north and the air is trapped by the Ajusco Mountains. The winter months are the worst for air pollution in the Valley of Mexico, due to fewer and lighter air currents. Cooler air temperatures create thermal inversions, which keep car exhaust and industrial emissions hovering just above ground level and can cause respiratory, eye, and throat irritations. In June the rainy season begins in earnest, and summer is considered to be the least polluted season.

The U.N.'s World Health Organization classifies Metropolitan Air Quality Index (Imeca) readings over 100 points as "unsatisfactory" and readings over 200 points as "dangerous." When the Imeca breaks 200 points, the city orders all outdoor activities for primary, secondary, and preschool children canceled as the young are more susceptible to the ill effects of bad air.

A Phase One alert (called when the Imeca breaks 250 points) doubles the "no circula" policy and 40 percent of privately-owned vehicles and half of all government vehicles are kept off city streets the following day. Industries are also ordered to reduce their emissions. Are the policies working? The number of days with Imeca readings over 200 increased in 1997, leading Homero Aridjis, leader of the Grupo de 100 environmental group, to criticize the government's strategies, saying that it depended more on the "Secretariat of the Wind" than anyone else to clear the valley of its polluted air.

In the late 1980s city politicians suggested constructing giant fans to stir up the air and push the pollution out of the valley. The idea is a flash of genius—or absurdity. Others have suggested drilling tunnels through the mountains to ventilate the valley. Most recently, a legislator suggested that all capital helicopters organize into a strategic formation to whip the smog out of town. Desperate times call for desperate measures. In fact, the city's success or failure over the next ten years will depend on the amount of political, cultural, and economic will exhibited by its citizens to bring Mexico City into balance with the environment.

ENVIRONMENTAL GROUPS IN MEXICO CITY

Mexico City hosts a number of environmental groups dedicated to raising environmental awareness. Activist groups such as **Grupo de los 100** continue to raise their voices for conservation and environmental balance. The **Environmental Education and Training Institute of North**

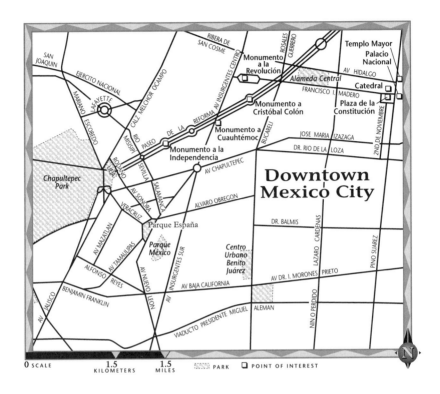

America (EETINA) focuses on environmental education and specialized training and works with U.S. and Canadian counterparts. (Contact information is listed in Appendix B.)

Luis Manuel Guerra hosts a daily radio program in addition to a 1-hour environmental talk show, aptly entitled *Ecocide*. Guerra, the founder of the independent environmental research institute **INAINE**, studies issues from water to air quality and offers technical advice. Call (5) 689-6885 for more information.

The **Mexican Institute for Renewable Resources** has a top-notch library, open to the public. Founded by Enrique Beltran, a co-founder of the International Union for Conservation of Nature and Natural Resources (IUCN), an independent assembly of scientists, the library itself is one of the best resources in Mexico City. Beltran's family continues to carry on the work of raising environmental awareness in Mexico. The institute is located at Dr. Vertiz 724; (5) 519-1633 or 519-4505, e-mail imernar@laneta.apc.org or ebeltra1@mail.internet.com.mx.

The **Centro de Ecología y Desarrollo** (**Cecodes**) is one of the more persistent of the academic centers that review environmental issues—it was briefly closed and then renamed under the Salinas administration. Cecodes produces numerous Spanish-language reports and studies on Mexican environmental issues, including studies on transportation in Mexico City, reviews of the nation's lakes and dams, and in-depth investigations of regions such as the Isthmus of Tehuantepec. These books are for sale, and students and scholars interested in further information can use the center's extensive library. The center is located at Chiapas 208, Dept. 7; (5) 264-8758 or 264-2138, e-mail cecodes@laneta.apc.org.

Naturalia, an environmental group led by Oscar Moctezuma, campaigns for endangered species of Mexico, including the Mexican wolf and the Zacatuche rabbit. Naturalia's crusade supports captive breeding programs, mounts expeditions to locate wild wolf populations, and conducts an environmental education campaign to dispel malicious wolf myths. "A myth widely spread by ranchers is that all wolves kill cattle," Moctezuma says. "But only a few do this and only because their natural prey is so scarce. On the other hand, studies have demonstrated the enormous value of the role the wolf plays in its ecosystem." Naturalia's campaign is funded through subscriptions to its bimonthly magazine and the sale of T-shirts, mugs, and posters. For information, contact Oscar Moctezuma at (5) 674-6678, e-mail naturalia@servidor.unam.mx.

Pronatura also sponsors public education campaigns and environmental trips. The group is 15 years old and has sister chapters in Xalapa, Veracruz, Hermosillo, Sonora, and Mérida, Yucatán. Their Mexico City office is located at Camino al Ajusco No. 124; (5) 630-1008.

TOURIST INFORMATION

SECTUR, Mexico's Tourism Secretariat, maintains a 24-hour telephone hotline: (5) 250-0123 or (5) 250-0151 with English-speaking operators. The main office, located at Avenida Presidente Masaryk 172 at the corner of Hegel in the Polanco district, is open Monday through Friday from 9 a.m. to 9 p.m. Information on ecotourism is slight, but may expand in the near future. On the bright side, the staff can help you make reservations anywhere in the country.

Another SECTUR office is located at Amberes 54 on the corner of Londres in the Zona Rosa and is open daily from 9 a.m. to 9 p.m. You will also find general tourism information at the international airport and at the city's bus stations.

THINGS TO SEE AND DO
IN AND AROUND MEXICO CITY

CHAPULTEPEC PARK

It's easy to spot Chapultepec Park from the air. The greenery of this 850–hectare (2,100-acre) oasis stands in sharp contrast to the gray urban zone surrounding it. The park dates to the 1420s, when Aztec kings created the first nature reserve in the Americas, complete with small forests, botanical gardens, zoos, and aviaries. Then known as Cerro de Chapultepec (Grasshopper Hill), it provided the drinking water for Tenochtitlán.

Today, on weekends and holidays, Mexican families picnic on the expansive green lawns, and there never seems to be a time when the park could be called empty. The park is home to a zoo (greatly improved since the days of Keiko the whale, star of *Free Willy*), a children's museum, an anthropology museum, and a small lake where you can rent a rowboat.

The **Museo de Antropología** (National Anthropology Museum) is an absolute must-see, combining anthropological studies of Mexico's indigenous groups with a mind-bending collection of artifacts produced over the past 3,000 years. Mexico's cultural diversity and artistic genius are showcased in 23 exhibition halls. It's easy to wander the museum yourself, or you can take a guided half-day tour.

Highlights include the Aztec Calendar Stone, giant Olmec heads made of basalt, and reproduced murals and tombs. Fortunately, there is a fine café on the lower level, where you can boost your blood sugar in the middle or at the end of your visit. Flash photography is not permitted in the museum. There is a $5 entrance fee for the museum, except on Sundays, when admission to all national museums is free. Student discounts are available only for students of Mexican universities and schools.

El Papalote (The Kite), the newest addition to Chapultepec Park, is one of the world's finest children's museums. It's filled floor to ceiling with science displays, a rain forest tree, a five-story maze, and interactive Spanish-language games. Papalote is a delight for young and old alike. It's also a hangout for Mexican celebrities, including El Cuaz, the adventure sports enthusiast whose exploits on Mexican cable television entertain thousands. The museum, which is located in the second section of Chapultepec Park, is open daily from 9 a.m. to 6 p.m., and is closed Mondays. The park is located at Av. Consitituyentes 268; (5) 237-1700.

THE RUINS OF TENOCHTITLAN

In February 1978 a ditch digger preparing a new line for the Metro struck something hard with his shovel. Scraping the dirt away, construction

Day of the Dead altar in the Tenochtitlán ruins

workers noticed it was an engraving. Work stopped immediately. When the engraving was unearthed, archaeologists were summoned, and the carved stone disk depicting the dismembered body of the goddess Coyolxauqhuix identified the site as the Templo Mayor, the Great Temple of the Aztec empire.

The temple is located at the very place where the Aztecs had the vision, promised by their god Huitzilopochtli, of an eagle perched upon a nopal (prickly pear) cactus devouring a snake. Upon the site the Aztecs erected a pyramid with two temples, one dedicated to Huitzilopochtli, the other to the agricultural rain god Tlaloc.

Another legend suggests that the temple is constructed on top of two caves that are filled with a primordial water. The caves are home to Huehueteotl, the ancient god of fire and lord of time who occupied the center of the earth. In building their pyramid on this visionary site, the Aztecs honored sacred space.

The Templo Mayor was the sacred mountain and sacrificial altar for the Aztecs. Diverse offerings were brought to this holy place as a result of conquests and tributes. Many of the caches were water-related. The temple integrates symbols of water, earth, sun, and sky, natural elements honored by all Mesoamerican civilizations. The Aztecs constructed the temple as not only a man-made structure, but as an equal partner in the natural order of things. The temple was believed to provide the greatest source of all, the energy of creation. Because of its cultural and religious value, the temple was destroyed by Cortés after the Spanish defeated the Aztecs.

For hundreds of years the location of the temple could only be guessed. After the discovery and archaeological work, the government opened the ruins and a new museum to the public. Located just behind the cathedral in the *zócalo*, the ruins and museum are open Tuesday through Sunday; on Sunday admission is free.

XOCHIMILCO ECOLOGICAL PARK

The highlight of any trip to Mexico City is a visit to one of the original breadbaskets of the Americas, the raised fields of Xochimilco Ecological

Park. (Consider this the ecological equivalent of the Basilica of Guadalupe.) Five hundred years ago this was the agricultural hub of Tenochtitlán, a metropolis of 235,000 inhabitants. Today, as in centuries past, a series of canals surround raised agricultural fields called *chinampas*. Since the Valley of Mexico is mostly wetlands and swamps, the chinampas were the most practical means of agricultural production. In the Aztec's Náhuatl language, the name "Xochimilco" means "garden of flowers." Not only were vegetables once grown in the raised beds, so too were the flowers that lined the streets of the city and its rooftop gardens.

There are two main parts to Xochimilco: a traditional, tourism-oriented area a few blocks west of the historical center of town, and the newer ecological park north of town. The 190-hectare (470-acre) park was created in 1993 as part of a multimillion-dollar "ecological rescue project" spearheaded by the municipal government. Visitors to the park can stroll the promenades to see examples of the trees native to the central valley of Mexico City. It's also an excellent area for bird-watching. Pleasant lagoons attract bulrushes, ducks, and egrets. There are poorly maintained gravel paths for walking or biking throughout the park; rental bikes are available nearby. If you want a better understanding of the area, Xochimilco is best appreciated on the extensive canal system. Take a leisurely boat ride in one of the brightly colored *trajineras*—squarish canoes that can carry up to a dozen passengers. The park is open from 10 a.m. to 6 p.m. Tuesday through Sunday. It has a small museum, but unfortunately it offers very little information on the environmental history represented by the canals.

Your other choice is to go to the traditional area of Xochimilco, where there are several *embarcaderos*, or piers, within a few blocks of the historical center of town. Weekends are lively times as families visit the park, and boats carrying musicians serenade young lovers. There are always plenty of vendors selling food and drink. The trajineras typically charge about $10 an hour. One could ride for a full day without seeing the whole park, however, 2 hours is usually sufficient.

Las Chinampas (The Agricultural Fields)

Between the eighth and tenth centuries, seven Nahua tribes arrived in the Valley of Mexico. The Xochimilca people founded their city at the southern tip of the valley. Another tribe, the Aztecs (also called the Mexica), founded Tenochtitlán and the Aztec empire farther north. Soon after the Aztecs' arrival, they conquered the Xochimilcas, whose agricultural fields, or *chinampas*, were used to provide the food for the growing Aztec empire. (Today the D.F. easily encompasses the once-distant cities.)

Chinampas are formed by alternating layers of aquatic weeds, muck, and earth packed inside rectangular cane frames firmly rooted to the lake floor. You may hear them called "floating gardens," but the term takes poetic license with the truth. Trees such as cypress *(ahuehuetes)* are planted every meter along the edges of the fields. Their roots have long anchored the beds securely to the lake bottom.

In the late 1540s, after the Spanish conquest, chinampas covered nearly 9,000 hectares (22,230 acres) on Lakes Xochimilco and Chalco. Each hectare (2.47 acres) could provide food for between 15 and 20 people, thus supporting most of Tenochtitlán's residents.

When the Spanish arrived, they imposed more traditional forms of agriculture and simultaneously began to drain the lake bed. What was the proud agricultural hub of Xochimilco became a neglected garden; hundreds of years later, in the 1970s and 1980s, it became a depository for the city's wastewaters. The many freshwater springs that once fed Lake Xochimilco were successively diverted to provide a water supply for Mexico City. More than two-thirds of the fields cultivated in the 1930s have been paved over by streets and homes.

Most of the water that reached the canals was contaminated by residential or industrial pollution and could not be used for food crops. The chinamperos chose to increase flower cultivation instead, using discarded

Trajineras await passengers in Xochimilco

oil cans filled with organic muck from the bottom of the canal. The area suffered from environmental neglect until 1990, when Xochimilco was declared an urban ecological park. The treated waters are now maintained year-round. The chinampas should not be seen as mere historical artifacts, but as a living example of alternative agriculture. Farmers continue to scrape muck and organic debris from the canals, using the muck as fertilizer for the agricultural gardens. *Chilicastle*, the plentiful, shiny blue-green algae that grows on the water's surface, is scooped from the water and placed on the earth to help maintain the soil's fertility.

To see chinampas where farmers actually cultivate corn and vegetables in the summer and flowers in the winter, you have to get off the beaten track. Geographer Phil Crossley, who has studied the chinampas for the past ten years, suggests traveling to San Gregorio, 20 minutes east of the final stop on the *tren ligero* (electric train). He writes, "There are several places you can walk out into chinampas being farmed in vegetables, mostly lettuce, spinach, and some other local faves, including *acelga* and *verdolaga*. The easiest one to find and get to is right beside the El Acuario restaurant. . . . Farmers are friendly and don't seem to mind visitors as long as you're careful about where you walk; greet and ask permission of everyone you meet."

Getting to Xochimilco
From central Mexico City, take the green Metro (line 2) to the end of the line at the Tasqueña station and change trains to the tren ligero (the signs are well marked), which runs directly to Xochimilco. From Xochimilco you have two options. You can take a taxi to San Gregorio or walk five blocks west of the central plaza to the Embarcadero Fernando Celada.

For more information, call the Xochimilco Ecological Park, (5) 673-8139, or the Mexico City office of SECTUR at (5) 250-0123 or 250-0151.

Near Xochimilco
After visiting Xochimilco, an obligatory stop is the nearby **Dolores Olmedo Patiño Museum**, set in a colonial mansion from the 16th century at 5843 Avenida México. It contains one of the best collections of artwork by Diego Rivera and Frida Kahlo. The museum is open Tuesday through Sunday from 10 a.m. to 6 p.m. Admission is $1.50. For information, call (5) 555-1016.

SAN NICOLAS PARK
For those spending more than a few days in Mexico City, an outing to the nearby Ajusco Mountains is an obligatory and rewarding trek. Despite its

recent urbanization, large parts of Mexico City and the surrounding valley are still rural areas, where the local people have not lost their connection to nature, nor their desire to share this blessing with their urban neighbors.

San Nicolás is located on the old two-lane Pichuca-to-Ajusco Highway, in southern Mexico City. The entrance is marked by the restaurant of Don Leonardo, Las Llantas, so named because the parking area is demarcated by large tractor tires buried in the ground. On weekends the parking area and the park itself is crowded. The entrance fee is $1, or $1.50 with guided service.

San Nicolás is just one of Mexico's many ejidos, large parcels of land turned over to communities of farmers by the government after the Mexican Revolution. Today ejidos make up 60 percent of Mexico's territory, and in the areas that the government has declared "protected," the ejidos comprise 90 percent of the territory.

San Nicolás was officially declared an ejido in 1924 and expanded 12 years later in 1938. Although it officially opens to the public in the beginning of 1998, it's already used by 1,600 visitors a week, almost half of whom are cyclists who use the well-made trails to explore and race through the mountain passes.

In preparation for better management of tourism, guides are being trained, and workshops are being offered for local residents. Says resident and local guide Santiago Martínes Castro, "We want to make this operation like a restaurant with a menu. We need to provide a variety of options for the traveler." Guides are trained to identify the native plants, which transform the forest into a combination pharmacy and multipurpose *tienda*. On my trip into the Ajusco, Martínes pointed out *perlilla*, used for making brooms; and the *sauco* tree, whose flowers are used in tea to relieve coughing.

San Nicolás has established areas for camping as well as easy trails for the elderly and children. Wisely, park managers want to make sure the hiking and biking trails are clearly defined. It's no fun to dodge slow-moving hikers if you're on two wheels and it's worse being hit by a fast-moving mountain bike if you're on foot.

In promoting environment-based tourism, the 2,340-hectare *ejido* of San Nicolás is also redefining how it wants to conserve its natural resources. The *ejidatario*'s primary income comes from the cultivation of agricultural crops—corn, wheat, beans, peas, potatoes, and a variety of other vegetables and fruit. Some of the land is used for ranching. About 80 percent of the forest is covered in a mix of pine and oak forests, with a scattering of *ocote* and *oyamel* trees. Approximately 2 million trees have been planted in the past 20 years.

The 340 families on the ejido are hoping that ecotourism can help pay some of the bills. When this pilot project formally debuts in the beginning of 1998, it may be one of the first working examples in Mexico of tourism connecting with local economic and environmental development.

The ejido of San Nicolás receives technical support and assistance from a group called Consultores Balam, a former tourism company (Balam Expediciones). "If you want to assure the conservation of these areas, you have to work with ejidos first," says Febo Suárez, who works with the group. Money helps, too. The project received a $50,000 grant from Fondo Mexicano, the country's environmental fund.

For more information about this project, contact Consultores Balam, Atlixco 55, Col. Condesa, Mexico City, (5) 286-9961 or 562 0270, e-mail febobalam@laneta.apc.org or juanci@mexred.net.mx.

Getting to San Nicolás Park
The park is located in the Ajusco Mountains, at the southern edge of Mexico City. Buses marked "Reina Ventura" and "Bosques" depart from La Universidad Metro stop. Ask to be dropped off at Don Leonardo's restaurant. If you are driving, take the *periferico* (the highway that more or less encircles the city) south from the center of town and exit at the Ajusco Highway (a good sign to look for is the brightly colored building of TV Azteca, one of the national networks). Pass the Azteca studios on your right and begin the slow ascent on the highway to the Ajusco. Don Leonardo's restaurant is on your right near the kilometer-20 marker.

OTHER THINGS TO DO IN MEXICO CITY
The **Basilica of Guadalupe,** shrine to one of Mexico's most famous icons, La Virgen de Guadalupe, attracts thousands of pilgrims daily, some of whom travel the last few hundred meters on their knees. Less known is that the original church was built on Cerro del Tepeyac hill, the exact site of the temple of Tonantzin, the Aztec mother goddess. If you're interested in earth-friendly spirituality, plan on spending part of a day at this national park and religious mecca.

Legend has it that in the winter of 1531 a vision of the Virgin Mary appeared to Juan Diego, an indigenous farmer and recent convert to Christianity. The appearance took place ten years after the Spanish triumph over the Aztecs. The grand city of Tenochtitlán was in ruins. Juan Diego, born in 1474, participated in Aztec ceremonies and witnessed the collapse of his civilization. What is important in the story is that Mary appears not to the Spanish conquistadores, but to the Mexicans. And it is to Juan Diego, a poor farmer, that she requests a church be built on this hillside, sacred to the Aztecs.

According to the story, Mary asked Juan Diego to ascend the hill where he would find special proof of the divine appearance to take to the

Hoy No Circula

Travelers should be aware of the "Day without a Car" program, especially if they plan to drive in Mexico City. The city government instituted the program in 1989 in an attempt to relieve Mexico of its daunting traffic by making drivers leave their cars at home one business day a week. The program has had mixed success. There are actually more cars on the street now than when the program began.

The government has targeted motor vehicles as the primary cause of pollution. Whether or not this is true is worthy of debate. Some studies place the blame not on cars but on the city's leaky canisters of household cooking gas.

Nevertheless, the restriction will affect you if you drive in Mexico City. If your license plate ends with the following numbers, do not attempt to drive on the day listed or you will be fined and your vehicle may be confiscated. If you have a novelty license plate that is all alphabetical letters, do not drive on Fridays. All vehicles may drive on Saturdays and Sundays and from 10 p.m. to 5 a.m. The schedule is as follows:

Monday: 5, 6
Tuesday: 7, 8
Wednesday: 3, 4
Thursday: 1, 2
Friday: 9, 0

bishop. On the top of the hill, Juan Diego surprisingly found flowers, in spite of the winter frost. He picked them up and put them inside his cloak. When he went to the bishop's house to give him the flowers, another surprise was in store: The image of the Virgin Mary appeared on the inside of his cloak. It is that portrait that hangs in the basilica today.

When you see the image, try to interpret it as a hieroglyph—the picture was read by the Aztecs 450 years ago. Mary stands on a crescent moon and is silhouetted by the rays of the sun—symbols of the Aztec gods. She is also pregnant, signified by the black cord around her waist. While contemporary viewers may see her folded hands as a sign of prayer, this was the indigenous symbol of gift giving. For whatever reason, the image resonated throughout Mexico and the Americas. You'll find Guadalupe shrines from U.S.-Mexico border towns to Brazil.

So many pilgrims visited the original basilica that a new cathedral was constructed next door. The image of *La Virgen* is hung above moving walkways that carry the visitors back and forth in front of it. A major festival takes place here each year on December 12. To get to the basilica, which is open daily during daylight hours, take the Metro to the La Villa station and walk two blocks north along Calzada de Guadalupe. The area surrounding the basilica is a national park, not because of the diverse wildlife, but for its historic value.

West of the zócalo, **Alameda Park** is named for the *alamos* (cottonwoods) that were first planted here in the late 1500s. Originally the site was an Aztec market. The Spanish converted it into a park, initially square and then enlarged between 1766 and 1771. In the late 19th and early 20th centuries, sculptures were installed.

The park appears the way it did a hundred years ago. The paths crisscross diagonally. Short metal fences do a poor job of keeping people off the grass, and the trees bloom with lavender flowers in the springtime. Visitors will notice a number of vacant lots on the park's southern side. The 1985 earthquake destroyed a slew of hotels that overlooked the park from their Avenida Juárez address.

On the western side of the park, a museum has been especially constructed to house the **Diego Rivera mural *Dream of a Sunday Afternoon in the Alameda***, which depicts key figures from Mexican history standing front and center in the park. If you go inside, a sunglass-wearing guard will show you into a darkened room where the mural is illuminated with cheesy lighting effects. Programs alternate between English and Spanish.

Mexico City has great **outdoor markets**, thanks to Ernesto P. Uruchurtu, who served as city mayor in the 1950s. If you want some fresh fruit or vegetables of if you want to talk with the growers and venders, the following places are within a short taxi ride from anywhere downtown. Note that often items are not priced, so be prepared to bargain.

At the top of the list is the **Jamaica Market**, specializing in live plants, cut flowers, and other imports from the nearby Xochimilco Ecological Park. The Jamaica Market is conveniently located near the Jamaica Metro station. I used to recommend La Merced, just a few blocks southeast of the zócalo, but it's cramped and claustrophobic, especially compared to the open-air coliseum of food found at the Jamaica Market.

A second favorite is the **Sonora Market**, which specializes in botanical cures and a wide variety of herbs. Those interested in witchcraft will find

71

A bicycle taxi ferries passengers in the Centro Histórico in Mexico City.

merchants happy to explain the powers of these herbs. Curiously, if you're looking for a boy's mariachi costume, this is also the place to go. The Sonora Market is a few blocks from the Fray Servando Metro station.

MEXICO CITY TRANSPORTATION

AIR SERVICE

The **Benito Juárez International Airport** is one of the most tourist-friendly airports in the world. If you pause and look bewildered, airport staff will usually offer assistance. In 1993 the international terminal was refurbished, increasing both its space and efficiency. There's plenty of parking, and an organized system of taxis ensures that no one gets ripped off. Inside the airport, there are several taxi kiosks. Tell the clerk where you are going, and you'll be sold a ticket, which you give to the taxi driver outside.

There are separate terminals for domestic and international travel. If your flight arrives at another city in Mexico, you will still go through international customs. As you approach the arrival area, an official will ask you for your customs card then point you to an exit, cleverly marked with a traffic signal. Press the button. If you receive a green light, you can go ahead. If you get a red light, customs people will examine your luggage. The airport is in the northeastern part of the city, roughly 6 kilometers (4 miles) east of the zócalo. It is located on Metro Line 5 at Terminal Area.

TRAIN SERVICE

Train travel is a romantic means of transportation, but until services improve, you should probably take the bus in Mexico. If you choose to ride the rails, the **Buenavista Railroad Station** is located on Avenida Insurgentes Norte at the intersection of Mosqueta, (5) 547-1097. You'll see the ticket windows when you first step inside. Trains carry passengers to the cities of Ciudad Juárez, Monterrey, Guadalajara, Veracruz, and Oaxaca. There is no convenient Metro or subway stop near the railroad station. The closest is **Metro Revolución**, eight blocks south.

LOCAL METRO AND BUS SERVICE

The Mexico City Metro is one of the best in the world. Metro tickets cost 15 cents. If you plan on traveling by Metro often, buy multiple tickets at one time so you don't have to stand in line each time you want to take a trip. *Colectivos* or *combis* are private minibuses that charge by the distance. When you get on, let the driver know where you're headed so he can charge you the correct price.

REGIONAL BUS SERVICE

Mexico has more than a dozen long-distance bus services and four bus stations to make connections to almost any city in Mexico: Terminal Norte (North); Terminal Sur (South); Terminal Oriente, also called TAPO (East); and Terminal Poniente (West). Here's a guide to the stations' primary destinations:

Terminal Norte
Address: Avenida de los Cien Metros 4907
Metro: Autobuses del Norte, Line 5
Destinations: Chihuahua, Guadalajara, Guanajuato, Mexicali, Monterrey, Querétaro, San Miguel de Allende, Tula

Terminal Sur
Address: Avenida Tasqueña 1320
Metro: Tasqueña
Destinations: Acapulco, Cuernavaca, Mérida, Puerto Escondido, San Cristóbal de las Casas

Terminal Oriente (TAPO)
Address: Calzada Ignacio Zaragoza 200
Metro: San Lázaro, Line 1
Destinations: Cancún, Oaxaca, Palenque, Puebla, Veracruz, Xalapa

Terminal Poniente
Address: Avenida Sur 122, at the corner of Avenida Río Tacubaya
Metro: Observatorio, Line 1
Destinations: Morelia, Toluca, Angangueo

TOURS AND OUTFITTERS IN MEXICO CITY

Al Aire Libre, Centro Comercial Interlomas, Local 2122, Paseo de la Herradura #5, 52760 Huixquilucan, Edo de Mexico, (5) 291-9217 or 291-9507, e-mail rchristy@compuserve.com. Individualized tours that feature outdoor hiking, climbing, and other adventure sports.

Descubre Mexico, Apartado Postal 77-282, (5) 294-2836, e-mail descubremexico@compuserve.com, Web site http://www.descubremexico .com.mx. A new travel agency that focuses its work on promoting tourism that actively supports conservation efforts.

EcoGrupos de Mexico, Centro Comercial Plaza Inn, Av. Insurgentes Sur 1971, Nivel Paseo, loc. 251, Col. Guadalupe Inn, 01020 Mexico, D.F., (5) 661-9121, fax 662-7354, e-mail ecomexico@compuserve .com.mx, Web site http://www.ecogrupos.com.mx. Offers group tours to destinations throughout Mexico. The office can be slow to respond to individual queries.

Grupo Advent, Fresno 293-A, Santa María de la Rivera, (5) 547-0649, e-mail advent@ienlaces.com.mx. Mexico City–based guided trips go to Teotihuacán, Ajusco, Tepotzlán, Valle de Bravo. Day trips cost $50, plus rental. Inquire about multi-day trips throughout the country.

Ogima: Exploradores de los Ocho Vientos, Alfonso Reyes 81 (Local 9), Esq. Zitácuaro 6, Col. Condesa, 06170 Mexico, D.F., tel./fax (5) 272 03 97, e-mail mag01@ienlaces2.ienlaces.com.mx. Contact Marjorie Gutiérrez for information.

Río y Montaña, Prado Norte 450-T, Lomas de Chapultepec, 11000

Mexico, D.F., (5) 520-2041 or 520-5018, fax 540-7870, e-mail rioymontana@compuserve.com.mx. River trips throughout Mexico.

WHERE TO STAY IN MEXICO CITY

Mexico City has a room for every budget and desire. The budget and moderate hotels are found in the heart of the city near the centuries-old zócalo, and near the Monument to the Revolution. Pricier hotels are found in the Zona Rosa and Polanco districts.

Hotel Bamer, Avenida Juárez 52, $40, (5) 521-9060. Faces the south side of the Alameda. Nearby hotels fell in the 1985 earthquake, but this one stood its ground.

Hotel Catedral, Donceles 95, $30, (5) 518-5232. Just a few blocks from the zócalo and the Templo Mayor, this hotel offers clean rooms and a sparkling lobby. The roof has one of the best views of downtown.

Hotel de Cortés, Avenida Hidalgo 85, $100, (5) 518-21-84 or, in the U.S., (800) 528-1234. Faces the north side of Alameda Park. Built in the late 1700s for Augustinian friars, the rooms are now remodeled with all of the amenities.

La Casa de los Amigos

The Quakers established **La Casa de los Amigos**, (Ignacio Mariscal 132, (5) 705-0521, e-mail casa@laneta.apc.org) for religious services and community work in Mexico. Not a typical hostel, the house offers space for peace and justice work as well as an extensive library that is open to the public. Throughout the year the Casa also holds various week-long seminars, some of which focus on environmental issues in the city.

Hotel Diligencia, Belisario Domínguez 6, Col. Centro Histórico, $15, 526-5840 or 526-5845, fax 512-2338. Two blocks from Garibaldi Plaza, the hotel maintains a quiet, family-friendly ambiance. Parking is next door.

Hotel Layfaette, Motolina 40 and 16 de Septiembre, Col. Centro Histórico, $10, (5) 521-9640. Clean, inexpensive hotel in the heart of town and across from one of the oldest vegetarian restaurants in Mexico.

Hotel Polanco, Edgar Allen Poe 8, $50, (5) 280-8082. Cozy hotel near Chapultepec Park.

Hotel Oxford, Ignacio Mariscal 67, $12, (5) 566-0500. Clean hotel in a quiet neighborhood very close to the Monument to the Revolution.

WHERE TO EAT IN MEXICO CITY

La Bombilla, Morelia 60, 511-0675. Typical Mexican foods and pre-Hispanic dishes. It's a gourmet restaurant so expect higher prices. There's live music on Saturday afternoons from 3 to 6 p.m.

Café Tacuba, Tacuba 28, (5) 512-8482. One of the classier restaurants in the city. Stop by for a meal or take a break in the afternoon to sample their famous tamales. Open from 9 a.m. to 10 p.m.

El Rinoceronte Ecológico, inside Parque Ecológico, Loreto and Peña Pobre at Av. San Fernando 765; breakfast buffet 33 pesos, lunch buffet 44 pesos; (5) 606-0809 or 666-7205. Beautiful location surrounded by gardens and large trees.

El Vegetariano, Filomeno Mata 13, (5) 512-1186. One of the oldest vegetarian restaurants in Mexico, it's a hidden gem on the second floor, so look up if you're looking for the sign. Serves heaping platters of healthy food.

La Casa de las Sirenas, Republica de Guatemala 32, Centro, (5) 704-3273. Tequila bar behind the cathedral. Choice spot on the roof for people-watching and observing the Aztec dances that take place outside of the Tenochtitlán ruins.

Panadería Ideal, Avenida 16 de Septiembre 18, (5) 521-6496. Not a restaurant, but a bakery with a cavernous interior. If you see people walking around town with boxes wrapped in light blue paper, you'll know they bought confections from this place. Ideal for early-risers, the bakery is open from 6:30 am. to 9 p.m.

Restaurant Bar Beatriz, Motolinia 32, Col. Centro Historico, (5) 510-1772 or 512-2704. Tacos are a specialty here, as is Aztec Soup (*Sopa Azteca*). The folk art paintings on the wall change regularly.

Sanborn's Casa de los Azulejos, Avenida Madero 4, (5) 518-6676. A downtown landmark. The patio of this 16th-century manor has been converted into one of Mexico City's most famous restaurants. This is the flagship of the Sanborn's restaurant chain, found in all of Mexico's larger cities. Less known is that the business was started by a pair of gringo brothers just before the Mexican Revolution.

Yug, near El Angel on Paseo de la Reforma at Varsovia 3. Tasty vegetarian food that's a bit more exotic than the fare served at El Vegetariano.

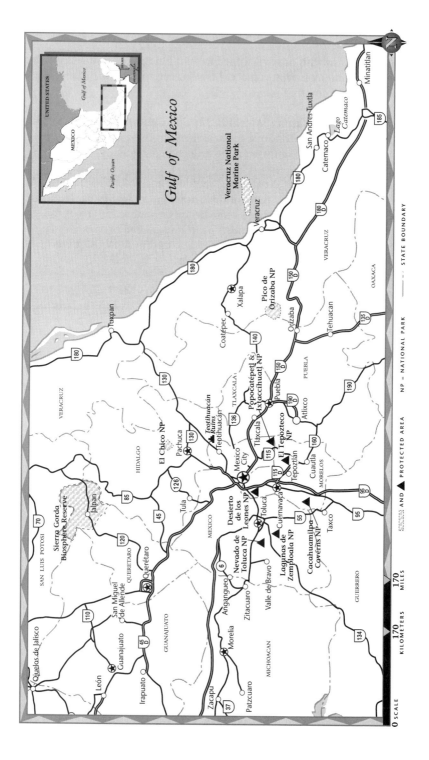

CENTRAL MEXICO

6

MEXICO, MORELOS, VERACRUZ, MICHOACAN, QUERETARO, AND HIDALGO

You're smart. You spend a few days or a week in Mexico City, but soon your lungs, desperate for fresh air, compel you to hightail it out of *El Monster Grande* (The Big Monster). If you walk around Mexico City long enough, you'll get fed up with the constant hassle of bumping into your 20 million neighbors.

Ready to stretch your legs without tripping over someone? There are several hundred environmental destinations within a few hours of Mexico City. For example, it's only a 6-hour drive or bus ride to either the Pacific or the Gulf coast. Whether you're looking for a day trip or a short excursion, this section will help you locate some great parks and protected areas to visit outside the capital city.

The regions surrounding Mexico City could not be more different from one another. To the north, in the states of Mexico and Guanajuato, the region is semi-arid, while to the east, Veracruz is one of the most tropical regions in the country and a storehouse for the country's water resources.

To the west, the state of Michoacán is set in a tropical and semi-humid region that provides the ideal climate for agriculture. Michoacán is the nation's leading producer of strawberries and avocados; farmers here also cultivate cotton, watermelon, sugarcane, lemons, and bananas. The state has 210 kilometers (130 miles) of Pacific coastline and is also home to mountains covered in coniferous forests. Among its most spectacular sites is the Monarch Butterfly Sanctuary, where orange and black butterflies from throughout North America spend each winter.

To the south is the state of Morelos, your best bet for travel to the nearby parks and caves. If you have a weekend in Mexico City and you want to trek through forests or explore some caves, Morelos offers these opportunities and more.

The Sierra Volcánica Transversal (Trans-Mexico Volcanic Axis) crosses Central Mexico from east to west for almost 1,000 kilometers (620 miles). Here are Mexico's highest peaks (Orizaba, Volcán Nevado de Toluca, Popocatépetl and Ixtaccíhuatl), which will be visited in this chapter. This mountainous region is home to various animals, including the Zacatuche rabbit (*romerolagus*), an endemic mammal that makes its home on the volcanic slopes above 3,300 meters (10,800 feet).

In true Mesoamerican fashion, which employed all five directions (west, north, south, east, and the center), we will use Mexico City as our center point. The following are trips that are easily made in three to five days, or can be combined for longer trips exploring Central Mexico.

WEST CENTRAL MEXICO

DESIERTO DE LOS LEONES NATIONAL PARK
Location: 24 km (15 mi.) W of Mexico City
Area: 2,000 hectares (4,940 acres)
Activities: Hiking, horseback riding
For More Information: SECTUR at (5) 250-0123 or 250-015 or the Mexico state tourism office

A short, one-day environmental side trip from Mexico City takes you to the fresh air and woods of Desierto de los Leones, which became Mexico's first national park at the beginning of this century. Here, in the foothills of the Cumbres de Ajusco, abundant springs were once the major source of water for the city. Today, as urban growth has exhausted many of these freshwater sources in the valley, the springs have been reduced to a trickle.

The name of the park, which translates to "Desert of the Lions," is misleading. While you might expect to see Lawrence of Arabia–type sands, this is actually not a desert but a pine forest. The Desierto is a pleasant retreat, made even sweeter by occasional Sunday concerts at the old Carmelite monastery (completed in 1611) in the center of the park. The Carmelites believed that they should worship in a "house in the wilderness" to honor their spiritual founder, Saint Elias. Two hundred years later the region was not remote enough for the spiritual pilgrims, so

Water Resources in an Arid Country

Guanajuato provides a good example of the country's most pressing environmental problem—its diminishing supply of groundwater. As in many other agricultural centers, the intensive use of water needed for the commercial production of vegetables for export has led to the depletion of the underground aquifers. State authorities have estimated that unless measures are taken to reverse this trend, these aquifers will run dry early in the next century. The solution lies both in water conservation and reforestation efforts, which safeguard the aquifers by preventing negative effects such as soil erosion. The forests surrounding Guanajuato are now being guarded and make for excellent bird-watching.

the monks moved to the town of Tenancingo and the Desierto de Los Leones monastery became an "ex-convent."

In the late 1880s, the Mexico City government was authorized to auction off land in the Desierto, provided buyers agreed to conserve the springs and not cut down trees protecting the underground watershed. In 1917 the area was decreed a national park by President Venustiano Carranza.

While the forests in this park and the Ajusco Mountains in general still function as the lungs of Mexico City, they are not immune to environmental degradation. Pollution contributed to a die-off of oyamel firs in Desierto de los Leones in the early 1980s, with trees in the southern forests of the park hardest hit by the prevailing wind patterns in the valley. Pollution weakens the trees, which are then plagued by small burrowing worms that lodge themselves between the bark and the trunk, interrupting the flow of sap. A new program called "S.O.S. Operation Desert"—begun in 1996— combines reforestation programs, agroforestry, and new natural management techniques to boost the trees' health. Woodpeckers are being reintroduced into the forests to help restore balance to the ecosystem.

Visitors to the park will easily locate the convent, behind which is a well-kept garden and the entrance to one of the best-maintained systems of hiking trails in all of Mexico. You can also inquire about horseback riding in the convent's cobblestone parking lot. Half-day trips can be arranged for $20.

This park is not known for its variety of species, but for its easy access from Mexico City. If you're hungry, vendors sell an assortment of barbecued meats and cooked corn at the food stands outside the park.

Getting to Desierto de los Leones National Park

Buses travel from the Observatorio Metro station in Mexico City to the park several times a day. From the road it's a 4-kilometer (2.5-mile) walk to the monastery. Via car, take Highway 15 toward Toluca and turn at the park sign (at Kilometer 24). The park is open daily from 6 a.m. to 5 p.m. The "ex-convent" is open every day except Monday, from 10 a.m. to 5 p.m.

NEVADO DE TOLUCA NATIONAL PARK

Location: 70 km (44 mi.) SW of Mexico City, 50 km (30 mi.) S of Toluca
Area: 51,000 hectares (126,000 acres)
Activities: Hiking, picnicking, swimming
For More Information: Contact SECTUR at (5) 250-0123 or 250-015 or the Mexico state tourism office for more information.

For tourists, Mexico's most easily accessible and popular volcanic destination is Nevado de Toluca National Park, home to the country's fourth-highest peak (4,558 meters or 14,954 feet). The mountain, named Xinantécatl, or "the naked man," is an extinct volcano with two craters that now contain lakes (poetically named for the sun and the moon). Visitors can reach the craters via a well-maintained two-lane state highway, so the area is a popular retreat.

The area was declared a national park in 1936 and now is spotted with fir and pine forests (much of the original cover has been deforested). Park wildlife includes the Zacatuche rabbit—which thrives on the volcanic slopes throughout Central Mexico—and coyote, white-tailed deer, bobcats, and woodpeckers.

While the more rugged Popocatépetl and Ixtaccíhuatl volcanoes are suited for experienced climbers only, hikers here do not need to be athletes to make the trek to the summit. There are plenty of trails that crisscross the area. If you want to climb either of the two peaks, take the trail along the rim of the crater upward. The park doesn't have guards, but people at the nearby Posada Familiar, located near the park entrance, can direct you. Make your trip to the crater early in the day, as it becomes cloudy in the afternoon.

The park also attracts divers, who explore the high-altitude lakes. (The less-adventurous can simply swim in them.) And during the winter it's reportedly possible to ski on the slopes. I have yet to confirm this first-hand. There is no infrastructure for skiing, so you'd have to bring your own skis and manage to find your own way up the mountain if you wanted to take multiple runs.

Tours and Outfitters
Odesea Circuitos Turisticos, Sacaranda 105-A, Toluca, (72) 70-33-13. Offers full-day tours of the park for $50.

Getting to Nevado de Toluca National Park
There is frequent service from Mexico City's western bus station to Toluca City. From Toluca, head west on Highway 134 and take the 27-kilometer (17-mile) State Road 10 north to Xinantécatl; at Kilometer 22 turn off toward the town of Sultepec. Seven kilometers (4.5 miles) further is a left-hand turn which loops to the east side of the mountain before entering the crater. There are no direct buses from Toluca to the park. The best you can do is take the bus from Toluca to Sultepec and ask to be dropped off at the turnoff and hitchhike from there. Drivers must pay a $3 fee to enter the park.

Where to Stay in Nevado de Toluca National Park
Camping is permitted in the park. In addition, you might try the following. Neither facility has a phone, and you should bring your own food.

Albergue el Pino Nevado de Toluca, 15 kilometers (9 miles) downhill from park entrance. Youth hostel.

Posada Familiar, near the park entrance gate, $5. Offers rustic accommodations.

THE MONARCH BUTTERFLY SANCTUARY
Location: 210 km (130 mi.) W of Mexico City
Area: 16,110 hectares (39,791 acres)
Activities: Hiking, butterfly viewing
For More Information: SECTUR at (5) 250-0123 or 250-015 or Mexico state tourism office

Each fall, in one of the most spectacular migrations in the world, millions of black and orange monarch butterflies fly from forests in the United States and Canada to winter in Central Mexico. And each year, from

November through March, thousands of people visit the Monarch Butterfly Sanctuary to walk among the butterflies and to observe these fascinating creatures up close.

The Monarch Butterfly Sanctuary, created in 1986, comprises five protected areas. Sadly, all of the reserves are showing signs of stress because of illegal logging. Some of the reserves have been almost completely deforested, and only two of them, El Rosario and Chincua, are open to the public. Chincua is open only when the National Institute of Ecology deems that public visitation will not greatly disturb the butterflies. El Rosario is open to the public every year during the butterfly season and it is the focus of this section.

While the Monarch Butterfly Sanctuary is Mexico's most visited protected area and one of its most prominent environmental attractions, it faces many of the problems common to environmental tourism throughout Mexico. Few services exist for the individual traveler interested in conservation. The tours that do exist are aimed at day-trippers who generally pack their own lunches, so the flood of tourists visiting the park provides few economic benefits to the community. If you'd like to contribute to the conservation of the region, plan on spending a night or two.

Monarch butterfly

Michoacán State Tourism Office

Visiting El Rosario

El Rosario receives 150,000 to 200,000 visitors each year. The best time to visit is between February and early March, and visitor traffic is lighter mid-week than it is on weekends.

El Rosario is accessible from the towns of Angangueo and Ocampo, with Angangueo, an old mining town, offering a better infrastructure for visitors. The town currently has 5,000 residents, down from 18,000 in 1987—when the price of silver bottomed out in the early 1980s, many residents of Angangueo were forced to look for work elsewhere. Tourism hasn't been enough to restore the town's former glory, but each weekend from November to March the town is full of tourists who come to see the monarchs.

In the reserve you will find a visitors center (one of the few in Mexico) where you are obliged to contract a local guide. The hike uphill into the forest area will take anywhere from 2 to 3 hours. You will likely find monarchs on the ground before you see the main colonies, but remember that touching the butterflies is prohibited. On overcast days, the monarchs cling to the oyamel trees. Branches sometimes break under the weight of hundreds of thousands of butterflies.

The sight of butterflies blanketing the trees is beautiful and downright ghostly, but not as majestic as when they glide through the forest. When the sun comes out and the temperature warms, the butterflies drop from the trees to fly and drink nectar from flowers and dew collected on the ground. In March, as the days get longer and the temperatures rise, the monarchs begin their northward trek, deserting the forests until the following autumn.

Butterflies

The Central Mexican valleys where monarch butterflies winter were "discovered" in 1974 when researchers from the University of Florida finally traced the butterflies' flight path from Canada. The news made the covers of *National Geographic* and *Scientific American*, which ran startling photographs of great pines veiled with thousands of monarchs. Of course, local residents of Angangueo knew of the monarchs, which at times would blanket the town. Now that the world was clued in, the town of Angangueo would begin its own metamorphosis.

In early 1997 an extended freeze killed many of the wintering monarch butterflies. Initial reports of a 33-percent death rate shocked the nation and the world, but the actual death rate, according to scientists, was less than 7 percent, well within the normal range of variability.

Ever-present threats to the monarchs include continued destruction of forest habitats and environmental changes along their migration paths throughout Mexico, the United States, and Canada. Farmers in the United States and Canada have declared milkweed (the plant that nourishes monarchs) a noxious weed and use herbicides to control it, resulting in reduced availability of the butterflies' major food source and place to lay their eggs. While the monarchs may not be endangered now, their survival depends on the cooperation of all three countries in North America.

Better efforts must be made to assist poorer communities if conservationists want local residents to protect the monarchs. Environmental groups such as Grupo de los Cien have suggested that the campesinos receive an annual fee for the conservation of the trees in these forests. If campesinos were paid even a minuscule amount to protect the forests, rather than the small income they make from destroying them, this reserve might stand a chance of protecting the monarch butterfly. As Mexican economist David Barkin said at a 1997 trinational conference on the monarchs, "There are two miracles in the monarch reserve area. One is that the butterflies have survived, and the other is that the campesinos have survived."

Tours and Outfitters

There are no local operators with whom to book a formal excursion, but **EcoGrupos de Mexico** (5/661-9121) offers frequent weekends trips from Mexico City during the butterfly season, and **Trek Mexico** (5/525-6813) books week-long trips that feature the reserve and nearby colonial cities. Both companies are based in Mexico City.

Getting to the Monarch Butterfly Sanctuary

From Mexico City, direct buses leave several times a day from the Terminal Poniente bus terminal (at the Observatorio Metro station) for Angangueo. Alternatively, take a bus from Mexico City to the larger town of Zitácuaro and make the switch to an Angangueo bus from there; buses leave from Zitácuaro for Angangueo every 15 minutes. If you're driving, take Highway 15 west. Turn at Zitácuaro to take the highway north to Angangueo.

Angangueo is the best-developed hub for travel in the reserve. Once you're in town, if you don't have your own transportation, find other travelers interested in seeing the butterfly sanctuary and rent a pickup. Prices are fixed by a local cooperative, and a 4- to 5-hour rental costs about $25, depending on the type of vehicle. This price is good for up to ten passengers, so it's obviously cheaper if more people split the cost of the vehicle. There is ample parking at the reserve. From Angangueo you can also travel to Chincua, another reserve on the Michoacán–Mexico state border. A second option is to travel to Ocampo, which also has a small road to El Rosario.

Life Cycle of a Monarch

Monarchs go through four separate life stages. They begin as eggs, hatch as larvae or caterpillars, become pupae (chrysalides or cocoons), and mature into adult butterflies. The eggs hatch in small batches of five to ten, depending on the ambient temperature. The caterpillars then devour their eggshells and begin the quest for food, feeding exclusively on milkweed. Each time they outgrow their exterior skin (called the cuticle), they molt, eat the skin, and continue growing. After four cycles of molting they attach themselves to the underside of a leaf and form a delicate and beautiful chrysalis. Inside the chrysalis a developing butterfly matures for several weeks. When it's time to break loose, the insect pushes its legs downward, splits the chrysalis, and sets itself free. The newly hatched butterfly pumps the fluid concentrated in its body into its wings, which then harden, allowing it to fly.

Once hatched, the butterflies then begin a migration north to spend their summers in North America. They mate several times over the summer and live from two to six weeks. At the end of the summer, the remaining butterflies head south, averaging 150 to 200 kilometers (90 to 125 miles) a day. The life span of the migratory butterflies is considerably longer—nine months longer—than that of their counterparts. The trip takes half a month, up to two months if winds or rain slow the butterflies' progress. The journey is considered one of the longest, greatest migrations in the natural world.

Why the butterflies, several generations removed from the ancestors that once wintered in the valley, migrate to the same place is a mystery. It has been suggested that regional magnetism stemming from nearby mountains (this is a former mining area) emits what in essence is a homing beacon for the monarchs.

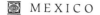

Where to Stay near the Monarch Butterfly Sanctuary

Don Brunos, Morelos 92, Angangueo, $20, (715) 60-026. Located on the main street coming into town, the hotel has simple rooms that surround a lovely courtyard with a well-kept garden. Rooms with fireplaces cost $5 more a night.

Hotel El Paso de la Monarca, Nacional 20, $10, (715) 80-187. In the center of Angangueo. Quiet hotel with ten rooms.

Hotel Margaritas, Morelos No. 88, Angangueo, $15, (715) 80-145. Located across from Don Brunos, this is a combination hotel and restaurant. The hospitable manager happily shares magazines and books on the monarchs and is always looking for new materials, preferably in Spanish. Some rooms are equipped with fireplaces.

John F. Kennedy Institute, Calle Adolfo López Mateos No.4, Pueblo Nuevo, Contepec, Michoacán, (447) 850-31, fax (447) 850-31, e-mail cuitlahuac.osornio@uia.mx. Camping is available on the spacious grounds of this local technical school. Contepec is about 50 kilometers (31 miles) north of Angangueo and is easily accessible from Highway 15, which runs from Toluca to Guadalajara. Guides can take you hiking in the oyamel forests on top of Cerro de Altimirano or point out the pre-Hispanic rock art depicting the monarchs. A two-day stay with meals and guide service costs $30. Extended stays can be arranged at a discounted price; large groups of campers can be accommodated. For more information, contact Gerardo Osornio.

NORTH CENTRAL MEXICO

TEOTIHUACAN RUINS

Location: 50 km (31 mi.) N of Mexico City
Area: 100 hectares (247 acres)
Activities: Archaeology
For More Information: SECTUR at (5) 250-0123 or 250-015 or the Mexico state tourism office

The impressive ruins of Teotihuacán make an easy day trip from Mexico City. The site boasts the third-largest pyramid in the world and the ruins of an ancient city whose original name and original inhabitants are not even known. When the Aztecs found Tenochtitlán, they adopted the ruins

Stone carving at Teotihuacán ruins

as a ceremonial ground and named the city "Teotihuacán," or "Place of the Gods."

Teotihuacán is located in the northeastern corner of the Valley of Mexico, on a plateau more than 2,000 meters (6,560 feet) high with a temperate, semi-arid climate. Water from the San Juan, San Lorenzo, and Huixulco Rivers, along with underground springs, allowed the city to flourish for roughly 1,000 years. Occupation of the area began around 500 B.C. and lasted until the sixth century. At its zenith, Teotihuacán was home to more than 200,000 people and was arguably the biggest city in the world.

Water sources have always been important in Mexico, a country which is nearly half desert. In this area the rivers and springs could adequately support the irrigation of more than one harvest a year. Mineral resources were also important in ancient times, and the nearby hills are rich in obsidian (used to create ceremonial knives and figures) and clay deposits (used for ceramics).

The basic structures of the city are still intact. It was originally divided into four quarters by two corridors. The north-south avenue is called Avenida de los Muertos (Avenue of the Dead), again named by the Aztecs who believed, incorrectly, that the buildings were tombs.

Teotihuacán's crowning glories are the Pyramid of the Sun and the Pyramid of the Moon. The Aztecs named the tallest structure the for the sun because its front wall faces the exact point on the horizon where the sun sets at the spring and autumn equinoxes. This pyramid—70 meters (230 feet) high with a 220-meter (720-foot) base—was built around A.D. 150. The neutral stone facade belies its former spectacle—originally it was painted bright red. The smaller Pyramid of the Moon was built between A.D. 250 and 600.

Teotihuacán traded with other Mesoamerican cities and evidently exerted a strong influence on its neighbors after the fourth century. Teotihuacán's ceramics, obsidian crafts, and architecture are found in distant cities such as Monte Albán (Oaxaca), Tikal (Guatemala), and Copán (Honduras); the goods and crafts of other cultures have been uncovered in Teotihuacán graves and caches.

Why did this city and its empire collapse? There is evidence of malnutrition and environmental neglect in the region, especially the deforestation of nearby hills. In the seventh century the city was literally torched and abandoned.

A recently inaugurated museum and botanical garden are located on the grounds of the site. The museum showcases excavated ceramics and sculptures. Admission is included in the entrance fee.

The ruins site is open from 10 a.m. to 5 p.m. Tuesday through Sunday. Entrance is $2, but free on Sundays. There is an extra charge ($5) to bring in a video camera.

Getting to the Teotihuacán Ruins

Various tour companies offer day-long excursions that can be arranged from any mid-priced hotel, but it's just as fun to take the bus from the Terminal de Autobuses del Norte station in Mexico City. The trip is less than an hour and costs $5. Drivers can take Highway 85D and pay a $4 toll, or take the free and often congested Highway 132D from Mexico City. The archaeological zone is well marked. There is a ring road surrounding the complex and five separate parking areas. The parking area closest to the museum and nearby restaurants is found on the western side at "Puerta No. 5."

Where to Eat Near Teotihuacán

Food is available from more than 20 reputable roadside cafes on the western side of the ring road. The best dining experience is found at **Restaurant La Gruta** (915/601-04), opposite "Puerta No. 5," where meals are served inside a decorated subterranean cave.

SIERRA GORDA BIOSPHERE RESERVE
Location: 175 km (107 mi) NE of Querétaro City
Area: 383,567 hectares (947,410 acres)
Activities: Bird-watching, hiking

For more Information: *Grupo Ecológico Sierra Gorda at (429) 6-02-42 or SECTUR*

Sierra Gorda Biosphere Reserve, declared a reserve in May 1997, is a difficult place to visit without a guide. However, for those willing to travel on lesser-known roads and practice their Spanish, the visit is well worth the effort. The reserve is in the state of Querétaro, bounded by the state of San Luis Potosí to the northeast, the Río Moctezuma to the southeast, the Río Estorax to the southwest, and the Río Santa María and the state of Guanajuato to the northwest. The city of Jalpan is located in its center.

Economically, this is a very poor area of the state. Environmentally, however, it's one of Mexico's hot spots. Its great variety of ecosystems range from coniferous forest to jungle to semi-desert. The Sierra Gorda is also a refuge for several animal species in danger of extinction: jaguars, tigrillos, jaguarundi, and the military macaw. Migratory species such as the monarch butterfly and the peregrine falcon trace their paths through the Sierra. In fact, the mountains' cloud forests and canyons shelter more than 300 species of migratory and native birds, including the euphonia, trogon (closely related to the quetzal), woodcreeper, and parrot. There are also more than 500 archaeological sites, many of which have yet to be studied and documented.

The local organization **Grupo Ecológico Sierra Gorda** (429/6-02-42) has been working since 1987 to protect the Sierra Gorda Queretana and is the only established tourism provider in the region. Ecotourism is being used to generate revenues as well as to provide environmental education for both locals and visitors.

Sótano de Barro

The Sierra Gorda is rife with wells and subterranean rivers that have burrowed through the area's soluble rocks over millions of years. Within the reserve is the famous Sótano de Barro (Mud Basement), a gigantic sinkhole 600 meters (1,970 feet) wide and 450 meters (1,475 feet) deep, called by some the second-deepest well in the world. At night a colony of military macaws roosts in the sinkhole. They emerge en mass at dawn the next morning.

To reach the well, you'll need to hike for 2 hours and climb 900 meters (2,950 feet) through an oak forest. You can arrange to make the trek with mules. Your best bet is to spend the night before your morning hike in the cheerful town of **Santa María de los Cocos**, 7 kilometers (4.5 miles) from the base of the Sótano de Barro. Here a bed in the simple hotel costs $20. Daily meals cost $10 per person. Guides offer trips to the Sótano de Barro for $15 per person, while an excursion to the more distant Ayutla Canyon costs $20 per person. You can rent a horse for an additional $10 per day. Santa María de los Cocos is 30 kilometers (19 miles) from Jalpan. If you are taking a bus from Mexico City, get off in Jalpan, where you can get a combi to Santa María de los Cocos. The lodging is just outside of town. For information, call Sabas Ledezma in Jalpan at (429) 602-22.

Tours and Outfitters
Grupo Ecológico Sierra Gorda, Juárez No. 9, Jalpan de Serra, Querétaro, C.P. 76340 Querétaro; tel./fax (429) 6-02-42 or, in the Querétaro City, (42) 13-84-28. Takes small groups of seven to 12 people on full-day tours that cost from $75 to $120 and can be tailored to individual interests. Profits from these trips are used for environmental education and sustainable development programs in the region. Destinations include the tropical deciduous forest near the Jalpan Dam, the Ayutla River Canyon, Escanela River, and El Sótano del Barro. For information, contact Martha ("Paty") Ruiz Corzo.

Woodrising Consulting, 132 Main St., Erin, ON N0B 1T0, (519) 833-1031, e-mail nbird@woodrising.com, Web site http://www.woodrising.com. Works closely with Grupo Ecológico and arranges trips from Canada throughout the Sierra Gorda. For information, contact Neil Bird.

Getting to the Sierra Gorda Biosphere Reserve
There is hourly (if not more frequent) bus service from Mexico City to Querétaro. From Querétaro, several buses daily make 4½ hour ride (3½ by car) to Jalpan via "the road of 700 curves."

Santa María de los Cocos is 30 kilometers (19 miles) from Jalpan. If you are taking a bus from Mexico City, get off in Jalpan, where you can get a combi to Santa María de los Cocos.

Where to Stay near the Sierra Gorda Biosphere Reserve
Hotel Hidalgo, Madero 11, $10, Querétaro, (42) 12-00-81. Colonial hotel one block west of Plaza Obregón. The management speaks English; free parking.

Hotel Plaza, Juárez Norte 23, $15, Querétaro, (42) 12-11-38. Great budget hotel on the west side of the Jardín Obregón.

Where to Eat near the Sierra Gorda Biosphere Reserve
La Casa de la Marquesa, Allende 6, Querétaro, (42) 12-00-92. Fine Mexican food; breakfast and lunch buffets.

La Oveja Negra, Boulevard Bernardo Quintana 110, Querétaro, (42) 13-72-64. Excellent barbecued sheep (hence the name, "The Black Sheep").

Restaurante Correo Español, Avenida Constituyentes 50, Queré taro, (42) 16-75-99. Authentic Spanish cuisine in a restaurant that has served fine food for more than 60 years. Don't come here expecting tacos.

SOUTH-CENTRAL MEXICO

CUERNAVACA/LAGUNAS DE ZEMPOALA NATIONAL PARK
Location: 90 km (56 mi.) S of Mexico City
Area: 4,669 hectares (103,791 acres)
Activities: Spanish language schools, fishing, hiking
For More Information: Tourism office, Avenida Morelos Sur 802

A popular destination with a population of about 1 million people, Cuernavaca boasts a mild climate, colonial architecture, and the lion's share of Mexico's Spanish language schools. A pleasant excursion from the town is Lagunas de Zempoala National Park, 25 kilometers (16 miles) to the northwest. Some of the park's seven lakes are stocked with game fish. In terms of biological diversity or even entertainment, this is adequate, but not representative of Mexico's grandeur. You'll find well-worn paths for hiking and even some areas for camping.

Getting to Cuernavaca
To get to Lagunas de Zempoala National Park from the highway between Mexico City and Cuernavaca, turn off the main road at Tres Marías and head west through the town of Huitzilac.

Where to Stay in Cuernavaca
Villa Calmecac, Zacatecas 114, $20, (73) 132-146, e-mail meliton @mail.giga.com. One of Mexico's few truly eco-friendly hotels is run by Meliton Cross, a founding member of AMTAVE, Mexico's ecotourism promotion association. The small hotel offers various workshops, as well as canoe and kayak trips on the Amacuzac River in southern Morelos. Meliton also offers full-day rafting or kayaking trips ($40) on the Amacuzac River from June to October, and mountain biking trips ($25) in the nearby pine and oak forests from October to May.

Where to Eat in Cuernavaca

Las Mañanitas, Linares 107, (73) 14-1466. The restaurant allows exotic peacocks to roam the gardens, and the staff keeps a watchful eye on children tempted to harass the birds. A fancy place, but well worth the extra pesos.

EL TEPOZTECO NATIONAL PARK

Location: 25 km (16 mi.) NW of Cuernavaca
Area: 24,000 hectares (59,280 acres)
Activities: Hiking, archaeology
For More Information: SECTUR at (5) 250-0123 or 250-015 or the
Morelos state tourism office

El Tepozteco National Park, along with Lagunas de Zempoala National Park, is part of the Ajusco-Chichinautzin Biological Corridor, which protects the southern side of the volcanic axis. Created in 1937, the park consists of a low-deciduous oak and fir forest. The highest peak is Volcán de Chichinautzin, which rises 3,450 meters (11,315 feet) above sea level.

The easiest access point to the park is from the town of **Tepoztlán,** which has a reputation for being a quiet, artistic, New Age community. Anyone who visits, however, will soon recognize that Tepoztlán is a sophisticated and complicated town. Sociologists have gravitated toward Tepoztlán because of its links to tradition—Robert Redfield based his studies here around the turn of the century, and these in turn led to the research of Oscar Lewis. Lewis put Tepoztlán on the map in the 1950s with his portrayal of the town and family life in his books *Five Families* and *The Children of Sánchez.*

You'll find a marked path at the end of Avenida Tepozteco leading up to a cliff 400 meters (1,310 feet) high and boasting the **Pyramid of Tepozteco,** constructed in the 1400s. The site honors Ometochtli-Tepoztecatl, the Aztec harvest god (also the god of fertility and of *pulque*). The feast of the Tepozteco takes place on the summit, at night, from September 7 to September 8. The walk uphill is slippery and takes more than an hour, but the view is rewarding. Outside of special festivals, watchmen enforce a 10 a.m. to 5 p.m. visitation time. There's a small admission fee to the park.

Preservation Prevails

Tepoztlán made headline news in 1995, when community residents protested the construction of an expensive golf course within the national park. The Committee of Tepozteco Unity (CUT) formed to block the development of the Club de Golf El Tepozteco, designed by a Cuernavaca business. This $300-million project would have included a hotel, tennis courts, 800 luxury homes, 592 condo units, and an industrial research park. The permitting process drew local criticism. The golf course would have been located inside the buffer zone of the national park (some of the 187 hectares purchased for development were private agricultural lands— mostly tomato fields owned by 78 families). Protesters also questioned the approval given by the city council and mayor for a project that would consume five times as much water as the town itself. And concerns were also raised about potential pesticide runoff from the golf course.

In August 1995, CUT protesters seized the city hall and blockaded the town. PROFEPA, the enforcement arm of Mexico's environmental secretariat, ordered construction to halt until it could review the environmental impact statement. So far, the citizens have prevailed: the golf course will probably never be built. In a town that prides itself on its historical identity, developers made a big mistake in not seeking community input.

Getting to El Tepozteco National Park
The town of Tepoztlán is 10 kilometers (6.2 miles) from Cuernavaca.

Where to Stay and Eat near El Tepozteco
There are several small restaurants in Tepoztlan, or food and lodging is accessible in nearby Cuernavaca.

CACAHUAMILPA CAVERNS NATIONAL PARK
Location: 22 km (14 mi.) from Taxco, in western Morelos
Area: 1,600 hectares (3,952 acres)
Activities: Hiking, caving
For More Information: SECTUR at (5) 250-0123 or 250-015 or the Morelos state tourism office

South of Cuernavaca and close to the silversmithing town of Taxco are the Cacahuamilpa Caverns (Grutas de Cacahuamilpa). The area attracted attention in 1995 when a Canadian developer announced he would create a sound-and-lights extravaganza (along with mechanically operated dinosaurs, à la *Jurassic Park*). The promotion fell through when environmentalists from Grupo de los 100 and other regional groups criticized the environmental damage such changes would cause as well as the permitting process, which was conducted behind closed doors.

The caverns are among the largest in North America, formed during the Jurassic Period when the Río dos Bocas carved through the land. When the river shifted course—it now flows 80 meters below the caverns—the cave drained.

Guided 90-minute tours take visitors inside the caverns, where they can see stalactite and stalagmite formations as well as an underground river. The natural history is downplayed on most tours. Instead, guides point out the human figures, animals, and fantastic creatures ("the face of the devil," "the face of the devil when he's older") the formations resemble. By the time the 2-kilometer (1.2-mile) tour is over, you can point out the "Aztec Calendar" and "Virgen de Guadalupe" yourself. Tacky? Perhaps. But the caves are stunning nonetheless. On your way out, be sure to take the short trek to the valley of Río dos Bocas, where two rivers flow out of the hillside.

The caves are open daily from 10 a.m. to 5 p.m.; the admission fee is $2. You can hire a guide for a private English-language tour for an additional $8. The best time to visit is in summer, when the rainy season keeps the caves moist. Try to avoid the park on the weekends, when the majority of tourists arrive.

Getting to Cacahuamilpa Caverns
The caves are located along Highway 16, which can be reached from Alpuyeca or Taxco. Cuernavaca has direct buses to the caves, or ask the bus driver to drop you off near the exit for the caverns en route to Alpuyeca or Taxco.

Where to Stay and Eat near Cacahuamilpa Caverns
There are some small restaurants (or comedores—basically food stands) outside of the caverns, but no lodging facilities. Accomodations may be found in Cuernevaca or nearby Taxco.

EAST-CENTRAL MEXICO

POPOCATEPETL AND IXTACCIHUATL VOLCANOES
Location: 70 km (43 mi.) SE of Mexico City
Area: 25,679 hectares (63,427 acres)
Activities: Mountain climbing
For More Information: SECTUR at (5) 250-0123 or 250-015 or the Mexico state tourism office

Clear days in Mexico City are measured by one's ability to see the surrounding snowcapped mountains and peaks. The spectacular vista was commonplace a generation ago when novelist Carlos Fuentes wrote his book *Where the Air is Clear*. But now—20 million people, more than 3 million cars, and thousands of manufacturing plants later—the days the surrounding mountains are visible are few and far between.

The most impressive of the mountains seen from Mexico City are the twin volcanoes, Popocatépetl (Smoking Mountain; 5,452 meters, or 17,888 feet) and Ixtaccíhuatl (The Sleeping Woman; 5,286 meters, or 17,343 feet). The last eruption of Popocatépetl (commonly known as Popo) occurred in 1802. Additional rumblings took place throughout the 1920s, then, after a long slumber, the volcano was awakened again in December 1994. Since then it has been off-limits to climbers. Popo was on red alert (indicating a high level of danger) for at least part of 1998. The volcano is monitored by the National Autonomous University of Mexico (UNAM).

Historically, the volcanoes have been used for a variety of natural resources. The Aztecs are said to have made trips to the volcano to fetch ice for Moctezuma's drinks. The ingenious Spanish conquistadors used the sulfur found in Popo's crater as a source for their gunpowder. According to one legend, a princess was waiting for the return of her warrior lover when she heard an erroneous report of his death. Grief-stricken, she poisoned herself and died. The warrior, still alive, returned from battle; finding his lover dead, he carried her body to the top of Ixtaccíhuatl. Holding her corpse in his arms, he jumped into the crater to his death.

Mexican volcanoes are higher than most U.S. mountains, but smaller than their South American cousins. Consequently, mountain climbers bound for South American volcanoes use this area as a training ground. Popo is the easier hike of the two (but probably off-limits for the next few years). It's best to climb either volcano between late November and early March during the dry season (which is also when Mexico City suffers thermal inversions—all the more reason to head for the hills), but it's possible to climb during the rest of the year. Climb early before the clouds roll in during the afternoon.

The town of Amecameca lies at the foot of the volcanoes. Further uphill is Tlamacas (3,950 meters or 13,000 feet), the staging ground for an ascent. You can stay at the Vicente Guerrero Tourist Hostel here. This is a perfect place to acclimatize and serves as a meeting point for climbers. Ice crampons—which you'll need—can be rented here.

A word about safety: You should not try to climb a volcano without rock climbing experience. If you're a novice, find a guide. Be sure to have crampons, rope, and an ice ax, and know how to use them. Be alert to the danger of snow blindness, and be sure to wear UV-protecting sunglasses while you're on the ice. Altitude sickness is potentially life-threatening; know the symptoms (severe headache, accelerated respiration). Allow a few days to acclimatize in Mexico City or Amecameca before climbing to an even higher elevation.

EL CHICO NATIONAL PARK
Location: 10 km (6.2 mi.) NE of Pachuca
Area: 2,739 hectares (5,876 acres)
Activities: Hiking, rock climbing, camping
For More Information: Contact SECTUR at (5) 250-0123 or 250-0151

Two hours northeast of Mexico City, El Chico (The Little One) was Mexico's first national forest reserve, decreed so by President Porfirio Diaz at the end of the 19th century. The area was deforested three centuries earlier, when the metal-working industry indiscriminately chopped down trees for firewood.

Today the park is filled with pine, oak, and juniper forests. Like other "developed" protected areas in Mexico, the hills all have fantastic names—The Nuns, The Rabbit, The Windows. Although the nomenclature may be cheesy, the area nevertheless translates into a great area for day hikes. During the summer rainy season, bring warm clothes and be sure to fill up on the delicious quesadillas and pecans in the town of El Chico.

Trails are well-marked in El Chico, although it's impossible to get a map of the region. Guides are neither needed nor available in the park. Weekends tend to bring a good deal of traffic from nearby Mexico City, but during the week the park is much more tranquil.

Declaring El Chico a park in 1898 was precedent-setting. It was the first time the government had enacted and followed through on a forestry law that authorized the establishment of reserves on national lands. In 1922 El Chico's designation was upgraded to that of a national park.

Tours and Outfitters
Al Aire Libre, Centro Comercial Interlomas 2122, Boulevard Interlomas No 5, Col. Lomas Anáhuac, 52760 Huixquilucan, Estado de Mexico, (5) 291-9217. This adventure-travel company teaches rock climbing techniques in El Chico National Park. Tours usually depart early on Saturday mornings, overnight in the park, and return the next day to Mexico City.

Getting to El Chico National Park
The park is most easily accessible via personal automobile. If you're driving, take Highway 105 from Pachuca (90 kilometers or 56 miles northeast

of Mexico City) toward Tampico. After 9 kilometers (5.6 miles), take the turnoff to El Chico. There are several buses a day from Pachuca, just 20 minutes away.

Where to Stay near El Chico National Park
Hotel de los Banos, Matamoros 205, Pachuca, (771) 3-07-00, $10. At the turn of the century, this hotel was the first in the city to have bathrooms inside the guests' rooms. Pleasant accommodations today.

Hotel Emily, Calle Hidalgo/Plaza de la Independencia, Pachuca, (771) 5-08-68, $20. One of the cleanest hotels in Mexico, located in the center of town. Parking is available and the restaurant serves great breakfasts.

Hotel Noriega, Calle Matamoros 305, Pachuca, (771) 5-1555 or 5-1591), two blocks south of the Plaza, $10. A budget favorite with a covered courtyard and restaurant. Rooms have television and parking is available nearby.

Where to Eat near El Chico National Park
Restaurant La Blanca, on the plaza near the clock tower, (771) 2-18-96. Complimentary *pastes* are served as an appetizer. The Cornish miners who brought soccer to Mexico also brought this delicious item—a pastry filled with ground beef and vegetables.

VERACRUZ

In terms of environmental travel, heart-pounding adventure, and cultural gems, Veracruz offers more than you could possibly see in one visit, unless you have a year to spare. The state lies on the Gulf of Mexico and boasts beaches, reefs, lagoons, valleys, and rain forests. The state has historic importance, as well: The Olmecs established their first city at San Lorenzo in what is now southern Veracruz around 1200 to 900 B.C. Twenty-five centuries later, in 1519, Hernán Cortés made his dramatic appearance on the Gulf Coast north of present-day Veracruz city.

The state is tropical from La Región Huasteca in the north to Los Tuxtlas in the south. The exception lies in the south: the snow- and ice-covered Pico de Orizaba—Mexico's highest peak and a favorite destination of mountain climbers. (See Pico de Orizaba section for details.)

Veracruz has more than 40 rivers and is one of Mexico's wettest regions. The state contains one-third of Mexico's hydrological resources, and its fisheries fleet is the largest in the country. Almost 12,000 boats head out to sea each morning to harvest shrimp, clams, crab, and sea bass, supplying 12 percent of the country's seafood needs.

RAFTING THE RIVERS OF VERACRUZ

In the mid-1990s rafting hit Veracruz by storm. While just five years earlier only intrepid adventurers and white-water enthusiasts bothered to check out the rivers in Veracruz, by 1997 there were four major companies running tours here. Xalapa is the base of operations, though many of the companies operate from other cities. Most of the companies focus their operations on the weekend travelers from Mexico City. Experience is not required.

The Antigua River offers some of the best rafting in the region. Tour companies have set up operations along its banks in the town of Jalcomulco and Aguas Termales del Carrizal. The river can be divided into three parts: the Antigua from Paso Limón to El Carrizal (where Veraventuras has set up a campsite), the Pescados below Jalcomulco (where Mexico Verde and Río y Montaña have operations), and the Barranca Grande.

A good river for an easy day trip is the **Actopan**. It's just north of Xalapa and has 11 kilometers of Class II and Class III rapids from the El Descabezadero (The Guillotine) waterfall to the town of Actopan.

Two hours from Xalapa is the **Filobobos River**, as famous for its archaeological ruins as its Class II to Class V rapids. The river passes by the El Cuajilote and Vega de la Peña ruins, dating from A.D 200 to 900.

Both complexes are recently discovered Toltec-Huasteco ruins, complete with stone carvings, ball courts, and pyramids. These sites were excavated only in the past decade. Many of the mounds are still mostly covered with soil, moss, and trees. El Cuajilote boasts a natural spring underneath one of its pyramids. Clearly water has always been important in this area. Excavations are continuing at both of these sites.

Tom Buckley

Veracruz Falls

RIVER OUTFITTERS

Mexico Edventures, World Trade Center, Ruiz Cortines 3497, 94290

Boca del Río, Veracruz. Specializes in academic trips and tailor-made environmental education trips throughout Veracruz.

Mexico Verde, José María Vigil No. 2406, Col. Italia Providencia, 44620 Guadalajara, Jalisco, (3) 641-5598, fax (3) 641-1005. Offers rafting trips throughout Mexico, but specializes in Veracruz.

Río y Montaña, Prado Norte 450-T, Lomas de Chapultepec, 11000 Mexico, D.F., (5) 520-2041, fax 540-7870, e-mail rioymontana @compuserve.com.mx. Another well-respected adventure tourism company which specializes in Veracruz. Most of the Veracruz trips leave on the weekends and feature two descents for $250.

Veraventuras, Santos Degollado No. 81-8, 91000 Xalapa, Veracruz, (28) 18-95-79 or 18-97-79, fax (28) 18-96-80. This local company tailors specialized tours throughout Veracruz. Veraventuras offers single-day, three-day, and week-long river trips. Three-day tours on the Pescados-Antigua and Actopan Rivers cost $125 to $225 depending on accommodations.

VERACRUZ NATIONAL MARINE PARK

Area: 52,238 hectares (129,028 acres)
Location: Off the coast of Veracruz City and Antón Lizardo
Activities: Diving, snorkeling, bird-watching
For More Information: SECTUR at (5) 250-0123 or 250-0151or the Veracruz state tourism office

Diving and snorkeling await you along the 17 reefs just outside of the Veracruz harbor. This is Mexico's first national marine park with decent snorkeling, given the murky waters. An added bonus are the sunken vessels that are submerged in the harbor. Locals say that the best time to dive is from May to September.

There are two main areas. The first lies in front of the Port of Veracruz and includes the following reefs: Gallega, Galleguilla, Anegada de Adentro, La Blanquilla, Pájaros, Hornos, and Ingeniero. These reefs skirt the small islands—Isla Verde and Isla de Sacrificios—outside the harbor. Wildlife includes brown pelicans, frigate birds, and green turtles. The depth of the reefs is about 37 meters (120 feet) and the trip from Veracruz Harbor takes about a half hour.

The second area is in front of Punta Antón Lizardo, 20 kilometers (12 miles) southeast of Veracruz and includes the following reefs: Giote, Polo, Blanca, Punta Coyol, Chopas, Enmedio, Cabezo, el Rizo, Santiaguillo,

Anegada de Afuera, Anegadilla, and Topetillo. Average depth—about 48 meters (157 feet)—is deeper here. Trips that originate in Veracruz City generally charge $10 more to visit the reefs further from the port.

The first action to protect the reefs took place in 1975 when La Blanquilla Reef was proclaimed a wildlife refuge. In 1992 President Carlos Salinas declared the entire system of reefs a national marine park.

Tours and Outfitters

La Casa del Mar, at the intersection on Camacho and Zapata, (29) 36-12-78. Specializes in snorkeling and diving trips.

Servicios Subaquaticos El Dorado, Blvd. Avila Camacho 865, Colonia Centro, (29) 31-43-05 or 37-00-14, e-mail dodiver@infosel.net.mx. Diving store that offers diving courses ($250), snorkeling ($20) and diving trips ($30-40) to the nearby reefs, and rental equipment.

Veracruz-Mexico Expeditions, Tiburón 1528, Boca del Río, (29) 21-15-50 or 21-46-70, e-mail iguanaexp@hotmail.com. They offer full-day rafting trips ($60), half-day snorkeling trips ($50), and customized trips for those interested in cultural and environmental travel. Contact Olga Díaz Ordaz for more information.

Getting to Veracruz National Marine Park

Veracruz is five hours from Mexico City, with frequent bus service from the eastern bus station (TAPO). Veracruz also has an airport with service to Mexico City, Campeche and Mèrida.

Where to Stay near Veracruz National Marine Park

Hotel Baluarte, Canal 265, Veracruz, (29) 32-6042, $30. Modern hotel with its own restaurant. Parking is available across the street.

Hotel Colonial, Lerdo 117, Veracruz, (29) 32-01-93, $20. A classic favorite in downtown Veracruz. Parking costs $2 extra.

Hotel Prendes, Independencia 1064, Veracruz, (29) 32-4854, $30. Facing the Plaza de Armas, this three-story hotel has nicely furnished rooms. Exterior rooms have balconies, which are great for people-watching, but these rooms can be noisy.

LOS TUXTLAS AND LAKE CATEMACO

Location: 150 km (91 mi.) S of Veracruz City
Activities: Swimming, hiking, bird-watching

Pronatura Veracruz

As bird-watching becomes popular in Mexico, the environmental group Pronatura Veracruz hopes that bird-loving tourists will bring much needed financial resources to support conservation in the region.

In the fall of 1996 Pronatura Veracruz biologists documented the greatest migration of hawks ever recorded in the world—4.5 million birds. According to chapter president Ernesto Ruelas, this "River of Raptors" is one of the greatest unsung natural phenomena on Earth. Twenty species of hawks fly over Veracruz on their north- and southbound journeys during the fall and spring migrations. These raptors include turkey vultures, Swainson's hawks, Mississippi kites, and kestrels. The birds signal the changing seasons, and now Pronatura is encouraging everyone to start looking up.

Pronatura is encouraging local Veracruzanos to protect the forests and rivers. Pronatura is working with a local group, Maderas del Pueblo, to establish a farmers' reserve in Uxpanapa, home of the last vast tropical forests in Veracruz. The region is home to 50,000 mostly indigenous people who resettled here in the 1970s after they were displaced by a hydroelectric reservoir.

For more information, contact
Pronatura Veracruz
Museo de Ciencia y Tecnológia
Avenida Murillio Vidal
Xalapa
(28) 12-88-44
e-mail verpronatura@laneta.apc.org.

*For More Information: SECTUR at (5) 250-0123 or 250-015 or the
Veracruz state tourism office*

Southern Veracruz is dominated by Los Tuxtlas, a chain of small mountains that preside over the marshy coastal plains. Incredible biodiversity
meets magical realism in this corner of Veracruz—just visit Lake
Catemaco, nestled between the two larger volcanoes.

Lake Catemaco is a popular tourist area that sees the majority of its
business during holidays and weekends. The oval-shaped lake is 16 kilometers (10 miles) long and is surrounded by the volcanic mountains. On
the northeast side of the lake is San Martha Volcano, a special biosphere
reserve. This entire region is noted for bird-watching, the most spectacular
of which takes place during the fall and spring migrations.

On the northern shore is **Parque Ecológico Nanciyaga** (294/3-
0666), an entertaining and educational 40-hectare (99-acre) park with a
great trail system and reasonably informed guides. It's a New Age center
of sorts with mud and steam baths (*baños de temascal*) and a good deal of
chanting. The officials here are targeting environmental restoration and
want to reintroduce crocodiles and turtles in the area. You can reach
Parque Ecológico Nanciyaga by road (30 minutes) or boat (90 minutes).

The region is known for its witchcraft and herbal medicine. It's also
the northernmost tropical rain forest in Latin America. If the towering
rain forest reminds you of a movie, you're probably recalling the 1986
Harrison Ford film *The Mosquito Coast*. The actual Mosquito Coast, in
Honduras, was too inaccessible for Hollywood crews, so the producer
chose southern Veracruz instead.

The Tuxtlas have had a long history of occupation, dating back to at
least 1400 B.C. The area abuts the Coatzacoalcos River Valley in the
southern part of the state on the border with Tabasco. This was part of
the Olmec heartland, and the Tuxtlas served as the quarries for the gigantic Olmec heads that can be seen today at various archaeology museums in
Mexico.

Tours and Outfitters

Tierra de Tucanes, Apdo. Postal 68, 95870 Catemaco, (294) 3-1032.
Ornithologist William Shaldack offers six-day tours through the Tuxtlas
for about $1,000. Gourmet lunches in the rainforest are included. Highly
recommended are individualized one-day trips that run $60.

Getting to Los Tuxtlas and Lake Catemaco

Bus service to Catemaco is available from Xalapa and Verzcruz City (both
of which have frequent service to and from Mexico City).

Besides the lakeside town of Catemaco, there are two main cities in the region where you can base your tours. The first, Santiago Tuxtla, is 27 kilometers (17 miles) from Lake Catemaco and features the Tuxteco Museum and Olmec sculptures. San Andrés Tuxtla is closer—only 12 kilometers (7 miles) from Lake Catemaco on Highway 180.

Bus service between San Andrés Tuxtla and Xalapa or Veracruz is frequent. From San Andrés Tuxtla local buses serve Catemaco. The only first-class bus station in the town of Catemaco is the ADO terminal on the corner of Aldama and Bravo.

Where to Stay in Los Tuxtlas

Hotel del Lago, Avenida Playa on the corner of Abásolo and Avenida Playa, Catemaco, $20, (294) 3-01-60. Clean rooms in a pleasant hotel with a restaurant.

Hotel Los Arcos, Madero 7 on the corner of Mantilla, $20, (294) 3-00-3. Friendly service. Rooms have private baths and wide balconies.

Hotel Michelle, Dr. Bernardo Peña 36, San Andrés Tuxtla (20 minutes away from the lake), $20, (294) 2-10-08 or 2-17-64. Located in the nearby town of San Andrés, the hotel has 40 clean rooms and provides good information on nearby reserves and beaches.

Playa Azul, kilometer 2 on the Highway to Sontecompan, Catemaco, $30, (294) 3-00-42 or 3-00-01, fax (294) 3-00-42. The owners cater to bird-watchers and promise guests that they can expect to see some 70 to 80 species of birds during a week's stay at the lodge. The hotel also rents bicycles and offers walking tours through the forest.

PICO DE ORIZABA

Location: East of Puebla and just north of Orizaba
Area: 19.8 hectares (48.9 acres)
Activities: Mountaineering
For More Information: SECTUR at (5) 250-0123 or 250-015 or the Puebla or Veracruz state tourism offices

If you'd like a serious challenge, consider Pico de Orizaba—at 5,746 meters (18,853 feet) it's the highest point in Mexico and the third-highest peak in North America. It is also called Pico de Citlaltépetl (*Pico* for "peak," and *Citlaltéptl* for "star"—the mountain's snow-covered peak does indeed resemble a star). You can buy basic food supplies and plan your trip in either Puebla or the town of Orizaba. Pico de Orizaba, Popocatépetl, and

Dangerous Coffee

Every year between November and April, untreated waste from coffee processing plants floods into Mexican rivers in the Gulf Coast state of Veracruz. It's a problem that is damaging the ecosystem, but finding a solution has been difficult.

"If the government steps in and enforces the national water laws, all of our state's coffee producers would have to go out of business," explains Fernando Celis Callejas, spokesman for the Coffee Producers Confederation (CNOC), adding that the coffee producers don't have the money to upgrade their facilities.

Veracruz produces 40 percent of Mexico's coffee supply. But the state's humid climate does not accommodate the traditional method of drying coffee beans in the sun. Instead, the beans are first crushed in a pulping machine and then fermented in tanks of river water. The liquid residue, called stillage, is dumped back into the rivers. For each kilogram of coffee produced, 6 to 8 liters of stillage are created as a byproduct.

According to biologist Eugenia Olguin of the Institute of Ecology, some Veracruz rivers are now biologically dead due to the growth of agricultural industries in the past several decades. The rivers are being overtaxed by the large amounts of organic material. The seasonal wastes rob the rivers of oxygen, leading to the suffocation of aquatic creatures. Fisherman complain that they have lost their livelihoods.

Olguin's department at the Institute of Ecology is working to develop low-cost technologies to treat the effluent in a way that could create spiraling, a type of algae that can be used as feed for livestock.

In the meantime, however, the coffee producers still cannot afford to purchase newer, more environmentally sound production equipment.

Iztaccíhuatl are the only three peaks in Mexico with permanent fields of snow. There's simple hiking on the lower slopes and a narrow trail with a steep slope to the peak.

For more information on climbing any of Mexico's volcanoes, check out *Mexico's Volcanoes*, a guidebook by R. J. Secor (Mountaineers Press).

Getting to Pico de Orizaba

Puebla is easily accessible from Mexico City with bus service available every 15 minutes. The trip to Puebla never takes more than an hour and a half. From Puebla, travel 2 hours east on Highway 150 to Tlachichuca. Just east of this town there are dirt roads (four-wheel-drive vehicle required) that lead up the north side of the mountain to an isolated alpine refuge called Piedra Grande. You can also travel from Orizaba, just 25 kilometers (16 miles) away from Tlachichuca.

Pico de Orizaba

National Institute of Ecology

Where to Stay near Pico de Orizaba

There are no hotels in the park, but accommodations can be found in nearby Puebla City or San Salvador El Seco.

Hotel Colonial, Calle 4 Sur 105, Puebla, (22) 46-4199, $20. Old-fashioned hotel one block east of the zócalo.

Hotel Imperial, 20 de Noviembre 101, San Salvador El Seco, (245) 1-0001, $8. Located just 30 kilometers (about 19 miles) from the park entrance, this small hotel has clean rooms and hot water available.

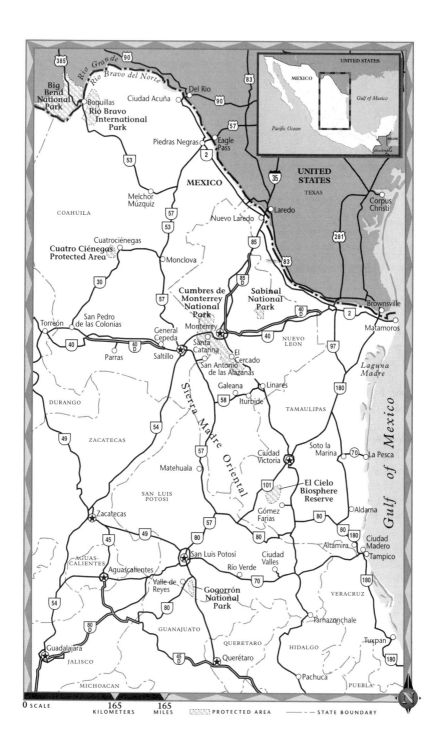

NORTHEAST MEXICO   7

TAMAULIPAS, NUEVO LEÓN, & COAHUILA

The northeastern corner of Mexico is a land of sharp contrasts: coastal dunes, the Sierra Madre Oriental, and a sizable portion of the Chihuahuan Desert.

Nestled between the Eastern and Western Sierra Madres, the Chihuahuan Desert is the largest desert in North America. Three-fourths of it lie in the Mexican states of Coahuila, Chihuahua, and Durango, while the remainder is in the United States. This is a high desert—the peaks are generally 1,500 meters (4,920 feet) high while the basins seldom drop to 700 meters (2,296 feet) above sea level. The desert is home to more than 250 species of cacti—hundreds of native species include the creosote bush, lechugilla, and candelilla. The best time to visit the desert is in the spring and autumn months: March through May or September through October.

The Sierra Madre Oriental (Eastern Sierra Madre) offers a high-altitude refuge from the desert heat. Visitors can refresh themselves in the mountains outside of Saltillo and Monterrey, where bird-watching, hiking, and horseback riding are popular.

In the Lower Rio Grande Valley, the area from McAllen, Texas, to where the the Rio Grande flows into the Gulf of Mexico, researchers have identified ten biotic communities, 115 vertebrate species, and 400 bird species. Author Roger Tory Peterson named the Lower Rio Grande Valley one of the top 12 birding hot spots in the United States. Groves of sabal palm once thrived here, along with dense thornbrush, mesquite,

Election campaigning in Saltillo

and huisache. The area is one of the most biologically diverse in the Americas, but cannot continue to support such a fragile ecosytem without a healthy Rio Grande. Fortunately, efforts are being made to curb future pollution of this endangered river. One such effort is the construction of a new (and first!) water treatment plant for the city of Nuevo Laredo.

The coastal region, along Tamaulipas, is an important fishing area for both commercial and sportfishermen and is renowned among avid bird-watchers. Part of the Gulf coast is home to the nesting grounds of the endangered Kemp's Ridley turtle. Bird-watching in Tamaulipas has yet to soar in popularity, but that will come as bird-watchers discover the coastal towns south of the border.

Bird-watchers aren't the only ones finding the northeastern part of Mexico to their liking. Tourism providers have noticed a steady increase in visitors from Europe and Asia who travel to the region to see cacti plants in their native habitats. Local markets haven't failed to notice this trend, either. Products made from cacti—such as jams, jellies, and liquors produced from *nopales* (prickly pear cactus)—are increasingly available in small towns and at roadside stands.

The region has changed a great deal during the 20th century. The once-forested plains have been replaced by almost impenetrable thorn-brush (*matorral*) and towering yucca, and the land has been systematically cleared for pastures, orchards, and cropland.

Industrialization and intensive agriculture not only deplete the top-soil, which helps the land maintain its nutrients, but also exhaust fresh-water reserves and lead to the extinction of local species. Human consumption of water resources has destroyed many of Northern Mexico's freshwater habitats.

STATE OF TAMAULIPAS

Tamaulipas has 430 kilometers (267 miles) of coastline on the Gulf of Mexico, with beaches well known for their golden sand and warm water. Five major rivers flow from the Sierra Madre Oriental into the gulf, creating coastal wetlands that attract numerous species of birds and marine animals. Nature tourism, per se, is not well developed here, but coastal towns provide basic services. The area is a bird-watcher's paradise, so bring your identification book.

The Laguna Madre, a brackish lagoon fed by the Soto la Marina, El Carrizo, and Conchos Rivers, separates mainland Tamaulipas from a series of barrier islands or sandbars—Barra los Americanos, Barra Jesús María, and Barra Soto la Marina (which includes the Barra de Tordo, the nesting area of the Kemp's ridley turtle). Manatees can be seen at the mouth of the Soto la Marina River in the autumn, before they migrate to the Yucatán Peninsula for the winter.

The Tamaulipas state government is promoting the development of an intercoastal canal that would connect the Texas border to Tampico, in southern Tamaulipas. Environmentalists have argued that this would destroy many of the unique ecosystems within the Laguna Madre. The federal government's National Institute of Ecology has approved the project, though it included 120 points with which builders must comply if the project is to pass environmental impact studies.

EL CIELO BIOSPHERE RESERVE
Location: 50 km (31 mi.) S of Ciudad Victoria
Area: 144,530 hectares (356,989 acres)
Activities: Hiking, bird-watching, caving
For More Information: Terra Nostra, 19 Mendez y Doblado #220-A,
(131) 6-83-52

111

The El Cielo Biosphere Reserve stretches from the eastern to the western slopes of the Sierra Madre Oriental. *Cielo,* "sky" or "heaven" in Spanish, is an apt name for this biologically rich forest, the northernmost cloud forest in Mexico. The advantages of visiting this park include superb hiking trails and excellent local guides who are proud to show off their backyard.

In 1987 the United Nations designated El Cielo an international biosphere under the Man and the Biosphere Program. Its importance is due to the fact that it lies on a climate transitional zone between North and Central America and boasts four distinct ecosystems: tropical jungle, mountain forest, pine-oak forest, and a chaparral-matorral forest on the lower western slopes that supports an arid forest of dwarf oaks. These four ecosystems are habitat to 524 plant species. The park contains 93 mammals, representing 70 percent of the mammal species found in Tamaulipas. Elevations range from 300 to 2,200 meters (984 to 7,216 feet) above sea level.

Tourism is relatively new in this area, created as an alternative to forestry when the Mexican government designated El Cielo a biosphere reserve in 1985. Most of the tourism options are centered in **Alta Cima**, a town just within the reserve that is a 90-minute uphill drive from Highway 85 (the north-south highway from Ciudad Victoria). Alta Cima's El Pino hotel and restaurant (see below) are new and their success may inspire other ejidos in the reserve to open similar services.

From half-day hikes to multi-day treks, there's something for everyone in El Cielo. Hiking options include not only a short interpretive trail, but also a day-long trip to Cañón del Diablo (a 4-kilometer jungle hike with excursions to a cave and an old sawmill); a hike of the same distance to El Salto, a canyon that in the rainy season ends in a waterfall; and Casa de Piedras, a 6-kilometer (3.5-mile) hike into the pine forests and meadows. The day hikes cost about $5 per person.

In Alta Cima, you can hire guides and mules at La Fe (The Faith), a combination store and restaurant that also sells locally produced honey and wine made from wild grapes. Both the guide service (Servicios de Guías) and animal transportation service (Servicio de Transportación Animal) are operated by a men's cooperative.

Beyond Alta Cima are other smaller villages, less frequented by visitors. A biological field station, **Canindo Station**, lies 7 kilometers (4.3 miles) beyond Alta Cima. To get there you must either walk or have a rugged four-wheel-drive vehicle. This is not a tourist facility, although you can get permission to stay here at the SEDESOL office in Ciudad Victoria (5/2-32-42). The caretaker of the research station is Don Goyo, who lives in the nearby town of San José, about a kilometer (half-mile) beyond Canindo. There are some nascent visitor services in this town. You can buy sodas, coffee, cookies, and tuna from a tiny store. Don Goyo's wife, Doña Romanita, serves coffee and will cook a meal of tortillas, beans, and maybe eggs for a small fee (about $1.50 per person). Primitive campsites are available.

Hikes in **San Jose** lead visitors to a variety of natural attractions, including large caves, a rock formation known as The Elephant (El Elefante), a canyon lush with vegetation, and a crystal-clear, spring-fed stream that runs along a 2.4-kilometer (1.5-mile) loop trail. Locals ask that you hire a guide if you want to visit the caves.

The ejido **Joya del Salas** (known as Ejido Veinte de Abril), also within the reserve, is witnessing the growing economic success of Alta Cimas, and local residents may construct similar rustic accommodations for the traveler.

Conservation and Tourism in El Cielo

El Cielo Biosphere Reserve is home to 2,500 people, many of whom hope that tourism will bring sustainable revenues to their communities. "We need to let people know that nature can be enjoyed responsibly," says Marcela Alvarez of Mexico's Tropical Forest Action Program (PROAFT). "There's nothing wrong with tourism, especially when it helps the local community develop its economy without damaging the natural resources. Too often scientists came here to conduct research, but they didn't assist the community."

Indeed, without leaving economic benefits to the local population, conservation of protected areas such as El Cielo are doomed. In 1993 the Ciudad Victoria–based environmental group Terra Nostra won a series of grants to begin community organization in the buffer-zone area of the reserve. This work brought forth the cooperatives and the locally-controlled tourism in Alta Cima. There are few examples as successful as this in Mexico.

Tours and Outfitters

Terra Nostra, 19 Mendez y Doblado #220-A, (131) 6-83-52. Can book reservations and assist travelers interested in visiting El Cielo Biosphere Reserve. Terra Nostra generally does not arrange transportation to the reserve but can provide a map or advice on local buses.

Getting to El Cielo

El Cielo is relatively close to the Texas-Mexico border. It's roughly a 3-hour trip from Brownsville or McAllen, Texas, to Ciudad Victoria; from there, it's a 2-hour drive on winding Highway 85 to the small town of Gómez Farías, at the foothills of the Sierra Madre (turn off just after you cross the steel-frame bridge over the Río Sabinas). Gómez Farías has a few restaurants and is a good information hub (try the police station).

Reaching Alta Cimas from Gómez Farías requires driving 4 kilometers (2.5 miles) on a rocky uphill rocky road. This leg of the trip takes about an hour. You won't need four-wheel-drive, but high clearance is necessary, and you should be especially cautious during the rainy season. If you travel to Gómez Farías by bus, you might be able to catch a ride up the mountain, but the price may be steep—around $40.

A topographical map of the reserve (Gómez Farías F-14-A-49) is available from the INEGI office at 22 Carrera Torres #601 in Ciudad Victoria; (131) 4-10-33.

Where to Stay Near El Cielo

El Patio Neotropical, 26 Bravo 438, Ciudad Victoria, (131) 51-722, e-mail hcavozos@tamnet.com.mx. This eco-minded ranch in nearby Gómez Farías can accommodate groups of four to 15 people in a series of rustic stone cottages. Owner Herberto Cavazos believes in promoting sustainable tourism in the region and leads trips to El Cielo Reserve. Most leave directly from Ciudad Victoria on Friday afternoons. The inclusive price for a weekend stay is $250 per person.

El Pino, Alta Cima, $10. Run by the town's Grupo de Hombres, this is a rustic hotel with hot and cold showers. Each room has four bunk beds and solar-powered fluorescent lamps. The group provides guide service to nearby scenic locations, and camping is available on the hotel grounds. A restaurant here serves very basic meals (tortillas, rice, eggs, black beans, and nopales, when in season) for about $2 each.

Research Station Canindo, next to the community of San José, 7 kilometers (4.5 miles) from Alta Cima, $10. Canindo is run by the state office of SEDESOL. This is an interesting research center, equipped with humble solar energy generators that provide lighting. Visitors need permission from the Ciudad Victoria office if they want to spend the night here. Access is difficult: Only sturdy four-wheel-drive vehicles can make the drive from Alta Cima, and the road can be very slick when it rains.

KEMP'S RIDLEY TURTLE RESERVE/ PLAYA RANCHO BEACH
Location: 200 kilometers (125 miles) southeast of Ciudad Victoria, between La Pesca and Barra del Tordo
Area: 1,760 hectares (4,347 acres)
Activities: Turtle conservation, bird-watching
For more Information: SECTUR or the Tamaulipas state tourism office (131/2-10-57 or toll-free in Mexico 800/57-100)

The Laguna Madre, a brackish lagoon fed by the Soto la Marina, El Carrizo, and Conchos Rivers, separates mainland Tamaulipas from a series of barrier islands or sandbars—Barra los Americanos, Barra Jesús María, and Barra Soto la Marina (which includes the Barra de Tordo, the nesting area of the Kemp's ridley turtle). Manatees can be seen at the mouth of the Soto la Marina River in the autumn, before they migrate to the Yucatán Peninsula for the winter. And sea turtles can be seen along the beaches.

The nesting season of the Kemp's ridley, the smallest and most endangered of sea turtles, occurs from April to September. During this period, teams of conservationists patrol 129 kilometers (80 miles) of Playa Rancho Nuevo (Rancho Nuevo Beach), located 24 kilometers (15 miles) from the town of San Rafael, from three to five times a day. They locate newly laid eggs and move them to fenced corrals for incubation. Hatchlings are released soon after birth to begin their lives at sea.

The hotels on both sides of the sandbar can arrange visits to these "turtle camps" for those interested watching the researchers work. Keep in mind that efforts here are focused on critical conservation strategies, not necessarily tourism. This means that researchers may or may not have time to answer questions. If you're interested in some hands-on work, see if volunteers are needed to patrol the beaches or help out during the peak season.

While the most famous of the turtle beaches is Playa Rancho Nuevo, there are two other camps, one 17 kilometers (11 miles) to the north in the town of Ostionales and the other 13 kilometers (8 miles) to the south in the town of Barra del Tordo. Visits to the turtle camps can be arranged via hotels, such as El Paraíso or Los Evanos Ranch (listed below). If you arrive during the high turtle season, you may be able to see baby turtles or even release them into the gulf yourself.

Plan to base your stay in either La Pesca or the town of Barra del Tordo. These towns are on the eastern edge of the sandbar. La Pesca attracts anglers because it's where the powerful Río Soto la Marina empties into the Gulf of Mexico. Local game fish are redfish, black drum, flounder, and striped mullet.

The Kemp's Ridley Turtle

The Kemp's ridley turtle was named for Richard Kemp, a fisherman who shipped specimens to Harvard University from Key West in the late 1800s. Also known as the Lora, the Kemp's ridley is the only turtle species that lays its eggs during the day. Females nest in a large group called an *arribada*. Each turtle digs a hole in the sand, deposits her eggs in the nest (or clutch), and returns to the sea. The young hatch in 50 to 55 days, then rush into the water.

As they mature, the turtles feed in bays and estuaries along the Gulf of Mexico in Texas, Florida, Louisiana, and the Bay of Campeche. The males spend their entire lives at sea, while almost all of the females return to Rancho Nuevo to lay their eggs.

Until the 1960s, scientists did not know where the turtles nested. In 1965 a 20-year-old black-and-white film was discovered that documented an arribada of at least 40,000 Kemp's ridleys nesting in broad daylight on a tiny stretch of Rancho Nuevo beach. Later it was found that the turtles lay almost all (95 percent) of their eggs on this length of sand between the mouth of the Soto la Marina River and the Altamira.

The turtle population has seen an alarming decline during the late 20th century. The number of nesting turtles at Rancho Nuevo had plummeted to 1,200 in 1975, from approximately 40,000 in 1947. The population continued its drastic decline until 1987, when only 748 nests were made at Rancho Nuevo. The numbers have increased since 1988, and scientists hope that the adult population will reach 10,000 by the year 2010.

In an effort to make that population increase more likely, scientists have developed technology to avoid conflicts between fishermen and the turtles. Increased use of Turtle Excluder Devices (TEDS) by the shrimping and fishing industry keeps turtles from suffocating in the nets. However, a new potential danger looms in the planned dredging of the Gulf Intercoastal Waterway from Brownsville, Texas, to Tampico, which would cut through the Laguna Madre. How increased barge traffic along this route would affect the surrounding ecosystems is unclear, but environmentalists have asked the government to be cautious.

Getting to the Turtle Reserve

Barro del Tordo is a 5-hour drive east from Ciudad Victoria on Highway 70. The town has its own small airstrip, and there is daily bus service from Soto la Marina. Inquire at hotels along the beach about visiting the turtle reserve.

Where to Stay and Eat near the Turtle Reserve

El Paraíso, 6 kilometers (4 miles) from the Gulf of Mexico on the shore of the San Rafael River or Carrizales, Barra del Tordo, $70, (12) 13-99-56 or (12) 13-87-73, e-mail fhaces@correo.tamnet.com.mx. This fishing lodge, owned by Francisco Haces, is a terrific base for both turtle-watching and bird-watching (yellow parrots, eagles, egrets, parrots, and hawks). Be sure to make reservations beforehand. The price includes overnight lodging, all meals, and the use of horses and kayaks. Five-day guided fishing trips cost about $600 and also include accommodations and meals.

From the town of Aldama, take the highway toward the gulf for 46.5 kilometers (29 miles). As the road nears the water, the scenery changes from marshland to gently rolling hills. A sign for "El Paraíso" is well-marked on the highway. Take a left and drive through the pasture. The lodge is set on a bluff overlooking the river. There are a dozen cottages with tiled bathrooms, electricity, and comfortable beds.

Los Evanos Ranch, near La Pesca, $80, (12) 27-20-59, e-mail acaso@correo.tamnet.com.mx. Owner Arturo Caso maintains this 4,000-acre cattle ranch that has three different ecosystems—deciduous forest, wetlands, and beaches. The ranch coordinates trips to the turtle camps as well as week-long bird-watching trips ($700) in the area. Among the avian species found are gray-crowned yellowthroats, red- and yellow-headed parrots, roadside hawks, squirrel cuckoos, and mottled and pygmy owls. Reservations must be made beforehand, and the ranch accommodates groups of at least five and no more than ten people.

NUEVO LEON

The state of Nuevo León has it all: forests, canyons, desert, and waterfalls, plus a variety of spectacular flora and fauna. Bird-watchers in Nuevo León have counted 388 different species (one-third of the national total). The state boasts 2,200 plant species, though scientists suggest the number might rise to 7,000 given adequate research. Included in that number are 19 different types of pine trees.

Bird lovers will enjoy *Aves de Nuevo León*, a book published under the auspices of the Nuevo León Advisory Council of Flora and Fauna (available at El Castillo bookstore on the pedestrian mall and at other bookstores in Monterrey).

CUMBRES DE MONTERREY NATIONAL PARK
Location: Surrounds the city of Monterrey
Area: 246,500 hectares (608,855 acres)
Activities: Hiking, rock climbing, bird watching
For More Information: Park information, (8) 335-6979, or the state tourism office at (8) 340-1080 or (01) 800-83-222 in Mexico

The city of Monterrey, with a population of 3 million people, is Mexico's third-largest city and the industrial capital of Mexico. Founded 400 years ago around the springs of Santa Lucía, Monterrey expanded rapidly,

Forested hillside in Nuevo León

especially at the end of the 19th century, when it became a ranching center, then an industrial center. Today residents call their city El Monster Chico (The Small Monster), as opposed to El Monster Grande, Mexico City.

Monterrey's signature skyline is a portion of the Sierra Madre Oriental that in 1939 was declared a national park, the 255,000-hectare (630,000-acre) Cumbres de Monterrey. Like the Cumbres de Ajusco park in southern Mexico City, the mountains here are the recharge zone for the underground aquifers that provide Monterrey with its water supply. The pine and oak forests capture the moisture in the soil. Hiking, mountain climbing, and bird-watching are popular activities at this pleasant getaway from the urban metropolis.

While Cumbres de Monterrey is large, most of it is undeveloped. There are four areas of interest to visitors within the park: Huasteca Canyon, García Caverns, and two privately developed parks within the national park: Chipinque and Horsetail Falls.

Chipinque

The closest and the easiest portion of the park to visit is Chipinque, located on the southwestern edge of Monterrey. Chipinque is managed by Patronato del Parque Ecológico Chipinque, a group of Monterrey businesses. The park also has a small restaurant.

A map of the ten hiking paths in Chipinque is available at the visitor's center near the park entrance. Hikes are in the easy to moderate range, and paths are well-designed and marked. Because it's so close to the city, the area surrounding the visitor's center is often swarming with noisy school children, but the human density lessens as you hike into the mountains.

Peaks in Chipinque range from 650 to 2,260 meters (2,130 to 7,415 feet). For rock climbers and mountaineers, there are five summits in the park (listed in degree of difficulty): the Pinar, 1,515 meters (4,970 feet); the Window, 1,955 meters (6,415 feet); the Antennas,

Sierra de Los Picachos

The Sierra de los Picachos mountain range, an outlying portion of the Western Sierra Madre north of Monterrey, is dotted with numerous caves, canyons, and waterfalls. On clear days the peaks of the Picachos can be seen from the U.S.–Mexico border.

Los Picachos functions as a biological mountain island, as it is isolated from similar habitats by a "sea" of drier brush and chaparral. U.S. Fish and Wildlife Service biologists have documented ferruginous pygmy owls, black-chinned hummingbirds, peregrine falcons, black-headed orioles, Montezuma quail, acorn woodpeckers, yellow-green vireos, and trogons in the region, while mammals found in the area include black bears, ocelots, mountain lions, and ring-tailed cats. Partnerships among Mexican and U.S. officials attempt to secure funding for biological corridors and research. While you may not see these animals—they're very shy—you might be able to spot their tracks.

The vegetation of Picachos is diverse, with Tamaulipan brushland on the eastern slopes, low chaparral on the northern slopes, and more dryland vegetation on the south and western slopes. According to researchers, the plant diversity might surpass that of El Cielo Biosphere Reserve.

2,015 meters (6,610 feet); the "M East," 2,020 meters (6,630 feet); and the Crest of the Eagle, 2,260 meters (7,410 feet).

The dominant tree species within the park are Chinese pine (*Pinus teocote*) and white pine (*Pinus pseudostrobus*). There are more than 20 species of mammals which inhabit this terrain, including bears, pumas, squirrels, and white-tailed deer. There are also 120 species of birds, including bluebirds and hawks.

Chipinque Park is 20 kilometers (12 miles) southwest of downtown Monterrey. Travel south of Avenida Manuel Gómez Morín and you'll find the well-marked entrance. The paved road winds upward into the foothills and takes you directly to the visitor's center. The entrance fee is

50 cents for pedestrians and cyclists and $2.50 for individual cars. The park is open daily from 8 a.m. to 8 p.m.

Horsetail Falls

The 25-meter (82-foot) Horsetail Falls (Cascadas Cola de Caballo), formed by small rivers rushing down the Sierra Madre Oriental, is located one hour south of Monterrey. As the water hits a series of rocks, the curving spray falls in the shape of a horse's tail. There are several marked dirt and gravel paths, including one that leads to the summit of the falls. The surrounding forest comprises poplars, oaks, and native pine species. The park is fairly small and privately owned. It features one of the few multipurpose recreation centers in the country—facilities include a lodge, a small restaurant, volleyball courts, picnic tables, and bathrooms.

Horsetail Falls Park is open Tuesday through Sunday from 9 a.m. to 5 p.m. The entrance fee is $5. The park is 6 kilometers (3.7 miles) from El Cercado, a small town 35 kilometers (22 miles) south of Monterrey on Highway 85.

García Caverns

The state's most famous caves, the García Caverns (Grutas de García), are found just west of Monterrey. The caves are estimated to be more than 50 million years old and were only discovered in the late 1800s. Marine fossils embedded in the walls provide evidence that the caves were once under the sea.

A guided tour follows a 2.5-kilometer (1.6-mile) path through the various chambers. Formations with poetic names such as Chamber of Clouds and The Eagle's Nest are illuminated. The tours, given on the hour, are conducted in Spanish. But English-language tours are available upon request for an additional fee. The caves are open from 9 a.m. to 5:30 p.m.

To reach the caves from Monterrey, drive west toward Saltillo on Highway 40. After the well-marked turnoff to the town of García, drive another 18 kilometers (11 miles) to the entrance.

You can arrange a ride to the caverns from Monterrey for around $30 to $50. Remember to negotiate price before agreeing to hire the driver. The Transportes Monterrey–Saltillo bus line goes to the caverns, but only on Sundays.

Huasteca Canyon

The famed Huasteca Canyon (Cañón de la Huasteca), a canyon west of Monterrey, boasts 300-meter-high cliffs and a park (with a children's playground) in the middle. Without a doubt, the 350-hectare (865-acre) park earns its classification as "semi-urban," but if you're not expecting solitude you'll have a great time. Among the highlights at Huasteca are the petroglyphs on the walls of the canyon. There are unlimited opportunities for rock climbing, but you have to bring your own equipment.

The Santa Catarina/Huasteca bus takes you from the corner of Padre Mier and Juárez in downtown Monterrey to the park. These buses run several times daily.

Getting to Cumbres de Monterrey National Park
Monterrey's international airport, just 30 minutes east of town, receives daily flights from major U.S. cities and larger cities in Mexico. The city's mammoth bus station (Central de Autobuses) is located downtown on Colón between Pino Suárez and Reyes. Monterrey is a major travel hub, and you'll find buses to nearby towns and larger cities including Nuevo Laredo, Saltillo, Ciudad Victoria, Querétaro, and Mexico City. The train station is a half-kilometer west of the bus station. There are daily trains to Mexico City, though service has declined in quality the past few years.

Industrial Monterrey has numerous parks and pedestrian malls

Mountain Hiking and Exploration

Aventurismo Guias Profesionales is a new travel agency offering a variety of nature-travel excursions in Saltillo and throughout northeastern Mexico. Three-day hiking or mountain-climbing trips run about $400. For more details, contact Mauricio Pérez Gómez at (84) 17-24-69 or 15-55-78, e-mail: avgps@mexnet.mcsa.net, Web site: http://www .mcsa.net/aventurismo/.

Where to Stay in Monterrey near Cumbres de Monterrey

Hotel Amado Nervo, Amado Nervo Nte 1110, Monterrey, $30, (8) 375-4632. Small, friendly, five-story hotel in the heart of downtown Monterrey. All rooms have air conditioning.

Hotel Hacienda Cola de Caballo, just out side the Horsetail Falls, (828) 50-660, http://www.coladecaballo.com, $100. Suites and conference center, environment-friendly management.

Hotel Los Reyes, Hidalgo 543 Poniente, Monterrey, $25, (8) 343-6168. Just west of the Zona Rosa, this is a clean hotel with parking.

Hotel Río, Padre Mier 194, Monterrey, $90, (8) 344-9040. Enormous hotel in the downtown area. Caters to business travelers and conferences.

Where to Eat near Cumbres de Monterrey

El Rey de Cabrito, Constitución 817 Ote at Calle Dr. Coss, Monterrey. This festive and cavernous restaurant serves traditional goat as well as other regional specialties.

Las Monjitas, at Calle Galeana 1018, Monterrey, off the pedestrian mall. Inexpensive *taquería* with great food, especially tacos. It takes some getting used to—the waitresses are dressed as nuns.

Sanborn's, Escobedo 90, Monterrey, on the pedestrian mall. A Mexican chain restaurant that also sells a miscellany of goods—newspapers, magazines, candies, tobacco, batteries, and hair dryers. If you're here for breakfast, order the Huevos Sanborn's, two eggs served in a tomato sauce with the three "C"s—chiles, cheese, and cream.

RENACER DE LA SIERRA LODGE
Location: 2 hours SW of Monterrey
Activities: Hiking, bird-watching
For More Information: For reservations, contact the Sánchez de la Peña family in Monterrey at (8) 353-9023

Renacer de la Sierra (Rebirth of the Mountains), Nuevo León's oldest environmental tourism lodge, is planted in the heart of the Sierra la Marta, part of the Sierra Madre Oriental. This portion of the Sierra boasts Cerro El Morro, Nuevo León's highest mountain at 3,740 meters (12,270 feet), as well as eight species of pine and two species of fir (one endemic to the area). Numerous *ecotonos*, where two separate ecosytems are found on the same hillside—one system supporting pine trees, another cacti, for instance—can be found here as well. Notice how the vegetation is more lush on the western side of the mountains and hills, as they receive the majority of the precipitation.

Revenues from Renacer's cabins support scientific research and conservation in the area. The area is rebounding from a regional wildfire that destroyed 8,000 hectares (19,760 acres) in 1975. Today the hills are alive with young pines and strands of golden aspen. Income is used to reproduce seedlings and for reforestation. "After the fire, some of the conifers came back, but it will take 800 years for complete recovery," says José Sánchez de la Peña, an environmental writer whose family runs the facility. Some 370,000 trees were replanted in 1979 and 1980, and another 17,000 were planted in the summer of 1995.

The lodge is as simple as the owners are friendly. There are eight rustic log cabins with indoor bathrooms, cooking stoves, gas heating, and oil lamps. The area is perfect for hikers and bird-watchers. No motor bikes, hunting, or loud noises are permitted. To make reservations, call the Sánchez de la Peña family in Monterrey at (8) 353-9023.

Getting to Renacer
Renacer is located 125 kilometers (78 miles) from Monterrey—115 kilometers (71 miles) on paved roads, the last 10 kilometers (6 miles) on a fairly good dirt road. From Monterrey take Highway 40 west toward Saltillo then head south on Highway 57, a toll road to Matehuala. Keep

your eyes open for signs to San Antonio de las Alazas; turn left and follow the road for 50 kilometers (31 miles). This is a beautiful valley and you will pass the small towns of San Antonio and Santa Rita. Continuing straight ahead, the pavement ends at a series of resort hotels. Five kilometers (3 miles) down the road you'll pass Los Oyameles cabins. After the lodge, turn right on a short road that leads to Renacer.

COAHUILA

RINCON COLORADO

Location: *44 km (27 mi.) W of Saltillo on Highway 40*
Area: *5,000 hectares (12,350 acres)*
Activities: *Dinosaur museum*
For More Information: *Paleontological Commission in Saltillo (941/49-544) or the state tourism office (84/30-0510)*

Millions of years ago, northern Coahuila was a tropical oasis, not an arid desert. It was also a favorite stomping ground of dinosaurs. Over the last

Museum of Paleontology, Rincón Colorado

20 years, Mexican scientists have unearthed secrets more than 70 million years old in this fossil site just outside the small town of General Cepeda. The most amazing discoveries at Rincón Colorado include egg nests, bone fragments, and skin impressions. These items, along with other fossils of marine organisms, shells, and tropical plants dating back to the Cretaceous Period, are on display at a small museum in the center of town. Visitors to Rincón Colorado can also take a self-guided walking tour of the excavation site. Admission to both areas is $5.

In 1992 a complete skeleton of a duckbill dinosaur called a kritosaurus was excavated in the area. A replica is on display at the University of Mexico's geology museum in Mexico City.

Getting to Rincón Colorado
There are well-marked signs to the museum and fossil site installed by INAH, the National Institute of Anthropology.

Where to Stay near Rincón Colorado
Hotel Imperio del Norte, Boulevard Carranza #3800, Saltillo, $20, (84) 15-00-11. Comfortable hotel and trailer park.

Hotel Rancho El Morillo, near the intersection of Calle Obregón Sur and Periférico Luis Echeverría Sur, Saltillo, about 3 kilometers (1.9 miles) southwest of downtown, $30, (84) 17-40-78. Restored hacienda with a pool, volleyball court, and chapel.

Hotel Urdiñola, Victoria Pte. 207, Saltillo, $20, (84) 14-09-40. Centrally located hotel with a lot of character. Parking is available down the street.

CUATRO CIENEGAS PROTECTED AREA
Location: 280 km (174 mi.) NW of Monterrey
Area: 84,347 hectares (208,338 acres)
Activities: Exploring gypsum dunes, lagoons, and cacti habitat
For More Information: City Hall, or Presidencia Municipal at (869) 6-06-50

Desert hikers will find the small town of Cuatro Ciénegas (Four Lagoons), with its rare white gypsum sand dunes and adjacent wildlife park, one of the most intriguing destinations in Mexico. This area is described by biologists as a "showplace of biodiversity" and an "irreplaceable treasure of Mexico." After spring and late-summer rains, the desert blooms and the effect is nothing short of spectacular. Unfortunately, the region is being destroyed due to intensified agricultural irrigation, livestock grazing, and mining of the dunes. The once 20-meter-high (65-foot-high) dunes have

Cacti of the Americas

The cactus plant is endemic to the Americas and can be found everywhere from Canada to Chile. Since there are no cacti fossils, it's considered a relatively new arrival to the plant kingdom. The cactus figures prominently in Aztec mythology. After receiving a vision of an eagle devouring a snake while perched on top of a cactus, the Aztecs built a temple to the warrior god Huitzilopochtli and founded Tenochtitlán, "the place of the prickly pear cactus." The Aztec king Moctezuma grew several varieties in his gardens in what is now Chapultepec Park in Mexico City.

Cacti are divided into three subfamilies: Pereskioideae, Opuntioideae, and Cactoideae. Cactoideae have no leaves (they would lose too much water through transpiration); they either stand like monuments with arms that stretch in different directions or they are globular. They conserve water within their thick, fleshy trunks. Almost 90 percent of all cacti are in this subfamily. The Opuntioideae, with more than 300 species, is more succulent. Its stems can be disc-shaped or cylindrical, and new growths link together like sausages. The Pereskioideae is the least evolved of the three subfamilies. It has both leaves and spines, and grows in the wetter portions of the desert as well as in the bush country.

Cacti are highly prized commodities; rare cacti are considered trophies by collectors. Some sell in Japan and Germany for thousands of dollars. But it's against the law to transport endangered species out of Mexico, and thieves are often heavily fined. Unfortunately, given the value of cacti, they represent a likely income source for rural Mexicans. Is there a sustainable way for the ejidarios to harvest a percentage of the rare cacti or their seeds for sale to cacti aficionados? That remains to be seen.

been reduced to 6 meters (20 feet) above the valley floor, because of excavation performed by the Proyeso, S.A. de C.V. gypsum mining company. Proyeso is part of Grupo Lamosa, a Monterrey-based industrial group that produces ceramics using the gypsum.

Declared a protected area in 1995, the Cuatro Ciénegas Reserve is located in an arid basin in the Chihuahuan Desert. Overlooking the valley are limestone sierras capped by conifer forests. Beneath the basin is a labyrinth of underground rivers, which has produced a large number of aquatic pools. These small ponds are home to species of fish and turtles found nowhere else on the planet. As the water in the pools and lagoons evaporates, it leaves behind the dried gypsum, which blows into the dunes. The Las Playitas lagoon is relatively easy to visit and has a number of ocotillo cacti colonies that are unbelievably beautiful after spring and summer rains. Because of the environmental fragility of the lagoons, avoid using suntan lotion or any kind of soap when swimming in them.

The dunes are only accessible with a registered guide. For a tour, it's best to ask at the city hall. Conservation efforts are now underway, as are negotiations with the local ejido that owns the property. Under normal circumstances you'll be required to provide your own transportation to and from the dunes.

The Sustainable Development for the Valley of Cuatro Ciénegas group at the Casa de la Cultura, west of the town square on Calle Hidalgo (869/6-08-96), promotes responsible business and tourism in the region. So far, however, tourism has floundered in Cuatro Ciénegas due to the lack of publicity and infrastructure. "We've seen scientists and tourists come here with their own food," says Susana Moncada, the town's former mayor. "They don't spend any money here, so how can we depend on them to support our economy?"

There is also a debate over what type of ecotourism to promote. Local guide Mendez pointed out that previous schemes at attracting tourists have not been environmentally friendly. "They want to develop the lagoons for water skiing," he says, "and this would have a terrible impact on the ecosystem." Mendez can be contacted at the Hotel Santa Fe, (869) 6-04-25.

Swimming in the Lagoons
After touring the white gypsum dunes, you can relax in one of the aqua-blue lagoons (there are actually more than four) that give this town its name.

A 10-minute drive south of town on Highway 30 brings you to a rustic interpretive center at Kilometer 90. Just behind the wooden building is a public pool or *balneario*. Other balnearios in the area include the Río

Cuatro Ciénegas Lagoon

Mezquites, a private facility located just before the interpretive center, and Poza la Bacerra, further down Highway 30 on the northern side of the road. The water at Poza la Bacerra is warmer and the park is a little more developed than at the other two balnearios, with white-sand "beaches" and bathrooms. Admission to either facility is $5. The facility is sometimes closed, so you might want to confirm the hours of operation at the city hall.

Things to See and Do in Cuatro Ciénegas

Cuatro Ciénegas is a very quiet town with few diversions, a pleasant zócalo, and a handful of ice-cream parlors. But locals go out of their way to make visitors feel welcome. Be sure to pick up a map at the city hall on the west side of the zócalo. You'll also find information on other attractions, such as the home of revolutionary hero and Mexican President Venustiano Carranza. The **Casa de la Cultura museum**, just west of the zócalo on Calle Hidalgo, has an intriguing display of ancient arrowheads found in this region as well as rare remnants of baskets woven more than a thousand years ago. Admission is $1.

Cuatro Ciénegas is home to the **Bodegas Ferriño winery** (whose most famous label is Sangre de Cristo, a very sweet red wine). You'll also find numerous homemade candies in the town's stores. Like most towns in Mexico, Cuatro Ciénegas has a definite sweet tooth.

Tours and Outfitters

Guardianas de Nuestro Valle (Guardians of Our Valley, 869/6-06-50) are local volunteers available from the city hall. They will guide you through the area in your automobile. Currently there is no charge for the service, but a $10 tip per person is considered polite. For more information on this group, ask for Ruben Flores or Gonzalo Zamora.

Getting to Cuatro Ciénegas

Cuatro Ciénegas is located on Highway 30. It is 74 kilometers (45 miles) or 1 hour west of the town of Monclova and roughly 235 kilometers (145 miles) on two-lane highways from Saltillo. The town is 320 kilometers (200 miles) or about 5 hours south of Piedras Negras near the U.S. border. Buses serve Cuatro Ciénegas from Saltillo, Monterrey, and Torreón. Autobuses Estrella Blanca and Autobuses Blancos offer service from the downtown square in Cuatro Ciénegas.

Where to Stay and Eat in Cuatro Ciénegas

El Doc, on the city square, Zaragoza No. 103, (869) 6-09-40. Great breakfasts; one of the favorite local establishments. The diner receives its name from its owner, a town dentist and the recently elected mayor, José Luis Fernández Hernández.

Finca Campestre, 1.5 kilometers (.9 miles) out of town on the highway toward Ocampo, $20, (869) 6-04-43. Owner Susana Moncada, who also directs the local SEDESOL environmental office, rents quiet and comfortable rooms at this hotel on the outskirts of town.

Hotel Ibarra, Zaragoza No. 200, $20, (869) 6-00-04. Small, comfortable hotel a few blocks from the downtown zócalo.

Hotel Santa Fe, Carretera Monclova kilometer 0.4, Juárez Avenue in town, $20, (869) 6-04-25. Small, clean hotel with parking. The hotel can arrange specialized guided trips with school teacher Héctor Méndez Campos.

Restaurant Valentino's, on the outskirts of town on Presidente Carranza (en route to the dunes), (869) 6-05-00. Valentino's has the best grill, or *parillada*, in all of northern Mexico.

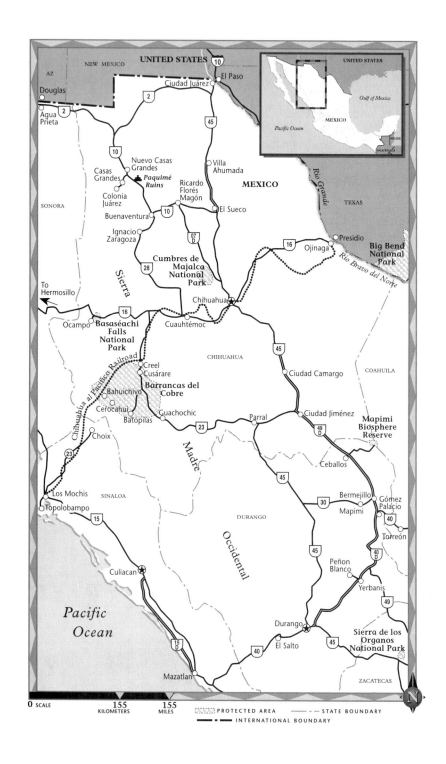

NORTHWEST MEXICO

8

CHIHUAHUA AND DURANGO

The 1,300-kilometer (806-mile) Sierra Madre Occidental Range—made famous in *Treasure of the Sierra Madre,* the novel by B. Traven—stretches from the U.S.–Mexico border to the states of Chihuahua and Durango. Blanketed by thick pine and oak forests, it presides over coastal plains to the west and the Chihuahuan Desert to the east. Copper Canyon is the principal natural attraction in the region, but be sure to take time to explore the archaeological ruins of Paquimé and the ever-mysterious Zone of Silence in Durango's Mapimi Biosphere Reserve.

The Sierra Madre Occidental (Western Sierra Madre) is one of the most ecologically diverse areas in Mexico. It is home to as many as 100 species of oak and 20 species of pine, including *Pinus ponderosa* and *Picea chihuahuana.* In addition, 30 percent of Mexico's land mammals are found in the Sierra Madre—visitors may see tracks of the black bear, mountain lion, otter, white-tailed deer, or Mexican wolf.

Numerous environmental trips are available in the area. Packaged tours of the Copper Canyon are becoming more and more common as individual travelers and travel agencies discover the park. But back-packers will find they have the edge in seeing the rural areas, far from the vista of the Chihuahua al Pacífico Railroad. Unfortunately, for the most part tourism here downplays conservation efforts. In fact, many of the hotel owners in the town of Creel, Copper Canyon's tourism hub, also own the sawmills. Forestry is still the state's number one industry, and tourism is just gaining a toehold. Genuine community-led ecotourism projects are just taking off in Cusárare and in Uruachi, deep in the heart of canyon country.

CHIHUAHUA AL PACIFICO RAILROAD

Mexico's most famous train runs through the Sierra Madre Occidental from Chihuahua City to Los Mochis, Sinaloa, on the Pacific coast. Many small canyon towns are served best by the train. You can get to Creel by road from Chihuahua, but if you're in this area, be sure to book a seat on this incredibly scenic rail journey.

The dramatic 515-kilometer (319-mile) trip takes 16 hours end to end and features 87 tunnels and 37 soaring bridges. The first-class run includes brief stops; there are longer and more frequent stops on the second-class service.

Windows facing south provide the best views of the canyons, but you can always leave your seat and check out the passing scenery from the loading area in between the train cars. Of course, there are times when the train is delayed due to washouts, rock falls, heavy snow, and derailments, and in these situations patience and a sense of humor, or a pack of playing cards, will serve you well.

You can purchase tickets in advance in Chihuahua City or in Los Mochis. If you want to make a reservation, reliable tourism offices (with personnel who speak English) charge only a small mark-up.

Chihuahua al Pacífico Railroad stop in Creel

The first-class train leaves from Los Mochis at 6 a.m. and from Chihuahua City at 7 a.m. For tickets and more information, contact **Turismo al Mar** in Chihuahua City at (14) 16-59-50, fax 16-65-89. In Los Mochis, **Viajes Flamingo** travel agency at the corner of Leyva and Hidalgo can help you; (681) 2-16-13, fax 8-33-93. To book formal tours on the Chihuahua al Pacífico railroad, contact **Chihuahua al Pacífico Tours**, Avenida Americas No. 303, Chihuahua, (14) 14-68-11, fax 13-73-60.

CHIHUAHUA

Chihuahua is Mexico's largest state. Its varied terrain includes spectacular canyons, towering mountains, and the Chihuahuan Desert. But Chihuahua is experiencing hard times. In the mid-1990s, while tropical storms battered Baja California and the Pacific coast, Mexico's interior, including Chihuahua, received very little rain. In 1996 total losses from the drought in Mexico were estimated at more than $1 billion. Chihuahua was one of the states hardest hit.

The drought has devastated Chihuahua's once-profitable cattle ranching industry. Yet while water levels are currently below normal, there are still green oases, and most signs indicate that the drought is coming to a gradual end. Meanwhile, the state's economic development office has begun to seek alternative ways to bolster Chihuahua's financial standing and now has a branch devoted to the promotion of ecotourism. The office is definitely worth a visit to obtain up-to-date information on natural attractions throughout the state.

Ecotourism in Chihuahua

The state's economic development office has a special office dedicated to developing and promoting a variety of ecotourism programs and destinations. The office also publishes the informative magazine *Conozca Chihuahua*. Contact Carlos Lazcano Sahagan, Chihuahua Dirección General de Fomento Economico, at Libertad No. 1300-1, Chihuahua City, Chihuahua; (14) 29-34-21, 29-33-00, or (800) 903-92; fax (14) 16-00-32.

CHIHUAHUA CITY

Location: 375 km (233 mi.) S of El Paso, Texas
Activities: Hiking, museums, travel hub for the Chihuahua al Pacífico railroad and Copper Canyon

For More Information: *(14) 29-34-21 or 29-33-00, fax (14) 16-00-32; in Mexico, (800) 903-92*

Chihuahua City (population 300,000) functions as the travel hub for those coming from or going to the canyons. Located at the junction of the Chiviscar and Sacramento Rivers, the city is on a high-desert plain surrounded by mountains. Its stately stone buildings—such as the Palacio de Gobierno on Calle Aldama—and its broad plazas resemble cities on both sides of the U.S.–Mexico border. Don't pass up the opportunity to look at its storied past before you head on to the mountains.

In October, Chihuahua holds its state fair and agricultural exhibition. Like state fairs in the United States, there are rodeos, rides, and concerts. For more information on fair events visit the tourist office.

Things to See and Do in Chihuahua City

Pancho Villa was a prominent historical figure in the region, and chose to settle down in Chihuahua at the beginning of the century. His stately residence, **Quinta Luz**, has been transformed into the **Museum of the Mexican Revolution**. The rooms have the original furniture from the early 1920s. Exhibits include period photos, many of Villa's personal weapons, and the 1922 Dodge in which he was shot and killed in 1923, complete with bullet holes. The museum is located at Calle 10 #3014 and is open Tuesday through Sunday.

The **Regional Museum of the State of Chihuahua**, at Paseo Bolívar 4 (14/10-5474), offers another good history lesson. The exhibits change on a frequent basis, but the house itself, built in 1910 as a replica of a French neoclassical mansion, is the main attraction. The museum is open Tuesday through Sunday from 10 a.m. to 2 p.m. and then again from 4 to 7 p.m.

The state capital also has numerous **arts and crafts markets**, including the Mercado de Artesanías (Aldama 519), Artesanías y Macetas en Barro (Díaz Ordaz 415), Artesanías y Gemas Naturales de México (Calle 10a No. 3015), and the Palacio de Artesanías Mexicanas (Victoria 319). The best is the **Casa de Artesanías** (14/37-12-92), at Avenida Juárez 705 next to the Hotel Apolo. You'll see a great deal of Tarahumara crafts and there are knowledgeable clerks who can answer your questions.

Getting to Chihuahua City

Chihuahua is well-connected via train, plane, and bus. The airport is 18 kilometers (10 miles) northeast of town off of Highway 15. There are two train stations: The station with service to and from Mexico City and Ciudad Juárez is located on Avenida División del Norte; the station for the Chihuahua al Pacífico line is at Calle Mendez and Calle 24. The bus

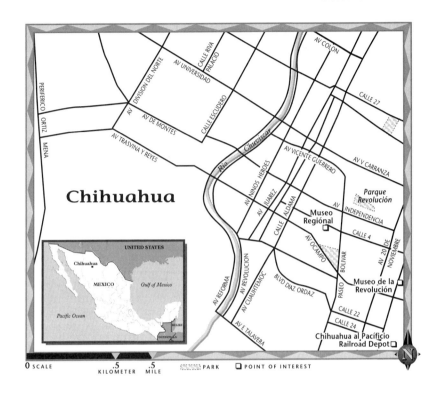

Chihuahua

0 SCALE · .5 KILOMETER · .5 MILE · ▦ PARK · ❑ POINT OF INTEREST

terminal is 8 kilometers (6 miles) from the center of town on Avenida Juan Pablo 2. There is frequent service to and from Ciudad Juárez, Durango, and Torreón, plus express trips to and from Mexico City (20 hours).

Where to Stay in Chihuahua City

Hotel Apolo, Av. Carranza 102 (at Av. Juarez), $15. Located next to the Palacio del Gobierno, this hotel has secure parking and rooms are air conditioned.

Nueva Hotel Reforma, Victoria 814, $5, (14) 12-58-08. Clean rooms in an old hotel with enclosed patio.

San Francisco, Victoria 504, $50, (14) 16-75-50 or, in the U.S., (800) 847-2546. Luxurious rooms very close to the downtown plaza.

Sicomoro Hotel, Boulevard Ortiz Mena 411, $65, (14) 13-54-45, or toll-free in Mexico (01-800) 14567. Located on the west side of town

near el Complejo Industrial. A convenient lodging for business travelers, this hotel has a heated pool and parking.

Where to Eat in Chihuahua City

El Leñador, Avenida Tecnológico y Ahuehuete, 13-61-91. Great tacos; daily breakfast and lunch buffet. The restaurant resembles a log cabin.

La Calesa, at the intersection of Aldama and Colon, 16-02-22. One of Chihuahua's more expensive restaurants, it's well-known for its steaks, fine *parilladas*, and superb service.

Tacos Orientales, Ortiz Mena 3427 and three other locations in town, 26-51-01. Top contender for having the best tacos and *antojitos* (appetizers) in town. Hot salsas, good prices, and clean and fast take-out service. Uses 100-percent Mexican beef and fresh veggies.

CUMBRES DE MAJALCA NATIONAL PARK

Location: 60 km (37 mi.) NW of Chihuahua, outside of Rivapalacio
Area: 4,772 hectares (11,787 acres)
Activities: Hiking, biking
For More Information: State tourism office, (14) 29-34-21 or 29-33-00

One of the oldest national parks in Mexico (protected since 1938), Cumbres de Majalca is famous for strange rock formations created through natural erosion and canyons created by the streams feeding into the Chuviscar and Sacramento Rivers. Its stony peaks are a favorite destination for rock climbers, and the park attracts hikers and cyclists as well.

While there may be more spectacular and more virgin parts of the Sierra to visit, none are as easily accessible from Chihuahua City as the Cumbres de Majalca National Park. The park has 33 kilometers (20 miles) of fire roads, which create a variety of cycling and hiking circuits. Many of the roads are marked, but there's no handy map of the area.

At an altitude of 1,600 to 2,500 meters (5,250 to 8,200 feet) above sea level, the park has pine and oak forests that provide habitat for black bear, coyotes, falcons, woodpeckers, and wild turkeys. Development has been minimal, so this is a great place for hiking and camping. Lodging is available in rustic cabins or in nearby motels along Highway 45. There's no park entry fee.

Getting to Cumbres de Majalca National Park

The park lies between Chihuahua and Ciudad Juárez on Highway 45. The turnoff is at Kilometer 35 and the park is 40 kilometers (25 miles) farther west on a secondary road. There is no bus service; the park is accessible only via car.

COPPER CANYON
Location: 480 km (300 mi.) W of Chihuahua City
Area: 7,350 sq. mi. (18,000 sq. km.)
Activities: Hiking, horseback riding, encounters with indigenous groups
For More Information: State tourism office, (14) 29-34-21 or 29-33-00

Copper Canyon is a world-renowned tourism destination. It's surrounding peaks are covered with pine and oak forests and reach 2,370 meters (7,775 feet). Yet Copper Canyon (Barranca del Cobre) itself is just one of more than 20 canyons that stretch west of Chihuahua City in the Sierra Madre Occidental, located between the high central plateau and the Sea of Cortez. The term "Copper Canyon" is often used to describe the entire region, which is also known as the Sierra Tarahumara, paying homage to the indigenous people who live here.

To journey into this rugged and isolated terrain with knowledge of its spectacular biodiversity and history is to experience one of Mexico's best adventures. Carl Lumholtz explored the Sierra Madre and the Barranca de

Copper Canyon, view from Divisadero

137

Sinforosa in 1892, and his well-documented adventures have inspired generations of canyon enthusiasts. The region offers everything from casual exploring and hiking to mountain biking and horseback riding. You'll also find a variety of climates—it can snow in the mountains while tropical temperatures reign in the valleys. The average altitude here is 2,275 meters (7,500 feet) above sea level, while the highest point, Cerro del Mohinora, is 3,306 meters (10,847 feet) and the lowest point, at the confluence of the Septentrion and Chinipas Rivers, is around 220 meters (720 feet). Copper Canyon receives about 15 inches of rain per year, most of it falling in July, August, and September.

A trip into the canyons and the Sierra requires a good base of operations. The town of Creel is most travelers' hub of choice. Multi-day treks are arranged by many of the hotels in Creel, though you can find independent guide services in any of the towns by asking hotel owners or visitors. The state department of tourism also has a list of qualified guides. But don't limit your visit to Creel. There are numerous towns along the railroad and in the valley—Batopilas, Cusárare, Divisadero, Bahuichivo, Cerocahui—that serve a similar purpose.

For detailed information on hiking and backpacking in the region, check out M. John Fayhee's *Mexico's Copper Canyon Country: A Hiking and Backpacking Guide* (Cordillera Press, 1994).

At present, Copper Canyon does not have federal status as a national park or as a biosphere reserve, but the plans and studies necessary to gain that designation were set in motion in February 1996, when Mexico's Environmental Secretariat (SEMARNAP) announced its intention to form a 2.2-million-acre biosphere reserve in the Sierra. CASMAC will be responsible for planning approximately 750,000 acres of this reserve in the upper Río Fuerte watershed in the Sierra Tarahumara

The Tarahumara

The canyons of the Sierra Tarahumara are home to 60,000 Tarahumara Indians (in their own language they are the Raramuri, "those who walk through life correctly"), many of whom find tourism intrusive. If you do visit, please respect their privacy. That said, many Tarahumara are qualified guides who want to help bridge gaps in cultural understanding.

When the Spanish arrived in the early 1500s, the Tarahumara lived in the fertile valleys of central Chihuahua. To evade the missionaries and Spanish settlers, they moved to the mountains. The Tarahumara are the second-largest indigenous group north of Mexico City (the Navajo in the United States are the first). They are famous for the long-distance running achievements of some of their members. The most elite of the athletes are capable of running nonstop for more than 20 hours.

The Canyons

Name	Depth (Meters/Feet)	Nearby Towns
Urique	1,870/6,135	Urique and Batopilas
Sinforosa	1,830/6,000	Guachochi and Batopilas
Batopilas	1,800/5,900	Batopilas
Candameña	1,640/5,380	Ocampo and Uruachi
Chinipas	1,600/5,250	Chinipas
Oteros	1,520/4,990	Maguarichi and Uruachi
Copper	1,300/4,265	Urique, Guachochi, and Bocoyna

The Tarahumara have an organic cosmology—a vital part of their religion is their belief that they are an integral part of the land and of the universe itself. Their settlements are very small and often seasonal. They traditionally live in caves or cabins along the canyon rims during the summer and move to the canyon bottoms during the winter. This is all geared toward a productive agricultural system in which specialized crops are grown for a specific altitude or type of soil. Corn is the major crop and the indigenous milpas, or fields, include more than six different strains, including blue, red and white corn.

Canyon History

The region's barrancas are not only some of Mexico's youngest geological formations, but are the largest in North America. They were formed 30 to 40 million years ago, during a period of intense volcanic activity in what is present-day northwestern Mexico. Thousands of volcanoes erupted, throwing lava and ash onto the surrounding plateau and creating the Sierra Madre Occidental. The tectonic activity also created deep fractures in the earth's crust. Because the rocks are relatively soft, the rivers originating in the high Sierra cut deep canyons on their descent to the Gulf of Mexico. The canyons bear the names of these powerful rivers: Chinipas, Candameña, Urique, Tararecua, Batopilas, and Verdes.

Flora and Fauna of the Canyons

The Sierra is one of the most biologically rich areas in Mexico, in part because there are two distinct environmental climates—one in the mountains and on the plateaus, and another at the bottom of the canyons. This terrain includes snow-covered mountain peaks and subtropical forests in the canyons.

The canyons are home to 290 recorded bird species (24 endemic and ten in danger of extinction) including the military macaw (*Ara milittaris*), the thick-billed parrot (*Rhynchopsitta pachyrhyncha*), and the eared trogon (*Euptilotis noxenus*). Almost a third of Mexico's land mammals are found in the region, including the black bear (*Ursus americanus*), the puma (*Felis concolor*), and the Mexican wolf (*Canis lupus baileyi*), which is in danger of extinction. Hunting has claimed many species. The grizzly bear is extinct, and the wild turkey and deer are now rarely seen.

More than 3,500 vascular plants are found in the region. Among them are tropical and temperate species as well as hundreds of endemic species, including at least 60 wild relatives of major crops and more than 400 wild medicinal plants—an irreplaceable genetic legacy. Most of these endemic plant species are endangered by logging and overgrazing. Ironically, ethnobotanists now estimate that the forests are more valuable as extractive reserves for medicinal plants than for timber. The *chuchupate* plant, used as a blood thinner in both traditional and modern medicine, is worth thousands of dollars per acre in virgin pine forest, but it is sparse in most of the Sierra due to overharvesting and deforestation.

Mixed forests of ponderosa pine and Douglas fir are found above 2,000 meters (6,500 feet), while juniper, piñon, and live oak are found at lower elevations from 500 to 1,500 meters (1,640 to 4,900 feet). Biologists have counted 15 species of pine and 25 species of oak in the canyon regions. Unfortunately, these forests have been commercially logged for 100 years, and only the worst trees have been left to generate new forest.

Ecotourism Outlook

In another example of how the word "ecotourism" changes definition depending on who's using it, Mexico's Tourism Secretariat (SECTUR) and the Chihuahua State Department of Tourism are promoting major infrastructure projects in the name of promoting tourism. One plan calls for the creation of 2,000 hotel rooms in the Copper Canyon region. Critics argue that environmental tourism should be small-scale and built from the ground up.

Advisory Council of the Sierra Madre

In 1992 Randall Gingrich, Edwin Bustillos, and indigenous leaders from the Sierra formed the Chihuahua City–based Advisory Council of the Sierra Madre (CASMAC). The groups programs support indigenous communities suffering loss of land, destruction of forests, and human rights abuses. Its mission is to return control of the forests to the traditional indigenous communities—especially the Tarahumara and Tepehuan—and to facilitate sustainable ecosystem management. They believe that conservation, sustainable agriculture, and defense of basic human rights are inseparable for the indigenous groups' cultural survival.

For more information or to support the work of CASMAC, contact the group at Division del Norte 2300, Suite CH44-0119, Colonia Altavista, Chihuahua; tel./fax (14) 155912; U.S. mailing address: 3815 Buckner "E," Suite CH44-119, El Paso, TX 79925; e-mail sierrarg@igc.apc.org.

According to government figures, approximately 90,000 tourists visit the Copper Canyon region each year. A new international loan of up to $380 million will assist in supplying infrastructure, including water treatment plants. However, according to researchers and Mexican journalists, no environmental impact study has been conducted to see how building the infrastructure will effect the area. And another danger, argue critics, is that the area does not have enough water to support such tourism facilities. Stay tuned: This is the major tourism development project of the current presidential administration.

Tours and Outfitters
Columbus Travel, Route 12, Box 382-B, New Braunfels, TX 78132, (800) 843-1060 or (800) 885-2000. Organizes multi-day package tours of the canyons. These trips are geared toward the higher-end bracket of the

tourism industry and receive many kudos from travelers. Hikers can request specilized information and the company will personalize tours with local guides. The seven-night "Western Explorer" trip from Los Mochis to Chihuahua City costs $1,100 and includes all hiking trips.

Outpost Wilderness Adventures (OWA), P.O. Box 511, Hunt, TX 78024, (830) 238-4383, fax (830) 238-4788 (summer: P.O. Box 7, Lake George, CO 80827, 719 748-3080). Schedules customized hiking and biking trips using hotels and local guides from Creel and Batopilas. Week-long trips cost $735 and include hotels, meals, guides, and transport from El Paso, Texas, and back.

Quezada Viajes, Aldama No. 316 Altos 4, Chihuahua, (14) 15-71-41, fax (14) 10-80-43, e-mail rquezada@infosel.net.mx. Arranges tours in the region and makes hotel and train reservations. Week-long trips cost $850 per person; discounts are offered to groups.

Sanborn's Viva Tours, P.O. Drawer 519, 2015 S. 10th Street, McAllen, TX 78705, (800) 395-8482. Offers a 6- or 11-day bus trip that puts travelers on the train from Chihuahua to Divisadero and then drives them back to McAllen, Texas.

Wilderness Expeditions, P.O. Box 40092, Tucson, AZ 85717, (602) 882-5341. Offers hiking treks throughout the Copper Canyon region.

Getting to Copper Canyon

The canyon is accessible from the Chihuahua al Pacífico railroad, the end points being Los Mochis, Sinaloa, and Chihuahua City, Chihuahua. From Chihuahua, you can take the train or bus to the town of Creel, which is the easiest hub for exploration of Copper Canyon country. Other towns on the railroad are developing tourism as well, particularly Divisidero, Bahuichivo, and Cerocahui.

CREEL

Location: 480 km (300 mi.) W of Chihuahua City
Activities: Hiking, horseback riding
For More Information: Contact the state tourism office, (14) 29-34-31 or 29-33-00

Creel is Mexico's ultimate small town (population 5,000). A 4-hour trip from Chihuahua City, it serves as a starting point for many tours of the canyons. If you stay here long enough (a few days) you begin to recognize almost everyone in town. The town is nestled high in the mountains at 2,338 meters (7,670 feet), and evenings here can be chilly, even in the warmer months.

Creel is a study in paradox—it is a logging village that supports environmental tourism. The town was named after the former state governor, Enrique Creel, son of the United States ambassador to Mexico in the 1930s, who founded timber works in the area.While the World Bank and SECTUR are developing "ecotourism" here, hardly anyone here knows of these efforts. The most noteworthy projects are those that not only involve but are run by the indigenous Tarahumara communities. Be sure to visit the ejidos of San Ignancio Arareko and Cusárare, just outside of town.

While its small hotels and restaurants offer something for every budget, the town is relatively quiet. Most everyone here is coming from somewhere else and heading in an altogether different direction. If you're looking for a guide, just ask around—either at your hotel or among your fellow travelers. Creel is also the hub of mountain biking in Mexico—the Mexican Mountain Bike Nationals are held here each summer. To rent a bike in town, check out **Expediciones Umarike**, located on the west side of the train tracks south of the train station.

A good spot in which to get your bearings is the **Casa de Las Artesanías**, located next to the train station. Run by the Catholic mission, this store promotes Tarahumara crafts and culture. They sell wooden dolls, drums, blankets, and photos of the Tarahumara, who would rather not be photographed by tourists. When you buy products here, you can be sure that all of the profits benefit the mission's hospital. The clerks are all knowledgeable and friendly locals. If you can speak Spanish, you'll find out all the news and gossip. If you don't speak Spanish, you'll still receive the same friendly service. The store is open Monday through Saturday from 9:30 a.m. to 1 p.m. and from 3 to 6 p.m. On Sunday it's open only in the morning.

Things to See and Do near Creel

The Complejo Ecoturistico Arareko (Arareko Ecotourism Complex), created by the local Tarahumara, is a successful tourism operation with rustic cabins, a scenic lake, and terrain honeycombed with hiking and cycling paths. The ejido has more than 20,000 hectares (49,400 acres) of pine and oak forests. Some of its Douglas fir trees are 430 years old. Swimming in the lake is discouraged because the water quality is not up to par. A guided tour of the lake via boat (*lancha*) costs $8 per hour.

Near San Ignacio de Arareko are bizarre rock formations with names like "Valley of the Mushrooms" and the "Valley of Penises." The

Valley of the Mushrooms, Ejido Arareko

"elephant" is just outside the ejido on the highway from Creel. If you hire a local guide, you won't get much beyond a colorful description of the local geology. After cycling past the Valley of the Penises, I asked my guide if the names had always been the same. "No," he said. "We just came up with the names when the tourists started coming."

In 1991 the state government attempted to expropriate the land in Arareko for tourism development. But this was foiled by the Tarahumara residents, who insisted that if tourism were to come to Arareko, they would develop it themselves. Since then a new state governor has taken office and has officially handed government properties over to the ejido.

Entrance into the ejido costs $1.50 per person. On the main highway, there is a women's cooperative store that sells handicrafts, clay pottery, wood carvings, and ritual drums.

The Recohuata Hot Springs, 10 kilometers (6.2 miles) south of Arareko in the Barranca de Tararécuam, make an excellent day trip from Creel, Arareko, or Cusárare. The springs are located at the bottom of Tararécua Canyon, a 450-meter (1,500-foot) drop that takes a few hours to trek. To get to the springs you have three options: hike (it can be done in a day, but with little time left for enjoying the springs), bike (not so difficult on the single track trails), or combine driving with hiking. Any hotel in Creel can fix you up with a ride, or you can look for your own way from the downtown plaza.

Cusárare, a Tarahumara community 20 kilometers (12.5 miles) south of Creel, is actively pursuing ecotourism as a means of generating income as well as protecting its stately 30-foot waterfall. The path to the waterfall is well-maintained by the local community. There's only one hotel in the area—the luxurious Copper Canyon Sierra Lodge. This community boasts an 18th-century church, Los Santos Cinco Señores de Cusárare. The church is dedicated to the Virgin de Guadalupe and the entire town celebrates the feast day on December 12th.

Tours and Outfitters
Complejo Turistico Arareko, on López Mateos, (145) 6-01-26. Rents bikes for $2 per hour and arranges reservations for the cabins in nearby Arareko.

Expediciones Umarike, located on the west side of the train tracks south of the train station on Avenida Ferrocarril, fax (145) 6-02-12. The company is run by Arturo Gutiérrez, who is fluent in English and married to a Welsh woman. The quality of the mountain bikes here is several steps above that at Arareko, and prices are higher as well. Day rental is $10. You can also book half-day, full-day, or multi-day guided trips with Arturo. The only downside: he sometimes closes up for the slow season (May–June).

Getting to Creel
Most visitors arrive via train; the station is located right on the town square. The train station has daily service to Chihuahua City and to Los Mochis, Sinaloa (see Chihuahua al Pacífico section, above). Across the tracks is the Estrella Blanca bus station, which has frequent service to Chihuahua City and Cuauhtémoc. A daily bus serves Ciudad Juárez on the border.

Where to Stay in and around Creel
Complejo Ecoturistico Arareko, Arareko, (145) 6-01-26. Accommodations in the ejido are available at the deluxe Segorachi Lodge, which costs $25 per night. The more rustic Batosarachi cabins run $6 per night. The lodge is part of a network of community-run hotels, coordinated by FONAES, a federal rural development agency. Guides are available for local treks ($10). Be sure to ask these local experts about environmental conditions.

Copper Canyon Sierra Lodge, Cusárare, 800-776-3942. Offers week-long packages for around $800, but does not rent rooms for individual nights.

Margarita's, López Mateos 11, Creel, $5–20, (145) 6-00-45. Just off the plaza, within sight and earshot of the train, this is the most famous hostel in Creel, and perhaps in all of Mexico. There are inexpensive dormitory accommodations and private rooms. This is clearly a favorite of international and Mexican backpackers.

Margarita's Hotel Plaza Mexicana, Calle Chapultepec, Creel, $30, (145) 6-02-45. An upscale version of the hostel, with the same friendly service.

Motel Parador de la Montaña, López Mateos 44, Creel, $30, (145) 6-00-75. Large hotel two blocks west of the plaza, with restaurant, bar, and parking.

BASASEACHI FALLS NATIONAL PARK

Location: 290 km (180 mi.) W of Chihuahua City, just S of Basaséachi
Area: 6,263 hectares (15,470 acres)
Activities: Hiking
For More Information: State tourism office, (14) 29-34-21 or 29-33-00

Some of the most incredible features of Copper Canyon are its waterfalls. At 453 meters (1,486 feet), **Piedra Volada** is the highest waterfall in Mexico and is located in Basaséachi Falls National Park in west-central Chihuahua, near the Sonora state border. Amazingly, these falls were discovered only in September 1995. Basaséachi Falls National Park also boasts at least four other waterfalls, as well as the beginning of the Candameña Canyon. The best time to see the falls is during the rainy season, from June to September. While trekking may be a bit slippery, the falls are most spectacular during this time.

Declared a national park in 1981, this is the only portion of the Sierra Madre Occidental that has status as a federal protected area. While the forests here have been grazed, there are still stands of old-growth trees, including a variety of pine species, Douglas firs, and Arizona cypress. Native fauna include white-tailed deer, mountain lions, pumas, and falcons.

The park's trails are well-marked. Most visitors want to take in the vista of the park's namesake waterfall, which is easier to visit than the Piedra Volada. Your best bet is a trail that goes from near the top of the Basaséachi Falls to the base. This is a hike for the more experienced hiker. It takes less than an hour to go down and about 90 minutes to ascend.

The town of Basaséachi has 300 inhabitants and limited services. Highly recommended is continuing on the 40-kilometer (25-mile) dirt

Native Seeds

The Arizona-based group Native Seeds/SEARCH has worked in the Sierra Tarahumara for many years. The group, which has studied and criticized forestry projects since the 1980s, strives to protect biological diversity.

Native Seeds supports the survival of native plants by distributing native plant seeds to farmers (and to individuals who would like to grow rare plants in their yards). Increasing distribution of the plants helps ensure that these species survive. It also helps demonstrate the value of native plants, which require less care than do exoctie specis introduced to the desert from other ecosystems.

If you'd like to cultivate plants of historical and biological value, contact Native Seeds/SEARCH, 2509 N. Campbell Avenue, Suite 325, Tucson, AZ 85719, (602) 327-9123, fax (602) 327-5821, Web site http://www.desert.net/seeds /home.htm.

road from Basaséachi to Uruachi, at the base of the canyon. Uruachi is home to a new tourism center run by the community. The region is a refuge for protected species such as cougars and the Mexican wolf. You might also see eagles, falcons, and wild ducks, which migrate annually from northern Canada.

Tours and Outfitters
LOBO, Turismo de Aventura, Avenida Francisco Villa No. 3700-10A, Col. Lomas del Sol, Chihuahua, (14) 21-56-26. Arranges hiking treks from Basaséachi to Uruachi. Contact Fernando Domínguez Arvizo.

Getting to Basaséachi Falls National Park
The park is located in between Cuauhtémoc, Chihuahua, and Hermosillo, Sonora. From Creel, take Route 330 northwest to the park. It is located just off of Highway 16. From Chihuahua City take Highway 16 toward Hermosillo.

Where to Stay near Basaséachi Falls National Park

There is a well-established campground at the park, or you can stay at a nearby hotel on Highway 16 in Basaséachi.

In Uruachi, lodging is officially available only by cabin, not per person or per bed. There are ten "regular-sized" cabins that accommodate six people. They cost $60 per night. The largest cabin accommodates 12 and costs $120 per night. Meals are an additional $8 a day. A 4-hour horseback ride with guide costs $10. For reservations or information, write to Fernando Domínguez, Parque Nacional de Basaséachi, Chihuahua, or contact the government's rural microenterprise development agency, FONAES, via e-mail: comsocl@fonaes.gob.mx.

BATOPILAS

Location: 140 km (86 mi.) S of Creel
Activities: Hiking
For More Information: State tourism office, (14) 29-34-21 or 29-33-00

Most travelers choose not to leave the Creel area until they travel to Batopilas via a harrowing road politely called one of the most scenic drives in the Americas. The town of Batopilas is a much quieter version of Creel and is nestled within a tropical valley. Although now a sleepy village of 800 souls, at the turn of the century Batopilas was one of the richest silver-mining towns in the world, with a population of 10,000 and more than 300 mines. The town retains a good part of its late-19th-century mining architecture. When the mines were depleted, the townspeople left and, for the better part of this century, Batopilas was a ghost town. The surrounding hills still are riddled with abandoned mine shafts. It may be hard to believe now that the town is a shadow of its former self, but in 1873 Batopilas was the second town in the country, after Mexico City, to have electricity.

The town is 500 meters (1,640 feet) above sea level, on the canyon floor. While the Sierra may be cold, Batopilas enjoys a semi-tropical climate year-round. Orange groves, mango trees, avocado, and papaya thrive here. Yards are landscaped with bougainvillea, and one plant or another is always in bloom.

Hikers have numerous options from Batopilas, including the old **Royal Road** between Batopilas and Urique, which passes many fantastic vantage points. It also includes a turn to the old mining town of Cerro Colorado. The walk takes from two to three days. To avoid getting lost, hire a local guide—ask your fellow travelers to recommend a good one. Also worth visiting is the 400-year-old Jesuit mission known as the **Lost Cathedral of Satevó**, a pleasant day hike 6.5 kilometers (4 miles) south of Batopilas.

Getting to Batopilas

The bus from Creel to Batopilas runs just three times a week, leaving at 7 a.m. on Tuesday, Thursday, and Saturday. The trip takes from 7 to 9 hours because when the road is curving, it's also plummeting. The road from Creel to La Casita (the halfway point) is paved; the remainder is gravel. The trip may leave you queasy, but remember, the adventure is supplemented with some of the best nose-to-the-window scenery in all of Mexico. The location of the bus stop in Creel is shifting as more travelers visit Batopilas, so inquire in town.

Where to Stay and Eat in Batopilas

Casa Real, located between Doña Mica's and the plaza, $20. There are six clean rooms and a gated courtyard.

Copper Canyon Riverside Lodge, $800 per week, (14) 15-82-14 or, in the U.S., (800) 776-3942. A two-story mansion restored as a hotel in the center of town. The lodge is booked only for eight-day package trips that combine a stay here with one at its sister lodge in Cusárare.

Hotel Mary, downtown Batopilas, $10, (14) 10-52-24. Inexpensive lodging at a friendly pensión. There are private and shared bathrooms with hot water. The hotel also has a small restaurant, the Patio Quinto, with the best food in Batopilas.

PAQUIME RUINS

Location: 340 km (211 mi.) from Chihuahua City, 7 km (4.3 mi) S of Nuevo Casa Grandes
Activities: Archaeological sites, museums
For More Information: SECTUR at (5) 250-0123 or 250-015 or the Chihuahua Tourism Office

The northwest section of Chihuahua is home to many archaeological sites, the most famous of which are the Paquimé Ruins. This conglomeration of adobe houses was home to the Paquimé civilization, which settled in northern Mexico between A.D. 900 and 1340. At the end of the 15th century it was destroyed by enemies and abandoned. Since then the roofs have collapsed, leaving only the walls, re-plastered in a brilliant white that contrasts strongly with the nearby vegetation. Some of the buildings were once three stories tall, much like those in Chaco Canyon to the north in present-day New Mexico. The layout resembles a maze. Respect the signs that indicate where you can and cannot go and do not bring food into the site.

The Paquimé were farmers and traders—visitors will see the remains of the adobe hutches where they kept their turkeys. Artifacts show that they exchanged goods with the Anasazi in the north as well as groups in Central Mexico. The Mesoamerican influence is apparent in the site's ball court and the monuments to Quetzalcoatl. One of the successes of the civilization was its production of multicolored pots made without a potter's wheel. You'll see examples in the museum. Local potters continue that tradition in the nearby town of Juan Mata Ortíz.

Paquimé Ruins

Be sure to visit the **Museum of Northern Mexico Cultures**, located next to the archaeological site. The museum exhibits artifacts from the Paquimé Culture as well as surrounding tribes, such as the Chichimeca, Mogollon, O'odham, and Anasazi. The museum has various fossils of mammals and a large collection of arrowheads from Clovis and Folsom. Photography is not permitted inside. The museum is open year-round Tuesday through Sunday from 10 a.m. to 5 p.m.

Getting to Paquimé Ruins

The location of the Paquimé Ruins is well marked. The ruins are just outside the town of Casas Grandes, 10 minutes from the town of Nuevo Casas Grandes, which is on Highway 10, midway between Buenaventura to the south and Janos to the north. Buses run between Nuevo Casas Grandes and Casas Grandes every 30 minutes, sometimes more frequently.

If you're coming from Ciudad Juárez, take Highway 45 south until you reach El Sueco, and then take Highway 10 west. If you're coming from Agua Prieta, Sonora, take Highway 2 east until you reach the town of Janos, then head south on Highway 10.

Where to Stay near Paquimé Ruins

Hotel Paquimé, Av. Benito Juárez 401, $25, (169) 4-47-20. Pleasant hotel in Nuevo Casas Grandes, 10 minutes from the ruins.

JUAN MATA ORTIZ

Location: 20 km (12.4 mi.) from Casas Grandes
Activities: Horseback riding, pottery, hiking
For More Information: Request a copy of the Friends of Mata Ortíz
newsletter from Mike Williams, U.S. (915) 544-2565, e-mail: mataort
@mindspring.com., web site: http://www.mindspring.com/~mataort
/matahp.htm

An excursion from Casas Grandes to the town of Juan Mata Ortíz is a definite must, especially if you truly enthused by artesania. In this village of adobe houses spread throughout a river valley, local potters use techniques and decorative styles similar to those used by the Paquimé, though many of the artists have developed a unique style of their own. There are currently about 300 potters in the area (up from 143 in 1990). The feather-light polychrome and black-on-black pottery here is not inexpensive—some pieces custom-ordered by art dealers cost as much as $3,000. Other museum quality pieces can be purchased for under $200 (those by Olga Quezada and Roberto Bañuelos are good examples), and good earthenware costs $40 to $50. The house of Juan Quezada, the most famous potter in the village, is well marked, just past the train station as you come into town.

Horseback riding costs $5 per hour or $12 for three hours. Three of the best guides are teenagers Miguel Gonzáles (English-speaking), Antonio Velóz, and Freddy Rodríguez. Contact the inn Posada de las Ollas for more information (see below).

You can also take side trips to the nearby **Swallow Cave** (Cueva de la Golondrina) and **Cave of the Pot** (Cueva de la Olla). Swallow Cave was inhabited as early at 5500 B.C. **Arroyo de los Monos**, with great rock art, is only 45 minutes from Mata Ortíz.

Tours and Outfitters
MataTours, 299 King's Point Dr. #124, El Paso, TX 79912, (915) 542-2871, e-mail mataort@mindspring.com. Mike Williams can arrange tours to Juan Mata Ortíz as well as horseback riding and excursions to archaeological sites in the Sierra.

Getting There
Follow the paved road through Casas Grandes to the Mormon community of Colonia Juárez, birthplace of former Michigan governor George Romney. Just past the plaza/basketball court, turn left and follow the road over a narrow one-lane bridge. Make an immediate left and pass the Latter Day Saints elementary school. Here the pavement ends but a

decent gravel road will lead you to Mata Ortíz, 20 kilometers (12.4 miles) away. The road takes you through the Palanganas Valley. You will pass a small agricultural community on your left (Cuauhtémoc). Soon you will enter San Diego, a small ejido known for its hacienda dating back to 1902 and built by the former Chihuahuan land baron Luis Terrazas. Remaining on the gravel road, you climb the hill and cross another plain for about 5 kilometers (3.1 miles) before descending into Juan Mata Ortíz.

Where to Stay in Juan Mata Ortíz
Posada de las Ollas, down the third street to the left after crossing the railroad tracks when entering the village. Fine accommodations at a small inn where lodging with three meals a day costs $39 single and $59 double.

DURANGO

Like Chihuahua, the state of Durango is a land of incredibly diverse geography. It's valleys are covered with fruit orchards, it's mountains with pine trees. (Durango produces roughly twice the timber output of Chihuahua, though this figure has declined in recent years.) The Chihuahuan Desert occupies portions of the south and southeastern sections of the state. Within the state of Durango, the Sierra Madre Occidental is called the Sierra Tepehuanes.

Travelers have long known of Durango's outdoor beauty, and like Chihuahua, the state is attempting to diversify its income base with tourism. Hollywood filmmakers came here in the 1940s to find locations that recalled the "Wild West" of the United States. Outside of the capital city (the city of Durango) you'll find at least three film sets. Inquire at the tourist office on locations and accessibility during the time of your visit.

MAPIMI BIOSPHERE RESERVE AND THE ZONE OF SILENCE
Location: 100 km (62 mi.) N of Torreón and Gómez Palacio
Area: Reserve is 123,000 hectares (303,810 acres)
Activities: Hiking, bicycling, cactus tours
For More Information: SECTUR at (5) 250-0123 or 250-015 or Durango state tourism office

The Mapimí Biosphere Reserve (and the Zone of Silence, which is

Sierra de los Organos National Park

The Sierra de los Organos National Park in northeastern Zacatecas was declared a national park for its spectacular beauty. Its isolation, however, keeps it a relatively unknown treasure in Mexico. The park's basalt organ pipe–like mountains were used as a backdrop for several John Wayne classics. While it's said the actor donated picnic tables and barbecue grills for visitors to use, I didn't see any such amenities when I visited the park. At any rate, the scenery is outstanding and the area is easy to explore. The park does have some paths, but nothing as developed as a hiking trail.

The entrance to the park lies 15 kilometers (9.3 miles) north of the town of Sombrete. This turnoff is well-marked, but you'll see the towering mountains long before you reach the junction. The road passes through the small village of San Francisco de los Organos. Turn east and take the dirt track which parallels the rock formations. While there are no restaurants in this village, there are several stores where you can purchase a soft drink or snacks.

For more information on Sierra de los Organos, call SECTUR at (5) 250-0123 or 250-015.

within the reserve) is located on the *altiplano* (high desert) at about 1,150 meters (3,772 feet) elevation near the Chihuahua-Coahuila border in the heart of the Chihuahuan Desert. The climate is semi-arid and local vegetation is dominated by the agave and creosote bush. This is a cactus lover's paradise, but there is no visitor's center, and there are no established hiking trails. The reserve is also home to the endangered Bolson tortoise.

Of the Mapimí Biosphere Reserve's 123,000 hectares (303,810 acres), 20,000 are administered by the Mexican government and 103,000 by the UNESCO Man and the Biosphere program. Official protection, however, is lacking under both designations. Work to establish the reserve began in 1974 and the protected area was founded in 1977.

Most of the land belongs to local residents, so the protection of resources depends on continued cooperation among scientists and the local community. The reserve supports a research station, El Laboratorio del Desierto (The Desert Laboratory), and has developed good relations with the local residents, especially ranchers. There are no accommodations for tourists here and there is no camping.

Note that the park is a slow 2-hour drive—mostly through private property—from the main highway. The gravel road is good, but it crosses numerous gates, which must be opened and closed along the way. The area is not tourist-oriented; travelers should not expect to find food, drinks, or gasoline en route.

Zone of Silence

So why do people go to this area? Co-existing within the reserve are the undefined boundaries of the mystic Zone of Silence (La Zona de Silencio). The Zone of Silence earned its name from the alleged difficulty of receiving or sending radio signals here. The area is said to be especially rich in minerals and meteorite fragments.

The Zone of Silence is just south of where the famous Allende meteor fell in 1964. The 13-million-year-old meteorite was composed of magnesium 26, an element that does not exist in our solar system. Mystics treat the Zone of Silence as a sacred place and consider it a hub for UFO travel. While I can't promise you an otherworldly experience here, this area is the perfect place to meditate on the subtle beauty and solitude of the desert.

Tours and Outfitters

Contraste Tours, Avenida Victoria No. 826 Sur, Gómez Palacio, Durango; (17) 15-20-51, 14-00-47, or 14-69-30; fax 14-04-40 or 15-00-03. This company offers five-night, six-day tours to the Zone of Silence, the Rosario Caves, and other areas in Durango for $900.

Pantera Excursions, Apdo 670, Durango, (18) 25-06-82, e-mail pantera@omanet.com.mx. This is perhaps your best bet for guided service in the region. Owner Walter Bishop knows the region well and has a planned cycling route in the area, with lodging at the nearby ranches. A three-day trip runs about $200.

Getting to the Zone of Silence

The Zone of Silence is well-marked on Highway 49 with an exit at the town of Ceballos, 87 kilometers (54 miles) north of Torreón. A dirt road leads to the ejidos La Flor and Santa Maria Mohovano. Again, there are no tourist facilities and there is no regular bus service.

Torreón has an airport which serves major Mexico cities. The bus station is on the east end of Av. Juárez and offers frequent service to Durango, Chihuahua City, Saltillo, and Monterrey.

Where to Stay near the Zone of Silence

Camping can be arranged inside the Zone, but only with permission of the ejidarios or ranchers.

Hotel Río Nazas, Av. Morelos No. 732 Pte., Torreon, $40, (17) 16-12-12. Comfortable hotel with parking garage and restaurant.

Hotel Calvete, Ramon Cornoa Sur No. 320, Torreon, $80, (17) 16-15-30 or 16-10-10, fax (17) 12-03-78. Four-star hotel with all amenities.

Motel Campestre, on Highway 40 at Blvd. Miguel Aleman 251 Ote, Torreon, $25, (17) 14-27-81. Friendly managers, clean rooms. RV campers can park here.

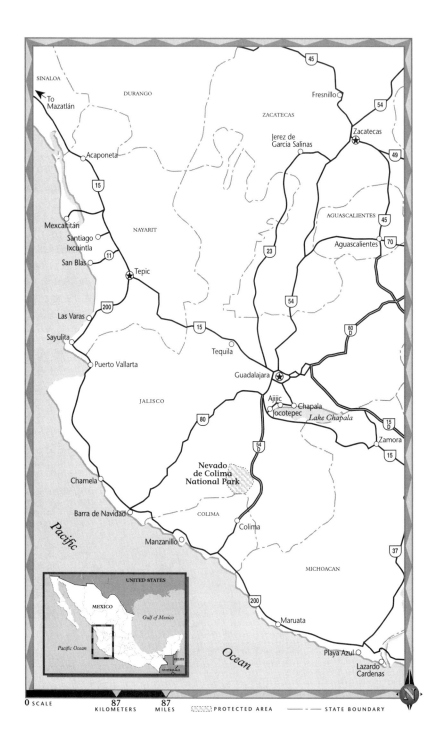

THE CENTRAL PACIFIC COAST

9

JALISCO, NAYARIT, AND COLIMA

Mexico's Central Pacific Coast boasts both environmental diversity and tourism pleasures. The states covered in this chapter (Nayarit, Jalisco, and Colima) are the agricultural powerhouses of the nation. Tropical Nayarit, for example, grows Mexico's greatest diversity of tropical fruit and accounts for 75 percent of the national production of tobacco. Jalisco is responsible for the world's production of blue agave, the plant used for tequila. This wild and mountainous landscape is home to a diverse group of Mexicans. Nayarit has sizable populations of Huichol and Cora Indians who know their mountains better than anyone.

Numerous sea turtle protection projects are underway along the Pacific coast of Mexico. Seven of the eight species of sea turtles in the world nest on Mexico's 11,000 kilometers (6,831 miles) of coastline. Often it's as easy as walking a few steps from your oceanfront hotel to the beach to see the tracks or the turtles themselves.

Environmental tourism and scientific research, such as that conducted by Open Air Expeditions in Puerta Vallarta or Mazunte in Oaxaca (see Chapter 12), may indeed represent the best way to protect the sea turtles. The presence of tourists discourages poaching, and the services they require provide alternative work for former poachers as tourism guides and hotel employees.

If you were inspired by the movie *Free Willy*—or if you just like whales—you'll find the Pacific coast an ideal setting for close encounters with these great beasts. The Pacific gray whale migrates along the

Arctic-Pacific corridor and during the winter moves to a breeding ground in the shallow coastal waters. The world population of gray whales is currently estimated at 26,000. The endangered humpback whale is much rarer, but can be seen in these waters as well.

One of the most interesting species on the Pacific coast is neither reptile nor cetacean: The aptly named strangler fig, or *matapalo*, starts out as a growth that eventually wraps around its host tree, finally choking it to death.

Mexico's Sea Turtles
Turtles that lay their eggs on the Pacific coast include the East Pacific green, the olive ridley, and the leatherback. Sea turtles take 20 to 30 years to reach sexual maturity and can live for 100 years. But their numbers have taken a dive in recent years. All species of sea turtles are considered threatened or endangered, vulnerable not only to human poachers but to natural predators such as crabs, raccoons, and skunks.

Turtle populations were sustainable when communities harvested only what they needed, but when savvy marketing accelerated national and international consumption, sea turtles became endangered. During the 1970s Mexico gave federal protection to some sea turtle species and established protection camps along the coasts. But it wasn't until

Turtle nursery, Rincón de Guaybitos, Nayarit

1990 that Mexico banned the killing of all sea turtle species. Since then, poaching has become common. In a country where most people earn 50 pesos a day, poaching is very profitable: Poachers receive 3 pesos (35 cents) per egg, a substantial sum considering many nests harbor more than 100 eggs.

The government tries to hire underemployed fishermen as technical experts in the turtle protection camps, but it lacks sufficient funds to provide work for all. Oscar Frey, who runs Cielo Abierto expeditions in Puerto Vallarta, says, "The next step is responsible, environmental tourism that attracts tourists to get involved in the programs and provides income for the camps and their technicians. You can get rid of the poachers by involving them in this program."

JALISCO

TEQUILA
Location: *70 km (43 mi.) N of Guadalajara*
Activities: *Tequila tasting, hiking*
For More Information: *Jalisco tourism department, (3) 613-1196 or 614-0123, or SECTUR*

Tequila, the birthplace of Mexico's national drink, offers an opportunity for "agricultural tourism." The town lies in the shadow of a volcano and is surrounded by fields of orderly rows of prickly blue plants known as *agave tequilana*. Approximately 100 million agave tequilana plants are cultivated on approximately 40,000 hectares (98,800 acres) and produce no less than 50 million liters of tequila each year, 40 percent of which is exported. There are many tours in this area, on which you will learn about the process of distillation from start to finish.

The drink tequila is a relatively new invention. While pre-Columbian Indians consumed various drinks made from agave plants, most notably *pulque*, the process by which the drinks were made did not include distillation. When the Spanish arrived they distilled the agave juice, naming the product *mezcal*. The mezcal produced in the town of Tequila enjoyed wide popularity and assumed the special name of tequila by the end of the 19th century.

To qualify as genuine tequila, the drink has to be manufactured in one of two municipalities, Tequila or Arandas, to the northeast of Guadalajara. Like mezcal, there are many qualities and distinct flavors of tequila; the best is not meant to be pounded down, but sipped.

El Cerro de los Enanos

It's only a short drive from the center of Tequila to the top of the volcano. Just follow Hidalgo Street south out of town. You'll cross the railroad tracks and get to the summit in 30 minutes. The top of the volcano is capped by a series of microwave towers. Locals call this area El Cerro de los Enanos (The Hill of the Dwarfs) because the trees at this altitude don't grow very large. Bird-watching here is great—more than 60 species have been documented.

Getting to Tequila

Tequila is only an hour's drive from Guadalajara along Highway 15, the main highway to Tepic. It's easy to arrange a bus trip, or you can hire a taxi for about $20 one way.

Where to Stay in Tequila

Tequila is just an hour away from Guadalajara, Mexico's second largest city.

Hotel Francés, Maestranza 35, Guadalajara, $30, (3) 613-1190. The oldest hotel in Guadalajara, founded in 1610. Rooms have private bathrooms, some with bathtubs.

Hotel Lafayette, Avenida de la Paz 2055, Guadalajara, $50, (3) 615-0252. Just west of Avenida Chapultepec in the Zona Rosa, this hotel is a high-end treat with air-conditioned rooms. Breakfast is included with the night's lodging.

Hotel Las Americas, Hidalgo 76, Guadalajara, $10, (3) 613-9622. Fairly modern rooms across from the Plaza Tapatía.

PUERTO VALLARTA

Location: On the Pacific coast, 418 km (260 mi.) W of Guadalajara
Activities: Bay cruises, whale-watching, bicycling, spas
For More Information: City tourism office, (322) 2-0242, on the SE corner of the main square at city hall

A romantic and popular town situated on the Pacific coast, Puerto Vallarta lies between the Sierra Madre to the east and Banderas Bay (Bay of Flags) to the west. While not normally considered a pure nature-travel destination, the city does offer excellent opportunities for whale watching and biking. It also has a number of high-quality tour operators and interesting tour opportunities.

Many of Puerta Vallarta's megaresorts were constructed at a time of lower environmental awareness and minimal regulations. Thus, they have done a great deal for the economy but little for conservation. Having learned lessons from the past, environmental groups are fighting to preserve the remaining mangroves.

On a positive note, the city department of ecology selected the olive ridley turtle for a conservation campaign because of its attractiveness to the local population and tourists. Other endangered species in the area are the green macaw, the green iguana, and the crocodile.

For the visitor, the city's investment of $33 million in a wastewater treatment plant means that the water in Puerto Vallarta's hotels and apartments is safe to drink. The concession of water services to the British company Bitwater is one example of the recent wave of privatization occurring throughout Mexico.

Things to See and Do in and near Puerto Vallarta

Don't miss the weekly **Río Cuale Nature Walk** sponsored by the Puerto Vallarta Library. A children's tour leaves the Centro Cultural, at the east end of Isla Río Cuale every Saturday morning at 10 a.m. A tour for adults is held at the same time on Sunday. Manuel Lomelí, a naturalist guide, leads the tours and points out plants, trees, and grasses. You'll spot the wild fig, the octopus tree, mangos, and butterfly palms. The tour features tidbits such as the fact that 12 of the 70 species of bananas in the world grow in Mexico. Depending on the group, the tours are in English or Spanish. A 20-peso donation to the library is requested. For information call (322) 4-99-66.

Ecotravelers can easily busy themselves at sea as well as on land. Banderas Bay is home to migrating humpback whales from December to April. Since 1991 the oceanologists from **Open Air Expeditions** (322/2-33-10) have documented individual whales by the distinct markings on their tails. Tourists get a firsthand view of mothers caring for their calves. On land, **Bike Mex** (322/3-16-80) offers cycling trips along the coast and into the mountains. With the recent addition of **EcoGrupos Vallarta** (322/2-66-06), this city is becoming a hub for nature-based travel in Mexico.

Most of Puerto Vallarta's tourism is based in mainstream cruises (often combined with all-you-can-drink liquor specials, and hence dubbed "Booze and Cruise" trips). Slowly, interest in presenting the natural history in tourism operations is increasing; the operators mentioned above are on the cutting edge of this market. That said, if you're interested in a commercial boat cruise, be forewarned that some vendors are not legitimate. You can avoid problems by purchasing tickets from a cruise company or a travel agency.

161

Tours and Outfitters

Several companies offer **horseback riding** in the Sierra Madre. Try **Rancho Amigo** (4-73-42), **Rancho Ojo de Agua** (4-06-07), or **Rancho Charro** (4-01-14). You can also make arrangements with the larger hotels or any of Puerto Vallarta's ubiquitous travel agencies.

B-B-Bobby's Bikes, Miramar 399, (322) 3-00-08, e-mail bbikespv @acnet.net, Web site http://www.cupertinobike.com/bobby.htm. Offers a variety of options including both guided and self-guided circuits ranging from $20 to $50. All mountain bike rentals and self-guided tours include a map and instructions, cycle computer, helmet, gloves, two filled water bottles, a mini-pump, and a fanny pack. The most frequently requested routes, Playa Grande and Río Cuale/Vallejo, pass through the cobbled streets of Vallarta's picturesque outlying villages. The rides cost $35 each and are about 20 kilometers (12 miles) long.

Bike Mex, Guerrero 361 in the Colonia Centro, Puerto Vallarta, tel./fax (322) 3-16-80, e-mail bikemex@vallarta.zonavirtual.com.mx. Bike Mex offers a variety of one-day or multi-day bike trips in the region. For the advanced cyclist, they offer the "Killer Donkey Trail," which climbs high into the Sierra Madre. Less-taxing trips stay closer to sea level.

EcoGrupos Vallarta, Ignacio L. Vallarta 243, (322) 2-6606, e-mail 74174.2424@compuserve.com. This office, run by Karel Beets and Astrid Frisch, was one of the first to offer natural history tours in Mexico. Tours include an 8-hour whale-watching trip from Punta Mita beach ($55), nighttime turtle-watching while patrolling the beach ($35), and a morning trek through the tropical forests surrounding Puerto Vallarta, where more than 70 species of birds live in their natural habitat ($35).

Open Air Excursions, in the center of town at Guerrero #339, (322) 2-33-10, e-mail openair@vallarta.zonavirtual.com.mx. This small company offers a variety of environmental trips, including sea kayaking, hiking, bird-watching, and whale-watching. Trips combine environmental education, scientific research, and tourism. The company is owned and operated by two oceanologists and professional adventure-tourism guides, Oscar Frey and Isabel Cárdenas. This business supports several conservation projects, including a program of Mexico's National Fisheries Institute that studies sea turtles. Another project is the photography of humpback whales that return to Banderas Bay each year. The photos document the relationships within whale families and help researchers understand migratory habits and territorial patterns.

Chamela-Cuixmala Biosphere Reserve

In the southern part of Jalisco, 3 hours south of Puerto Vallarta and 25 miles north of Barra de Navidad, the 13,142-hectare (32,461-acre) Chamela-Cuixmala Biosphere Reserve protects a dry tropical forest and one of the most species-rich areas in Mexico. Managed by a private NGO, the Cuixmala Ecological Foundation, it is frequently used for biology training courses and receives support from the U.S. Fish and Wildlife Service.

Chamela's forest stretches across the west coast of southwestern Mexico. It is considered to be the driest tropical-dry forest in Latin America. The deciduous and semi-deciduous forest and mangroves are home to 750 species of plants, 64 species of mammals, 85 species of amphibians and reptiles (among which is the Mexican bearded lizard, one of only two venomous lizards in the world), and approximately 200 species of birds.

The reserve is used primarily for scientific investigation. Earthwatch has a special program that surveys small carnivore species, as well as the coyote and jaguar. For more information, call them at (617) 926-8200 or (800) 776-0188.

Puerto Vallarta Hot Air Balloons, Morelos 536 Centro, 3-20-02 or 3-05-76. Two-hour sunrise and sunset trips over Banderas Bay. The pilots are all licensed by the FAA and have 15 years of experience.

Terra Noble, Miramar 276, Puerto Vallarta, (322) 3-03-08, e-mail terra@vallarta.zonavirtual.com.mx. An "art and healing center," Terra Noble is located on the hillside overlooking the city. Its cool, clay-colored architecture blends into the landscape. The center offers workshops in pottery and painting, tai-chi classes, therapeutic massage, and a sweat lodge that utilizes the Temazcalli ceremony, a tradition that dates back 2,000 years. Contact owner Ana María Platas for more information.

Getting to Puerta Vallarta

As one of Mexico's favorite coastal destinations, Puerto Vallarta is well-connected. The Gustavo Díaz Ordaz International Airport is 7 kilometers (4 miles) north of downtown and serves both U.S. and domestic Mexican flights. There is no central bus station, but most of the individual stations are downtown south of the Río Cuale along Avenida Insurgentes. Regular service is provided to Guadalajara, Tepic, and Mexico City.

Where to Stay in Puerta Vallarta

Hotel Villa del Mar, Francisco I. Madero 440 on the corner of Jacarandas, (322) 207-85, $15. Few amenities—no TV or phones in the rooms—but this hotel has a longtime following and friendly management.

Los Cuatros Vientos, Matamoros 520, (322) 201-61, $30. Located north of the Rio Cuale, this hotel has simple rooms and offers a continental breakfast.

Posada Rio Cuale, Serdan 242, (322) 204-50, $30, is a clean hotel with a swimming pool and a large secluded patio.

Where to Eat in Puerta Vallarta

Chianti's Spaguetteria, Olas Altas 509. Located in the old part of town, this is one of your best bets if you're hunting for pasta.

Ocho Tostadas, corner of Calle Niza and Lucerna, one block from Las Palmas Boulevard, (322) 433-18. Great seafood cocktails. The famous tostadas give the restaurant its name.

Papaya 3, Abasolo 169, (322) 203-03. Serves up vegetarian options just two blocks north of the Hard Rock Cafe.

MAR DE JADE LODGE

Location: In Chacala Bay, 2 hours N of Puerto Vallarta
Activities: Hiking, wildlife, sea kayaking, and more
For More Information: Call (372) 20-1-84 or write to the address below.

Mar de Jade is a rustic jungle lodge that focuses on health programs and environmental conservation. Founded in 1983, the lodge is run by Laura del Valle, a doctor who started a community clinic in nearby Las Varas in 1983. Mar de Jade hosts a combination work/study program for doctors who want to learn Spanish and contribute to the community health center. Guests with non-medical skills are welcome to participate in other programs

Nayarit coastline

in the community. Rooms are spacious and airy, and come with the sounds of the gently roaring ocean. Shared accommodations and three meals cost $50 per day. The one-week Spanish/vacation program costs $400, and a 21-day program that combines Spanish lessons and community work costs $950. Available activities include sea kayaking, hiking, bird-watching, whale-watching, surfing, horseback riding, and meditation. Acupuncture and massage is also provided. For information or reservations, write to Apdo. 81, Las Varas, 63715 Nayarit; (372) 20-1-84; e-mail marjade @pvnet. com.mx, Web site http://www.puertovallarta.com/mardejade/.

COLIMA

Colima is one of the smallest states in Mexico, though it boasts the requisite variety of ecosystems, ranging from snow-covered volcanoes to tropical lagoons. The Náhuatl name Colima means "the place where the old god is dominant."

NEVADO DE COLIMA NATIONAL PARK
Location: 20 km (12.4 mi.) from Colima
Area: 22,200 hectares (54,834 acres)

Activities: Hiking
For More Information: Colima State Tourism Office, phone (331) 2-4360 or 2-8360

This park boasts two volcanoes, the extinct Nevado de Colima (4,200 meters or 13,375 feet) and the younger, active Volcán de Fuego de Colima (3,850 meters or 12,625 feet), which has erupted several times during the past 450 years. The latter can be climbed as long as it's not showing any signs of activity, in which case the park is closed.

While the lower levels have been deforested, toward the top the lush coniferous forests are home to endemic birds such as the Aztec thrush, long-tailed wood partridge, highland guan, thick-billed parrot, and stygian owl.

According to OCEAN, a conservation group based at the university in Colima, the volcanoes provide a cool oasis of subtropical montane and temperate forests rising up from the hot and dusty lowlands. Besides its diversity of birds, the park is also home to the endangered Mexican bobcat (*Lynx rufus escuinapae*). The bobcat hunts rodents on the older lava flows and avalanche deposits that tumble down from the summit of Volcán de Fuego. In turn, the isolation at high altitudes and the inaccessible nature

Maruata 2000

One hundred kilometers (62 miles) west of Colima, Highway 54 runs into the town of Tecoman on the Pacific coast. Between Tecomán and Lázaro Cárdenas, Michoacán, is the town of **Maruata**. The beach here is a refuge for sea turtles, and the local community has undertaken an eco-tourism project called Maruata 2000 by building 14 cabins and offering camping facilities for $5 per person. Daily meals cost $10. You can rent a horse for about $6 per hour, a bicycle for $4 per hour, or a boat for sportfishing or snorkeling. The water is off-limits to speed boats. Buses run to Maruata from both Tecomán and Colima City. For more information, call Ezequiel García at (332) 503-68.

of the middle-elevation montane and temperate forests, where deep canyons descend to lower elevations, provides suitable habitat for the elusive cougar, now endangered throughout much of Latin America. These volcanoes, and the big cats and unique flora and fauna that live here, are in urgent need of protection.

OCEAN director Andrew Burton suggests monitoring the ranging behavior of radio-collared cougars to determine the boundaries of a proposed reserve that would encompass the volcanoes and the interconnecting corridors to nearby mountain ranges. Travelers interested in the project should contact Andrew Burton via e-mail at Andrew@bciencias.ucol.mx.

Getting to Nevado de Colima National Park

From Colima City travel 90 kilometers (56 miles) north on Highway 54 to Ciudad Guzman and then another 83 kilometers (52 miles) upward to Joya. There is also a road from Atenquique (midway between Colima and Ciudad Guzman) that leads to Joya. From Joya there are simple trails and some friendly locals who can point the way.

Where to Stay near Nevado de Colima National Park

The nearest accommodations to the park are located in Colima City.

Flamingos Hotel, Avenida Rey Colimán 18, Colima City, (331) 2-2525, $15. Spartan hotel with clean rooms, many with balconies.

Hotel America, Morelos 162, Colima City, (331) 2-0366, $35. Half a block west of the Jardin Núñez, this modern hotel has a swimming pool and parking.

Motel Los Candiles, 1.5 kilometers (1 mile) northeast of Colima City on Highway 54, (331) 2-3212, $30. Three-story hotel with guarded parking and coffee shop.

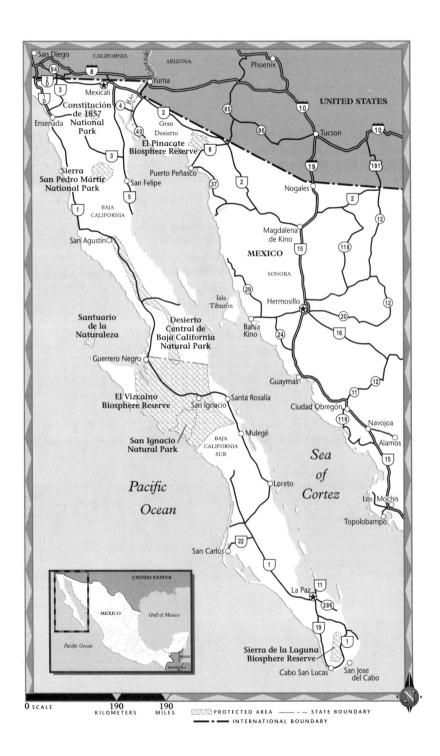

10

THE BAJA PENINSULA AND SONORA

The split between Baja California and mainland Mexico is a result of the San Andreas Fault. At one time, millions of years ago, the two lands were connected. The Sea of Cortez, now between them, formed as they separated. Consequently, the ecosystems on the eastern coast of Baja have a great deal in common with those across the sea on the mainland.

THE SEA OF CORTEZ

Bordered by the states of Sonora, Sinaloa, and Nayarit, and to the west by the Baja California Peninsula, the Sea of Cortez was named by Spanish explorer Francisco de Ulloa. Ulloa sailed the sea's perimeter in 1539 and 1540 under the orders of Hernán Cortés, a man who 20 years earlier lead the conquest of the Aztec Empire. The Mexican government renamed the sea the "Gulf of California" early in this century, though map makers are divided about which name to use. "Sea of Cortez" seems to be the preferred title used by conservationists and Baja aficionados.

By any name, the sea is 1,400 kilometers (868 miles) long and 210 kilometers (130 miles) across at its widest point. Its northern reaches are shallow and highly saline. To the south, where the lava breaks through along the fault line, about 3 inches of new sea floor are created each year as magma extrudes to fill the gap. The peninsula began to separate from the mainland 130 million years ago, during the Mesozoic era. Scientists predict that the peninsula will be completely separated from the continent in a few million years.

Option G

Sea of Cortez

The floor of this sea is one of the steepest in the world. Underwater canyons often reach more than 3 kilometers (1.9 miles) in depth. These abysses cause large tidal margins, especially in the northern half of the sea around the mouth of the Colorado River.

There are nearly 100 islands in the Sea of Cortez, and 53 of them have been protected since 1978 as a special biosphere reserve. The islands were formed primarily by submergence of the surrounding territory, though some, like Isla Coronado, were created by volcanic activity. The largest, at 1,000 square kilometers (620 square miles), is Isla Tiburón (Shark Island).

The islands receive only 1 inch of rainfall per year, yet they boast 3,500 species of plants, many of them found nowhere else on the planet. Half of the 120 species of cacti on the islands are endemic. A number of animals have taken to the islands as well, including rattlesnakes, chuckwallas (2-foot-long lizards), and Cimarron goats. Over 95 percent of the world's elegant terns and Herman's gulls breed on Rasa Island near Bahía de los Angeles in Baja California. Other birds include blue-footed and brown boobies and the endangered brown pelican.

The coast along the Sea of Cortez is generally more tranquil than that on the Pacific side. The desert of the Baja Peninsula is known as

the Gulf Coast Desert and is an extension of the Sonoran Desert
across the Sea of Cortez.

Overfishing in the Sea of Cortez

With more than 800 species of marine vertebrates, the Sea of Cortez
may biologically be the richest body of water in the world. This high biological diversity is due to it's nutrient-rich water and the fact that this
region gets plenty of sunshine—the sea receives more sunlight than any
other in the world. These riches have not been ignored by the fishing
industry, and certainly one of the biggest environmental threats in the
region is overfishing.

Commercial ships with nets or long lines of hooks have depleted
much of the stock, so it's not surprising that the main proponents of
stricter conservation measures are coming from the sportfishing sector.
The gill nets used in commercial fishing are indiscriminate in what they
catch, and lost nets often become floating deathtraps for fish. Some
ships use long-liners, which are essentially long strands of baited hooks.
Like gill nets, these hooks catch enormous amounts of fish and are
blamed for the decline in big-game fish such as marlin and yellow tail.
Trawlers catch shrimp by dragging cone-shaped nets along the seafloor.
However, for every pound of shrimp netted, the trawlers catch 10
pounds of other marine species, most of which die.

According to a report by the United Nations Food and Agriculture
Organization (FAO), "about 70 percent of the world's marine fish stocks
are fully to heavily exploited, overexploited, depleted, or slowly recover-
ing." Unfortunately, the commercial fishing industry appears to be doing
little to mend its ways.

In an excellent series of articles about the Sea of Cortez, in 1995
Sacramento Bee reporter Tom Knudson pointed out the problem with
free market environmentalism. "Fishing is supposed to be done conserv-
atively to protect stocks," he writes. "But in poverty-stricken Mexico,
another rule applies: If you will buy it, they will kill it. They will liqui-
date their sea."

While the area remains a biologically diverse area, it is nothing like
the Serengeti of the sea that it was two decades ago. Back then "it was
like diving into an aquarium," a Baja California real estate agent told
Knudson. Today, things have changed. Overfishing has reduced both
the number and diversity of species.

If there is a bright spot in the Sea of Cortez story, it is that sport-
fishers are taking note of the dramatic changes and working to put things
back into balance. Fishing guide Fernando Arcas is trying to persuade
the government to declare the area near Loreto a national marine park,

which would make it off-limits to industrial-style fishing. "We're not saying fishermen can't work. We just don't want them to kill everything," he told the *Sacramento Bee*.

BAJA CALIFORNIA

The Baja California Peninsula is 1,260 kilometers (781 miles) long and generally less than 130 kilometers (81 miles) wide. The peninsula supports four types of ecosystems: woodlands, deserts, tropical forests, and wetlands. A mountainous spine extends lengthwise from the northwest to the southeast. The mountains give way in the center to a broad plain that forms the Vizcaino Desert.

Highway 1 connects Tijuana, on the U.S. border, to Cabo San Lucas at the southern tip of Baja. The road was paved in 1973, and many old-timers fondly recall the pre-concrete days of tough but exceptionally beautiful travel. Today, travel in the Baja is a leisurely affair. Travelers have two options—they can opt for destinations closer to the U.S.-Mexico border, such as Sierra San Pedro Mártir or the El Vizcaíno Biosphere Reserve, where whale-watching is superb, or they can head further south (where international air connections are better) to resorts such as La Paz or Cabo San Lucas and the nearby Sierra de la Laguna Biosphere Reserve.

Among the animal species that inhabit the peninsula are coyotes, cougars, lynx, bobcats, badgers, and skunks. There are also numerous rabbits, which often end up as meals for the carnivores. There are nearly 300 species of native and migratory birds found on the peninsula, and the coasts are considered a major "flyway" for migratory fowl. One commonly seen bird is the brown pelican, which simply thrives in the Baja. Watch the bird as it swoops into the ocean for its catch.

The region is especially rich in cacti. The landscape sometimes erupts with forests of *cardon*, *garambullo*, *biznaga*, *pitahaya*, and opuntia (which includes the nopal, or prickly pear cactus, and the cholla). The cardon is the largest cactus in the world. Individual plants can weigh as much as 10 tons! All of these plants have mastered the art of survival. Nothing lives in these deserts unless it finds a way to capture and retain the precious life fluid that is water. Some cacti have adapted a wool-like covering that traps moisture from the occasional humidity.

Pro Esteros

Extending from San Ysidro to Bahía Magdalena, the coastal estuaries of Baja California are home to mangrove forests and highly salt-tolerant grasses, and serve as rest areas for migratory birds using the Pacific fly-way. Millions rest and feed in these wetlands from October to January each year.

In 1988 citizens from both Mexico and the United States formed Pro Esteros, an environmental group dedicated to the conservation of these wetlands, working across sectors with environmentalists, government authorities, and private property owners. A few years ago the group helped win ecological reserve status for Estero de Punta Banda near Ensenada.

Baja California's largest bay is the Bahía de San Quintín. An enormous number of migratory and resident species find refuge and food here throughout the year, and the bay supports the most successful system of aquaculture on the peninsula. Because of its warm climate and beautiful beaches and marshes, it's an attractive tourist destination. Pro Esteros warns that uncontrolled tourism will jeopardize the fragile equilibrium of this ecosystem.

Pro Esteros continues its work of surveying coastal bird species and mapping the wetlands using Geographic Information Systems (GIS) technology. Membership costs $20 a year; a year's subscription to their newsletter costs $10 a year. For more information, contact Grupo Pro Esteros, Avenida Ruiz #1686, Zona Centro, Ensenada, Baja California; (61) 78-60-50; U.S. address: c/o Alan Harper, Treasurer, 5187 Saddle Brook Drive, Oakland, CA 94619; e-mail proester@telnor.net, Web site http://www.cicese.mx/~proester.

Getting to Baja California

There is ferry service between Guaymas (on the Mexican mainland) and Santa Rosalia and from Topolobampo and Mazatlán on the mainland to La Paz. Irregular flights serve Tijuana, Loreto, La Paz, and Los Cabos. The border has several land crossings, the most popular of which are Tijuana and Mexicali.

SIERRA SAN PEDRO MARTIR NATIONAL PARK

Location: *100 km (62 mi.) E of San Telmo and 150 km (93 mi.) SE of Ensenada*
Area: *20,000 hectares (49,000 acres)*
Activities: *Hiking, stargazing, camping*
For More Information: *Contact Horacio de la Cueva, Bosques de las Californias, e-mail cuevas@cicese.mx.*

The highest point on the Baja Peninsula is **Picacho del Diablo** (Devil's Peak), which stands 3,050 meters (10,000 feet) above sea level. The peak can be seen from as far away as the mainland in Sonora. The mountain is covered by the pine and oak forests of the Sierra San Pedro Mártir. Despite the biological richness of the area, it's not a terribly frequented park. But it's well worth the visit. Through rustic, there's a beautiful camping area (bring your own food and water), rock climbing, and some good hikes, including one (for experts only) that climbs up Devil's Peak. Trails are not always well marked, so bring maps and a compass.

The park has a rustic office used by guards, but it does not function as a visitor's center. Ten kilometers (6.2 miles) from the park entrance is La Tasajera, the main camping area. The park guard can point the way and provide you with options. Mexico's National Autonomous University has established an observatory here with a 2.1-meter (6.9-foot) reflecting telescope. Stargazing is one of the park's many pleasures, though nights can be cold, so be sure to dress warmly.

The Sierra San Pedro Mártir range is one of the most important biological and cultural treasures of Baja California. It's home to several rare, endemic, and endangered species, such as the desert bighorn sheep, the San Pedro Mártir rainbow trout, and the mountain cypress. At one time it was also home to a number of California condors, but the species recently became locally extinct. Biologists are currently considering whether to reintroduce the bird to the area. During the last decade Mexican and international scientific communities have expressed an interest in obtaining biosphere reserve status for the Sierra San Pedro Mártir under UNESCO's Man and the Biosphere Program.

In December 1995, a binational meeting on strategies for the conservation of the Sierra San Pedro Mártir was held in Ensenada, with the aim of presenting the Sierra biosphere reserve initiative to the public. A local NGO, Forests of the Californias/Bosques de las Californias, continues to support this effort. The mountains in Northern Baja are part of the peninsular range that includes the Cuyamaca, Palomar, and San Jacinto Mountains across the border in California. The goal of this organization is to preserve the biological diversity not only in the Sierra San Pedro Mártir, but throughout the region.

In the short term, the group is participating in the preparation of the park's management plan; within a year or two they plan to establish an interpretive center. If you are interested in supporting this work, the group offers a quarterly newsletter and an annual report for $20. Contact them in the U.S. at Bosques de las Californias c/o Horacio de la Cueva, treasurer, P.O. Box 189003, Coronado, CA 92178, e-mail cuevas@cicese.mx. In Mexico: Bosques de las Californias, c/o Ernesto Franco, Monaco 153, Fracc., Mediterráneo, Ensenada, B.C. 22810, e-mail cmontes@cicese.mx.

Tours and Outfitters
Expediciones Ecotur, Kilometer 16 on the highway to Ensenada, (66) 36-11-83, U.S. fax (619) 662-1720. This reputable company offers a number of travel packages. A five-day hiking trip costs $95 per person; a five-day horseback trip costs $295.

Expediciones Ecotur, south of Tijuana at Kilometer 16 on the highway to Ensenada, (66) 36-11-83, U.S. fax (619) 662-1720. Friendly and informative nature trips led by well-respected guide Manuel Sánchez. Tours include hiking and horseback trips in the San Pedro Mártir, Baja's Central Desert, and the Sierra Juárez. Prices are very reasonable. A week-long horseback trip in the Sierra San Pedro Mártir costs $300.

Getting to Sierra San Pedro Mártir National Park
From Highway 1 go east just north of Colnett Bay, which is 130 kilometers (81 miles) south of Ensenada. The dirt road to the park is 100 kilometers (62 miles) from the highway. Look for the signs marked "Observatorio." This is an infrequently visited area, so remember to stock up on provisions. There is an entrance station in an area called La Corona de Abajo and, at the time of this writing, there is no fee to enter the park. While the park is easy to get to most of the year, the road can be closed by snow in the winter

EL VIZCAINO BIOSPHERE RESERVE
Location: From Laguna San Ignacio, Guerrero Negro, and Isla Cedros across to the Sea of Cortez
Area: 2,546,790 hectares (6,290,571 acres)
Activities: Whale-watching, archaeology
For More Information: SECTUR or the Baja California Sur tourism office

El Vizcaíno, declared a reserve in 1993, is Latin America's largest biosphere project. The Mexican government manages a buffet of environmental and cultural heritage sites in this park that spans the middle of the Baja Peninsula. Its most famous reserves are the lagoons frequented by whales in winter. The park also protects animals such as the lynx and puma. This area, which has been designated a World Heritage Site by UNESCO, receives 12,000 visitors each year.

This colossal reserve includes three lagoons and one bay on the Pacific coast. Tourists come here in growing numbers to watch gray whales (*Eschrichtius robustus*) calve and nurse their young in the warm, shallow waters. The lagoons are some of the most magical places in the entire country. The gray whales, which sometimes measure more than 18 meters (60 feet) in length, migrate from the Bering Sea to Laguna Ojo de Liebre and Laguna San Ignacio to the south. The best time to see the whales in the lagoons is from February to early April. In the later months, the calves are older and are less hesitant to approach the open boats (*pangas*).

There is no guarantee that you will be able to touch or interact with the whales, so do not pressure the *pangero* to do so. If the whales want to interact, you'll know—many seek tactile encounters and will approach the boat. Always remember that the mothers are quite protective. If a calf approaches your boat, it's likely that the mother is nearby, possibly directly underneath you.

Guerrero Negro and San Ignacio

Guerrero Negro was founded in the 1850s when the whales were "discovered" by whale hunters, among them one Captain Charles Melville Scammons. Scammons made a fortune from whale oil, and the Scammon's Lagoon in this area now bears his name, though it is better known by locals as Laguna Ojo de Liebre (Eye of the Hare). Before the turn of the century, tens of thousands of gray whales had been slaughtered. (Incidentally, Guerrero Negro owes its name to a U.S. whaling ship, the *Black Warrior*, that sunk in the lagoon at the end of the 1800s.)

Guerrero Negro doesn't pretend to be a tourist town—its economy is based on supporting the world's largest solar salt-evaporation operation.

Option G

Iron Eagle Monument, Baja Norte–Baja Sur border, Guerrero Negro

Nevertheless, it's a terrific gateway to the lagoon. The official whale-watching season lasts from December 15 to April 15. You can arrange a whale-watching trip with a pangero or you can make arrangements at **Malarrimo Restaurant and RV Park** (115/70-1-00). Boats leave in the mornings and early afternoons. By mid-afternoon, winds come up and the whale-watching conditions deteriorate. Locals report that during the 1996–1997 season there were over 1,000 adult whales in residence, and nearly 400 babies.

From the shore you may be able to see or at least hear the whales blowing. The mothers and calves stay in the shallower waters while the males cavort near the entrance of the lagoon. Camping is permitted on the beach of Laguna Ojo de Liebre. The best place to camp is at the far west end, close to the nursery channel. It's not uncommon to find whale bones on the shores of the lagoon, especially at low tide.

North of Guerrero Negro is the exceptionally quiet **Malarrimo Beach**, which faces north on the Vizcaíno Peninsula. The point juts out into the southbound currents of the Pacific Ocean and is reputedly a beachcomber's dream. You'll need a four-wheel-drive vehicle to reach the beach. The dirt road intersects with Highway 1 near the Kilometer 116 marker and winds 44 kilometers (27 miles) through streambeds until it reaches the beach—16 kilometers (10 miles) of shoreline sand running from an *estero* on its eastern end to rocky cliffs to the west.

Another town adjacent to the Vizcaíno Biosphere Reserve is **San Ignacio**. Summers can be extremely hot here (as in all of Baja), but the town is pleasant in the winter. There are hotels and restaurants, including La Posada, a simple establishment a few blocks from the center of town. The town functions as the hub of travel to the San Ignacio Lagoon and the petroglyph rock art in the mountains near **San Francisco de la Sierra**.

San Ignacio Lagoon, a large bay frequented by calving gray whales, is 50 kilometers (31 miles) southeast of San Ignacio. Laguna San Ignacio provides habitat for the second-highest number of gray whales after Laguna Ojo de Liebre. Whales here are friendlier than those at Scammons Lagoon, and come closer to shore. Tours ($20) can be arranged in the town of San Ignacio with the guides at Ecoturismo Kuyima, (115) 4-00-26, or at the Hotel Posada, (115) 4-0313.

Only licensed guides are allowed to take travelers into the lagoon during the calving season (January–April). Guides have been trained to keep a safe distance between the boats and the whales, and to make sure that the whales approach the pangas, not the other way around.

Local conservationist Serge Dedina recommends four local "camps." At Campo La Laguna, where the road from San Ignacio meets the lagoon, Francisco "Pachico" Mayoral will take you out among the whales. The second camp, Campo La Base, enjoys the services of Maldo Fischer, a knowledgeable guide. He can also arrange nearby camping. Antonio Aguilar, an excellent guide, presides at Campo La Fridera, and his wife prepares great meals. At the fourth camp, Punta Carey, there are rustic accommodations run by Ecotourism Kuyima (115/4-00-26, fax 115/4-0070).

If you choose to go directly to the lagoon, get there early. Most of the boats leave by 10 a.m., if not earlier. The advantage of taking a tour is that money goes to the guides and their extended families. Tours last about 4 hours. It's a long way by boat to the mouth of the lagoon, where most of the whales congregate. Trust your guide to know what the best options are.

The world-famous **Indian cave paintings** in the Sierra north of town, which have been declared a World Heritage Site, are also popular

Baja's Saltworks

Mexico is the world's seventh-largest producer of salt. The country's largest saltworks company, Exportadora de Sal (ESSA), is in Guerrero Negro, site of Laguna Ojo de Liebre (Scammon's Lagoon). The operation is the community's main source of income.

An expansion of this business, financed by the Mitsubishi Corporation, targets San Ignacio Lagoon. While it has the support of the Mexican government, the project is under heavy criticism by environmentalists, including Mexico's respected Grupo de los 100. They argue that the expansion would upset the ecosystem's balance and possibly endanger the turtles that seek sanctuary here during the winter. Among the chief complaints: construction of giant evaporation ponds will pump thousands of gallons of water out of the lagoon; a proposed concrete pier would cut across the path of migrating whales, and finally, the coming and going of additional ships and diesel tankers would disrupt whale movement. There is also the danger of a fuel spill.

The company now collects more than 6 million tons of salt annually around the shores of Laguna Ojo de Liebre, enough to make it the largest solar salt-evaporation operation in the world. Water is moved from pool to pool as it evaporates under the relentless sun. Road graders push the mountains of salt out of the crystal beds. As envisioned, production will increase from 6 to 7 million tons of salt per year, and include 50,220 hectares (124,000 acres) of evaporation ponds just north of the lagoon entrance.

attractions. The most amazing of the murals is the Cueva Pintada in the Santa Teresa Canyon. Hundreds of figures are drawn on the walls of this 160-meter-long (525-foot-long) gallery. You can arrange tours in town with La Posada Motel or Ecoturismo Kuyima (115/4-00-26), or by asking for a guide at one of the local stores in the small village of San Francisco de la Sierra.

If you go on your own, head north on Highway 1 for 45 kilometers (28 miles) and then take a graded dirt road 37 kilometers (23 miles) to San Francisco de la Sierra, the jumping-off point for trips to the caves. It's always a good idea to hire a local guide and, in this case, it's the law. Some guides here do speak English and they provide a wealth of information on the cave paintings and the local environment. Just register with the National Anthropology and History Institute (INAH) representative in town. Guide service runs $5 a day, twice that with meals, and tipping is a good idea. You can also rent burros for another $5 a day. Camping is available on the canyon bottom at an INAH-designated site.

Evaporative saltworks

Tours and Outfitters

If you go on your own and hire a local operator in Guerrero Negro or San Ignacio, the whale-watching tours cost about $25 per person. Organized tours are much more expensive, though less complicated. Guides are also bilingual, which can help if your survival Spanish isn't up to par.

Baja Discovery, P.O. Box 152527, San Diego, CA 92195, (800) 829-2252, e-mail BajaDis@aol.com, Web site http://www.bajadiscovery.com/. With more than 20 years experience in the region, this company offers luxury nature-tourism, including "safari-style" camping in San Ignacio.

Baja Expeditions, 2625 Garnet Ave., San Diego, CA 92109, (800) 843-6967, fax (619) 581-6542, e-mail travel@bajaex.com, Web site http://www.bajaex.com/. Just a few years older than Baja Discovery, this company offers a variety of nature-based trips in the region. Seven-day trips run around $1,100.

Ecotourism Kuyima, San Ignacio, on Plaza San Ignacio, (115) 4-00-26, fax (115) 4-0070. Located across from the mission, this agency is run by the local ejido and a fishing cooperative. While these people are not long-term locals, they are well respected and have a good reputation in the community.

Expediciones Ecotur, Kilometer 16 on the highway to Ensenada, (66) 36-11-83, U.S. fax (619) 662-1720. There are a number of travel packages available from this reputable company. A five-day hiking trip to the Sierra de San Francisco costs $295. The trip can be combined with whale-watching. This Tijuana-based company works very closely with the guides at **Ecotourism Kuyima**.

Malarrimo Eco-Tours, 1.4 kilometers (1 mile) west of Highway 1 on the edge of Guerrero Negro, (115) 70-1-00. Offers two trips to Laguna Ojo de Liebre a day, leaving at 8 a.m. and noon. Tours cost about $40 and include a box lunch and beverage.

Getting to El Vizcaíno Biosphere Reserve

Guerrero Negro is just south of the northern border of Baja California Sur and 750 kilometers (465 miles) from Tijuana. To get to Laguna Ojo de Liebre, drive 8 kilometers (5 miles) south of Guerrero Negro then turn right at the sign for "Parque Nacional de Las Ballenas Gris," close to Kilometer 208. The following 24-kilometer (15-mile) dirt road is open during the whale-watching season. A side road belongs to the local salt company and is closed to public use. The road ends at the edge of the lagoon. There is a small parking fee.

The town of San Ignacio is 145 kilometers (90 miles) south of Guerrero Negro and 72 kilometers (45 miles) to the east of the lagoon.

Where to Stay and Eat in El Vizcaíno Biosphere Reserve

El Parador Trailer Park, off Highway 1 at Kilometer 74, San Ignacio, $5. Sites have electricity and water.

Hotel El Morro, Blvd. Emiliano Zapata, Guerrero Negro, $15, (115) 7-0414. Clean and basic budget hotel.

Hotel La Pinta San Ignacio, off Highway 1, San Ignacio, $50, (115) 4-0300. Comfortable rooms and good service.

Hotel Posada San Ignacio, Av. Venustiano Carranza 2, San Ignacio, $20, (115) 4-0313. Friendly and economical lodging. A Baja institution. If you need a guide or a recommendation, contact the Fischer family here.

Malarrimo Restaurant and RV Park, 1.6 kilometers (1 mile) west of Highway 1 on the edge of Guerrero Negro, $20 for hotel, $10 for camping, (115) 70-1-00, fax (115) 70-1-00. This is a combination hotel, restaurant, and travel agency (Malarrimo Eco-Tours). Owner Enrique Achoy is bilingual and very helpful, and the seafood at the restaurant is always excellent.

LA PAZ
Location: On the shore of the Bahía de la Paz in Baja California Sur
Activities: Boating, whale-watching, snorkeling, sea kayaking, scuba diving
For More Information: State tourist office booth at the intersection of Calle 16 de Septiembre and Paseo Alvaro Obregón

Nestled in the crescent of the Bahía de la Paz, La Paz is the capital of the state of Baja California Sur. Originally named Puerto de la Santa Cruz, the name was changed in 1596 to reflect the tranquillity of the area's waters. Ironically, the town's history has been less than peaceful. Indians revolted against the Jesuits in the 1700s, and pirates sought refuge in the bay later in the century.

Things are much calmer now, and tourists are welcome year-round, especially during the Festival of the Whale in March. The climate is pleasant from October through May when the days don't get so hot. This may be a quiet town, but between diving, whale-watching, and old-fashioned beach lounging you'll find plenty to do.

Things to See and Do in La Paz
The bigger hotels offer boat trips to the sea lion colonies at **Isla Espíritu Santo** and **Los Islotes**, just north of town in the bay. These are two of a small cluster of islands that you can visit via sea kayak. The snorkeling and diving off both are excellent. **Punta Prieta** and the waters off **Punta Bonanza** offer great snorkeling adventures as well. If you want to enjoy deep-sea fishing, you can arrange a skiff (panga) via the travel agencies that operate along the *malecón*, a charming 5-kilometer (3.1-mile) promenade along the sea.

Be sure to check out the history of the region at the **Museum of Anthropology**, located at 5 de Mayo and Altamirano. Check out the photos of the prehistoric cave paintings found in Baja and the exhibits of the region's geological history. The museum is open daily from 8 a.m. to 6 p.m.

The **Center for Biological Research** (CIBNOR), located

16 kilometers (10 miles) north of La Paz on the road to San Juan de la Costa, is dedicated to aquacultural and agricultural study throughout northwest Mexico. More than 150 biologists work here. The institution houses a library and has test farms open to the public.

Tours and Outfitters

Baja Expeditions, Calle Sonora 586, (112) 5-38-28). Offers whale-watching trips.

Baja Quest, Sonora 174, (112) 3-53-20. Offers scuba diving, sea kayaking, whale-watching tours, and natural history cruises.

The Cortez Club, Kilometer 5 on the highway toward Pichilingüe at the La Concha Beach Resort, (112) 1-61-20, fax 1-61-23. Offers PADI diving certification courses, whale-watching, and fishing.

National Association of Ecotourism and Adventure Guides, Nicolás Bravo y Marcel Rubio, La Paz, Baja California Sur 23000, (112) 5-22-77 or 1-15-60, fax 1-15-15. Excellent referral source for local guides as well as nature tourism guides throughout Baja California. The group is headed by Renato Calo Mascarella.

Getting to La Paz

La Paz has ferry service across the Sea of Cortez to Topolobampo, Sonora, and Mazatlán, Sinaloa. The port is located at Pichilingüe, 16 kilometers (9.5 miles) northwest of downtown. The Marquéz de León International Airport (LAP) is 18 kilometers (11 miles) southwest of the city on Highway 1 and has international service to Los Angeles as well as nonstop flights to and from Culiacán, Guadalajara, Hermosillo, Loreto, Los Mochis, Mazatlán, and Mexico City. The bus terminal is southwest of downtown at Jalisco and Héroes de Independencia, and has service to Ciudad Constitución, Guerrero Negro, Cabo San Lucas, Tijuana, and Mexicali.

Where to Stay in La Paz

El Meson, Felix Ortega 2330, (112) 5-7454, $30. Small rooms in a quality hotel. Guarded parking is available. Lodging includes continental breakfast.

Hotel Mediterrane, Allende 36-B, (112) 5-1195, $30. Small hotel popular with Europeans and foreign travelers.

La Paz Trailer Park, Brecha California 120, 2 kilometers (1.2 miles) south of town, (112) 4-87-87, $14. Helpful management. Amenities include a pool and a book exchange.

Pensión California, Degollado 209, (112) 2-28-96, $10. Simple budget favorite.

Where to Eat in La Paz
Bismark 2, corner of Degollado and Altamirano, (112) 2-48-54. Everyone's favorite seafood restaurant. A family-run establishment with great ceviche.

El Quinto Sol, corner of Avenida Independencia and Belisario Domínguez, (112) 2-16-92. Health-food market and popular vegetarian restaurant.

SIERRA DE LA LAGUNA BIOSPHERE RESERVE
Location: Southern edge of the peninsula, between La Paz and Cabo San Lucas
Area: 112,500 hectares (277,875 acres)
Activities: Hiking, camping
For More Information: National Association of Ecotourism and Adventure Guides, (112) 5-22-77

Declared a biosphere reserve in 1994, the Sierra is a narrow range that rises to 2,090 meters (6,850 feet). The area, which includes many hiking trails, makes a nice respite for visitors to Cabo San Lucas. Desert scrub covers the base of the Sierra here and the vegetation changes with elevation. The slopes support a dry tropical forest, the middle elevations have oak forests, and oak and pine blanket the Sierra above 1,500 meters. Because of its high degree of unique species, scientists speculate that the area was at one time an island. The Sierra boasts the highest endemism on the mainland peninsula. It is home to mountain lions, lynx, and deer. There are 250,000 people living in the area, most near the beaches.

Tours and Outfitters
National Association of Ecotourism and Adventure Guides, Nicolás Bravo y Marcel Rubio, La Paz, Baja California Sur 23000, (112) 5-22-77 or 1-15-60, fax 1-15-15. Excellent referral source for local guides as well as nature tourism guides throughout Baja California.

Getting to Sierra de la Laguna Biosphere Reserve
There are several access points from Highways 1 and 9 in the towns of Santiago, San Antonio, and San Jose del Cabo.

Where to Stay and Eat in Sierra de la Laguna Biosphere Reserve
A variety of restaurants and accomodations are available in both La Paz and Cabo San Lucas.

BAHIA MAGDALENA

Location: 240 km (150 mi.) NW of La Paz on the west coast of the peninsula
Activities: Whale-watching, windsurfing, camping
For More Information: SECTUR or the Baja California Sur state tourism office

Bahía Magdalena (often referred to as Mag Bay) is filled with whales January through March. Industrial and mining activities, as well as the recent construction of a thermoelectric plant, have impacted the bay in environmentally destructive ways. Tourism here is also on the upswing, and the influx of visitors could cause more harm. In an effort to curb problems before they begin, local environmentalists are asking tourism operations to strive to preserve the ecological balance of the bay.

Pangeros offer 2-hour boat tours from this area for $25 per hour per person. Tours can be arranged on the beach at Puerto López Mateos and Puerto San Carlos. Puerto López Mateos has limited facilities. Puerto San Carlos is a small town with about 5,000 residents, a gas station, a cafe, and three hotels (Las Brisas, Marlin, and Palmar). Camping and RV parking are available on the northern and southern ends of town. Windsurfing is popular south of Puerto López Mateos.

Tours and Outfitters
Baja Expeditions, 2625 Garnet Ave., San Diego, CA 92109, (800) 843-6967, fax (619) 581-6542, e-mail travel@bajaex.com, Web site http://www.bajaex.com/. This company offers a variety of nature-based trips in the region. Seven-day trips to Bahia Magdalena cost about $1,100.

National Association of Ecotourism and Adventure Guides, Nicolás Bravo y Marcel Rubio, La Paz, Baja California Sur 23000, (112) 5-22-77 or 1-15-60, fax 1-15-15. Excellent referral source for local guides as well as nature tourism guides throughout Baja California. The group is headed by Renato Calo Mascarella.

Getting to Bahía Magdalena
The bay is 240 kilometers (150 miles) from La Paz. Head north on Highway 1 then west from Ciudad Constitución to the town of San Carlos on

▲ Boojum trees on the Baja Peninsula (Option G)

▲ Los Cabos, Baja California Sur (National Institute of Ecology)

▼ Bicycling in the Complejo Ecoturistico Arareko, Chihuahua (Ron Mader)

▲ Relief on a Mitla wall, Oaxaca (Ron Mader)

▼ Monument to Quetzalcoatl, Teotihuacán (Ron Mader)

▲ Tropical frog (National Institute of Ecology)

▼ Colorful window in Guanajuato (Ron Mader)

▲ Crafting handmade paper in
San Cristóbal de las Casas
(Ron Mader)

▲ Nayarit coastline
(Ron Mader)

▼ Great Maya Reef (National Institute of Ecology)

▲ Día de los Muertos altar in Tenochtitlán ruins (Ron Mader)

▼ Swimming in a lagoon near Cuatro Ciénegas (Ron Mader)

▲ Popocatépetl Volcano (National Institute of Ecology)

▼ Colonial Guanajuato's State University (Ron Mader)

▲ Calakmul forest (National Institute of Ecology)

Highway 22. Ciudad Constitución has frequent bus service to and from La Paz, Loreto, and Guerro Negro.

Where to Stay in Bahía Magdalena

The nearest accommodations are in Ciudad Constitución, 50 kilometers (31 miles) to the west.

Campestre La Pila RV Park, 1 kilometer (1.6 miles) south of town near the power plant, (113) 2-05-62, $10. Follow the dirt road west before it heads south. This popular camping site has hot showers and a swimming pool.

Hotel Conchita, Blvd. Olachea 180 near Hidalgo, (113) 2-02-66, $20. Long-time budget favorite. Clean rooms.

Maribel Hotel, Guadalupe Victoria 116 near Blvd. Olachea, $20. Comfortable rooms with TV and in-room phones.

SONORA

Across the Sea of Cortez lies Sonora, one of Mexico's largest and wealthiest states. The majority of Mexico's copper is mined here and agriculture is booming. Like other border states, Sonora faces threats to its ecology and biodiversity, including depletion of groundwater, illegal collection of fauna and flora (especially cacti), and urban encroachment. The border region as a whole has an annual population growth rate of 4 percent. It will take some time to determine whether this growth compromises conservation or provides new funds for environmental initiatives.

The Sonoran Desert is the third-largest North American desert, extending from the California-Nevada border south to the tip of Baja California and occupying most of the state of Sonora. Two-thirds of the desert lies in Mexico. The surface is a mix of volcanic and metamorphic rock. One of its most spectacular sites is within Sonora's Pinacate Biosphere Reserve, marked with craters and lava fields produced by volcanic activity as recent as 1,300 years ago.

According to researchers, the great Sonoran Desert appeared about 10,000 years ago, during the Holozoic era. The climate became warmer and drier as ice masses retreated. This change produced the Southern Shield, which forms part of the 2,000 square kilometers (1,240 square

Hermosillo's Centro Ecológico de Sonora

Centro Ecológico de Sonora (62/50-10-34, fax 50-11-37) is a well-maintained, state government–run ecological park and research institution founded in 1985. The center is 4 kilometers (2.5 miles) south of town and includes a 2.8-kilometer (1.7-mile) path over desert terrain. The walk provides visitors with information on 300 plant and 200 animal species including falcons, eagles, peacocks, owls, monkeys, antelopes, camels, deer, bighorn sheep, and a large variety of fish and reptiles.

Exhibits showcase the ecosystems found in Sonora: mountains, grassland, desert, and the Sea of Cortez. The center's botanical garden grows plants native to the Sonoran Desert, especially those that are endangered. The park is open Wednesday through Sunday from 8 a.m. to 5 p.m. The turnoff to the park is 2.5 kilometers (1.6 miles) south of Hermosillo on Highway 15.

Hermosillo is a pleasant 240-kilometer (125-mile) drive from the U.S. border on Highway 15. The Centro is is 4 kilometers (2.5 miles) south of town.

miles) of desert and mountainous area within El Pinacate. The highest elevations in the volcanic field—about 1,200 meters (4,000 feet)—occur in this region.

The king of the desert is the saguaro cactus, its stickman-like appearance sometimes towering six stories high. For some reason it attracts gunfighters, eager to do battle with an unarmed cactus.

EL PINACATE BIOSPHERE RESERVE

Location: *South of the Arizona border, 480 km (300 mi.) from Hermosillo*
Area: *Pinacate: 714,556 hectares (1,764,953 acres); Gran Desierto de Altar: 31,000 hectares (77,000 acres)*

Activities: *Hiking, exploring the Cerro Colorado and Elegante Crater area*
For More Information: *SECTUR or the Sonora state tourism office*

If you're crossing the border at Lukeville, Arizona–Sonoyta, Sonora, you
might think you're in an "empty" desert. You're not. Humans have
inhabited the region for thousands of years. The Pinacate Reserve and the
abutting **Gran Desierto de Altar Reserve** are less than a day's drive
from the border. Together, the two contiguous reserves protect the sea,
coast, and inland desert. El Pinacate stands out for its easy access and
surreal beauty.

El Pinacate is the most arid site in North America. The 30-mile-wide
volcanic field is named after a beetle that when threatened sits vertically
on end and emits a foul odor. More loveable wildlife in the area include
puma, deer, antelope, wild boar, Gila monsters, bighorn sheep, prong-
horn, quail, and red-tailed eagles.

The park's chief attraction is its bizarre and mind-boggling scenery.
About 3 or 4 million years ago, an erratic series of volcanoes erupted in
what is now the the Pinacate lava field. Today, hundreds of blank cinder
cones and craters mark the surface. You can visit some of the largest,
including El Elegante, from the park entrance off Highway 2. To reach
the crater, it takes a 2- to 3-hour hike along a well-marked path. Once
there the view is simply awesome. The crater is 1,400 meters (4,600 feet)
wide from rim to rim and 140 meters (460 feet) deep.

Some of these lava fields were used to train U.S. astronauts heading
to the moon during the Apollo space program. While the craters definitely evoke an otherworldly terrain, what is amazing is not the sterility,
but the fertility of the land. The desert blooms in February and March
after spring rains. You'll see many cacti, including saguaro, ocotillo, and
cholla. Dune sunflowers, verbena, and desert lilies blossom in the sand.

Visitors to this new park will find a rustic information center staffed
by personnel from Mexico's Institute of Ecology. They'll be happy to
offer you information on guides. There are few paths in the region, but
you can climb on the volcanic cones to observe the craters. You are urged
to travel with someone who knows the area, such as an experienced
guide, and to explore the area in a four-wheel-drive vehicle, as the roads
are of dubious quality. The park's dune fields can be accessed via
Highway 8 and a 4-kilometer (2.5-mile) dirt road that heads west near
the Kilometer 73 marker.

Birth of Two Reserves

Mexico declared this area a biosphere reserve in 1993, at the urging of
Ezekiel Escurra, then-director of Mexico's protected areas. Escurra

had performed his graduate research here years before and knew the importance of the local biodiversity as well as the park's larger role in the Sea of Cortez region. Management authority for El Pinacate rests with IMADES (Instituto del Medio Ambiente y Desarrollo Sustentable del Estado de Sonora).

El Pinacate and the Upper Colorado Gulf in the Sea of Cortez were jointly declared biosphere reserves. One of the reasons was to protect the *vaquita* and *totoaba* species. The totoaba resembles white bass and is considered a delicacy; consequently, it has been overfished. The vaquita has perished in fishermen's nets and is now one of the rarest marine mammals on earth.

A highly commercial fishing industry thrives in the middle portion of the Sea of Cortez. By protecting the breeding grounds, officials hope to be able to sustain future marine production.

Tours and Outfitters

Ajo Stage Lines, 1041 Solano, Ajo, AZ 85321, (520) 387-6467 or (800) 942-1981. Offers both day-long journeys ($70) and customized group tours, including overnight camping with gourmet cuisine. Bill Nelson, who has run Ajo Stage Lines for several years, has a good reputation for environment-friendly natural history tours throughout the Sonoran Desert.

Pathfinder Travel, Blvd. Benito Juarez 320-B, (638) 3-44-20, fax (638) 3-40-32, e-mail @pathone@pathfinder-travel.com.mx, Web site http://www.pathfinder-travel.com.mx. U.S. mailing address: P.O. Box 784, Lukeville, AZ 85341. Pathfinder's half-day trip includes an English-speaking guide, soft drinks, and transportation from Puerto Peñasco. Longer hiking trips to Cero Colorado and El Elegante cost $45. Overnight trips can be arranged for $100.

Getting to El Pinacate Biosphere Reserve

The entrance to El Pinacate is 50 kilometers (31 miles) west of Sonoyta, Sonora, on Highway 2. If you're approaching the park from the U.S., be sure to visit the Organ Pipe Visitor's Center on the Arizona border for up-to-date information.

Where to Stay in El Pinacate Biosphere Reserve

The best selection of hotels and restaurants are found in Puerto Peñasco.

Hotel Costa Brava, overlooks the malecón, Puerto Peñasco, (638) 3-41-00, $40. Rooms have great views of the sunset on the Sea of Cortez.

Hotel Paraiso del Desierto, corner of Calle Constitución and Calle Morua, Puerto Peñasco, (638) 3-21-75, $20. Just off the highway, this is a pleasant hotel with pool. Rooms have air-conditioning.

Playa de Oro RV Park, Playa Miramar, Puerto Peñasco, (638) 3-26-68, $15. Popular RV parks with restaurant and boat storage.

SONORA'S BEACH TOWNS: PUERTO PENASCO, BAHIA KINO, AND GUAYMAS

Location: South of the Arizona border on the coast of the Sea of Cortez
Activities: Fishing, bird watching, museums
For more information: Contact the Sonora tourism office (62) 14-84-07 or (800) 4SONORA from the United States.

A good way to get to know the Sea of Cortez is via three of Sonora's coastal cities: Puerto Peñasco, Bahía Kino, and Guaymas. All three offer boat trips as well as a smattering of natural history museums.

Puerto Peñasco (also known as Rocky Point) is just south of El Pinacate Biosphere Reserve. Tours can be arranged via Pathfinder Tours, (638) 3-44-20. The town is home to **Center for the Study of Deserts and Oceans** (CEDO), which plays an important role in the conservation of animals in the area. In addition to a 55-foot whale skeleton, the site displays the "Earthship CEDO," a solar-powered building constructed of old tires, sand, and aluminum cans that is a model of alternative housing. Tours are available. CEDO also manages a research center and can accommodate large groups of students or those interested in natural history. The center is located in the southern side of town in the Fraccionamiento los Conchas neighborhood. The museum is open Monday to Friday from 9 a.m. to 5 p.m. and donations are requested. Contact CEDO for more information, P.O. Box 249, Lukeville, AZ 85341, (638) 201-13.

The seaside town is also a jumping off point for **Isla Tiburón (Shark Island)**, a 120,800-hectare (298,376-acre) park decreed a special biosphere reserve in 1963. Mexico's largest island, it boasts beautiful beaches. Two mountain chains cross the island from north to south and reach rocky summits up to 1,200 meters (3,900 feet) in height.

For more than 100 years, the island has been home to the nomadic Seris Indians, who were attracted by the dependable inland water supply. Battles in the mid-1800s, sparked by greedy cattle ranchers, drove the Seris from inland Sonora to the island.

Bahía de Kino, directly across from Isla Tiburón, is another departure point for the island. About a quarter of the population of this town are Seris. The **Museo de los Seris** offers a good introduction to

189

The Sonoran town of Alamos

the culture. It's located at the corner of Calle Progreso and Av. Mar de Cortéz and is open from 10 a.m. to 1 p.m. and 3 to 6 p.m. Admission is free but, again, a donation is recommended.

Several Seris working with the National Institute of Ecology in Bahía de Kino have been trained as ecotourism guides and offer tours and boat trips to Isla Tiburón. The guides are all bilingual, speaking in Seri and Spanish. Individual guides who have been certified include Alfredo López Blanco, Roberto Molina Herrera, Ernesto Molina Villalobos, Francisco Molina Sesma, and Cornelio Robles Barnett. Contact them via Francisco Navarro at the National Institute of Ecology, (624) 2-01-05.

Guaymas is a charming port town whose local oysters are famous throughout Mexico. There are many possibilities here for the ecotraveler, but so far plans are mostly on paper. Diving is good in the Sea of Cortez, and **Naviera Guaymas** (622/1-01-24) can arrange trips.

Guaymas is home to the **Center for Conservation and Development**, sponsored by Monterrey Tech University (ITESM). The center conducts research in the Sea of Cortez and hosts the Museum of Invertebrates, Fishes and Marine Mammals. The museum's collection includes rare specimens such as the endangered vaquita. The museum also houses one of the world's largest collections of gray whale skulls. The center is on the ITESM campus 10 kilometers northwest of downtown on Bacochibampo Bay.

Tours and Outfitters

Guias de Bahía Kino, Bahía de Kino, (624) 2-01-05 or 2-01-06, contact Francisco Navarro at the National Institute of Ecology. Individual guides offer boat trips to Isla Tiburón. Three-day trips combining an introduction to Seri culture and nature hikes run about $1,000 per group of four.

Naviera Guaymas, Carretara Kilometers 1983/1984, Col. Loma Linda, (622) 1-01-24, fax 1-03-47. Arranges seven-day diving trips in the Sea of Cortez for $1,400. Reservations can be made in Mexico City through Subaquatec, (5) 611-3517, fax 598-4300, e-mail subaqua@inetcorp.net.mx.

Pathfinder Travel, Blvd. Benito Juarez 320-B, (638) 3-44-20, fax (638) 3-40-32, e-mail pathone@pathfinder-travel.com.mx, Web site http://www.pathfinder-travel.com.mx. U.S. mailing address: P.O. Box 784, Lukeville, AZ 85341. Offers a variety of trips to the Pinacate Biosphere Reserve, Copper Canyon, and Guerrero Negro in Baja California.

Getting to Sonora's Beach Towns

Puerto Peñasco is 100 kilometers (62 miles) south of Sonoyta, opposite Lukeville, Arizona, on Highway 8. There is bus service to Sonoyta, Hermosillo, and San Luis Río Colorado. Bahía Kino is 117 kilometers (73 miles) west of Hermosillo on Highway 16. There is bus service to Hermosillo. Guaymas is 135 kilometers (84 miles) south of Hermosillo or 6 hours south of Nogales. The town has a small international airport 10 kilometers (6.2 miles) northwest of town. There are three small bus stations with frequent service to Hermosillo, Guadalajara, Mazatlán, and Mexicali. The ferry that runs to Santa Rosalia, Baja California, departs from a terminal on Avenida Serdán at the east end of town. The ticket office is open from 7 a.m. to 2 p.m.

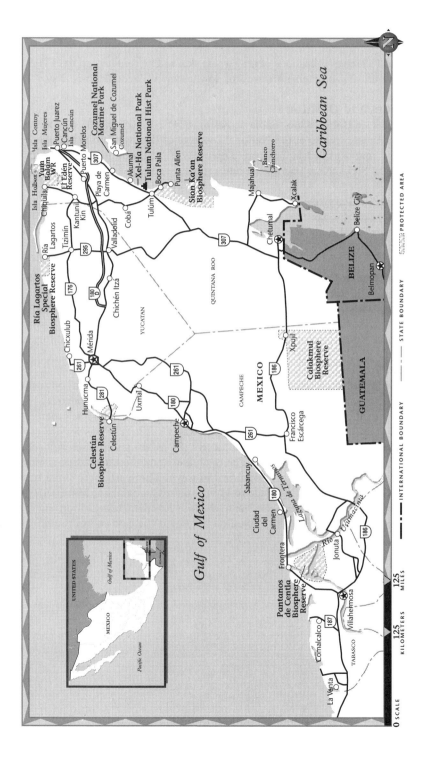

SOUTHEAST MEXICO: THE YUCATÁN PENINSULA

11

All regions in Mexico differ greatly from each other, but some are profoundly—if not cosmically—different. The Yucatán Peninsula is one of Mexico's newest territories; it emerged from the sea roughly 60 million years ago as the result of a tremendous meteor crash. Today the peninsula juts into the Caribbean and the Gulf of Mexico. Politically speaking, the peninsula's territory is sliced like a pie and shared among the states of Yucatán, Quintana Roo, and Campeche.

The terrain is limestone coated with minimal topsoil. Where there are small hills (often no more than a few feet high), the ground can support hardwood trees such as kapok, ebony, and zapotes. Locals call these natural mounds *petenes*. *Zapote* trees produce the chicle used in chewing gum, and travelers can see the traditional form of chicle harvesting in the Yum Balam Biosphere Reserve or at the botanical garden in Puerto Morelos. Zapote wood is so solid that it is reputed to sink in water. The Maya chose it for their support beams, some of which are still intact a thousand years after they were built.

Northeastern Yucatán is a region of seasonal extremes and high biodiversity. Major ecosystems include marine grasslands, mangrove swamps, rain forests, savannas, wetlands, and sand dunes. The wetlands are particularly important for migrant birds, which can be found in Ría Lagartos, El Edén (a private reserve open to the public), and the incomparable Sian Ka'an Biosphere Reserve.

The northcentral Yucatán was the home of the ancient Mayan

capitals, now the spectacular ruins of Uxmal, Chichén Itzá, and Tulum. In contrast to today, the population density was very high in the region during the peak of these empires. The Maya were experts at scattering residential areas around their cities, and most homes also had agricultural fields. You'll see some interesting and mysterious markers throughout the region, especially in El Edén.

On the gulf side of the peninsula, visitors will find migrating birds among the murky waters. The brightest and most popular with tourists are American flamingos, also known as Caribbean flamingos because they are found on both sides of the Yucatán. Like storks, flamingos are wading birds.With angular beaks and dentated tongues, they feed by straining mud for nutrients. Flamingos are not always pink—in fact, chicks' feathers are white when they hatch. As they age, their plumage takes on the familiar pink hue.

On the Caribbean side, flocks of frigate birds and spoonbills nest in the abundant mangroves. This "Turquoise Coast" also attracts anglers. Reputable operations offer catch-and-release fishing. Enthusiasts come hoping to achieve the "triple slam" of sportfishing: hooking bonefish, permit, and tarpon.

The shorelines are blanketed with mangrove thickets, which have until recently been an obstacle to coastal development. Several varieties of mangroves, including red, black, white, and buttonwood, can be found here. Red mangroves surround the lagoons and bays, while the black mangroves are found closer to shore. All are home to numerous species of birds and an abundance of aquatic life.

The southern part of the peninsula, which borders Belize and Guatemala, is more mountainous than the northern part. In Campeche, the Calakmul Biosphere Reserve abuts two international parks in the adjoining countries. Two species of monkeys live here: the howler monkey, so named for the racket it makes, and the spider monkey.

Quintana Roo (pronounced "row") is Mexico's newest state. Less than 25 years old, the state now boasts Mexico's most visited tourism destination: the former fishing village of Cancún, now the nation's most ambitious tourism megaproject. The state has plans to extend its tourism facilities and services southward to the Belizean border on the Costa Maya.

CENOTES, UNDERGROUND RIVERS, AND CAVES
The Yucatán Peninsula does not have any surface rivers. Instead, water filters through the porous limestone and finds its way to underground streams. The pure limestone ground sometimes dissolves, creating large freshwater pools called cenotes, or *aguadas*. The Mayan cities often used the cenotes as water sources. Today's tourists find they also make great

Henequen plantation near Mérida

swimming holes. Perhaps the most famous cenote is near Chichén-Itzá. Unfortunately, this sacred cenote is little more than a hole in the earth capped by green pond scum and litter. Other cenotes include the Zaci and Dzitnup near Valladolid, Kikil in Tizimin, and Mukuyche in Abala. Many of the cenotes are linked by some of the longest underground rivers in North America, including Nohoch Na Chich, Naharon, Cristal, and Calavera.

Cave diving is becoming especially popular, but it demands the utmost respect from *trained* divers. Souvenir hunters and clumsy adventurers often destroy what they've come to visit. Chichén Itzá is the site of the enormous Balancanche cave system.

DEVELOPMENT IN THE YUCATÁN PENINSULA
In the Classic and post-Classic Maya period, the Yucatán Peninsula boasted numerous metropolises, many of which were still inhabited at the time of the Spanish conquest. The Maya conquered the peninsula around 500 B.C. and have called the region home ever since. The bitter wars between the Maya and the Spanish transformed into conflicts between the Maya and the Mexicans in the 20th century. The Maya kept the invaders at bay, even hiding their main city of Chan Santa Cruz. When it was

discovered at the turn of this century, the Mexican army destroyed it. In the 1930s President Lázaro Cárdenas implemented a major ejido system in Quintana Roo that returned half the land in the territory to Mayan communities. Chan Santa Cruz was rebuilt and renamed Felipe Carrillo Puerto, in honor of President Cárdenas' land commissioner.

If the deforestation it caused had not been so severe, henequen would continue to be a popular crop among the region's cooperatives. Made from the sisal agave cactus, which is related to Jalisco's famed tequila agaves, henequen is used to make twine and was the economic mainstay of the Yucatán from the mid-1800s to the mid-1900s. At that time, large haciendas controlled the fates and fortunes of the local peasants. Later, the revolution transformed many of these operations into ejido-controlled cooperatives. Unfortunately, the rise of synthetic materials in the 1960s proved disastrous for the sisal industry. Today, while the sisal agave requires little maintenance and no special irrigation—perfect for the areas of the peninsula where rainfall is seasonal and then sporadic—only one local cooperative continues to harvest henequen.
Because of the slash-and-burn practices of the henequen farmers, what was once high jungle in the Yucatán is now dry, secondary vegetation.

Sugarcane plantations also boomed in the early part of the 20th century, but the harvests soon depleted the shallow topsoil. As they did with henequen, the plantations utilized slash-and-burn farming in which crop yields last for a few years until the soil nutrients are exhausted. Traditional farming calls for four years of fallow and then the process is repeated. The peninsula continues to look for a sustainable economic base.

Could tourism be the best catch of the day? The peninsula's economy thrives on tourism, and the newspapers cover travel company news as diligently as political squabbles. The region is a spectacular destination, though the price of its development has often been environmental conservation.

The Yucatán has always attracted international attention. Sylvanus Morley was an archaeology student at Harvard who spent time in the Yucatán in the early 20th century. He developed a plan for restoration of Chichén-Itzá and was a strong defender of the Yucatán Maya until his death in 1948.

The success of the Sian Ka'an Biosphere Reserve and a more commercial endeavor, Xcaret, have encouraged other areas to promote local ecotourism.

"The entry port of Cancún works beautifully to facilitate massive tourism," said Barbara MacKinnon de Montes, a former president of Amigos de Sian Ka'an. "This is a tremendous infrastructure advantage for small ecotourism projects. The only problem is harmonizing the tourist image of Cancún with the idea of nature-based tourism."

This challenge will present itself in the years to come. How will Mexico reconcile its financial success in megatourism with the small-is-beautiful approach of community-based ecotourism? The philosophies of megatourism and ecotourism are not compatible. Rather than following top-down strategies, ecotourism demands the participation of local communities, which have the most to gain if they conserve their natural resources.

ENVIRONMENTAL GROUPS IN THE YUCATÁN

A combination of Mexican scientists and international expatriates lead the Yucatán's environmental groups. Five of the most formidable organizations are Pronatura Peninsula Yucatán (PPY), Amigos de Sian Ka'an, Planeta Limpio (Clean Planet), Lu'um K'aa Nab, and Yaxche, Arbol de la Vida (which works with the Chiapas-based Maya Ik).

PPY, a private, nonprofit conservation group in Mérida, was formed as a regional chapter of the Mexico City–based Pronatura in 1988. The group became an independent "civil association" in 1990, and today receives financial and technical support from The Nature Conservancy. In 1992 PPY received TNC's prestigious Clifford F. Messinger Award for "outstanding conservation achievement in Latin America." The group dedicates much of its resources to local communities and developing sustainable, environmental tourism in the Celestún and Calakmul Biosphere Reserves.

Amigos de Sian Ka'an was created in conjunction with the Sian Ka'an Biosphere Reserve in 1986 and is based 2 hours north of the reserve in Cancún. The association has always been instrumental in the studies of regional biodiversity. In 1996 Amigos was the winner of the Condé Nast Ecotourism Award. In 1997, however, Amigos received negative press when community members suggested that the group had stronger ties to tourism developers than to the communities in the biosphere itself.

Lu'um K'aa Nab (987/10-117) is based in Puerto Morelos, a town it would like to establish as the "First Ecological Port on the Mexican Caribbean." The program assists the local botanical garden and works with beach clean-up projects. The organization's sister group, Maya Echo (987/10-136), works to support community tourism. They take international visitors to a *chiclero* community, Central Vallarta, where women hand-make embroidery and show visitors their medicinal plants.

Yaxche, Arbol de la Vida works with Mayan communities throughout the Yucatán and assists in community development from the ground up, promoting sites such as the Cenote Cristal near Tulum. Yaxche's main office is in Felipe Carrillo Puerto, (983) 40842. There is a second office in Cancún, (98) 847-987.

THE CARIBBEAN COAST

Mexico's Caribbean Coast is also known as the Turquoise Coast because of its impossibly blue waters. Along the shore runs the Northern Hemisphere's longest barrier reef, much of which is officially protected as a marine park. For the beauty and diversity of its life forms, the reef can be considered the aquatic equivalent to a tropical rain forest.

In 1996 40,000 hectares (99,000 acres) of reef were added to those already recognized in the Sian Ka'an Biosphere Reserve—in Punta Cancún and Punta Nizuc, and off the west coast of Isla Mujeres. As a result of these additions, almost 20 percent of the state of Quintana Roo enjoys some form of environmental protection; the state is second only to Campeche in its amount of protected land and coast.

There is frequent bus service on Route 307 from Cancún to Tulum. But if you want to be more adventurous, or if you wish to visit Punta Allen, you should probably rent a car. The highway cuts through the peninsula's forest of shrubs in what is known as the Corredor Turístico. Hotels in the area are big and geared toward mass tourism, but there are thousands of potential day trips and longer journeys into the interior that can whisk you away from civilization.

CANCUN

Location: Northwest tip of the Yucatán Peninsula, 315 km (195 mi.) NE of Mérida
Activities: Snorkeling, hiking, bird-watching
For More Information: SECTUR office, Avenidas Coba and Nader, (98) 83-2184

Cancún is by no means a pure ecotourism destination—government officials and investors created the city less than 30 years ago to attract the growing market of sun-seekers from the United States. The city receives 3 million visitors each year. Still, the city is plunked in the middle of nature and, with terrific infrastructure, it's a prefect hub for travlers headed to less congested areas and more nature-oriented areas, such as the Sian Ka'an Biosphere Reserve, Ría Lagartos, and Celestún.

Some words of warning: Vendors at the tourism kiosks generally receive commissions from large businesses, so they rarely have information on community-based or eco-friendly projects. And don't expect to find true ecotourism in the glossy *Now Cancún* magazine you'll receive (free) at the airport. Though it bills itself as an ecotourism magazine, its ads are for golf courses, jet skis, and condos, which don't fit the bill. Don't accept these mass-market tourist attrations as the best the state of Quintana Roo has to offer.

Developing Cancún

To better understand the glamorous image Cancún has sculpted for itself, it's necessary to review its relatively short history. In 1968 the only town in the area was the small fishing village of Puerto Juárez, population 500. That year FONATUR, the national tourism development agency, announced that it would develop a megaresort in this relatively new federal territory (Quintana Roo became a state in 1973). The first resort hotel opened in 1974 and the rest, as they say, is history.

The original management plan for Cancún called for a great number of green areas that were to be left as open space. But the success of the hotels called for expansion, and urban encroachment won out over conservation. The financial success of Cancún's development plan has colored the notion of "ecotourism" in the region. The focus has been on creating environmentally friendly megahotels that cater to the affluent elite of the ecotourism market—those who can afford to pay $1,000 to $3,000 a week for a room.

Smaller efforts are simply drowned out by the chorus of loud advertisements and sales promotions at the Cancún airport or at information kiosks. Ask for information on the Sian Ka'an Biosphere Reserve or smaller parks, and you'll likely elicit a blank stare. As tourism agents don't get commissions from such places, they're not that interested in distributing information about "alternative" tourism.

In 1996 Mario Villanueva Madrid, the governor of Quintana Roo, proposed a Maya Coast ecotourism corridor. The project attempts to replicate the success of the tourism corridor between Cancún and Tulum. The effort to construct environmentally friendly hotels is noteworthy and commendable, but unless the development also supports conservation measures and includes and benefits local communities, it's hard to classify the project as "ecotourism."

Environmentalists in the coastal area have long complained that cruise-ship traffic along Quintana Roo's tourist corridor could damage the Maya Reef. In December 1997 those fears were realized when the *Leeward*, a member of the Norway Cruise Line, sailed directly over Los Cuevones Reef, part of the Isla Mujeres Marine Park near Cancún. The impact shaved off 80 percent of the reef.

Authorities filed charges against the cruise line and environmentalists mourned the destruction. The damage is said to be far worse than that inflicted by typical hurricanes; some believe it will take 500 years or more for the reef to recover.

Things to See and Do in Cancún

The most popular area for snorkeling and diving in Cancún is **Punta Nizuc**, a national marine park. It became a protected area in July 1996 along with the west coast of Isla Mujeres and Punta Cancún. A portion of every tourist dollar spent at the park supports monitoring and conservation efforts.

Biologists call this a "sacrificial reef," because it is visited by thousands each year. Although snorkelers are given instructions on how to explore the reef without harming it, they often disregard them. Many tourists come and destroy the coral, snatching pieces of it for *recuerdos* (souvenirs). Guides do their best to discourage such plunder, and efforts are underway to beef up vigilance and improve environmental education. It's amazing that the reef is in as good a condition as it is.

One of the natural highlights of the Cancún area is **Isla Mujeres** (Island of Women), another case study in the dangers of excessive tourism. Of the millions of people who visit Cancún each year, many take a day trip to the island. As a result, the island's El Garrafón lagoon is slowly dying, a victim of its own appeal. When you snorkel here, it's more common to see someone else's fins than to spot tropical fish, which have swum elsewhere to avoid the churning waters.

Long, narrow **Isla Contoy**, established in 1961 as a special biosphere reserve, is one of the most important bird refuges in the Mexican Caribbean. Fortunately for the island and its wild inhabitants, the lack of freshwater supplies have kept it free of human settlements. The island has extensive coastline, interior lagoons, and mangrove swamps that are home to 70 species of birds including frigate birds, brown pelicans, and double-crested cormorants. Visitors are charged an entry fee that supports the management of the reserve. The island is just an hour's boat ride from Cancún. For more information on Isla Contoy, call the local office of SEMARNAP at (98) 83-07-44.

Tours and Outfitters

Aero Costa, Calle Jaleb #8, (98) 84-04-03. Offers a variety of single-day environmental and archaeological trips in small airplanes.

Rent Me Sport Bike, Avenida Juárez and Calle Morelos. A good spot to rent bikes for exploring the island.

Venture Out, Hotel Canto, Avenida Yaxchilán, e-mail venture-out @geocities.com, Web site http://www.geocities.com/TheTropics/Cabana /4465/. Trips include a hike to Rancho Loma Bonita ($60) to explore cenotes, caves, and subterranean rivers. Excursions leave at 8 a.m. and 2:30 p.m. Also offers a full-day trip ($340) to Rancho San Francisco and the flamingo sanctuary at Ría Lagartos. The trip includes a leisurely stop at the chicle tappers' community of Kantunil-Kin.

Yaxche, Arbol de la Vida, Altos SM 4, (98) 847-987, e-mail ekab @cancun.com.mx. Not a traditional tourism agency, this group works with indigenous groups throughout the Maya world. Not surprisingly, its commitment to grassroots organizations puts it at odds with the government's Mundo Maya program. Yaxche is an excellent source of information on local guides. There is a second office in the city of Felipe Carrillo Puerto headed by Carlos Meade, who organizes ethnic and agricultural tourism trips. Call (983) 40-842 for details.

Getting to Cancún

Cancún boasts one of the busiest international airports in Mexico, 16 kilometers (10 miles) southwest of the city on Highway 307. You can get great deals if you choose a package tour and extend your stay. Note: Beware of changing money at the airport, where the exchange rate is notoriously low. It's best to change money before you arrive or wait until you get downtown.

There is frequent bus service to Tulum, Chetumal, Mérida, and Villahermosa. The central bus station is downtown at the intersection of Calles Tulum and Uxmal, across from the Plaza Caribe Hotel. If you are looking for your own wheels, there are numerous car rental agencies in Cancún, but the rates are much lower in Mérida. Offices are downtown and at the airport.

Where to Stay in Cancún

Casa Maya, Blvd. 5.5 Kukulcan, $100, (98) 83-0555 or, in the U.S., (800) 262-2656. Luxury hotel located on the beach. A five-night minimum stay is required.

Hotel America, Avenida Tulum and Calle Brisa, $40, (98) 84-75-00, fax 84-19-53. Large hotel in the downtown area with restaurant. Just a few blocks away from the headquarters of the Amigos de Sian Ka'an environmental group.

Villa Juvenil Cancún, Paseo Kukulcan kilometer 3.2, $15, (98) 83-13-37, fax 83-04-84. Youth hostel with separate rooms (and wings) and a campground. The hostel is located on a beach near the bus route.

Where to Eat in Cancún

100% Natural, in the Plaza Terramar at Paseo Kukulcan kilometer 8.5,

(98) 83-11-80. This is a fast-growing vegetarian restaurant chain. Thirsty? Try a veggie or fruit *liquado*.

Los Almendros, in front of the city's bull ring at Avenida Bonampak and Avenida Sayil, (98) 84-13-22. Tasty Yucatecan cuisine.

EL EDEN RESERVE
Location: 70 km (43 mi.) NW of Cancún
Area: 1,492 hectares (3,685 acres)
Activities: Hiking, bird-watching, scientific research, crocodile-watching
For More Information: Contact Marco Lazcano in Cancún, tel./fax (98) 80-50-32; e-mail mlazcano@cancun.com.mx

El Edén Reserve is the first privately owned protected area dedicated to biological conservation research. It was established in 1990 by a group of Mexican scientists including Arturo Gómez Pompa and Marco Lazcano. The area is administered by the El Edén NGO and provides numerous options for environmental travelers.

El Edén is situated in a remote area and is accessible only by high-clearance four-wheel-drive over a humble dirt road that leads through rain forests and marine grasslands. This region is known as Yalahau, a Mayan word meaning "where the water is born." The reason for the name becomes apparent as you drive through the fields where Cancún's major pumping stations (*bombas*) are located.

Lodging at El Edén consists of rustic cabins with hot water, clean bathrooms, and mosquito nets. The central dining area boasts a sturdy tower you can climb for an amazing view of the forest and nearby savanna. The Maya ruins in the reserve are not an ancient cosmopolitan city but remnants of residential areas and water diversion lines. Under current study, the wetlands here could have been a highly managed resource for agricultural production.

There's ample opportunity for both daytime and nocturnal explorations here. And since Edén is so far from civilization, it's the perfect place for stargazing on warm, tropical nights.

Animal Residents
La Savanna research station provides facilities for scientists and an ideal setting for conservation training courses. The region of Yalahau, including Yum Balam, Ría Lagartos, and Contoy Island, has the highest number of endemic species on the Yucatán Peninsula. El Edén reserve has recorded 205 species of birds, which represent over one-third of the species known to live on the peninsula. A number of endangered species also inhabit the area. You may find the tracks of ocellated turkeys, great curassows,

pumas, jaguars, ocelots, Morelet's crocodiles, spider monkeys, and others. Two collared peccaries given the names Pumba and Timon were released in the reserve and occasionally come to the station with their offspring. All are tame and friendly.

Getting to El Edén

Reservations must be made ahead of time with El Edén manager Marco Lazcano in Cancún; tel./fax (98) 80-50-32, e-mail mlazcano@cancun .com.mx. Two-day tours cost $235 and depart Monday through Friday. A better choice is the three-day tour for $315. Once you get there, you'll want to stay for a while. Prices include meals and transportation to the reserve.

El Edén Reserve

YUM BALAM WILDERNESS RESERVE

Location: *50 km (31 mi.) NW of Cancún*
Area: *154,000 hectares (380,380 acres)*
Activities: *Hiking, bird-watching*
For More Information: *SECTUR or Yum Balam on Avenida Adolfo López Mateos 403 in Kantunil Kin, (987) 500 -12*

The northern edge of El Edén abuts Yum Balam, a wilderness reserve (*Area de Protección de Flora y Fauna*) created in 1994 when residents of the area asked the government to give their region protected status. The park stretches from the interior of Quintana Roo to the coast and includes Holbox Island. Yum Balam is home to four municipalities and 5,000 people, mostly of Mayan descent.

The Yum Balam NGO, based in the town of Kantunil Kin, is currently developing tourism in the region. Spectacular forests and lagoons are now accessible via local guides, and a tourism infrastructure, including small cabins and composting toilets, has been constructed. Outside of town an agricultural school grows medicinal plants and collects honey. One of the best developed trails in the reserve is the Sendero Magico (Magic Path), a one-day excursion that can be arranged with local guides

Chicle harvest in Yum Balam Reserve

in the village of Solferino, just 30 minutes north of Kantunil Kin. Ask for Avelino Cahun Cohuo, Jose Quintal Olivar, or David Morales Olivar.

If you come to the reserve you'll have the opportunity to witness chicle production. Raw chicle, the basic ingredient in chewing gum, comes from the sap of the common chicozapote tree. Chicle extraction takes place during the rainy season and, if harvested sustainably, does not destroy the tree. *Chicleros* climb the tree and use a machete to cut grooves along the bark. As the juice oozes out, it flows down into a canvas bag tied at the base of the tree. Trees are allowed to recover for three to five years before they are tapped again.

In the north, the reserve extends into the Gulf of Mexico to **Holbox Island** (pronounced "hol-bosh"). In 1996 city leaders cleared an airstrip on the island to provide a convenient means of access, and today cabins and *palapas* are being constructed in preparation for small-scale tourism. The key attractions of the island are the numerous aviaries and rookeries. Holbox Island is only 75 kilometers (47 miles) from Ría Lagartos.

Getting to Yum Balam

The Isla Holbox airstrip services flights from Cancún and Mérida. There is also ferry service to the island from the town of Chiquila on the mainland. The best entry point to the interior portion of the reserve is in the town of Kantunil Kin, 130 kilometers (80 miles) northwest of Cancún.

PUERTO MORELOS

Location: 34 km (21 mi.) S of Cancún
Activities: Swimming, snorkeling, botanical gardens
For More Information: SECTUR or Quintana Roo tourism office

The coral reefs that fringe the coast near the small fishing village of Puerto Morelos were recently declared a national marine park as part of the Great

Maya Reef. The area has long been frequented by snorkelers and divers, but the number of actual "attractions" is small. The town is the base of operations for the Lu'um K'aa Nab environmental group, which works with Maya communities and keeps a watchful eye on the cruise ship industry.

Be sure to visit the **Dr. Alfredo Barrera Marín Botanical Garden**, at the Kilometer 38 turnoff for Puerto Morelos on Highway 307. The gardens, occupying 65 hectares (161 acres), represent the only land that has been set aside for conservation on the corridor between Cancún and Tulum. The ecosystems range from mangrove swamps to semi-evergreen tropical forests. In the tropical heat, the garden is a cool and well-shaded oasis.

Native plants are fostered in the nursery, which has an important mission given the daily deforestation of the surrounding region. There are 3 kilometers (2 miles) of marked trails. The gardens include a chicle tree and a re-creation of a chiclero camp, as well as a Maya ruin named The Altar that dates to the post-Classic period (A.D. 1400). You'll also find local medicinal and culinary herbs identified by their Mayan, Spanish, and Latin names. The park also attracts wild creatures—if you're lucky you might spot an agouti, a large rodent that grazes like a rabbit. The botanical garden is open from 10 a.m. to 5 p.m. A small admission fee is charged.

Tours and Outfitters
Maya Echo, Av. Rojo Gómez, (987) 10-136, e-mail starseed@ cancun.com.mx. Headquartered in the Amar Inn Bread & Breakfast, Maya Echo works to bridge the gap between international visitors and the local community. The group takes tourists on day trips ($40) to the botanical garden, the town of Central Vallarta, and the nearby chiclero communities.

Getting to Puerto Morelos
There is frequent bus service between Puerto Morelos and Cancún and Chetumal.

Where to Stay in Puerto Morelos
Blue Parrot Inn, six blocks north of the plaza, (987) 3-00-83, $40.

Isla Holbox

205

Small hotel. Rooms have fans and mosquito nets. Dives and snorkeling trips can be arranged at the dive shop here.

Caribbean Reef Club, Villa Marina, (987) 1-0191, $270. Luxurious accommodations in this in all-inclusive resort set on the beach.

COZUMEL NATIONAL MARINE PARK
Location: 70 km (43 mi.) *south of Cancún*
Area: 11,850 hectares (29,269 acres)
Activities: Swimming, snorkeling, diving
For More Information: SECTUR or Quintana Roo state tourism office

Cozumel Island is a diver's mecca and one of Mexico's most famous islands. Much of the west coast of the island has been protected as a marine park since 1980, but there's a great deal of confusion over the exact boundaries and enforcement has been minimal. The main attraction of the park, Paradise Reef (Arrecife Paraiso), is more than 32 kilometers (20 miles) long; a portion of it is composed of rare black coral. There are also more than 200 species of tropical fish and hundreds of underground caverns. The reef was the subject of one of Jacques Cousteau's earliest documentaries (1961) and has inspired marine biologists and conservationists around the world.

More than 1,500 visitors use the park in some fashion each day. The most popular diving reef is Palancar, accessible only by boat. The best sandy beach is Playa San Francisco, on the southwestern side of the island. **Aqua Safari** offers dive trips and rents diving gear and cameras (on Cozumel Island between Calles 5 and 7 on the waterfront; 2-01-01 or 2-31-01; e-mail dive@aquasafari.com). The PADI certification course costs $350, and a two-tank dive trip to two different reefs costs $50. Boats depart at 8:30 a.m. and return around 1:30 p.m.

Other attractions include the **Museum of the Island of Cozumel** (Calle 6 Norte and the malecón), which sponsors night excursions May through September to watch turtles lay their eggs. The museum is housed in a pink colonial building and has displays on local history and wildlife.

Chankanaab Lagoon Park features a botanical garden, a small museum, a crescent-shaped beach, and, of course, a natural lagoon, connected to the Caribbean Sea by underground tunnels and caves. The name "chankanaab" means "small sea" in the Mayan language. The lagoon, which used to be full of colorful tropical fish, is currently off-limits to visitors as scientists hope to restore the dying coral.

Take a moment while you're here and let your mind visit the past. A thousand years ago, Maya women made pilgrimages to the island to worship Ixchel, goddess of fertility. San Gervasio ruins are on the eastern side of the island, accessible via the Transversal highway. A side road from the highway leads to the ruins, a set of seven groups of buildings, the largest site on the island.

Getting to Cozumel National Marine Park

Cozumel Island has an international airport offering frequent service to Miami, Cancún, and Mexico City. The island also has direct ferry service to Playa de Carmen on the mainland. Boats leave all day from 6 a.m. to 8 p.m., and the trip costs about $5 per person. Playa de Carmen has an airport servicing domestic flights, in particular those to local environmental and archaeological destinations via **Aero Saab**, (987) 3-08-04. Playa de Carmen also has frequent bus service to and from Cancún and Chetumal.

Where to Stay near Cozumel National Park

Hotel Mesón San Miguel, Avenida Benito Juárez 2, (987) 2-02-33, $30 Located on the zócalo, some of the rooms have terraces that overlook the square.

Hotel Pepita, Avenida 15 Sur 2 at Calle 1 Sur, (987) 2-00-98, $20. Rooms have fans, insect screens in this hotel with a nice garden.

Hotel Vista del Mar, Avenida Melgar 45 at Calle 5 Sur, (987) 2-05-45, $40. Small hotel with a swimming pool.

AKUMAL

Location: 35 km (22 mi.) S of Playa del Carmen
Activities: Diving
For More Information: Contact SECTUR or the Quintana Roo tourism office

"Akumal" means "land of the turtles" in Mayan. And sure enough, thousands of sea turtles bury their eggs on beaches in this town, just south of Playa del Carmen at the Kilometer 255 marker on the Cancún-Chetumal highway. The beaches are excellent for collecting shells, and the nearby reefs are famous for diving (there are nearly 30 dive spots in the region). If you are interested in learning diving speleology (cave exploration), this is the best place on the peninsula. There are two PADI-certified centers with Mexican and U.S. dive masters. Two weeks with the instructors will leave you certified and a cavern-diving expert.

Tours and Outfitters

Akumal Dive Center, Kilometer 104 on the Cancún-Tulum Highway, (987) 5-9025, e-mail akumal.dive@mail.caribe.net.mx, Web site http://www.akumaldivecenter.com. Respected company offering dives off the reef ($18.50), cenote dives ($55), and night dives ($32).

Akumal Dive Shop, Apdo. Postal 1, 77710 Playa del Carmen, Quintana Roo, (987) 2-2453 or, in the U.S., (800) 777-8294. One of Akumal's oldest dive shops, they'll take you to the Caribbean's choice spots.

Getting to Akumal

Buses run from Cancún and Playa del Carmen to Akumal several times a day.

Where to Stay in Akumal

Most of the accommodations in Akumal are condos. You can ask a manager if there is a place to rent. One recommended place is **Hacienda de la Iguana** on the northern end of Half Moon Bay. Iguana #5 is a 2-bedroom, 2-bath condo. Depending on the season, the cost runs from $90-$225 per night. For information, call Marty Klein at (818) 769-4168 or e-mail JadanA@aol.com

XEL-HA NATIONAL PARK

Location: 120 km (75 miles) S of Cancún
Area: 100 hectares (247 acres)
Activities: Snorkeling, archaeological sites
For More Information: Contact SECTUR or the Quintana Roo tourism office

Just over an hour south of Cancún at the Kilometer 245 marker is the small Xel-Ha National Park. The transparent blue waters of this natural aquarium are filled with parrot, angel, and butterfly fish; barracuda; stingray; and some 50 other species. Glass-bottomed boats carry non-snorkelers across the waters. Snorkeling is allowed in the lagoon, and you can either bring your own equipment or rent equipment here. The use of water-polluting suntan lotions and sunblock is prohibited.

If you are taking the tour bus, most operations that visit the pyramids at Tulum (see below) also go to Xel-Ha. If you're traveling on your own, note that the crowds arrive around 11 a.m. The entrance fee is $10.

TULUM NATIONAL HISTORIC PARK

Location: 130 km (81 mi.) S of Cancún
Area: 664 hectares (1,640 acres)

Activities: Archaeology, nearby snorkeling
For More Information: SECTUR or the Quintana Roo tourism office.

Tulum is the most visited Mayan ruin in Mexico. Perched on a limestone shelf facing the Caribbean, it is the only Mayan city built on the coast and sits in a neotropical forest—a mix of coastal shrubs and jungle. The Mayas named this city "Tulum," which means "city of the new dawn," in honor of Kukulcán, their god of the sun. During its occupation thousands of years ago the city was brightly painted—the blinding white buildings that stand today were once red and blue. Still, what carvings and paintings remain easily recall the city's former splendor. Archaeologists believe Tulum was occupied at the time of the Spanish arrival in1518. A mural depicts the Maya rain god, Chac, riding a horse, an animal the Spanish introduced.

The 60 buildings at Tulum date from A.D. 1200. The tallest structure, known as The Castle, is a watchtower that sits above the complex on the limestone cliffs. Other notable structures include the Temple of the Descending God and Temple of the Initial Series.

Visitors are advised to wear sunscreen and a hat with a wide brim. Because of Tulum's popularity, guides offer tours in several languages. Admission is $5, free on Sunday and holidays.

Things to See and Do near Tulum

Next to Tulum are two cenotes managed by the local ejido. Visit **Cenote Cristal** and **Aktun-ha**, two fragile environmental systems open to

Central Cultural "Dos Palmas"

Central Cultural "Dos Palmas," south of Xel-Ha at kilometer 307, is a pleasant stop for travelers. Run by the Jacinto Paat ejido, this ecological reserve features underground grottos and ponds, caves, and cenotes of great beauty and historical and scientific interest. It's perfect for swimming, snorkeling, and diving. There are some rooms available as well as a craft workshop, museum, gardens, and a school of Mayan culture and cooking. For more information, contact Antonio Rivero Aguilar at (987) 1-21-32.

The ruins at Tulum

responsible travelers. The caves can be used to practice underwater speleology, but you must be PADI-certified. There are also botanical gardens
and a bird-watchers tower nearby. Cenote is only 4 kilometers (2.4 miles)
from the village of Tulum. Admission is about $1 if you want to swim or
snorkel. The cost is higher for divers, who must also hire guides.

Just a little more than 40 kilometers (25 miles) inland from Tulum
are the ruins at **Coba**, a major Mayan capital that thrived from A.D. 600
to 900. Coba boasts more than 20,000 structures, most of which are
buried under the tropical vegetation. What seem to be small hills dotting
the landscape are often pyramid ruins. A 30-minute hike takes visitors into
the forest to the striking Nohoch-Mul pyramid. One of the largest Mayan
structures in the Yucatán, it was taller than those at Chichén Itzá and
Uxmal. There are a number of paths leading to various ruins that allow
visitors to see a variety of wildlife. Lodging is available, or you can stay at
Tulum.

Near Coba, the Mayan village of **Punta Laguna** contains a 192-
hectare (475-acre) sanctuary that attracts spider monkeys. The visitor's
center has been developed with support of Pronatura Peninsula de
Yucatán.

Getting to Tulum

The Tulum ruins are easily accessible from Highway 307 where it intersects with the highway to Coba. Tulum has frequent bus service to and

from Cancún, Felipe Carrillo Puerto, and Chetumal. Coba also has service to Tulum, Cancún, and Felipe Carrillo Puerto.

Where to Stay in Tulum
El Crucero, junction of Highway 307 and the access road to Tulum, $20. Clean and simple rooms.

Nohoch Tunich Cabañas, 15-minute walk from the ruins of Tulum, $15. Simple cabins, communal toilets, and hot-water showers. Pleasant managers and always a diverse group of travelers. Be sure to eat at Doña Tina's restaurant, which serves food typical of the region.

SIAN KA'AN BIOSPHERE RESERVE
Location: 60 km (37 mi.) S of Cancún
Area: 607,500 hectares (1.5 million acres)
Activities: Fishing, bird-watching, archaeology
For More Information: Amigos de Sian Ka'an, (98) 84-95-83, fax 87-30-80

South of Tulum and 2 hours south of Cancún lies the Sian Ka'an Biosphere Reserve, one of the finest of its kind in the world. Sian Ka'an is Mayan for "where the sky is born." Such poetic language perfectly suits this lovely reserve of tropical forests and wetlands.

Most travelers opt for Punta Allen with its sportfishing and funky (but not cheap!) hotels. Everything must be brought to this remote town, including the diesel for the generator that provides electricity for about 4 hours every night. The park has no visitor's center to speak of and few traditional services. Instead, the directors entrust the Amigos de Sian Ka'an environmental group and the hotel managers to provide park services. Punta Allen is the last village one can actually drive to, and the only settlement with a sewage treatment system and potable water.

Sian Ka'an was established as a reserve in 1982 thanks to studies conducted by the Centro de Investigaciones de Quintana Roo (CIQRO). The region received full status as a biosphere reserve in 1986, and in 1994 the Bahía de Espíritu Santo—a large bay in the southern part of the reserve—was declared a wilderness refuge of 89,000 hectares (219,830 acres).

Within the park there are lagoons and sinkholes that possess unusually high levels of biodiversity. There are 318 species of butterflies and 345 (and counting!) species of birds, including roseate spoonbills, white-fronted parrots, egrets, belted kingfishers, blue and boat-billed herons, frigate birds, and jabiru stork, the world's largest flighting bird. The park is home to a number of endangered species including jaguar, puma, tapir, manatee, and the spider monkey. Loggerhead, hawksbill, and green turtles come ashore to nest between June and August.

There are 1,200 plants and 230 species of trees found in the reserve, 14 percent of which are endemic to the peninsula. Sand dunes support plant species similar to those on the Antilles Islands.

Geology and Archaeology

The reserve rests on the youngest geological segment of the peninsula, which emerged from the sea less than 2 million years ago. The park is roughly one-third tropical forest, one-third wetlands, and one-third a marine environment. There are three core zones: Muyil in the north,

What Isn't Ecotourism: Xcaret

Each year, more than 600,000 people visit this "eco-archaeological park" 80 kilometers (50 miles) from Cancún (between Playa del Carmen and Akumal) on Highway 307. Xcaret boasts a well-groomed environment and a smattering of archaeological ruins. If you visit Cancún, Playa del Carmen, or Cozumel, you will be bombarded with Xcaret brochures and advertising.

It's hard to believe someone would bomb "nature's sacred paradise," but that's what happened here. In order to place lighting and ventilation in the underground river, Xcaret was dynamited. If this place is truly sacred, the actions here were tantamount to blowing up part of a cathedral in order to improve it.

While it's a far cry from ecotourism, Xcaret perhaps offers eco-inspired tourism as it assists in local environmental education programs. The park also has an engaging museum with replicas of the major Mayan temples, a sea turtle rescue program, and a swinging night show that amuses cruise ship passengers and local tourists alike. Admission is $25 for adults. The nighttime theatrical revues cost extra.

Cayo Culebras in Ascensión Bay, and Uaimil, the largest. The highest areas are only 20 meters (65 feet) above sea level. There are nearly 30 archaeological sites in the reserve, most from the late post-Classic period (A.D. 1200–1500). In 1987 UNESCO declared it a World Heritage Site.

Sian Ka'an Biosphere Reserve

Diversifying Park Support

Sian Ka'an is linked with other environmental reserves, both public and private. It receives financial and technical support from the Amigos de Sian Ka'an, an NGO created at the same time as the reserve. "We have tremendous support from Amigos," says reserve director Alfredo Arellano. "For example, as a park we are prohibited from collecting financial donations, but Amigos, as an *asociación civil*, can receive tax-deductible donations to be used in conservation and educational projects."

Unlike parks in the United States, which are mostly uninhabited, Sian Ka'an is a lively home to more than 5,000 people, 80 percent of whom depend on lobster harvests for their economic survival. The population is a mix of wealthy landowners and campesinos. Because of the pronounced differences among the classes, the area is always ripe for conflict.

There are some arrangements, though, which underscore the responsibility of the hotels that are located here. The Casa Blanca fishing lodge, as well as others to a lesser degree, are funding the reserve's four-year coral reef study which will be used to produce a management plan for public use and conservation. The lodge has funded a beach clean-up project and study of what type of trash washes up on the reserve's shores. Plastic debris was found from sources as far away as Honduras and Texas. Additional information about this study can be obtained by contacting Casa Blanca in the United States at (800) 533-7299, fax (713) 526-4302.

Sportfishing in Sian Ka'an

The Sian Ka'an Biosphere Reserve boasts two exceptional bays, Ascension Bay and Espiritu Santo Bay. The vast estuary system and adjacent reefs enclose the bays and provide shelter for a large number of species.

The reefs provide shelter to small fish and crustaceans, which in turn attract larger predators.

When the reserve was created, landholders were permitted to remain. Catch-and-release fishing was promoted while hotel owners worked to eliminate gill nets in Ascension Bay. You can book a fishing trip from the Boca Paila Lodge, Casa Blanca, or Ana y José's.

Catch-and-release fishing allows anglers to go after the most challenging of fish—bonefish, permit, and tarpon—without depleting the stock. Bonefish prefer shallow water because the flats provide the crabs, shrimp, and mollusks that they like to eat. The shallow water also provides protection from sharks and barracuda. Bonefish as large as 33 inches have been caught and released in the bays. Permit are found in both shallow and deep waters and are more difficult to catch than bonefish. Tarpon are the largest fish found in the bay. They prefer brackish water, which the reserve's mangrove coasts provide.

Tours and Outfitters
Amigos de Sian Ka'an. Coordinates full-day tours that include interpretation of the region's ecology, an opportunity to swim in freshwater springs, and a visit to the Chunyaxche Lagoon, a waterway used by the ancient Maya that connects with Boca Paila. Amigos tours are handled by Lomas Travel in Cancún, (98) 87-19-70 or 87-19-71.

Getting to Sian Ka'an
There are several access points to the park. The 60-kilometer (37-mile) paved and then dirt road from Tulum to Punta Allen and Highway 307 to Vigia Chico are good choices.

Where to Stay near Sian Ka'an
Boca Paila, located midway down the Punta Allen peninsula before the Boca Paila bridge, $2,500 per week, (987) 872-0053 or, in the U.S., (800) 245-1950. Oldest fishing lodge in the area, with eight expensive cabañas.

Casa Blanca, Punta Pajaros, on Ascension Bay in the middle of the reserve, $3,000 per week, (800) 533-7299, fax (713) 526-4302. This sportfishing lodge can be reached only by small plane or a long and often cold boat trip from Punta Allen. The property used to be a coconut plantation. The lodge is owned by a Mexico City corporation and managed by a U.S. firm interested in developing eco-friendly accommodations on the island.

Cuzan Guest House, in the fishing village of Punta Allen, $60, fax

The Costa Maya

Coastal towns are difficult to visit and generally come with rustic accommodations. But that may change soon as the giant tourism-development company Grupo Posadas plans to build as many as 1,200 rooms in eight "ecological hotels" along the southern half of Quintana Roo's coast— from Tulum to Chetumal—by the end of this century. The plan is a greener version of the tourism corridor that stretches from Cancún to Tulum. Time will tell how sensitive to the environment this project will be.

According to 1996 news reports, Grupo Posadas plans to invest $90 million and employ 1,500 people.

(983) 40383. Definitely the funkiest of the fishing resorts, Cuzan boasts whimsical palapas and a down-to-earth approach.

CHINCHORRO BANK

Location: *Across the bay from Chetumal*
Area: *46 km by 15 km (29 miles by 9 miles)*
Activities: *Diving, swimming, snorkeling*
For More Information: *SECTUR or Quintana Roo tourism office*

One of Mexico's most spectacular set of reefs is the Chinchorro Bank (Banco Chinchorro). At 46 kilometers (29 miles) long and 15 kilometers (9 miles) wide, it is shaped like an enormous bracelet. The reefs of Chinchorro Bank, protected by the government, enclose four distinct cays and are just 30 kilometers (19 miles) or a 2-hour boat ride offshore from Xcalak. The barrier reef has claimed some 20 ships over the centuries; the horizon is littered with the silhouettes of these wrecked vessels. It's a mecca for divers and underwater photographers alike.

While the area is being developed as part of Mexico's "Costa Maya," there are few facilities for tourists. This may be because the coast is covered with mangroves, not the white beaches that are found north of the Sian Ka'an Biosphere Reserve. In the simple fishing villages of Punta Río Indio Mahahual and Xcalac, travelers can arrange trips with the local fishermen. But if it's snorkeling you're interested in, you don't even have to go out to the reef—you'll find beautiful water just 100 meters from the shore. Camping can be arranged on the beach or you can stay at the one hotel in Mahahual, the Mahahual Caribe.

Tours and Outfitters
Ogima: Exploradores de los Ocho Vientos, Alfonso Reyes 81 (Local 9), Esq. Zitácuaro 6, Col. Condesa, 06170 Mexico, D.F., tel./fax (5) 272-03-97, e-mail mag01@ienlaces2.ienlaces.com.mx. Ogima offers several diving packages to Mahahual for about $1,000 (with discounts for non-divers). Packages include all dives, meals, and accommodations, and transportation from Cancún or Chetumal. For more information contact Marjorie Gutiérrez.

Getting to Chetumal and Chinchorro Bank
Chetumal is connected by domestic flights. To reach either Xcalac or Mahahual, take Highway 307 north; after 100 kilometers (62 miles) take the marked paved road east to the coast, where it dead-ends at Mahahual. A dirt road continues another 65 kilometers (40 miles) to Xcalac.

Where to Stay near Chinchorro Bank
Nearby accommodations are found in Xcalak or inland in the Quintana Roo capital, Chetumal.

Costa de Cocos Resort, 50 kilometers (31 miles) south of Mahahual on the highway to Xcalak, U.S. phone (800) 443-1123, $100. Six cabañas with private baths. Price includes meals. Dive packages can be arranged.

Hotel Los Cocos, Avenida Heroes 134 at Calle Chapultepec, Chetumal, (983) 2-0544, $55. Pleasant hotel with well-maintained gardens and a swimming pool.

Hotel Principe, Avenida Heroes 326, Chetumal, (983) 2-4799, $30. Large rooms with a pleasant courtyard.

Playa Chinchorro Beach and Dive Resort, Xcalak, U.S. phone (800) 768-0053 , $100. Ten cabañas with mosquito netting and private bath. Rate includes all meals.

TRES GARANTIAS
Location: 126 km (78 mi.) from Chetumal, in the rain forest south of Nicolas Bravo

Area: *162 hectares (400 acres)*
Activities: *Bird-watching, hunting, hiking*
For More Information: *Sociedad de Productores Forestales Ejidales de Quintana Roo, (983) 2-92-02, e-mail ppf1@balam.cuc.uqroo.mx*

Tres Garantías, in a semi-evergreen tropical forest 32 kilometers (20 miles) south of Nicolas Bravo, is a 162-hectare (400-acre) reserve. As part of a community-based ecotourism project, an ejido of Maya chicle tappers have set aside half of their forest as wilderness area. The Society of Ejido-based Foresters spend more of their time trying to attract hunters to the region than they do hikers.

The region houses numerous species, including howler and spider monkeys, pacas, jaguars, tapirs, collared peccaries, and ocellated turkeys. Peccaries are wild pigs that generally travel in large packs. They can be very aggressive, so keep your distance.

Where to Stay in Tres Garantías
Campamento La Piramide, is a rustic, screened cabin owned by the ejido and can be rented for $45 per day. Reservations must be made ahead of time by contacting the office in Chetumal at Carmen Ochoa de Merino No. 143, Col. Centro, 77000 Chetumal, Quintana Roo, (983) 2-92-02.

THE NORTH COAST

The north coast of the Yucatán Peninsula does not have clear, turquoise waters. Instead, the murky and nutrient-rich waters of the Gulf of Mexico lap along the shore. This area is a birder's paradise. The resplendent flamingo has settled in several areas, mainly at Ría Lagartos Special Biosphere Reserve and the Ría Celestún Biosphere Reserve. The migratory flamingos are found in Bocas de Dzilam on the gulf and on Isla Holbox, and a few travel as far south as the Sian Ka'an Biosphere Reserve.

In 1993 some flamingos began nesting in the adjoining state of Campeche. The state government responded and created the 23,517-hectare (58,087-acre) Petenes Celestún Reserve, consisting of mangroves and petenes, south of Celestún. But the swamps don't only provide protection for flamingos. Other wading birds make their home there as well. The petenes are home to birds that are found in the more mountainous areas of the peninsula.

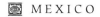

The Mexican flamingo population climbed from 8,000 in 1979, when the nesting and feeding areas were first protected, to a high of 26,000 in 1988. Then, that same year, Hurricane Gilbert caused a setback for the population.

Chief supporters of these wetlands are Pronatura Yucatán; The Nature Conservancy, which has targeted the area as part of their Parks in Peril Program; Ducks Unlimited of Mexico; and the North American Wetlands Council.

RIA LAGARTOS SPECIAL BIOSPHERE RESERVE

Location: *50 km (31 mi.) N of Tizimin on Highway 295*
Area: *57,000 hectares (140,790 acres)*
Activities: *Bird-watching*
For More Information: *SECTUR; Yucatán state tourism office; or Pronatura Yucatán, (99) 44-22-90 or 44-35-80, e-mail ppy@pibil.finred.com.mx*

Thousands of pink flamingos nest each winter in this reserve near the fishing village of Ría Lagartos. Officially designated a special biosphere reserve in 1979, it's the only one in Mexico that is part of the Convention on Wetlands of International Importance (commonly known as RAMSAR). In the late spring the vast majority of the region's flamingo population build their nests in this estuary. But flamingos aren't the only birds found in the area—270 other bird species call Ría Lagartos home. In addition, non-winged species such as hawksbill and green turtles arrive in September and October to lay their eggs.

Ría Lagartos is not a river but a collection of shallow lagoons and coastal beaches where the Maya have extracted salt for centuries. Even today, salt-mining operations continue to work here. A short trip to Los Colorados, a village northeast of Ría Lagartos, offers views of salt deposits and multicolored pools.

West of Ría Lagartos are two other flamingo nesting areas: **Dzilam de Bravo** and **El Palmar**. Trips can be arranged from Ría Lagartos or **Progreso**, a lively resort town that offers a nice beach and plenty of amenities.

Getting to Ría Lagartos

The quaint town of Ría Lagartos offers local bus service to Valladolid, 100 kilometers (62 miles) or 2 hours to the south. From Valladolid there are frequent connections to Cancún and Mérida.

Where to Stay near Ría Lagartos

Small cabañas are available for rent in this area. Ask the locals for more information.

Hotel Nefertiti, on the waterfront, $20. Photos of flamingos decorate the lobby, and a bust of the Egyptian queen rules over the courtyard.

MERIDA
Location: *Northwestern part of Yucatán state, 315 km (195 mi.) SW of Cancún*
Activities: *Archaeology, museums, bird-watching*
For More Information: *SECTUR or the state tourism office, (99) 224-9290*

The state capital of Yucatán is a wonderful hub for both ecological and archaeological travels. Curiously, despite its tropical atmosphere, Merida is north of Mexico City.

The city began as the Maya metropolis of T'ho; built of white limestone, it has been referred to since as "the White City." T'ho was conquered and dismantled by the Spaniards in 1542 under the command of Francisco de Montejo. Montejo named the new city after Mérida, Spain. On the south side of the plaza is the Casa de Montejo, the conqueror's former residence. Like so many other one-time aristocratic homes, it is now a bank.

In the spring of 1996, Mérida's last cenote, along the famed Paseo de Montejo, was destroyed when it was filled in to build a parking lot. According to the locals, the cenote had been a refuge for wildlife including fruit bats and vultures.

Things to See and Do in Mérida
If you visit, prepare yourself for a downtown mobbed with *ambulantes* (vendors). While a few ambulantes may be okay, you'll find that several dozen are an annoyance. Mérida has numerous cultural attractions that spotlight regional history and culture as well as the local *artesenia*. The **Casa de las Artesanías** (government craft store) is located at Calle 68 x 64 y 66, next to the Iglesia de Monjas. It offers a great introduction to the local handiwork, *jipi* palm hats and hammocks. They are perhaps the most famous and most comfortable in Mexico. The store is open daily from 8 a.m. to 8 p.m.

Huun is the Mayan word for paper and for the tree that was used by the ancient Maya in papermaking. The craft had disappeared from the Yucatán until 1985 when a sustainable development community project called Huun was begun. The producers use only cultivable and renewable plant resources. Visit **Huun Handmade Maya Paper**, Calle 19 313-A y 36, Col. Carranza, tel./fax (99) 27-32-47.

The **Regional Museum of Anthropology** is housed in a giant white mansion on the corner of Paseo de Montejo and Calle 43. Exhibits span time from prehistory to modern day. The museum is open Monday through Saturday 8 a.m. to 8 p.m., and Sunday from 8 a.m. to 2 p.m. Admission is free. Another must-visit is the **Casa de la Cultura del Mayab**, on Calle 63 between 64 and 66. Local artists hold exhibitions here. The last time I visited there was an exhibit consisting of shells (*conchas*) and other natural materials from Celestún.

Tours and Outfitters

Ecoturismo Yucatán, Calle 3 #235 between 32-A and 34 in Colonia Pensiones, (99) 25-21-87 or 20-27-72, e-mail ecoyuc@minter.cieamer.conacyt .mx, Web site http://www.imagenet.com.mx/EcoYuc/home.html. Run by Alfonso Escobedo, a professional guide, and his wife, Roberta Graham de Escobedo, this company was founded in 1989 and offers customized nature tours that combine bird-watching, archaeology, and glimpses into the living culture of the Yucatán.

Getting to Mérida

The first-class bus station is located at Calle 70 between 69 and 71. The second-class station is at Calle 69 between 68 and 70. It's easy to rent a car, either from the airport or at downtown locations. The airport is a short distance southwest of the city on Highway 180.

Where to Stay in Mérida

Hotel Caribe, Calle 59 #500, $30, 24-90-22l or toll-free in Mexico (800) 20-003. Rooms have either air conditioning or ceiling fans. You pay more for a/c—worth the expense in this tropical city. The building overlooks Parque Hidalgo.

Hotel Flamingo, Calle 57 between 56 and 58, $10, (99) 24-77-55, fax (99) 24-70-70. Clean hotel several blocks away from the downtown plaza.

Pablo's B&B, Calle 54, # 453 between 51 and 53, (99) 23-90-91, $25–35 per day (depending on season) with weekly rates available, e-mail pablos@pibil.finred.com.mx, Web site http://finred.pibil./rmpresas /pablos/pablos.htm. Paul (Pablo) Caldwell is a U.S. expatriate offering personalized tours and day trips. His bed-and-breakfast is about eight blocks from the town center; individual apartments have their own entrance, full kitchen, and private bath.

Where to Eat in Mérida

Los Almendros, Calle 50 #493 between Calles 57 and 59, (99) 21-28-51. Yucatecan cuisine, including *pavo relleno* (stuffed turkey) and *cochinita pibil* (pork wrapped in banana leaves and baked in a fiery pit).

This establishment is the parent restaurant of the Cancún franchise. Every Friday evening they have a regional show, complete with local music and dance.

Restaurante Amaro, Calle 59 #507 between 60 and 62, (99) 28-24-51. This wonderful eatery is housed in the colonial home of Quintana Roo patriot, poet, and namesake Andrés Quintana Roo. Specialties include vegetarian dishes and, of course, Yucatecan cuisine.

CELESTUN BIOSPHERE RESERVE

Location: 80 km (50 mi.) east of Mérida
Area: 464,130 hectares (1,146,000 acres)
Activities: Bird-watching
For More Information: SECTUR, the Yucatán state tourism office, or Pronatura Yucatán, (99) 44-22-90 or 44-35-80, e-mail ppy@pibil.finred .com.mx

Decreed a wildlife refuge in 1979 and a biosphere reserve in the 1980s, this is a great place to see anhingas, egrets, and the famed American flamingos. This seaside town was founded in 1718, and the economy thrives on the fishing industry.

The reserve itself is of major importance as a wintering zone for migratory birds, being the first stop on two of the four migratory flyways. Ducks Unlimited of Mexico (DUMAC) has a research station here, and this is a priority area for the North American Wetlands Conservation Council.

The American flamingo is the reserve's main attraction and can be observed from boats rented on the left-hand side of the bridge as you come into town. More than 320 species have been identified in the biosphere reserve, of which many are permanent residents. For the true birdwatcher, the best time to visit is in the winter when migrants abound.

One tour heads north from the bridge and takes you to see the flamingos on Isla de Pájaros, where cormorants, frigate birds, and great egrets take turns nesting. You also stop at an *ojo de agua*, a freshwater spring, for a swim and a possible view of the elusive tiger heron. Heading south you won't always see flamingos, but there are other points of interest such as the Petrified Mangrove Forest and Real de Salinas, a recently abandoned ghost town.

You'll see numerous fishermen in the estuary. SEMARNAP ordered formation of a cooperative to net shrimp as activities have changed from subsistence to commercial operations. The cooperative has 180 members; 95 additional applicants are awaiting acceptance. As many as 500 fishermen have worked in the estuary in the past.

Chicxulub Impact Crater

One of Mexico's most spectacular natural wonders is something you'll never see. Offshore of the town of Progreso lies the Chicxulub Impact Crater, buried beneath hundreds of meters of sediment. Some 65 million years ago, an iridium-rich asteroid struck Earth. Scientists estimate that, upon impact, more than 200,000 cubic kilometers of the Earth's crust was instantly vaporized, melted, or ejected from the crater. The impact left a stratum of iridium—an element rare on this planet but common in asteroids and comets—around the Earth.

The existence of the crater was first suspected during offshore petroleum explorations in the 1950s when Mexico's federal oil company, Petróleos Mexicanos (PEMEX), found sediment that did not correspond with that of the surrounding area. The crater was named after the nearby Maya village of Chicxulub. Geologists continue to study the area today.

Estimates of the crater's width range from 200 to 300 kilometers (124 to 186 miles)—numbers vary according to how scientists read the deviations in gravitational and magnetic field lines. Regardless of its exact dimensions, researchers say that Chicxulub could be the largest impact crater to form on Earth in the last billion years.

Whether or not the meteor's impact was responsible for the demise of the dinosaurs (first proposed in 1980 by Walter Alvarez of the University of California at Berkeley) is argued in scientific circles, but an obvious consequence of the impact can be found in the nearby geography. Scientists have described a 177-kilometer-wide ring of cenotes outlining the crater. The ring of fractured bedrock strikes the coast at Celestún and Bocas de Dzilam. These springs provide fresh water to the lagoons and the animals that live in them.

Tours and Outfitters

Some of Mérida's larger hotels arrange trips to the reserve. You can also arrange a trip yourself by simply heading to Celestún. At the entrance of the town you'll see signs for the dock where boatmen (*lancheros*) take groups of tourists through the mangroves. Boat trips arranged this way cost about $25 and can accommodate five to eight people.

David Bacab is an excellent local guide. He can be reached through **Ecoturismo Yucatán**, (99) 25-21-87 or 20-27-72 or in Celestún at (991) 62-049. If he's booked he can recommend other trained guides from the town.

Getting to Celestún

Celestún is easily reached from Mérida via Highway 281. Buses leave Mérida almost every hour on the hour, starting at 5 a.m. You can catch the bus in Mérida at the station on Calle 70 between 69 and 71. The second-class bus station is located on Calle 69 between 68 and 70.

Where to Stay in Celestún

Hotel Eco Paraíso Xixim, 8 kilometers (5 miles) from Celestún on the road to Sisal; $2,000 per week; contact Ecoturismo Yucatán at (99) 25-2187 for more information. Eco-friendly hotel with 15 rooms. The establishment, a sister hotel to the Eco Paraíso Caribe in Playa del Carmen, is geared toward foreign tourists who want four-star accommodations. Rooms have ceiling fans instead of air conditioning.

Hotel Gutiérrez, Calle 12 #127, $18, (99) 24-6348. Large rooms with ceiling fans.

María del Carmen, Calle 12 at Calle 15, $18, (99) 28-6978. Owners Doña Carmen and Don Lira are the founders of Grupo Ecológico Celestún, a local environmental group. Check out the material on local wildlife in the lobby.

CAMPECHE

CALAKMUL BIOSPHERE RESERVE

Location: On the border between Quintana Roo and Guatemala
Area: 723,185 hectares (1,786,266 acres)
Activities: Hiking, archaeology, bird-watching
For More Information: Calakmul Biosphere Reservation Information

Line, (981) 6-33-00; or Pronatura Yucatán, (99) 44-22-90 or 44-35-80, e-mail ppy@pibil.finred.com.mx.

The Calakmul Biosphere Reserve is one of the largest protected areas in Mexico, covering more than 14 percent of the state of Campeche. It retains the largest share of virgin rain forest in Mexico. The best time to visit is during the dry season that runs from November through March, though the area is greener during the rainy season from May to November. The southern section receives most of the seasonal deluge.

Calakmul is Mexico's grand "eco-archaeological" experiment. The reserve surrounds the ruins of what may be the largest city built by the Maya. If you want to combine bird-watching or treks with archaeology, this is the place to start. In 1993 the Mexican government paved a road through the forest to facilitate excavation of the ruins. Now this road allows easy access for tourists from Cancún or Mérida.

President Carlos Salinas de Gortari declared Calakmul a biosphere reserve in 1989. In a watershed agreement, Mexico's federal government

Chichén Itzá

One of the most spectacular of the classic Mayan cities is Chichén Itzá, about 120 kilometers (75 miles) east of Mérida off of Highway 180. This is the best-restored of the Mayan sites on the peninsula.

A spectacular event takes place each year on the vernal equinox. The Maya applied the science of geomancy in the construction of their cities. The goal was to create physical points of reference to assess seasonal changes, vital to a society fueled by agriculture. The main temple at Chichén Itzá is placed in such a way that on the first day of spring a serpent-like shadow descends the stairs. Not coincidentally, the temple was dedicated to the plumed serpent deity Kukulcan.

You can find accommodations in the nearby village of Piste. Staying here allows for more convenient early-morning tours than if you day-trip from Mérida. For more information on visiting Chichén Itzá, call the Mérida tourism office at (99) 224-9290.

transferred the management of the reserve to the state of Campeche, which agreed to jointly administer the park with the environmental group Pronatura Yucatán. In 1993 the reserve became part of the Man and the Biosphere Program. Calakmul will be joined by Guatemala's Maya Biosphere Reserve and Belize's Río Bravo Conservation Area to form the proposed international Maya Peace Park, which will attempt to protect the remaining forests in the Petén.

It's easy to visualize the scope of the reserve. From the top of the pyramid here, you can see across the border into Guatemala. See if you can find the top of the Danta pyramid in Guatemala's El Mirador Ruins.

There are more than 7,000 archaeological structures in Calakmul, 108 stelae, a mural 6 meters (19 feet) high, and two tombs. Occupation dates from the pre-Classic (700–600 B.C.) to the Classic period (A.D. 900). At its height, the city of 60,000 inhabitants was larger than either Palenque or Tikal at their zeniths.

Ten endangered species of large mammals live in the reserve, including five of the six felines found in Mexico. Nearly all are nocturnal. You may come across their tracks but sightings are uncommon. There are also anteaters, tapirs, white-lipped peccaries, and two species of deer. At least 30 different species of birds of prey, including the king vulture and ornate hawk-eagle, make their home here, as do the great curassow, ocellated turkey, and hundreds of other bird species.

Xpujil, occupied by the Maya since A.D. 400, serves as one gateway to the Calakmul Biosphere Reserve. The area does not receive many tourists, but in 1993 cabañas were built behind the local restaurant. The ruins of the ancient city are on the outskirts of the town.

There are numerous attractions nearby. The greatest concentration of blue-crowned motmots in the Yucatán are found near Xpujil. The **Río Bec** archaeological site is only 15 kilometers (9 miles) south of Xpujil, but it's a 2-hour drive by four-wheel-drive vehicle. A few kilometers north of Xpujil is the town of **Zoh Laguna**, which boasts a small zoo with native fauna including an ocelot and pumas.

Living in Calakmul

Population growth is the greatest danger to the reserve, and there continues to be considerable in-migration, particularly from the state of Chiapas. The major land uses within the area include logging, small-scale farming, and chicle extraction. Resources from the reserve are used by the surrounding 27 ejidos in both sustainable and non-sustainable manners.

Nearly 50 percent of the reserve is ejido property. The other half belongs to the federal government. There are nearly 24,000 inhabitants in the region. Four thousand of them live in the reserve, another 6,000 depend on the reserve's forest products, and more than 13,000 live in the surrounding area. The principle economic activity in the area is farming. Farmers cultivate corn, beans, and squash, and produce jalapeño and chipotle chiles for commercial sales.

Various strategies are being pursued to boost the livelihoods of the local Maya. These are the people who in fact have been guarding and protecting the ruins and the forests. The Canadian government is providing technical expertise in the creation of a model forest. This would not preclude forestry, but aim toward sustainable harvests—often ignored in the competitive world marketplace. Another plan, sponsored by The Nature Conservancy, is the creation of a company that distributes "Jungle Honey." Made by ejidal cooperatives, it would be available at the park.

Getting to Calakmul Biosphere Reserve

The reserve is located on Highway 186 between the town of Escárcega and Chetumal. Access is available from the small village of Conhuas, 60 kilometers (37 miles) west of Xpujil. The junction is well-marked and there is a booth that collects an entry fee of $2 per person. A narrow road leads to the site from Conhuas.

Where to Stay near Calakmul Biosphere Reserve

Chicanná Ecovillage Hotel, near the village of Xpujil, $65, (981) 6-22-33. Run by the Ramada corporation, this hotel receives high marks for its solar energy, rainwater collection, and recycling systems.

El Mirador Maya, west of Xpujil, $25, (983) 2-91-63. Simple restaurant and bungalows. Friendly service.

TABASCO

Tabasco is a state of countless lakes and lagoons, beautiful rivers, and rich vegetation. The Olmec civilization took root on the shores of the Gulf of Mexico here 2,000 years before the Aztec empire. Their crafts document their technical sophistication and artistic talent. From exquisite jade carvings to the colossal "Olmec heads," Olmec art is on par with classical sculpture. Without a doubt, Tabasco is the cradle of Mesoamerican civilization.

Tabasco has one-third of the hydrological resources of the country, including two of the most powerful rivers in Mexico, the Usumacinta and the Grijalva. The Usumacinta River, which begins its journey to the east in Guatemala, flows into the gulf here. The coasts have sandy beaches and lagoons such as El Carmen, Pajonal, Machona, and Tupilco.

Indigenous Past

Both the Olmec and later the Maya found ways of cultivating food without harming the local biodiversity—at least in the beginning. These cultures offer model ways to preserve life in all its forms while sustaining a fairly dense population.

Agroecologist Ronald Nigh praises the Maya civilization's expertise in producing abundant foods while preserving the environment. "I think the kind of technology that allowed a high population to produce high amounts of food they needed and not reduce the biodiversity, not to deforest, is a kind of technology we have a lot to learn from," he says.

The hydrology of the lowland coastal plane is so complex it's nearly impossible to predict what the floodwaters will do from year to year. The Maya simply adapted their fields to flooding. Flooding was accepted as a part of the natural cycle and recognized as beneficial in removing weeds and replenishing the soil with nutrients.

After the region was ruled by the Olmecs, it was home to a host of civilizations, including the Toltec, Chichimec, Tapanec, and Aztec. In the Aztecs' Nahuatl language, Tabasco means "flooded land."

Oil Industry

Tabasco is home to some of Mexico's richest petroleum fields and, consequently, to the most severe pollution. Communities next to the oil fields have not reaped the economic rewards.

While it was known that Tabasco had large oil reserves, exploration and drilling did not take off until the mid-1970s. An oil boom produced enormous wealth for the state, though at the cost of contamination of the lower marshlands and rivers. A study by the state ecology department found that 80 percent of Tabasco's water is polluted.

The national oil company, PEMEX, although protesting that environmental compensation is unjustified, gave 277 million pesos to the Tabasco government in 1995. Communities have asked for direct payment, saying that the state government has not placed the money in the communities affected by pollution. PEMEX is also repairing petroleum ducts and working with oyster-repopulation programs.

PANTANOS DE CENTLA BIOSPHERE RESERVE

Location: 50 km (31 mi.) NE of Villahermosa
Area: 302,706 hectares (747,683 acres)

Activities: Bird-watching, archaeology
For More Information: SECTUR or the state tourism office, (93) 16-3648

More than 30 percent of Mexico's fresh water drains into the Usumacinta–Grijalva Delta, directly north of Villahermosa and stretching to Ciudad del Carmen and the Laguna de Terminos. The Centla wetlands, declared a reserve in 1992, consist of mangroves, marshlands, jungles, and lagoons. These hot, humid wetlands are a refuge for the endangered marsh crocodile and manatee. The reserve is valued in Mesoamerica for its high biological productivity and aquaculture potential, and because it contains both Mayan and Olmec ruins. The Olmec site, near Jonuta on the border of Tabasco and Campeche, is of particular interest to archaeologists.

In the village of **Frontera**, 80 kilometers (50 miles) from Villahermosa, you can hire a lancha on the Usumacinta River for an informal tour of the swamps. To schedule a guided trip from Villahermosa, contact **Universo Maya**, (93) 14-59-58 or 12-11-11, ext. 1030.

Adjacent to the Centla reserve in the state of Campeche is the **Laguna de Terminos** protected area. Together, these reserves form a region of exceptional biological wealth. There are 190 species of birds that reside or winter here and numerous mammals, including howler monkeys and jaguars. The reserve is also home to 20,000 people, most of whom are Chontal Maya and live in small villages. These residents are being entrusted with the protection of the reserve. The government has designated 169,111 hectares (417,704 acres) as the biosphere reserve's buffer zone, which can be used for sustainable and ecologically sound projects. For more information about trips on the Usumacinta River, see Chapter 12, Southern Mexico.

Tours and Outfitters
Universo Maya, Avenida Ruiz Cortines 907 in the Hotel Maya Tabasco, (93) 14-59-58 or 12-11-11, ext. 1030. Offers day-long tours of the Pantanos de Centla, a two-day tour to the rain forest in Humanguillo, Tabasco, and week-long tours to various archaeological sites and parks in Tabasco and Chiapas.

Getting to Pantanos de Centla Biosphere Reserve
Take Highway 180 north 80 kilometers (50 miles) from Villahermosa to Frontera.

Where to Stay near Pantanos de Centla Biosphere Reserve
Hotel Cencali, 1.5 kilometers north of Villahermosa on Highway 180, $50; (93) 15-19-99. Three-story hotel that overlooks Laguna de las Illusiones behind the Parque La Venta.

Hotel Maya Tabasco, Avenida Ruiz Corines 907, Villahermosa, (93) 14-44-66 or, in the U.S., (800) 528-1234, $65. First-class hotel that attracts a growing number of travelers interested in the Mundo Maya.

Hotel San Francisco, Madero 604 between Zaragoza and María del Carmen, Villahermosa, (93) 12-31-98, $15. Rooms have air-conditioning in this six-story budget favorite.

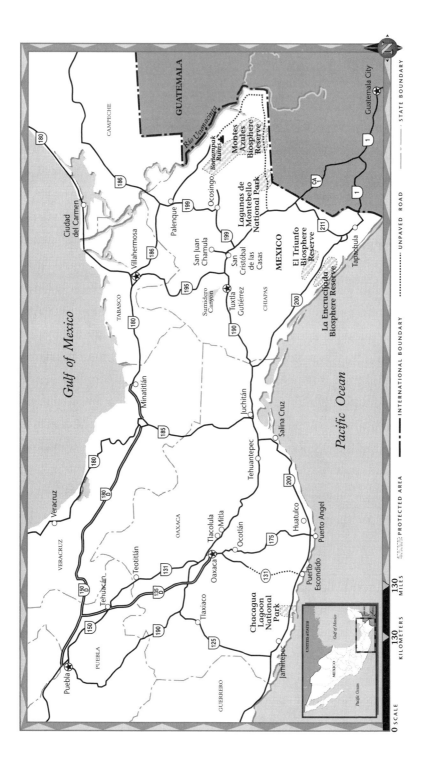

12

SOUTHERN MEXICO

OAXACA AND CHIAPAS

In both environmental and cultural terms, Southern and Southwestern Mexico share as much with neighboring Guatemala as with Central Mexico. You'll hear the festive marimba music in the plazas, and the Maya tongue becomes more predominant as you approach the southern border. Both Oaxaca and Chiapas are promoting and encouraging rural tourism. While the capital and coastal cities receive large numbers of tourists, the smaller towns are relatively unvisited. If responsible tourism can generate income in these rural pueblos, the campesinos will be less likely to migrate to the big cities in pursuit of a living wage.

OAXACA

Oaxaca, known as "Tierra del Sol" or "Land of the Sun," is a large, rambling state blessed with mountains, lakes, and miles of beautiful Pacific coastline. Human occupation dates back to the Olmecs, who probably lived in or visited this region around 1000 B.C. Subsequent Mixtec and Zapotec civilizations were conquered by the Aztecs, but the towns are still home to descendants of those peoples, who continue to keep their cultures alive.

Part of the state is located on the Isthmus of Tehuantepec, a narrow strait of land in which only 210 kilometers (130 miles) separate the Gulf of Mexico and the Pacific Ocean. Three mountain ranges dominate the landscape: the Sierra Madre del Sur, the Sierra Madre Occidental, and the Sierra Atravesada. Because the surface pressure is generally greater in the Gulf of Campeche than in the Pacific, the Tehuantepec region usually has strong, warm winds blowing from the north and remains humid most of the year. The clash of Pacific and Caribbean weather systems also brings strong winds and heavy rains to this region, setting it apart from the northern reaches of the state, which are cooler and drier.

Seventeen of Mexico's 56 different ethnic groups live in Oaxaca. The state's diverse population includes Zapotecs, Mixtecs, Mixes, Chinantecos, Mazatecos, Chatinos, Huaves, Chontales, Zoques, Tacuates, Amuzgos, Triquis, Nahuas, Cuicatecos, Chochos, Ixcatecos, and descendants from African slave populations.

Like other Mexican states, Oaxaca seeks to complement its agricultural income with tourism. The state is a prime tourist destination, with attractions ranging from the beaches of Puerto Escondido and Puerto Angel to colonial gems such as the city of Oaxaca and ancient archaeological wonders like Monte Albán and Mitla. There are enough things to do here to easily keep a tourist occupied for a week. One option is to spend a few days at the beach and then take a tour of the valleys surrounding Oaxaca City. There are even rural hostels (called Tourist Yu'us, described in this chapter) and cultural tours that take visitors to community museums.

Despite the mountains, this is tilled land; nearly one-third of Oaxaca supports agriculture. Fields of *higuerilla* tower 3 meters (10 feet) over homes. For centuries the oil from this plant has been harvested for fuel and used to treat leather goods. It offers a viable alternative energy source for local producers.

Although the region depends greatly on agriculture, it lacks even a modest system of irrigation or water treatment facilities. Due to the lack of water, the patchwork quilt of crops blanketing the rural landscape is mostly brown outside of the summer rainy season.

Hurricane Pauline

In October 1997 Hurricane Pauline lashed the southern coast of Oaxaca and Guerrero. Puerto Angel, where the hurricane made landfall, was particularly hard hit. Nearby Zipolite beach also suffered great damage from the storm and all palapa-type structures (made of palm fronds and bamboo) were wiped out. But the advantage of palapas is that they're not expensive and are easy to rebuild.

At the Mexican Turtle Center, which keeps track of turtles on nearby Escobilla Beach, a survey showed that 6 million turtle eggs were

Tourist Yu'u, Benito Juárez

destroyed by the storm, roughly 20 percent of those in the sand. But turtles are a resilient species, and the storm did nothing to deter their maternal instincts. Only two weeks after Pauline, a wave of 100,000 turtles crept up onto the beach to lay their eggs.

THE TOURIST YU'U PROGRAM

The state tourism agency, SEDETUR, has created the Tourist Yu'u Program to promote nature-oriented tourism in the Central Valley. Through this program, the first of its kind in Mexico, small tourist houses—known as Tourist Yu'us—have been established in nine Indian villages, including Benito Juárez in the northern Sierra, Teotitlán, Tlacolula de Matamoros, Quialana, Tlapazola, Santa Ana del Valle, Santa Cruz Papaluta, San Sebastian Abasolo, and Hierve el Agua. These houses offer simple, authentic accomodations for travelers who wish to explore rural villages and cultures. Services provided at each Tourist Yu'u vary, but each hostel is locally operated.

The Tourist Yu'u villages are in areas that have been severely deforested and have suffered various forms of environmental deterioration. Officials from SEDETUR hope that the promotion of tourism

233

can reintroduce a respect for local traditions, reduce stresses on the environment, and ultimately improve both living and environmental conditions. (Tourist Yu'u houses are generally the only lodgings available in the villages).

Each tourist house manages its own nursery and raises trees to help reforest the valley. An orchard near the Santa Ana house, for example, is already well underway. Tourist Yu'u visitors are encouraged to explore these areas on foot, bicycle, or horseback. Special trips allowing visitors to learn more about local arts and culture can be arranged with a local Tourist Yu'u administrator.

The cost for staying at a Tourist Yu'u is low: $4 per person per night in a shared cabin or $4 for a campsite. The biggest obstacle for tourists will be locating the houses. The maps printed by SEDETUR are rather sketchy, so make sure you get good directions from the office in downtown Oaxaca. Contact SEDETUR at Independencia 607; (951) 6-01-23, 6-48-28, or 1-50-40; fax (951) 60984.

The Tourist Yu'u at Hierva el Agua

Two hours away from Oaxaca lies one of the most interesting geological formations in Southern Mexico, **Hierve el Agua**, a rock formation with petrified waterfalls.

About 2,400 years ago, nomadic people settled in the region near Hierve el Agua and its consistent supply of thermal waters. They found the springs were easy to divert for crop irrigation. An elaborate network of canals fed terraced crops over half a square kilometer. Wells were constructed every 3 meters (10 feet) along the canals. Research dates the construction of the irrigation system from somewhere between 420–310 B.C. to A.D. 1500. The calcium carbonate and magnesium content of the water was so high that the deposits literally petrified the canals. Remarkably, the spring still produces 2 liters of water per second during the summer months, and the water continues to flow through part of the ancient canal system.

The formations at Hierve el Agua are one of the most popular attractions in the Central Valley. The Tourist Yu'u facility in Hierve el Agua boasts several guest houses as well as a thermal swimming pool with mud famed for its therapeutic and cosmetic properties. Numerous *comedores* feed hungry travelers, and visitors can purchase local art made with palm leaves. This is a clean, well-managed area with well-tended bathrooms.

Getting to Hierve el Agua

Take Highway 190 south from Oaxaca City. At Mitla drive 17 kilometers (11 miles) toward Ayutla along a stretch of road that climbs through the deforested mountains. The final stretch leads through the narrow streets of

San Lorenzo Albarradas, a small community where locals dry their surplus corn on the roofs of their modest houses. Eventually you'll pass through agricultural land where the fences are made of stone and cactus.

Other Tourist Yu'u Sites in the Central Valley

Some of most interesting Tourist Yu'u facilities are located in the following towns or villages.

El Tlacolula is the central town in the Tlacolula Valley. The valley is home to more than 60,000 Indians who speak the Zapotec language, and the town is home to more than 10,000 people. Rough residential dwellings are interspersed with numerous colonial buildings. The Sunday market, reported to be one of the oldest in Mesoamerica, is also the area's largest.

San Bartolomé Quialana is a small community of 2,500 people. The villagers make nets from the fibers of the agave and distinct black and white woolen blankets.

Santa Ana del Valle is downhill from Quialana, 34 kilometers (22 miles) from Oaxaca on Highway 190. The villagers earn their living from agriculture and weaving. The town has a community museum with various archaeological objects from the Zapotec period, as well as exhibits on the local experience of the Mexican Revolution, the Danza de la Pluma (Feather Dance), and traditional Zapotec weaving techniques using natural dyes.

San Marcos Tlapazola is a village of 1,500 people, though many of the men have emigrated to the United States to become farm workers. Women have started a cooperative to make clay pots. The Tourist Yu'u is outside of town and overlooks fields of agave plants.

San Sebastian Abasolo is a relatively prosperous farming community of 1,700 people. The fields surrounding the town produce three seasonal crops (corn, garlic, and chile) each year. The region's high water table allows for irrigation.

Santa Cruz Papalutla is about the same size as Abasolo. Residents make baskets from *carrizo*, a reed grass. "Papalutla" translates as "field full of butterflies," and the Tourist Yu'u displays a butterfly design to honor the town.

Teotitlán del Valle is world-famous for its traditional woven wool blankets. Natural dyes, derived from local plants and minerals, are slowly being replaced by cheaper artificial colors. The cochineal insect, for example, which produces a somber red, is very expensive, and consumers have asked for colors brighter than those the squashed bug can provide. In recent years weavers have begun to create rug versions of paintings by Picasso, Matisse, and Diego Rivera. If you have the time, the weavers can even work from a photograph to produce a personalized pattern.

235

Benito Juárez is a mountain community and the only Tourist Yu'u location that is not in the Central Valley. The town's unique health clinic harvests medicinal plants from its small garden. A 30-minute walk takes you to El Mirador, which offers a stunning view of the Oaxaca Valley and, to the northeast, a glimpse of Pico de Orizaba, Mexico's highest mountain.

In the same mountain range, you can also visit the Chinantec Indian communities of **Santiago** or **Comaltepec**. Part of this area is a Pleistocene refuge, formed during the last ice age. Within the area are diverse arrays of

Oaxaca's Northern Sierra

The Northern Sierra of Oaxaca, also known as the Sierra Juárez, offers visitors a wealth of natural attractions. From the tropical deciduous forests with cacti and high endemism (one-third of the plant species live only in a small area), you can trek through some of the most diverse pine and oak forests in the world to mountains topped with sub-alpine prairies. Zempoaltépetl, at 3,400 meters (11,150 feet), is the highest peak in the range and is the sacred mountain of the Mixe.

A community group is now arranging hiking treks and cultural exchanges from the town of Ixtlán de Juárez, 60 kilometers (37 miles) north of Oaxaca City. Iztlán and other towns in the Sierra have ancient histories. They were first settled by the Zapotecs and later controlled by the Spanish. Ixtlán de Juárez boasts a spectacular colonial church built in 1734.

To visit Ixtlán, take Highway 175 from Oaxaca to Tuxtepec. You will pass through the town of Guelatao, where Benito Juárez was born, just before you get to Ixtlán. There are six bus departures daily to and from Oaxaca City.

For more information contact Gustavo Ramírez Santiago or Angélica Montes Rodríguez, Avenida General Fidencio Hernández #19, Ixtlán de Juárez, Oaxaca, 68725 Mexico, C.P., (955) 3-60-75 or 3-61-11, e-mail grsixt@antequera.com.

flora and fauna, although forestry threatens the region. Particularly destructive is "high grading," which harvests the best timber and leaves the rest to regenerate, impoverishing the forest. With the pines cleared, scrubs invade the open spaces and disallow natural pine regeneration.

THE COMMUNITY MUSEUM PROGRAM

Cultural tours have always been popular in Oaxaca. An association called **Museos Comunitarios de Estado de Oaxaca** offers ecological and cultural tours to traditional communities in the Central Valley and the Mixteca region. Travelers who arrange tours with this group can be assured of personal contact with local artisans, who offer craft demonstrations and are happy to explain how they learned and practice their craft. The focus of these tours is on human talents such as firecracker making, baking, traditional healing, and pottery. Options for travelers include visiting Zapotec weavers, Mixtec potters, and valley stone carvers.

Villagers are happy to explain to visitors the many uses of natural resources. They collect materials for natural dyes, plants for healing, and maguey for pulque (a fermented alcoholic beverage), and harvest cinnamon bark, ginger root, and coffee beans. Small groups can be provided bicycles and horses for some of the tours. Tickets are available at the SEDETUR office at Independencia 607, and at the Unión de Museos Comunitarios de Oaxaca, Tinoco y Palacios 311-16, (951) 6-57-86, e-mail muscoax@antequera.com.

The following is a list of community museums found in towns without Tourist Yu'u projects. These may be visited independently or through the Museos Comunitarios de Estado de Oaxaca organization.

San José el Mogote, Kilometer 12 on Highway 170. This is a farming community. Archaeological investigations began in 1966, and many artifacts are housed at a new community museum located in an old hacienda. The museum has some intriguing displays of Olmec art that dates back 2,000 years.

Santiago Suchilquitongo, Kilometer 33 on Highway 170. This museum offers exhibits of local stone carvings as well as an explanation of nearby tomb No. 5 of Cerro de la Campana, which describes eight generations of a pre-Hispanic ruling family.

San Pablo Huitzo, Kilometer 35 on Highway 170. This town is surrounded by alfalfa fields. The main square and the city hall are being restored by the state tourism office. Attention is currently focused on improvements at a Dominican church (which houses the museum) built in 1546 and to the central park, which is being replanted with locally grown palms, pine, and ficus to complement Huitzo's own 300-year-old cypress.

San Pablo Huixtepec, 40 kilometers (25 miles) from Oaxaca City on Highway 131. The museum has archaeological artifacts and a description of the town's main fiesta, which takes place at the end of May and early June.

San Martín Huamelulpan, about 10 kilometers (6.2 miles) north of the small city of Tlaxiaco on Highway 125. The museum here presents an extensive archaeological collection. Local healers take visitors on a hike to collect medicinal herbs and teach them how to prepare an herbal bath.

San Miguel del Progreso, 15 kilometers (9 miles) south of Tlaxiaco. This museum displays historical photographs and documents concerning land tenure, exhibits on the craft of weaving with the back-strap loom, and archaeological artifacts. Community guides take groups to a natural spring, show and explain the use of the terraces for agriculture, and demonstrate how the maguey is harvested.

Santa María Yucuhiti, 30 kilometers (19 miles) south of San Miguel, on an unpaved road. Local archaeological finds and Mixtec weavings are displayed; the town's historic struggles over land tenure are documented.

OAXACA CITY

Location: 450 km (280 mi.) S of Mexico City
Activities: Archaeology, museums, artesenía, horseback riding, hiking
For More Information: State tourism office, Independencia 607, (951) 4-17-78.

Located 5 hours south of Mexico City in a picturesque valley at an altitude of 1,546 meters (5,072 feet), Oaxaca's capital city enjoys a spring-like climate year-round. Two branches of the Sierra Madre Occidental converge in the center of the state of Oaxaca to create this fertile valley. The region produces a multitude of crops, including the maguey plant, which is used to make mezcal, a less-refined version of tequila.

Oaxaca's name comes from a mangled version of the Aztec settlement Huaxyacac (place of gourds). The Spanish occupied the area as early as 1521 and established their new settlement in 1529 around the present-day zócalo. Oaxaca was at first named Antequera, after a city in Spain. Antequera, however, was rechristened Oaxaca in 1532, and the city quickly became one of the most important agricultural and trading centers in the region.

Oaxaca was the birthplace of Mexico's only Indian president, Benito Juárez. Dictator Porfirio Díaz was also born in Oaxaca. Yet despite the importance of these leaders, political noblesse never fully translated into a national powerbase.

Oaxaca's pleasant subtropical climate drew nomadic families to Mitla

and nearby caves 10,000 years ago. Farming communities evolved in Abasolo, Tomaltepec, and El Mogote. The Zapotec kingdom Monte Albán emerged in 500 B.C., constructed on the site of a mountain that was leveled by the city's builders. For hundreds of years, the Dynasty of Monte Albán ruled this region. In the last years of the reign, Zapotec power became increasingly decentralized until it was abandoned around A.D. 700. At the city's peak, more than 25,000 people lived here. Many of the descendants continue to raise corn on terraces surrounding the ruins. The ancient city had a sophisticated water system that allowed the Zapotec to take advantage of every drop.

The best time to visit Oaxaca City is during the summer rainy season, when the surrounding cornfields are green. During the rest of the year, Oaxaca reverts to an ash-brown color.

Things to See and Do in Oaxaca City

In the center of Oaxaca City is one of the most charming zócalos in Mexico. The state tourism office, one block away at Independencia 601, is staffed by exceptionally helpful and well-informed personnel who can

239

Mitla ruins, near Oaxaca City

even field questions on nascent ecotourism developments. To the south of the zócalo are the **food markets**, where an entire block of the city resembles a giant kitchen. Vendors sell fresh local produce and regional specialties. Here, or in the local restaurants, you can try *la comida Oaxaqueña*—fried grasshoppers in chocolate and a spicy and intricate mole sauce.

Mid-winter can also be pleasant in Oaxaca and the Christmas season is a joy. On the night of December 23, a long line of visitors spirals around tables placed in the zócalo to take part in the **Noche de Rábanos** (Night of the Radishes). Legend tells of two Spanish friars who encouraged the Indians from the area surrounding Oaxaca to cultivate produce in the lowlands irrigated by the Atoyac River. One of the monks suggested that the farmers carve the radishes into grotesque shapes. This would entice people to visit the market and buy the produce. Whether his ploy worked or not is unclear, but the custom hangs on in this state where traditions reign. People come to admire the bizarre shapes local Oaxaqueño farmers have given to their radishes.

Just east of town and a $1 taxi ride away is **Ciudad de las Canteras**, a former quarry that has been converted into a pleasant city park. In the 1950s the mineral veins were diminishing and the quarry was abandoned.

Later it was used as a makeshift garbage dump. In 1992 the state government cleaned up the area and converted it into the gardens (complete with waterfall) you see today. This is a perfect place for picnics or leisurely book reading.

Santa María del Tule

The most famous tree in Mexico, and some say the largest cypress in the world, grows near Oaxaca City in the town of Santa Maria del Tule. This is a frequent stop on packaged tours of the region, but don't let its popularity deter you from visiting.

The cypress, known in Spanish as *ahuehuete*, is Mexico's national tree. According to legend, Hernán Cortés cried beneath the boughs of a cypress after the Aztecs (temporarily) defeated the Spanish on La Noche Triste (The Sad Night).

The town, 10 kilometers (6.2 miles) from Oaxaca en route to Mitla, boasts not just one, but eight extremely large and ancient cypress trees. The largest is more than 2,000 years old and has a circumference of 50 meters (164 feet). Imagine—this tree was a sapling at the time the civilization at Monte Albán flourished.

The trees are unique natural monuments, attractions for both locals and visitors alike. Unfortunately, the cypress trees are also case studies of how environmental changes have affected Oaxaca. Urbanization and increased irrigation for farming have diverted water from the aquifers. During the dry season the water table drops more than 6 meters (20 feet). According to the local environmental group Mi Amigo el Arbol, if only two of the underground micro-river basins were restored, there would be sufficient recharge of groundwater supplies to ensure the survival of these trees. But agricultural and urban expansion continue to claim the underground rivers, jeopardizing the trees' future.

There is frequent bus service from Oaxaca's second-class terminal to Santa Maria del Tule. If you take a package trip to the ruins, a brief stop here is usually included.

Tour Operators

San Felipe Riding Club, 10 minutes from the center of Oaxaca on the road toward Chigolera, (951) 5-68-64. Horseback riding costs $7 per hour. The trails weave through the valley floor and along the Atoyac River. Overnight packages are available.

Viajes Turisticos Mitla, Francisco Mina 518, (951) 4-31-52. Half-day tours ($10) combine visits to archaeological sites and regional markets; guides provide detailed explanations.

Getting to Oaxaca

Oaxaca's airport is 8 kilometers (5 miles) south of the city and has frequent flights to Mexico City, Tuxtla Gutiérrez, and other destinations. The city's first-class bus terminal is north of downtown on Calzada Niños Héroes de Chapultepec. Second-class bus service is available nine blocks west of the zócalo on Calle Trujano. It takes about 5 hours on a new tollroad to travel between Oaxaca City and Mexico City (sometimes it takes an hour just to get out of Mexico City).

Where to Stay in Oaxaca

Hotel Central, 20 de Noviembre 104, $5, (951) 6-59-71. Simple, clean rooms just a few blocks from the zócalo.

Other Villages in the Central Valley

There are several other villages in the region that are worth visiting for their unique arts and crafts.

*Artists in **Arrazola** produce the world-famous, brightly colored wooden animals known as alabrijes.*

***Ocotlán** is the home of painter Rodolfo Morales. The state tourism office, SEDETUR, is refurbishing the Palacio Municipal, which displays early paintings by Morales. Unfortunately, during repairs, several works were damaged when they were moved to a storehouse. The Palacio will be converted into a library and museum.*

***Santa María Atzompa** is just 20 minutes south of Oaxaca City. Artisans here make distinctive, utilitarian pottery. The town's eight-year-old cooperative has been a terrific success. Oaxaca's famed black pottery, the color of which comes from both the clay and the traditional baking process, is found at **San Bartolo Coyotepec**. Most homes in this region contain family pottery workshops. Buses and taxis are frequent.*

Hotel Gala, south of the zócalo at Bustamante 103, $30, (951) 4-22-51. Very clean and quiet hotel.

Hotel Señorial, Portal de Flores 6, $25, (951) 6-39-33. Pleasant hotel on the zócalo. Offers a great breakfast and lunch buffet.

Marqués de Valle, 5 de Mayo 300, $40, (951) 6-06-11 or, in the U.S., (800) 722-6466. Easily the best hotel in Oaxaca due to its elegance and location (right on the plaza).

Where to Eat in Oaxaca
La Catedral, Morelos 602, (951) 6-3285. Tables are arranged in a beautiful courtyard. The food is exceptional.

La Primavera, on the zócalo. Sample a large platter—enough for four people—of delicious Oaxaqueño specialties for $8. The restaurant is on the plaza, just below the overrated Cocina de Abuela.

MAZUNTE
Location: Near Puerto Angel on the Pacific coast, 50 km (31 mi.) east of Puerto Escondido
Activities: Turtle-watching, bird-watching, tours of nearby coffee plantations
For More Information: SEDETUR, Oaxaca's state tourism office

The small town of Mazunte is famous and infamous for sea turtles. The fishing village is home to the **Mexican National Turtle Center** (Centro Mexicano de la Tortuga, or CMT, 958/43-055, fax 958-43-063), a laboratory/aquarium dedicated to the study and protection of sea turtles. Facilities include a small gift store. Located in town on the Avenida Principal, the center is open Tuesday through Saturday from 10 a.m. to 4:30 p.m., and Sunday from 10 a.m. to 2:30 p.m. Tours are led by multilingual guides.

Nearby Escobilla Bay, where hundreds of Golfina and olive ridley turtles come to lay their eggs, is now a tourist attraction. The nesting season usually begins in May and lasts for several months. The turtles come to the beach in large numbers for a few nights after the full moon. The number of turtle nests increased from 60,000 in 1988 to nearly 700,000 in 1995. There is nothing particularly fancy here—a cooperative of ten families has constructed some rustic bungalows—and the town makes sleepy Puerto Angel look like a metropolis. But everyone is friendly and happy to share their stories of how Mazunte has changed.

Before the 1960s villagers would harvest only enough eggs to satisfy

La Reserva Indígena Los Chimalapas

The rural communities of San Miguel and Santa María Chimalapas, in the state of Oaxaca, have created their own biosphere reserve, La Reserva Indígena Los Chimalapas. This is one of the few examples of a community taking a leadership role in the creation of a federally recognized ecological reserve. Traditionally the government has simply told communities that a park was to be established. There are still numerous conflicts in the region, pitting logging interests against Zoque Indians. If you enter the reserve, be sure to go with a local.

Los Chimalapas is the northernmost example of a high perennial forest on the American continent. The region covers parts of three states: eastern Oaxaca, southeastern Veracruz, and western Chiapas. Of the approximately 2 million hectares (4,940,000 acres) of tropical forest remaining in Mexico, Chimalapas and its neighboring regions make up nearly half. It is also one of the richest and most productive ecosystems on the planet. One hectare (2.47 acres) of untouched tropical vegetation can house up to 900 plant and 200 animal species. The region's rugged topography ranges from lowland plains 200 meters (656 feet) above sea level to mountain peaks of nearly 2,400 meters (7,900 feet). Chimalapas forms the upper basin of the Coatzalcoalcos and Grijalva River systems, through which nearly one-fourth of Mexico's total surface water flows into the Gulf of Mexico. On the Pacific side, Chimalapas forests feed Mexico's most important coastal lagoons.

Unfortunately, a series of fires in the spring of 1998 broke out and claimed 165,000 hectares of this forest, which biologists estimate will take three centuries to recuperate. A citizen group, Maderas del Pueblo, has taken the lead in restoration and can use financial assistance. Contact Miguel Angel Garcia at (5) 605-5242 or at e-mail: pacto@laneta.apc.org.

the local demand for food and aphrodisiacs. But commercial trade and a boost in international demand raised the price on turtles, and the slaughterhouse became the town's major source of income. Then, in 1990, a national ban on killing sea turtles nearly destroyed the town's economy. To avoid going under, the town shifted its economy from turtle slaughter to turtle preservation—a practice, incidentally, much more attractive to tourists.

Plans remain down-to-earth. "We want to develop something practical, a little at a time—not stratospheric plans," says Mazunte Mayor Mario Corella. Locals point out that while all turtles should be cared for, the green turtle (*Chelonia mydas*) is relatively abundant while the leatherback turtle (*Dermochelys coriacea*) requires more protection.

As part of the economic plan, Ecosolar, a Mexico City–based environmental group, drew up details for sustainable development in the area. Another cooperative, Cosméticos Naturales de Mazunte, began making shampoo, hair conditioner, body oils, and deodorants from locally cultivated agricultural products.

Down the road is the successful Rincón Alegre coffee processing plant, run by the Cien Años de Soledad ejido. The Mazunte cooperative can arrange tours. Tours of the region's waterways and lagoons are also available.

Tours and Outfitters
Hidden Voyages Ecotours, Puerto Escondido, (958) 207-34. An experienced environmental travel company run by Canadian ornithologist Michael Malone.

Mazunte Cooperative, (958) 4-07-14, fax 4-04-72, Web site http://www .laneta.apc/mazunte. Offers lodging, guided turtle tours, and trips to nearby coffee plantations.

Getting to Mazunte
Mazunte is just west of Puerto Angel on Highway 200. There is local bus service about every half hour. Puerto Escondido is 50 kilometers (31 miles) to the west of Puerto Angel, and Pochutla is about the same distance to the east. Mexico City's southern bus station has a direct bus to Pochutla, which is just a 30-minute bus ride from Mazunte. Puerto Escondido has the closest domestic airport.

Where to Stay near Mazunte
The following are convenient places to stay for anyone exploring Oaxaca's Pacfic coast:

Hotel Soraya, Playa Principal, Puerto Angel, 958-43009, $25. Located across from the pier and next to the telephone company. Small hotel with air-conditioning and a restaurant with a good view of the water.

Posada Cañón Devata, Puerto Angel, (958) 430-48, e-mail lopezk@spin.com.mx, $30. The owners have reforested the canyon, which offers terrific half-day hikes. Their restaurant serves organic fruits and vegetables, cultivated either on the premises or in the sierra.

Rancho Cerro Largo, Pochutla, between Zipolite and Mazunte; $50, (958) 4-30-63. Deluxe cabins on an isolated beach. Gourmet food and vegetarian fare.

CHACAGUA LAGOON NATIONAL PARK
Location: 70 km (43 mi.) W of Puerto Escondido
Area: 14,175 hectares (35,000 acres)
Activities: Bird-watching, boat trips through the mangroves
For More Information: SECTUR or SEDETUR, (915) 4-17-78

This national park (also spelled Chacahua) comprises a series of lagoons and beach shoreline between the towns of Santiago Jamiltepec and Puerto Escondido, west of Highway 200. The park includes savannas, coastal dunes, and mangroves. Local fauna include white egrets, iguanas, croco-diles, shrimp, and freshwater crabs. Crocodiles may be viewed in captivity at the park's small research facility (consisting of a large fenced-in area and a hut).

The native species of crocodile in the Chacagua region is the Ameri-can crocodile (*Crocodylus acutus*); however, most of the specimens held in captivity at Lagunas de Chacagua are Morelet's crocodiles (*Crocodylus moreleti*), also known as Central American crocodiles (*cocodrilo de pántano* in Spanish). This species is not native to the Pacific coast—its natural distribution is along the Gulf of Mexico drainage including coastal areas and the Yucatán Peninsula into Belize and Guatemala. It was brought in for farming and some turtles escaped and established a population in the wetlands.

Chacagua is a perfect place for bird-watching. The best months are March and April, when wood storks and roseate spoonbills nest. Locally managed canoes, or lanchas, take travelers for 2-hour tours of the man-groves from the town of Zapotalito on the eastern side of the park. Boat-men charge about $50 for a day-trip for up to ten passengers. A bargain, but you probably won't get an English-speaking guide. Request a visit to Cerro Hermoso beach, where you can swim and snorkel. There is also a

Touring the Coffee Towns

Oaxaca's coffee-producing plantations and towns offer spectacular views, colorful butterflies, exotic birds and plants, and friendly people. Plume Hidalgo, for example, a town of 4,000 located high in the Sierra, north of Puerto Angel and Huatulco, is famous for the "Café Pluma" coffee grown nearby. Town residents would like to see agricultural tourism contribute to the economy of the village. The community hopes to reintroduce populations of native mammals such as deer and river otter. The growers would like the government to declare their 30,000 hectares (74,000 acres) an ecological reserve.

Almost 90 percent of coffee producers in Oaxaca cultivate fewer than 5 hectares (12.4 acres). The producers grow organic coffee, which requires traditional agricultural techniques and sells for 15 cents more per pound than regular coffee. Unlike Central American plantations, which are cultivated in a manner that destroys the forest, the plantations in Oaxaca are sheltered within the existing forest canopy. Traditional coffee culture techniques do not clear-cut or use commercial pesticides, chemical fertilizers, or harvesting machines. Hand labor is essential for carefully removing competing shrubs, planting new coffee bushes, pruning the coffee and shade trees, and harvesting the beans. The farms are typically family managed.

Coffee farms can be excellent birding sites. The uppermost canopy provides habitat for insects, which are consumed by the birds. The trees also support epiphytes, which are home and watering holes for the spiders, frogs, and snails in the forest.

For more information on coffee producing towns and plantations, contact Alberto Pérez Mariscal at the Unión Estatal de Productores de Cafe, Posada la Casa de la Tía, Cinco de Mayo 108, Centro, Oaxaca 68000 Oaxaca.

scientific research center where researchers are breeding crocodiles. You can arrange a tour on site or from Puerto Escondido's larger hotels.

You might also want to visit **Laguna Manialtepec Lagoon**, 10 kilometers (6.2 miles) toward Puerto Escondido. During the rainy season the Manialtepec River breaks through the sandbar, turning the mangrove-fringed lagoon into a populated estuary. Like Chacagua, this area attracts hundreds of birds, including cormorant, anhinga, heron (including great blue, little blue, and black-crowned night heron), ibis, parrots, egrets, ducks, and jacanas (lily walkers).

Tours and Outfitters
Turismo Rodemar, Av. Pérez Gasca 905, Puerto Escondido, (958) 207-37 or 207-34, fax 207-89. Full-day trips to Chacagua National Park and the Sierra Madre Sur jungle from $20 per person.

Getting to Chacagua
To get to the park, travel southeast from Santa Rosa on Highway 200. At Kilometer 82, turn south onto the dirt road to Zapotalito. The park entrance is off this dirt road.

Where to Stay near Chacagua Lagoon National Park
See "Where to Stay near Mazunte."

CHIAPAS

Chiapas is a magical state with outstanding natural resources and abundant biodiversity. But older *Chiapenecos* can remember when the landscape was even greener and the wildlife more abundant. Such is the legacy of the 20th century.

Chiapas was a disputed territory in the 19th century, claimed by both Mexico and Guatemala. While Chiapas forms part of the Mexican Republic, it is the only state with legal authority to separate from the Republic, much like Texas in the United States. In Chiapas, ecological zones and cultural traditions easily cross borders.

Chiapas is the country's primary producer of coffee and bananas; the climate here is tropical and humid. The state accounts for almost a quarter of Mexico's water resources and houses Mexico's three largest dams, at Malpaso, Chicoasén, and Angostura, which generate almost 20 percent of the nation's electricity. Unfortunately, the dams created lakes that submerged more than 200,000 hectares (494,000 acres) of productive farm-

The Miguel Alvarez del Toro Zoo in Tuxtla Guttiérez features wildlife from Chiapas

land in the Central Valley. Campesinos were crowded even more, leading to further deforestation in the surrounding hills. Plans are underway to dam the Usumacinta River to provide energy for both Mexico and Guatemala.

On January 1, 1994, several hundred rebels of the Zapatista National Liberation Army (EZLN) seized towns in central and eastern Chiapas. Within two weeks the government's forces had forced the EZLN into retreat. A dialogue ensued that spurred the nation and the world to review Mexico's official policy toward indigenous peoples, land tenure issues, and agriculture. Ironically, instead of halting or diminishing tourism, the rebellion sparked a renaissance in political tourism.

The Zapatistas' key demand is for land and land tenure. In a review of the subject, Chiapaneco environmental scholar Hugo Guillén Trujillo concludes that conflicting land tenure rights have caused much of the ecological destruction and that only by resolving land-use and land-rights issues is conservation possible.

Chiapas became chic in the 1990s. Currently, San Cristóbal de las Casas (one of the towns seized by the Zapatistas) depends on tourism for 95 percent of its income base. The question now is whether this rise in tourism can be sustained and, more importantly, if there are ways for the income to go directly to the lower- and middle-class Chiapenecos. Traditional tourism mostly has benefited the rich residents of San Cristóbal and Tuxtla Gutiérrez.

The development of the cattle industry in the early 1950s sparked a battle between ranchers and native communities in Chiapas. From 1950 to 1985, both agricultural cultivation and the state's population growth quadrupled, but the number of cattle sextupled. In a practice that continues today, ranchers would rent land from ejidatarios, clear it of trees, then, when the land was completely grazed, move on to other untouched areas. This inefficient grazing method has turned these once-beautiful forests into wastelands.

More species of birds have been identified in Chiapas (600 in total) than in all of Europe. Tropical birds here include the toucan, scarlet macaw, flamingo, parrot, hummingbird, pheasant, quetzal, and wild turkey.

A Rich Land, a Poor People

Because it's situated at the intersection of tropical weather systems, southern Chiapas receives abundant rainfall, which keeps the region exceptionally green throughout the year. With fertile farmland, robust pine and oak forests, and an abundance of flora and fauna, southern Mexico is, at least environmentally speaking, a rich land. Yet despite the wealth of natural resources, most of the people here are poor and are caught up in a struggle for social justice.

There are many examples of environmental paradox (or economic injustice) in this state. Although the state is a leading producer of beef, this commodity is simply beyond the budget of most Chiapenecos. Second, while Chiapas provides half of Mexico's hydroelectric power, only a third of the state's households are hooked up to the electricity grid. In addition, prices for hooking up to the grid are higher in Chiapas than in other regions of Mexico, prompting several towns to stop paying their electricity bills and demand fair treatment. Because few of the homes are wired for electricity, this necessitates the collection of firewood for fuel and threatens nearby forests with deforestation.

Is This Region Safe for Travlers?

Travelers heading to Chiapas should be aware that the region is the epicenter of political problems in southern Mexico and there have been outbreaks of violence in recent years. However, since the 1994 Zapatista insurrection, tourism has increased, not decreased in this region. Be sensitive to the realities and the dangers here. If traveling in the forests, take a local guide or participate in an organized tour. Bus travel and in particular organized tours offer safe transportation to many of the destinations described in this book.

TUXTLA GUTIERREZ

Location: Western Chiapas, 83 km (51 mi.) N of San Cristóbal de las Casas
Activities: Zoo, museums, boat rides in the Sumidero Canyon
For More Information: Tourism office, west side of town on Belisario Dominguez 950, (961) 3-9396, 3-9397, or toll-free in Mexico 91 (800) 28-035

Tuxtla Gutiérrez (population 240,000) has been the capital of Chiapas since 1892. Entrenched in the tropics, the city is 526 meters (1,725 feet) above sea level and can be very hot. If you pass through town without stopping, you're missing some of the best that Mexico has to offer ecotourists.

The city is world-famous for its **Institute of Natural History** and the **Miguel Alvarez del Toro Zoo**, a modern transformation of a zoo originally founded in 1942 by Eliseo Palacios. Located 15 minutes south of downtown on the El Zapotal hillside, the 139-hectare (343-acre) zoo contains only animals from Chiapas, including boars, mountain deer, badgers, pheasants, tapir, black jaguars, and *pavones* (the *pavon*, a large turkey used as the symbol of the zoo, is endemic to Chiapas and in danger of extinction). "Natural" barriers are used instead of cages, and the animals' surroundings mimic their native habitats. Of the zoo's 213 species, 90 percent are in danger of extinction.

The zoo even has its own jungle, with *zapote*, *amate*, *jocotillo*, and cedar trees. A 2.5-kilometer (1.6-mile) trail winds through the forest and allows visitors to see animals in natural enclosures. A half-million people visit every year, yet it never feels crowded. This could be the finest zoo in all of Latin America. It is open Tuesday through Sunday from 8:30 a.m. to 5 p.m. There is no entrance fee, but voluntary contributions are welcome.

Taxis from the center of Tuxtla Gutiérrez to the zoo cost around $3. Buses leave three times every hour from the corner of 1 Ote Sur and 7 Sur Ote, seven blocks south of the zócalo. Take the bus marked "Cerro Hueco."

Another attraction in the city is the **Faustino Miranda Botanical Garden,** located in Madero Park. The garden was created under the direction of Faustino Miranda, author of the book *The Vegetation of Chiapas*, a classic text for those interested in the state's environment. The garden covers 4.4 hectares (10.9 acres) on the banks of the Sabinal River and showcases local species. It is open Tuesday through Sunday from 7 a.m. to 6 p.m.

Getting to Tuxtla Gutiérrez
Two airports serve the city. Aeropuerto San Juan is 35 kilometers (22 miles) west on Highway 190; Aeropuerto Terán is closer to town and is being remodeled to accommodate larger planes. There is no central bus station in town. The Omnibus Cristóbal Colón is on the corner of 2 Norte Ote and 2 Pte Norte, just two blocks northwest of the zócalo. The ADO station is on the corner of 5 Sur Pte and 9 Pte Sur.

Where to Stay in Tuxtla Gutiérrez
Most of the downtown hotels appear a bit ragged compared to what Oaxaca and San Cristóbal have to offer.

251

Gran Hotel Humberto, Avenida Central Pte 180 at 1 Pte Norte, $25. Next door to the Hotel Esponda.

Hotel Esponda, 1 Pte Norte 142, a block from the zócalo, $15. The staff is helpful and local phone calls are free.

SUMIDERO CANYON NATIONAL PARK

Location: 15 minutes S of Tuxtla Gutiérrez
Area: 21,789 hectares (53,819 acres)
Activities: Boat trips through the reservoir
For More Information: SECTUR, (961) 3-9396, 3-9397, or toll-free in Mexico 01 (800) 28-035

The spectacular, 1,000-meter-deep (3,300-foot) Sumidero Canyon was the stage for an epic battle between the Spanish and the Chiapanecan Indians, who chose to jump into the sacred canyon rather than submit to the invaders. More recently, engineers tamed the whitewater by building the Chicoasén Dam, the fifth-highest dam in the world.

The canyon offers spectacular scenery for visitors, who can visit by road or by river. A paved road has five different lookouts offering peaceful

Boating in Sumidero Canyon

views of the canyon: La Ceiba, La Coyota, El Roblar, El Tepehuaje, and Los Chiapas; the final site is located just 22 kilometers (14 miles) from the state capital. Here, most tours stop at the La Atalaya restaurant, which serves typical food and beverages.

Two- to 3-hour boat trips through the reservoir can be arranged from the Cahuare resort pier on the Grijalva River, outside the town of Chiapa de Corzo. The launches speed through the reservoir and take tourists to various rock formations along the canyon walls. It's 35 kilometers (22 miles) from the pier to the Chicoasén Dam, where walls 900 to 1,000 meters (2,900 to 2,300 feet) tall tower over the river.

"Christmas Tree" rock formation in Sumidero Canyon

The trips, which cost $25 total for all those on board, can accommodate up to ten passengers.

A variety of birds are abundant here—including white herons, cormorants, and kingfishers—as are monkeys, raccoons, iguanas, and crocodiles. The area is also famous for its butterflies. The vegetation is rich due to the area's high humidity and fertile soil. At the canyon's entrance are the ruins of a Chiapanecan ceremonial center, which some archaeologists suggest may have been dedicated to a water goddess.

Please note that the river is not suitable for swimming. Tuxtla Gutiérrez lacks a water treatment plant and instead diverts its sewage into El Sabinal River, which empties into the Grijalva.

Getting to Sumidero Canyon National Park

If you don't have your own transportation, you can take the bus from Transportes Cañón del Sumidero at 1 Norte Ote 1121, eight blocks east of the zócalo.

SAN CRISTOBAL DE LAS CASAS

Location: 83 km (51 mi.) S of Tuxtla Gutiérrez, in the Valley of Jovel
Activities: Hiking, bike riding, horseback riding, Spanish instruction
For More Information: SECTUR, (961) 3-9396, 3-9397, or, toll-free in Mexico, 91 (800) 28-035

The favorite town for travelers in Chiapas is San Cristóbal de las Casas, much smaller (population 90,000) and quieter than Tuxtla Gutiérrez. This colonial gem, complete with cobblestone streets and numerous plazas, churches, and traditional architecture, was founded by Spanish conqueror Diego de Mazariegos in 1528. Fray Bartolomé de las Casas, for whom the city is named, was the first Episcopal Chair. He was also one of the first and greatest defenders of the indigenous population. San Cristóbal was the original capital of Chiapas until 1892. The town serves as the commercial center for the indigenous villages in the surrounding area.

If you fortunate enough to have a bicycle, definitely ride what Eric Ellman, author of *Bicycling in Mexico*, calls the "highway to heaven." The trip from San Cristóbal to Palenque couldn't be more scenic. For information about bike rentals, see "Tours and Outfitters," below.

Things to See and Do in San Cristóbal de las Casas
The **Huitepec Ecological Reserve** is located just 3.5 kilometers (2.2 miles) from the center of town on the road to Chamula. The reserve is located on the eastern side of the Muktevitz volcano, one of the highest peaks (2,700 meters or 8,860 feet) in the Central Chiapas mountain

Materials for handmade paper production

range. A 2-kilometer (1.2-mile) interpretive trail winds through the pine-oak forest of the 135-hectare (333-acre) nature reserve. The area boasts 60 local species of birds and 40 migratory species that nest here during the winter. The reserve is managed by the local environmental group Pronatura Chiapas, at María Adelina Flores 21.

A very interesting workshop is open to the public and shows how paper is recycled in an artistic fashion. **Taller Leñateros** (Flavio Paniagua No. 54, 967-8-51-74) is an artisan society of Maya who have produced handmade paper, books, and block prints for than 20 years. The raw material comes from the nearby fields and forests. The paper makers use flowers, lichen, and banana fronds, along with recycled newspaper and rags.

La Pared bookstore has both English- and Spanish-language books. Owner Dana Burton is an enthusiastic supporter of the local chapter of Pronatura. La Pared is located at Miguel Hidalgo, a block from the zócalo; tel./fax (967) 8-63-67.

Na Bolom

Na Bolom (which means "house of the jaguar" in the language of the Tzotzil, one of the indigenous groups that populate the Chiapas highlands) is a research center committed to the protection and reforestation of the Lacandón forest and its indigenous inhabitants. Located at Guerrero 33 on the corner of Chiapa de Corzo, in the northwest section of town, the center provides information about and maps of the forest. The center is housed in a 19th-century colonial building that was the residence of founders Franz and Gertrude Blom. Franz was a Danish-born archaeologist who came to Mexico in 1919 to work for a Veracruz oil company. In 1943 he met Gertrude Duby, a Swiss journalist. They married in 1950 and began to convert their house into an institute for scientific studies. At first, the Bloms' extensive work with the Lacandones was anthropological. But as the deforestation of the Lacandón forest accelerated, their focus shifted to conservation.

Since 1975 the center has supported a nursery that gives away trees to people in Chiapas. Na Bolom plants some 35,000 trees each year. In 1978 Blom and other conservationists urged the government to create the Montes Azules Biosphere Reserve to protect the Lacandón rain forest.

Tours and Outfitters

Agencia de Viajes Chincultic, Real de Guadalupe No. 34, (967) 8-09-57. Offers three-day tours of the Lacandón forest via the town of Lacanja. The cost is $130 per person. The agency is part of the Posada de Margarita, a friendly home away from home for backpackers.

Altura Tours, 1 de Marzo 6D at Cafe Altura, San Cristobal de las Casa, (967) 8-40-38. Offers walking tours of the region that visit the Huitepec Reserve, an ecological center just 3.5 kilometers (2.2 miles) from town, and the nearby Zinacantan Valley. Cafe Altura specializes in organic food and owner Roland Lehman is fluent in German, Spanish, and English. The cafe also operates as a small tour company, offering ecotours in the Soconusco region of Chiapas. Three-, four-, or seven-day trips visit the Finca Irlanda coffee plantation and the Rancho Tepuzapa organic cocoa and fruit plantation. The seven-day trip also visits El Cabildo mangrove swamp.

ATC Tour Operators, Avenida 16 de Septiembre #16, (967) 8-25-50 or 8-25-57, fax 8-31-45, e-mail atc@sancristobal.podernet.com.mx. This agency offers a variety of tourism packages, including four-day trips ($250) to the more notable destinations in central Chiapas—Sumidero Canyon, Agua Azul, and Chamula. An eight-day trip that ventures farther east to the Yaxchilán ruins and Palenque costs $600.

Bicirent, Belisario Domínguez 5B. Rents bicycles.

Los Pinguinos, Avenida 5 de Mayo 10B. Rents bicycles.

Viajes Pakal, Cuauhtémoc 6-A, at the corner of Hidalgo, tel./fax (967) 8-28-19, fax 8-28-18. Offers packaged tours of the Mundo Maya. Arranges single-day and multi-day rafting trips in the Sumidero Canyon.

Getting to San Cristóbal de las Casas
The Cristóbal Colon bus station occupies the corner of Insurgentes and the Pan American Highway on the south end of town. There is frequent service to Tuxtla Gutierrez as well as Palenque and Comitán.

Where to Stay in San Cristóbal de las Casas
Hotel Real del Valle, Calle Real de Guadalupe 14, $10, (967) 8-06-80, fax (967) 8-39-55. Clean hotel with an atmospheric patio. Also offers walking tours of the region ($6) that include visits to the Almononga scenic overview, the Fogotico-Arcotelte River, Huitepec, and the Rancho Nuevo caves. Tours are offered daily except Sunday, from about 9 a.m. to 2 p.m. A similar 5-hour horseback trip ($7) travels to Chamula and the Rancho Nuevo caves.

Posada Vallarta, Hemanos Pineda 10, $9, (967) 8-0465. Located three blocks from the Cristóbal Colón bus station, this is one of the cleanest and best-run inexpensive hotels I've ever stayed at in Mexico.

Where to Eat in San Cristóbal de las Casas

Casa de Buen Cafe, Avenida Cristóbal Colón #9B. Owner Patricia Luna serves coffee from cooperatives in Motozintla.

Centro Cultural El Puente, Real de Guadalupe 55, 2½ blocks from the zócalo. The center houses the Centro Bilingue language school, a fine vegetarian restaurant, a small cinema, and an art gallery.

La Casa del Pan, Dr. Navarro 10 (north of the zócalo), e-mail danamex @mail.internet.com.mx. Serves whole-grain breads. Check out the altar to the Virgin of Guadalupe, Buddha, and Zapata. The cozy restaurant is also the place to check into environmental tours to Laguna Miramar in the Lacandón forest.

La Selva Café, Crescencio Rosas 9, (963) 2-18-87. Serves internationally certified organic coffee in a coffeeshop that is usually clean, even by the high standards of San Cristóbal. The store has a rack of the most recent newspapers and magazines. The coffee is produced by a group of coffee growers in Chiapas called Cafes Orgánicos de Chiapas. For information on the project, call the café or send an e-mail to uncafesur@laneta.apc.org.

CHIAPAS WATERFALLS

On the road east from San Cristóbal to Palenque, travelers will pass through cattle and coffee country. The first major town is **Ocosingo**, 86 kilometers (53 miles) from San Cristóbal and 95 kilometers (59 miles) from Palenque. According to Russell Greenberg, ornithologist and director of the Smithsonian Migratory Bird Center, more than 140 species of birds have been found in the shaded, traditionally managed coffee farms of Ocosingo. In stark contrast, research done in other countries shows only five or six species inhabiting full-sun coffee fields.

Between Ocosingo and Palenque, you will find a series of impressive waterfalls: Misol Ha, Agua Azul, and Agua Clara. These are all located within an easy day trip by bus from San Cristóbal or Palenque. There are also rustic accommodations. If you're going to pass through this part of the country, spend a day or two.

Agua Azul National Park is located on Highway 199, 45 kilometers (28 miles) south of Palenque and 40 kilometers (25 miles) north of Ocosingo. This national park was designated as such for its indescribable beauty. The falls are formed by the indigo-blue Yax River cascading down a staircase of 500 individual falls. There is a swimming area, and the water is warm. Be cautious: Whirlpools and underwater currents can be fatal. Admission is $1 per car or 50 cents per person.

Agua Clara, a converted cattle ranch just 8 kilometers (5 miles) from Agua Azul National Park and 58 kilometers (36 miles) west of Palenque, offers alternative lodging. The ranch is right on the Shumulha River and is accessible from the highway to Ocosingo. Guests may rent kayaks and small boats to explore the river or trek 2 kilometers (1.2 miles) through the reserve to a quiet natural pool created by the confluence of the Tulija and Shumulha Rivers.

Agua Clara is a new project, established in the summer of 1996, that seeks to restore former pasture and protect the existing forest. Optional tours include horseback rides to the town of La Junta, where the Shumulha and Tulija Rivers join. The cost is $10 per person. You can also hire a guide for bird-watching.

The waterfalls at **Misol-Ha** are about 20 kilometers (12 miles) from Palenque. They stand at an impressive 40 meters (131 feet) high. This location is less touristy than Agua Azul, but it's definitely not isolated. Watch your step on the slippery trail to the natural pool and falls. From a distance the mist generated from the waterfalls seems to hide the attraction from view, but you'll hear the roar of the falls. Amenities here include a restaurant and lodging. The entrance fee is about $2.

Getting to Chiapas Waterfalls

It's fairly easy to visit the waterfalls. Buses stop either at or within a short walk of the falls from either Palenque or San Cristóbal. From Palenque, combis take passengers for a quick stop at Misol-Ha and a 3-hour break at Agua Azul before returning to Palenque. But if you have more than a few hours, plan on staying the night.

Where to Stay near Chiapas Waterfalls

Agua Clara, contact Sociedad de Trabajadores Agrícolas de los Altos de Chiapas (STAACH), Tuxtla Gutiérrez, (961) 1-14-10, e-mail jkinalti @chisnet.com.mx or staach@laneta.apc.org. There are nine rooms ($30/night) and a restaurant.

Misol-Ha. Cabins for two people cost $25 per night, those that accommodate four are $55. Daily meals cost $10. Camping is allowed and hammocks are available for rent.

Rancho Esmeralda, Ocosingo, about halfway between San Cristóbal de las Casas and Palenque, in the Ocosingo valley. The 10.5-hectare

(26-acre) guest ranch is located in a tropical highlands setting just a 10-minute walk from the Tonina Maya ruins.

The ranch offers horseback riding, hiking, and bird-watching. Cabins, which do not have electricity or phones, cost $22 for two people. March through May are the "driest" months, but visitors should be prepared for showers throughout the year.

PALENQUE
Location: *143 km (88 mi.) from Villahermosa, Tabasco, in NE Chiapas*
Activities: *Archaeology, hub for travel to Agua Azul and Misol-Ha to the west and Bonampak and Yaxchilán to the south*
For More Information: *Tourism office in Casa de la Cultura at Jimenez and 5 de Mayo in Palenque, (934) 5-08-26*

With a population of 70,000, the modern-day town of Palenque (this is a new name; locals still call it Santo Domingo) is the staging area for trips further into the Lacandón forest. Historians and archaeologists compare the splendor of Palenque to the classical cities of Greece and Rome. This was one of the most powerful of the late-classic Maya cities and is home to one of the most intimate sets of ruins in Mexico.

While the most spectacular buildings have been cleared of their forest cover, more than 300 structures remain buried. Palenque became famous after its description by author John Lloyd Stephens and illustrator Frederick Catherwood in the 1841 best-seller *Incidents of Travel in Central America, Chiapas and Yucatán.*

The most impressive building here, and perhaps Mexico's most ornate pyramid, is the Pyramid of Inscriptions. Unlike the majority of Mesoamerican pyramids, which do not include secret passageways or tombs, this one has contained the tomb of Lord Pacal since his death in A.D. 683. Pacal's heirs ruled the empire for several generations, but Palenque was abandoned around A.D. 900. Visitors can go walk through the passages and visit the tomb area.

From the ruins you can see the low-lying coastal plains which stretch north to the Gulf of Mexico. To the south are the Selva Lacandona and the Montes Biosphere Reserve. These tropical evergreen forests are home to about 350 bird species. You don't have to be a checklist bird-watcher to appreciate the wildlife.

Tours and Outfitters
There are a great deal of travel agencies in Palenque offering tours to Yaxchilán, Bonampak, and a border crossing to Flores, Guatemala. Tour quality varies, so ask others for advice.

Turismo Quetzal, Av. Juarez 135, (934) 506-01. Offers tours to Yax-chilán and to the nearby waterfalls.

Getting to Palanque
National and international airlines fly to Villahermosa and Tuxtla Gutiérrez. From Villahermosa it's just 143 kilometers (88 miles) by car or bus to Palanque.

Where to Stay in Palanque
Hotel Casa de Pakal, Avenida Juarez 10, (934) 5-0393, $30. Modern four-story hotel. Rooms have air-conditioning.

Hotel Kashlan, Avenida 5 de Mayo 105 near Allende, (934) 5-0297, $20. Clean rooms with ceiling fans.

SELVA LACANDONA

South of Palenque lies the Selva Lacandona (Lacandón forest), which includes the Montes Azules Biosphere Reserve, four natural protected areas (Bonampak, Yaxchilán, Chan Kin, and Lacantum), and the communal reserve La Cojolita (originally called Yaxbe). On the fringes of the reserve are ejidos which cater to tourists. Here it is evident that nature tourism has the potential to bring a much-needed economic boost to rural communities throughout Mexico. While political pressures have erupted in the past few years in this state, tourists are generally safe. To offset potential problems, hire a Lacandón as a guide. That way the money stays in the community and the campesinos have a chance to earn a sustainable living.

Deforestation in this region has been severe. The Selva Lacandona originally occupied about 1.5 million hectares (3.7 million acres), most of it tropical rain forest. Less than one-third of the original forest remains. Currently, ecotourism is not strong enough to replace logging as the region's economic base. Still, environmental tourism is taking a big leap forward, and your visit will help. Ask questions. Support the operations that support the local communities and conservation.

MONTES AZULES BIOSPHERE RESERVE
Location: SE Chiapas, between the Northern Sierra and the Usumacinta River
Area: *331,200 hectares (818,064 acres)*

Activities: Hiking, archaeology, cultural tourism, bird-watching
For More Information: Conservation International-Chiapas, (96)
151951, e-mail CI-Chiapas@conservation.org

After long and persistent pleas from environmental groups, in 1978 the Mexican government declared this large chunk of Lacandón rain forest the Montes Azules Biosphere Reserve. Together with the Petén rain forest in Guatemala, the Lacandón forest forms the largest tract of tropical rain forest north of the Brazilian Amazon.

Lacandón people call themselves Hachack-Winick (The True People), and a community bond remains strong. The forest is rich in precious woods, and animals that live here include howler monkeys, jaguars, tapirs, crocodiles, and toucans.

Travelers can access the reserve from both the eastern and western sections. On the eastern and southern side, the best access is from Lacanja or **Frontera Corozal**, towns with access to the **Bonampak** and **Yaxchilán** archaeological sites. On the western side, a community project sympathetic to the Zapatistas is located near Miramar Lagoon.

The Road South from Palenque

In 1985 the Mexican government constructed an unpaved highway along the Chiapas/Guatemala border. This road leads to the Maya ruins of Bonampak, famous for its murals, and to Frontera Corozal, the departure point for the 45-minute downriver boat trip to Yaxchilán, famous for its sculptures and for its location on the Usumacinta River. Trails are cut through the jungle that lead to various acropoli. Via Frontera Corozal you can also travel to Flores, Guatemala, and visit the ruins at Tikal National Park.

Getting to the Montes Azules Biosphere Reserve

Buses leave daily from Palenque to Lacanja Chansayab and Frontera Corozal. Small airplanes can also be contracted from Palenque, Comitán, Tuxtla Gutiérrez, and San Cristóbal de las Casas.

Where to Stay near the Montes Azules Biosphere Reserve

Accommodations in the Selva Lacandona are primitive. Because of continuing changes in Chiapas, it's a good idea to ask your fellow travelers what they recommend. The following locations are all community-based tourism centers. They offer rustic cabins, good guides, and a chance to see a beautiful forest.

Ara Macao, south of Escudo Jaguar; contact Enrique Galvez in Tuxtla

Gutiérrez, (961) 534-76, fax 265-05. Located in tropical rain forest on the Lacantun River, the town of Ara Macao has recently opened an eco-tourism center that includes cabins and a restaurant. Among the rare species in the area are crocodiles, ocelots, and the scarlet macaw. A cabin for four people costs $85 per night; a cabin for two, $60. Daily meals cost about $25. Renting a boat to explore the Lacantun River costs $10. Guides organize trips into the Montes Azules Biosphere Reserve for $10 per person. From Palenque, take a bus to Pico de Oro and, from there, a minibus to Ara Macao. There are also buses from Frontera Corozal to Ara Macao.

Escudo Jaguar, 20 kilometers (12 miles) from the highway intersection of Crucero Corozal in the town of Frontera Corozal. This tourism center offers rustic lodging and a restaurant. Simple cabins for two people cost $67 per night, "duplex" cabins for four cost $85 per night, and daily meals cost $24. The community also offers tours to Yaxchilán for $8 per person or to the Isla Frontera for $4.

To reach the Escudo Jaguar center, take a bus from Palenque to Frontera Corozal, 147 kilometers (91 miles) away. Just before the town is a dirt road that leads to Escudo Jaguar, 20 kilometers (12 miles) away. For reservations and information, contact Luis Arcos Pérez, *domicilio conocido*, Frontera Corozal, Chiapas, (934) 5-03-56.

Lacanja Chansayab, 120 kilometers (75 miles) south of Palenque and 30 kilometers (18 miles) west of Frontera Corozal. Three of the 60 families in this town have set up bungalows for ecotourists; they also offer guided tours to the Bonampak ruins and environmental trips into the forest. Kim Bor has been spearheading ecotourism in this region for the longest time.

Las Guacamayas, Sociedad de Trabajadores Agrícolas de los Altos de Chiapas (STAACH), Tuxtla Gutiérrez, (961) 1-14-10, e-mail jkinalti @chisnet.com.mx or staach@laneta.apc.org. This new ecotourism resort is in the ejido Reforma Agraria 225 kilometers (140 miles) from Palenque. The town is on the same highway as Frontera Corozal. You'll pass San Javier, Zamora, and Pico de Oro before you come to a marked intersection, from which the remaining 45 kilometers (28 miles) to the ejido is a dirt road. The rustic tourism complex offers 5-hour hikes ($10) and trips on the Lacantun River. One of the trips includes a short pilgrimage to a 200-year-old ceiba tree more than 30 meters in diameter. This trip lasts 90 minutes and costs $40 for the lancha for a group of up to ten people.

LAKE MIRAMAR
Location: Part of the Montes Azules Biosphere Reserve
Area: 19 sq. km (12 sq. mi.)
Activities: Swimming, boating, hiking
For More Information: Dana Foundation at La Casa de Pan restaurant,
Dr. Navarro 10, Barrio El Cerrillo, San Cristobal de las Casas, (967) 8-04-
68, fax (967) 8-43-07, e-mail danamex@mail.internet.com.mx

A new community ecotourism project has begun in the ejido Emiliano
Zapata, near Lake Miramar, the largest (19 square kilometers) lake on
the western portion of the reserve. It sits within a ring of mountains
southeast of Ocosingo. Here you'll find caves, archaeological sites, and
hiking in a high evergreen forest. The ejido is surrounded by mountains,
humid tropical jungle, the San Quintin Valley, and the Jataté, Perlas, and
Azul Rivers.

Tourist access is through the community of Emiliano Zapata. It's
another 7-kilometer (4.5-mile) hike to the lake, where you'll find a
traditional-style communal house for travelers. The area is also suitable
for tent camping. The ejido has a number of common-sense rules for visitors: (1) Use the established latrines, (2) Separate garbage and deposit it
in the appropriate location, (3) Do not use detergent in the lake, and (4)
Do not use drugs or drink alcoholic beverages.

The ejido has a cooperative store where staples can be purchased.
There are also handicrafts for sale. This is the interior jungle, so if you
want to buy anything, bring cash, not traveler's checks or credit cards.
The project helps provide financial resources for the protection and conservation of the Lacandón forest.

Tours and Outfitters
Fernando Ochoa, Dr. Navarro 10, Barrio del Cerillo, San Cristóbal de
las Casas, (967) 80468, e-mail jovel@sancristobal@podernet.com.mx.
Fernando Ochoa leads groups of five to ten people into the area. A four-
day trip from San Cristóbal costs $180 per person using ground trans-
portation or $280 per person using air and ground transportation. The
trip includes a boat ride to a small island on the lake and a visit to its
archaeological site.

Getting to Lake Miramar
Take the bus from Ocosingo to San Quintin/ejido Emiliano Zapata. The
trip takes about 5 hours and costs $5. You can also contract a small air-
plane from Ocosingo or Comitán, or travel by motorboat from Atatitlán
via the Jataté River.

LAGUNAS DE MONTEBELLO NATIONAL PARK

Location: 60 km (37 mi.) SE of Comitán
Area: 7,000 hectares (17,290 acres)
Activities: Picnicking
For More Information: SECTUR, (961) 3-9396, 3-9397, or toll-free
in Mexico, 01 (800) 28-035

Created in 1959, this national park was the first in Chiapas. Located
3 hours southeast of San Cristóbal de las Casas, the park contains 59
lakes. Chains of former cenotes scattered throughout pine and oak groves,
the multicolored lakes range in hue from emerald-green to a dark violet.
The colors vary due to several factors including the type of soil on the bottom of the lakes and light refraction. The easiest lake to visit is Laguna de
Colores. Also in the park is a natural arch named San Rafael. Here a
stream disappears into subterranean caverns.

A dirt road provides access to the Montebello Lakes Canada, Pojoj,
Tziscao, and Dos Lagunas. While these other lakes are more difficult to
visit, they also provide more solitude. Tziscao is located almost on the
Guatemalan border and is one of the largest of the lakes.

The dirt road continues into the Lacandón forest, and the intrepid
traveler will find the Santo Domingo River waterfalls and Lake Miramar,
the largest natural body of water in Chiapas.

Derek Parent, author of the guidebook *La Mosquitia*, suggests that
adventurous travelers take the bus from Comitán to the Tziscao village in
Lagunas de Montebello, the last stop on the run. Lodging is available at a
simple hostel. From Tziscao it's a 7-hour bus ride to the village of Flor de
Cafe. From there a guide can take you on a 2.5-hour walk to the village of
Pico de Oro, from which you can take a boat from the Lacantun River to
the Usumacinta River. It takes three days to travel from Pico de Oro to
Yaxchitlán. Some of the water is very rough (Class IV). Be forewarned:
This area has experienced conflicts between the government, landholders,
and indigenous people. Always travel with a guide.

Getting to Lagunas de Montebello National Park

Buses from San Cristóbal de las Casas drop off passengers at Laguna
Monte Azul or Laguna Montebello. The park can also be reached from
Comitán, 50 kilometers (31 miles) away.

Where to Stay near Lagunas de Montebello National Park

Camping is allowed only at the Laguna Bosque Azul. There is a restaurant
and toilets. Currently, no fee is charged. Hotel accommodations can be

Isthmus of Tehuantepec

The Isthmus of Tehuantepec is a biologically rich area where the flora and fauna of both North and South America can be found. It is known as a contact zone between the Nearctic and Neotropical biological zones. At this narrow waistline of Mexico, the Pacific and the Gulf of Mexico are just 210 kilometers (130 miles) apart. The strategic importance of this land (it offers the shorest land route between the Gulf and the Pacific) was valued by the Spanish conquistadors.

The central part of the isthmus supports both Nearctic and Neotropical zones. Conservationists consider the Uxpanapa and Chimalapas forests in the isthmus to be critical areas. The region's biggest threats have been the introduction of cattle ranching and colonization, and to some extent, exploration and drilling by the petroleum industry.

found in San Cristóbal de las Casas, if you want to make a quick trip to the lakes or from Comitán.

Hotel Delfin Pension, on the west side of the zócalo on Avenida Central, San Cristóbal de las Casas, (963) 2-00-13, $10. Spacious rooms in a comfortable hotel.

Hotel Real Balún Canán, Avenida 1 Pte Sur 7, (963) 2-10-94, San Cristóbal de las Casas, $20. Rooms have private baths and telephones.

EL TRIUNFO BIOSPHERE RESERVE
Location: N of Tapachula, Chiapas
Area: 119,177 hectares (294,367 acres)
Activities: Bird-watching, hiking
For More Information: SECTUR, (961) 3-9396, 3-9397, or toll-free in Mexico, 01 (800) 28-035

This reserve in the southwestern corner of Chiapas, near the Guatemalan border, protects one of the richest and most biologically important sections of the Sierra Madre. Named for an inactive volcano, El Triunfo was declared a biosphere reserve in 1990. In 1993 the park was included in the UNESCO's Man and the Biosphere Program.

El Triunfo is located in the highlands of the Sierra Madre de Chiapas, a mountainous chain of steeps and pinnacles surpassing 2,000 meters (6,600 feet), surrounded by wide and numerous valleys that reach 1,000 meters (3,300 feet) above sea level. The reserve is almost constantly covered with clouds—this is one of Mexico's wettest places. The area supplies the water for nine rivers that supply more than 20 towns, including a large area of coffee plantations and the La Angostura Dam.

The area's climate varies from the dry and hot lowlands to the cool and humid western slopes and highlands. Here in the forest thicket, resplendent quetzals flash their green feathers as they dart through the canopy. More than 300 species of birds live here. Besides quetzals, the national symbol of Guatemala, you may see the horned guan, hummingbirds, flycatchers, forest falcons, manakins, or the azure-rumped tanager. The horned guan (*Oreophasis derbianus*) belongs to a group of birds found only in this region. The reserve also attracts the blue morpho, a large and fairly common blue butterfly. In addition, the reserve's extreme humidity favors the abundance of tree-like ferns, some reaching up to 15 meters in height.

The reserve is divided into five core zones measuring about 25,000 hectares (61,750 acres) each. A 90,000-hectare (222,300-acre) buffer zone surrounds the core zones. Management regulations prohibit any kind of productive or extractive activities in the core zones, which are dedicated to conservation and research programs.

The reserve has 12,000 residents who live in 37 ejidos. The population increases significantly during the coffee harvesting season. The highlands of Chiapas are one of Mexico's most significant coffee-growing regions. Coffee arrived in the region at the end of 19th century, when European investors, invited by the government, installed the first plantation. The prevailing climatic conditions favored the new crops (as it does the cultivation of cacao), so coffee plantations increased in number and in size. In turn, large numbers of Indians migrated from the highlands of Chiapas, Oaxaca, and Guatemala to pick up the additional work.

The economic success of cattle ranchers coincided with the ecological destruction of the area. Fortunately, in the 1940s, research by Miguel Alvarez del Toro provided the evidence needed to protect the area. But it wasn't until 1972 that the first protective policies emerged and the Natural History Institute of Chiapas took over direction of the area.

Tours and Outfitters
Tours are best organized by the **Institute of Natural History** in Tuxtla Gutiérrez; (961) 1-39-04, e-mail inhreservas@laneta.apc.org.

Getting to El Triunfo Biosphere Reserve
The park only accepts visitors that have permission from the Institute of Natural History in Tuxtla Gutiérrez. From Tuxtla Gutiérrez, take the Angel Albino Corzo Road. One route leads from Tapachula a short distance to the outskirts of the reserve and includes a 17.7-kilometer (11-mile) hike to a campsite. Another 12.8-kilometer (7.9-mile) path goes through Jaltenengo (also known as Angel Albino Corzo) and the forest of Finca Prusia.

LA ENCRUCIJADA BIOSPHERE RESERVE
Location: *Near Escuintla on Chiapas' Pacific coast*
Area: *144,868 hectares (357,824 acres)*
Activities: *Bird-watching, boat rides through the mangroves*
For More Information: *SECTUR, (961) 3-9396, 3-9397, or toll-free in Mexico 01 (800) 28-035*

On Chiapas' southern Pacific coast, La Encrucijada's ecosystem consists of mangrove estuaries, semi-deciduous tropical forest, and seasonally flooded forests. It forms one of the largest marine fishery spawning areas on Mexico's southwest coast and is also the winter habitat for many North American birds.

The park is accessible from Highway 200 from the town of Escuintla, about 90 kilometers (56 miles) north of Tapachula. There are no developed tours, but you can arrange an informal visit with the fishermen. You'll see an amazing collection of bird life and mangrove stands that often reach 22 meters (72 feet) in height. The region supports a large population of jaguars (the second- or third-largest in Mexico), as well as ocelots, jaguarundi, spider monkeys, boa constrictors, and American crocodiles and caimans.

There is a potential threat to these wetlands: The Chiapas Coast Hydraulic Program, implemented by the National Water Commission (CNA), is constructing 350 kilometers (217 miles) of dikes to divert freshwater to nearby agricultural areas.

Tours and Outfitters
The local coffee producers union is beginning an ambitious ecotourism project. Contact ISMAM for more information: 1a Avenida Sur #3, Motozintla, Chiapas; (964) 1-02-13 or, in Tapachula, (962) 5-24-04 or 5-45-37.

Getting to La Encrucijada Biosphere Reserve

From Escuintla, take the road to Acapetahua. There, cross the train tracks and follow a dirt road 18 kilometers (11 miles) to Las Garzas. From Las Garzas you can hire a boat to take you to the fishing village of Las Palmas.

Where to Stay near La Encrucijada Biosphere Reserve

Hotel Don Miguel, Calle 1 Pte 18, Tapachula (962) 6-11-43, $30. Modern hotel in the center of the city. It also has a restaurant.

Hotel Santa Julia, Calle 17 Ote 5, Tapachula, (962) 6-31-40, $20. Clean, comfortable rooms with TV and phone. Located next door to the Cristóbal Colón bus station.

Hotel Toledo, Avenida Alvaro Obregón 10, Escuintla (962) 4-0106, $10. Simple hotel with friendly management.

APPENDIX A
TRAVEL BASICS

ENTRY/EXIT REQUIREMENTS

All foreigners must carry a tourist card, issued at embassies and consulates and, for most travelers, on the airplane itself. If you're traveling across the border, the card is available at the official crossing point. You must supply proof of citizenship, such as a passport, to obtain the tourist card. If you are a resident of the United States, your birth certificate will do. Customs officials usually grant a 30-day stay; ask for a longer period if that's necessary. The maximum length of stay as a tourist is 180 days. Renewal of tourist cards is granted by the Secretaría de Gobernación, Albañiles 19, Colonia 20 de Noviembre, in Mexico City.

U.S. tourists visiting border towns do not need a tourist card for local, cross-border visits of less than 72 hours. While Mexico does not require formal visas from most countries, it does for travelers from France, Hong Kong, South Africa, and Andorra. Application procedures vary, so check with the Mexican embassy or consulate.

A $12 airport departure tax is issued on all international flights. Generally, but not always, the tax is included in the price of the ticket.

CUSTOMS

You can bring your camera or video camera, but you are limited to 12 rolls of film (or 12 blank cassettes). You can also bring a personal computer or other electronic goods. Tripod and flash equipment require special permits at many of the archaeological sites and monuments. Gifts up to a value of $300 can be brought into Mexico. For more information, call the Mexican Customs office in Washington, DC, at (202) 927-6724.

If you take animals into Mexico, you must have a certificate signed by a veterinarian stating that the animal is in good health and has been inoculated against rabies within the past six months. It is illegal to bring any products from endangered species into the United States. Also banned are products made from coral, ivory, tortoise shells, crocodile, lizards, sea turtles, marine mammals, or wild cats. For information about what products can be brought into the United States, contact the Division of Law Enforcement, U.S. Fish and Wildlife Service, P.O. Box 3247, Arlington, VA 22203-3247.

Note that archaeological relics may not be taken out of Mexico.

WHAT TO PACK

Considering the range of Mexican climates—hot and humid on the coasts, cool and smoggy in the nation's capital—you'll want to bring shorts, long pants, and swimsuits. Alternate good hiking boots with sandals. Umbrellas and ponchos are required equipment during the rainy season.

Here's my short list of what to bring: passport and passport copy, traveler's checks (bigger cities accept credit cards and you get a better exchange rate if you have cash, but they are a good form of insurance), alarm clock, pocket knife, insect repellent/anti-itch gel, antibiotic lotion, flashlight, dental floss, candy, Spanish dictionary, plastic bags for packing toiletries, gifts for new friends (local music, video tapes, and books are good bets).

Bring a camera! You'll see things in Mexico that you'll find nowhere else in the world. If you're not certain how many rolls of film to bring, don't worry. Unless you are using a special brand, you'll find film in camera stores across the country.

IMMUNIZATION AND HEALTH ISSUES

Specific immunizations are not required for travel in Mexico. If you're traveling in rural areas, it makes sense to get tetanus, typhoid, and polio shots. When in doubt, ask your family doctor. If you are taking special medicine, be sure to bring enough for your trip. Also, if you have a serious condition, you might want to bring along a copy of the prescription just in case your medicine runs out.

Diarrhea is commonly known in Mexico as *turista*. While some Mexican cities have modern water-treatment plants, often the water is contaminated by leaky pipes. Bottled water is generally safe; so is water that's been boiled for 20 minutes. Make sure that the food you eat has been well cooked. If you want to eat salad, lettuce, or tomatoes, make sure they have been washed in purified water. If you're traveling into remote areas you should take water purification tablets with you.

Another common complaint is of the air pollution. It's particularly bad in Mexico City, but it's also severe in Guadalajara and Monterrey. The most affected are children and the elderly. Unfortunately there is no pill to take, so your best bet is to take it slow and easy. If you do need medicine, pharmacies in Mexico are generally well stocked. It's easy to get prescription drugs, often at a lower cost than abroad. Be specific about what you are seeking, but also be smart and think ahead. Take the common remedies (aspirin, antacid tablets, bandages) with you. (See my list of things to take, above.)

Your body is in for a shock, so be kind to it. Avoid water unless it is bottled or purified. Coffee and tea are generally fine, and you won't get sick from pop (*refrescos*) or beer (*cerveza*). Moderation is suggested, but that's advice easier preached than practiced. Germs are easy to catch, so listen to the far-off voice of your parents and wash your hands before meals.

If you'd like more practical suggestions, there are two excellent guides. *Staying Healthy in Asia, Africa and Latin America*, by Dirk Schroeder (Moon Publications), is a handy, pocket-size book. *Where There is No Doctor*, by David Werner (The Hesperian Foundation), is a highly recommended handbook for anyone staying in remote villages.

SAFETY

Safety concerns are familiar to anyone who has traveled in a developing country. Travelers have wealth. Don't be ostentatious. A developing country is not the locale in which to display an expensive watch or briefcase.

Beware of crowded situations. The Mexico City metro, for example, moves 5 million people a day, and it's also the location for numerous robberies. Avoid the metro during the rush hours (8 to 10 a.m. and 4 to 7 p.m.). It's hard to beat the 15-cent ticket price. Travelers should note that officials frown upon taking large objects onto the metro—this includes backpacks and suitcases.

MEDIA

There are two English-language newspapers published in Mexico City that are distributed throughout the country. *The News* is the oldest paper. It's published by Grupo Novedades, famous for its comic books and *telenovelas* (TV soap operas). *The News* has shown a strong commitment to environmental reporting since the late 1980s.

The newcomer is the *Mexico City Times*, which had a brief life in 1963. It was resurrected in 1995, and although most of the reporters and editors resigned or were let go in 1997, the paper continues. The most recent rumor is that El Universal will purchase the paper. *Guadalajara Colony Reporter* is an informative weekly newspaper that covers the Pacific coast region. There are also local tourism broadcasts such as *Puerto Vallarta Today.*

Strangely enough, Mexico City cannot support an English-language radio station. *Radio Express* went off the air in 1995 and there is no dependable station for English-language radio. You might want to bring a short-wave radio if that's important to you.

Many Mexican cities have regional newspapers in English, published expressly for the visitor. You'll find these newspapers and magazines in Puerto Vallarta, San Miguel de Allende, Playa del Carmen, Oaxaca, and Cancún.

Tourists should check out tourism-oriented newsletters before they visit. An excellent option is the bi-monthly *Mexican Meanderings* (P.O. Box 33057, Austin, TX 78764, e-mail mexplore@valise.com). The Spanish-language *Mexico Desconocido* (Editorial Jilguero, Administración de Correos 10, 11000 Mexico, D.F., e-mail exdesco@compuserve.com.mx) is a highly-recommended, Spanish-language magazine that alerts travelers to the wonders of "unknown Mexico." It promotes responsible travel and an appreciation of Mexico's long history and diverse ecosystems.

TIME
Daylight saving time is in effect from the first Sunday in April to the Saturday before the last Sunday in October. Clocks are set forward by 1 hour. There are three time zones in Mexico: South, Central, and Eastern Mexico are on Central time (Greenwich mean time minus 6 hours). Nayarit, Sonora, Sinaloa, and Baja California Sur are on Mountain time (Greenwich mean time minus 7 hours). Baja California Norte is on Pacific time (Greenwich mean time minus 8 hours).

ELECTRICITY
Electricity is supplied at 110 volts AC, 60 Hz. The outlets used in Mexico are the same as those used in the United States and Canada.

METRIC CONVERSIONS
1 mile = 1.6 kilometers
1 foot = 0.3 meters
1 pound = 0.45 kilograms
1 gallon = 3.8 liters

1 kilometer = $3/5$ mile
1 meter = $3^1/3$ feet
1 kilogram = $2^1/2$ pounds
1 liter = $1/4$ gallon (or 1 quart)

CURRENCY, BANKING, AND CREDIT CARDS
Mexico's currency is the peso, and prices are indicated by the "$" sign. The peso is divided into 100 centavos. Coins come in denominations of ten, 20, and 50 centavos and one, two, five, ten, and 20 pesos. Notes are worth two, five, ten, 20, 50, 100, 200, and 500 pesos.

You can exchange foreign currency at banks or at exchange houses (*casas de cambio*). Exchange rates will vary, and often you'll get a better rate if you exchange currency instead of traveler's checks. The exchange rate is particularly poor at hotels. I've found that while the Mexico City airport offers a good return, the Cancún airport offers one of the worst. Be cautious.

You can easily get a cash advance from an ATM machine at one of the major banks. While you will be charged a greater fee from your credit card company, the process is relatively hassle-free. Make sure you have your access number, because most companies have a policy of not reporting the number over the phone. Note that ATMs offer the best interbank exchange rate.

When traveling in rural Mexico, always make sure you have Mexican currency (cash). Don't expect to find currency exchanges or places that accept travelers checks outside of the country's main cities.

TELEPHONING

Telephone service in Mexico has improved a great deal the past few years. Most public phones now take calling cards instead of coins, but just when you're prepared to find one, you'll come across the other. Ladatel calling cards are sold in either 20- or 50-peso denominations. They can be found at various stores and restaurants.

To call other cities in Mexico, use the "01" national code and then the number. To call the United States or Canada from Mexico, dial "001" first, then the area code and number. To call other countries, dial "00" first. Call international numbers collect by dialing "090," or national numbers collect by dialing "020." If you already have an account in the United States, the phone number for AT&T Collect is 01-800-112-2020; MCI is 01-800-021-1000.

If you are calling Mexico from another country, the international code is "52." Phone numbers cited in this book include only the city code. For example, the city code for Mexico City is "5." Thus, to call a Mexico City phone number from the United States, dial "011-525" and then the seven-digit number. To keep this complex, some cities in Mexico have a seven-digit number, while many smaller towns have just five or six digits.

TIPPING

Generally, you should leave a 10- to 15-percent *propina* (tip) in restaurants. Mexicans generally leave a 10-percent tip. Good service deserves recognition. Also, double-check that your restaurant bill does not already include a propina. In Chihuahua I ran into a budget-obsessed traveler who said that the Mexicans don't expect a tip. Obviously, he'd never worked as a waiter. If you get good service, be generous.

BUSINESS HOURS

Mexicans are among the hardest-working people in the world. Businesses usually are open from 9 a.m. to 2 p.m. and then reopen again from 4 to 7 p.m. These hours can vary with location. It's easy to find people still at work in Mexico City at 11 p.m., though they might not come back to work until 10 a.m.

Archaeological sites and museums are usually open from 9 a.m. to 5 p.m. State and federal museums are usually free on Sunday and holidays; most are closed on Monday.

MEXICAN HOLIDAYS AND FESTIVALS

January 1
New Year's Day—Año Nuevo

February 5
Constitution Day—Día de la Constitución

February 24
Flag Day—Día de la Bandera

Spring
Holy Week (before Easter)—Semana Santa

March 21
Anniversary of Benito Juarez' Birth—Día de Nacimiento de Benito Juarez

May 1
Labor Day—Dia del Trabajo

May 5
Cinco de Mayo—Anniversary of Mexico's 1862 victory over France in Puebla; this holiday is celebrated more in the United States than in Mexico.

September 16
Independence Day—Día de Independencia (Commemoration of Mexico's War of Independence with Spain)

October 12
Columbus Day—Día de la Raza (Commemorates the founding of the Mexican (mestizo) people

November 20
Revolution Day—Día de la Revolución (Anniversary of the 1910 Revolution)

December 25
Christmas—Día de Navidad

TRANSPORTATION TO AND WITHIN MEXICO

TRAVEL TO MEXICO
Mexico is one of the easiest countries in Latin America to which to travel. Direct flights leave regularly for Mexico City and other major tourist destinations. Savvy travelers will not overlook discounted flights to Cancún or Acapulco. Certainly, the beach megaresorts are over developed and often superficial compared to the cities with, say, 400 years of history, but they do represent terrific gateways to other destinations.

TRAVEL WITHIN MEXICO
Mexico offers an array of travel options. The country's first-class bus service puts Greyhound to shame. In addition, a network of second-class buses traverses the entire country. It's easy to go wherever you want. If you're short on time, you can fly. And if you don't want to rent a car, by all means hire a taxi for the day. It will generally cost you a lot less.

Bus Service
Bus travel in Mexico is the among finest in the world. Bus stations, called *central caminoneras*, are comparable to European train depots. The United States will have strong competition when high quality Mexican bus companies enter the U.S. market (one of the gifts of NAFTA) by the end of the century. The quality and frequency of Mexican buses will delight any traveler.

Some cities have a central caminonera for all of the bus lines, while other cities have individual bus stations for each company or for first- and second-class buses, respectively. This information is included in the destination chapters.

If you are traveling between major cities, you have a choice between first-class and second-class travel. First-class buses have working toilets and generally show a movie or two during the trip. You pay a little more for such amenities. If you're visiting smaller towns, you'll usually have to take second-class buses.

Train Service
The national railroad service, Ferrocarriles Nacionales de Mexico, maintains 24,000 kilometers (15,000 miles) of railroad. But privatization is

coming swiftly, and the more lucrative routes will soon be sold off. Riding the rails can be an exciting way to see the country, but unfortunately, the service has slacked off in the past few years. According to the Mexican Association of Importers and Exporters, two-thirds of the railways in Mexico were built before the 1910 Revolution.

That said, there are still several good options for train travel. Among the overnight trains are El Jarocho (which operates between Veracruz and Mexico City), El Tapatio (between Guadalajara and Mexico City), El Oaxaqueño (between Oaxaca and Mexico City), and El Purepecha (between Morelia and Mexico City). There are also lines between Mexicali and Guadalajara, and Monterrey and Mexico City. And if you're traveling across the Copper Canyon region, the Chihuahua al Pacifico train is the best way to go.

Officially, there are two classes of service: Primera Especial (first class) and Segunda Clasa (second class). With first-class service you get an air-conditioned car, reclining seats, and free boxed meals. Sleeping facilities are available on overnight trains, though they cost more. For reservations in Mexico City, call (5) 547-8655.

Airlines

Since Mexico is quite a large country, the best option for a long trip is via air travel. The two largest Mexican airlines—Aeromexico and Mexicana—both offer good service. Although they are owned by the same holding company, they're operated as separate companies.

International airlines operating in Mexico include American Airlines, America West, Continental Airlines, Delta, Lufthansa, United, and Varig. Mexico's Aviacsa offers trips in Southern Mexico, including Chiapas and the Yucatán. The airline is linked with Aero Exo, based in Monterrey, which serves northern Mexico. Aero California serves Baja California and the Pacific coast region. Aeromar serves northern Mexico.

If you are traveling in the southern part of Mexico and Guatemala, note that Mexicana has a discounted fare program called Mayapass with various links in Southern Mexico and Central America.

The 800-numbers listed below work from within Mexico.

Aerocalifornia	207-1392
Aeromar	207-6666
Aeroméxico	133-4000, 021-4000
Aviacsa	559-1955, 575-2181
Mexicana	448-0990, 502-2000
Taesa	227-0700, 758-1487
American Airlines	209-1400, 904-6000

America West	511-9779
Continental	280-3434
Delta Airlines	202-1608
Lufthansa	202-8866, 90-600
United Airlines	624-0222, 00-307
Varig	591-1744, 70-310

The international airports use a lottery system to determine which passengers have their luggage inspected. Be prepared to press a button at the customs desk. If you receive the green light, walk on through. If you receive a red light, you'll have to open your luggage for a quick inspection.

Each of the international airports has a different character. By far, the friendliest is in Mexico City. If you land at the airport in Monterrey late in the afternoon, you might have problems changing money. If you land in Cancún, you'll be able to change your money, but you'll get a terrible exchange rate. (I think that if my first impression of Mexico were of the Cancún airport, I wouldn't have come back a second time.)

Taxi Service

The majority of taxis in Mexico City are green-and-yellow Volkswagen bugs (known in Mexico as *sedans*). In the 1980s the green "eco-taxis" were introduced as a more environmentally friendly automobile. Make sure that the taxi meter is working or agree upon a set rate before you begin your journey. The U.S. Embassy recommends that visitors take taxis only from established taxi stands outside of the major hotels. I've never done this personally. The cost of these taxis is much higher than the normal taxis people simply hail from the street.

If you want to be safe, make sure the photo displayed in the top right corner of the windshield matches the driver. If you don't see the photo or it doesn't look right, don't get in the cab.

Most taxis outside of Mexico City do not have a taxi meter. If you are unsatisfied with the rate offered, wave the taxi on and hail another one.

Bicycling

Heavy traffic is the only obstacle for cyclists. Roads in Mexico are very good, but few have shoulders. Consult the book *Bicycling in Mexico* (Hunter Publishing) for specific advice. Author Eric Ellman claims that Mexico is perfect for cycling. The country offers great mountain roads—ideal for mountain biking—and flat coastal roads in the Yucatán and Baja. There's something for everyone's skills and desires.

Driving to and within Mexico

In 1995 nearly 2 million tourists entered Mexico by car. Drivers must have proper paperwork, including a driver's license and automobile registration, as well as photocopies of these documents. Once in Mexico, drivers must leave the paperwork with a border official at the Banjercito, the government's customs bank run by the treasury office (Hacienda); pay an $11 fee by credit card; and get a windshield sticker for a six-month multiple-entry permit. Credit cards must be Visa, MasterCard, or American Express, and must be in the same name as the registration.

You must return the car to the border at the end of the six months. If you need to leave the country and wish to leave the car at the airport, it's generally no problem. If you have any problems with this arrangement, call the customs office in Mexico City at 604-1240 or, toll-free in Mexico, (01) 800-001-48.

If you do not possess a credit card, a bond must be paid to ensure the car's return to the Banjercito office, usually in the customs complex, where the permit will be canceled. You do not have to go to the same border station where you entered.

Extra precaution is required while driving in Mexico. The highways have narrow shoulders and sharp curves, and many are in need of repair. Relax and just slow down. The major roads have good signage displaying highway numbers and the upcoming towns and cities. Missing are signs that indicate turns or impending danger. The best precaution is to avoid driving at night. Most highways are not illuminated and you stand a good chance of running into a pothole or a black cow that has strayed from the field. Hitting either can cause a terrible accident.

In the 1990s Mexico started promoting toll (*cuota*) highways. Most have four lanes and resemble any U.S. highway. Tolls are calculated by the number of axles on the vehicle. They can be expensive, but they are time-saving. Since the roads are privately financed, tolls can vary from region to region. Many of these toll-roads are free of trucks and buses, which opt for the free highways that generally have two lanes instead of four.

Watch the level of gas in your tank, and be sure to keep it at least half full. While there are plenty of gas stations along the major highways, in rural areas they are less common. Gasoline is sold by the liter—just a little less than a quarter of a gallon. Gas is available in two grades—Nova (leaded, 81-octane fuel) and Magna Sin (unleaded). It is customary to tip the service attendant a peso or two.

One terrific service should be mentioned here. Mexico's "Green Angels" (Angeles Verdes) are trained mechanics who traverse the nation's highways in their forest-green trucks with one mission: to assist travelers whose vehicles have broken down. The mechanics charge for parts or gasoline, but the service is free, courtesy of SECTUR, Mexico's Tourism Secretariat. It doesn't hurt to leave your Green Angel a tip, but that's completely voluntary.

If you are a member of the American Automobile Association, you can request information or assistance from the **Association Mexicana Automobilistica**, Orizaba No. 7, Col. Roma, 06700 Mexico, D.F., (5) 511-6285.

Your insurance company will not cover driving in Mexico. You'll need to purchase a separate policy from a company in Mexico. The **American Automobile Association** will help its members. Contact AAA Headquarters, 1000 AAA Dr., Heathrow, FL 32746-5063, (407) 444-8122.

Other services include **Discover Baja Travel Club**, 3089 Clairemont Dr., San Diego, CA 92117, (619) 275-4225 or (800) 727-BAJA; and **International Gateway Insurance Brokers**, 3450 Bonita Rd., #103, Chula Vista, CA 91910, (619) 422-3057 or (800) 423-2646, which offers house, boat, and car insurance.

Sanborn's Mexico Insurance Services offers a mile-by-mile travel guide to all of Mexico's major highways. The company has been an ardent promoter of ground-based travel and explorations in Mexico for the past 40 years. Sanborn's also offers health and legal insurance. Contact Sanborn's at P.O. Box 310, McAllen, TX 78505, (210) 686-0711 or (800) 222-0158, Web site http://www.hiline.net/sanborns/.

Whatever insurer you choose, make photocopies of your policy and keep the originals and copies in separate places.

Rental Cars

Rental agencies are abundant throughout Mexico. Agencies include Avis, Budget, Dollar, Hertz, and National. Many offer promotional fares, but be wary of these discounts. Some companies have only a few cars available with this offer, and chances are they won't have the vehicle you want when you want it.

You have to be 25 years old and have a valid driver's license and credit card to rent a car. Check with your credit card company to find out what type of insurance is automatically covered when you rent a car abroad. Cash payments for car rental are not allowed.

ENVIRONMENTAL VOCABULARY

arroyo - stream
bahía - bay
biological diversity - number of species that occur in a geographic area
biosphere reserve - management category for areas of high biological diversity
campesino - farmer
cenote - limestone sinkhole; found throughout the Yucatán Peninsula
chinampa - a raised garden
ejido - a farming community created by the Mexican government after the 1910 Revolution. The ejidos are governed by a general assembly.
endemic - native to a particular geographic area
fauna - animals
flora - plants
gruta - cave
henequen/hemp - tough fiber produced from the henequen agave plant
laguna - lagoon
llano - plains
maguey - agave or century plant
malecón - waterfront
milpa - cornfield
nopales - prickly pear cactus (served as a food—after the spikes are removed)
palapa - thatched hut or shelter
pajarao - bird
sendero - path
río - river

ACRONYMS USED IN THIS BOOK

CECODES	Center For Environment And Development
CITES	Convention on International Trade in Endangered Species of Wild Flora and Fauna
FONATUR	National Fund For Tourism Development
INE	National Institute of Ecology
IUCN	International Union for Conservation of Nature and Natural Resources
MAP	Man and the Biosphere Program
RAMSAR	Convention on Wetlands of International Importance

SECTUR	Secretariat of Tourism
SEDESOL	Secretariat of the Environment (Salinas administration)
SEDETUR	State Tourism Office of Oaxaca
SEDUE	Secretariat of Urban Development and Ecology (De la Madrid administration)
SEMARNAP	Secretariat of Natural Resources, Environment, and Fisheries (Zedillo administration)
SINAP	System of Natural and Protected Areas
UNEP	United Nations Environmental Programme

SPANISH LANGUAGE SCHOOLS

The cultural and linguistic immersion available at Spanish language schools in Mexico has numerous benefits. The Directory of Spanish Language Schools is regularly updated online at the Eco Travels in Latin America Web site (http://www.planeta.com).

CHIAPAS

Centro Bilingue
Calle Real de Guadalupe 55
San Cristóbal de las Casas,
    Chiapas
Contact: Roberto Rivas,
Director
Phone/Fax: (967) 83723
    or, in the U.S.,
    (800) 303-4983

Instituto Jovel
Maria Adelina Flores 21
Apdo Postal 62
San Cristóbal de las Casas,
Chiapas
Phone/Fax: (967) 84069

COLIMA

Language Institute of Colima
Colima, Colima
Phone: 2-05-87 or 4-57-86
U.S. Address:
P.O. Box 459,
Garberville, CA 95542-0459
Phone: (800) 604-6547

GUADALAJARA

Centro de Estudios para Extranjeros
Universidad de Guadalajara
Apdo Postal 1-2130
44100 Guadalajara,
Jalisco
Phone: (3) 653-60-24

Spanish Language School
1443 La Ermita
Col. Chapalita
45040 Guadalajara, Jalisco
Phone: (3) 121-4774
e-mail: spanscho@acnet.net
Web site: http//www.spanschool
.com.mx
Contact: Julia de Barba

GUANAJUATO

Academia Hispano Americana
Mesones 4
37700 San Miguel de Allende,
GTO
Phone: (415) 2-03-49
Fax: (415) 2-23-33

Instituto Falcon
Callejon de la Mora 158
Guanajuato, GTO 36000
Fax: (473) 2-36-94
e-mail: falcon@bajio.infonet
.com.mx
Web site: http://www.infonet.com
.mx/falcon
Contact: Jorge Barroso

Instituto "Habla Hispana"
Calzada de la Luz #25
37700 San Miguel de Allende,
GTO
Phone/Fax: (415) 2-07-13
e-mail: hhispana@iname.com or
74054.1400@compuserve.com
Web site: http://wwwvms.utexas
.edu/~kcargill/index.html
Contact:
Angelica Rodriguez,
Director

MICHOACÁN

Baden-Powell Institute
Antonio Alzate 565
58000 Morelia, Michoacán
Phone: (32) 24070

**Centro de Lenguas y
Ecoturismo**
Navarrete 50 Centro
61600 Patzcuaro, Michoacán
Phone: (434) 2-47-64
Fax: (434) 2-08-52 or 2-33-68

**Centro Mexicano Internacional
(CMI)**
Calz. Fray. Antonio de
San Miguel 173
Morelia, Michoacán
Phone: (32) 12-4596

MORELOS

**Cemanahuac Educational
Community**
Colonia Las Palmas
San Juan #4
Cuernavaca, Morelos
Mailing Address: Apartado 5-21,
Cuernavaca, Morelos
Phone: (73) 18-6407 or 14-2988
Fax: (73) 12-5418
e-mail: 74052.2570@compuserve
.com
Contact: Vivian B. Harvey

**Center for Bilingual
Multicultural Studies
"Centro Bilingue"**
San Jeronimo # 304, Col. San
Jeronimo
62170 Cuernavaca, Morelos

Phone: (73)17-10-87; after 5 p.m.
(Central time) call (73) 13-04-02;
in U.S., call (800) 932-2068
Fax: (73) 17-05-33
e-mail: admin@bilingual-center
.com
Web site: http://www.bilingual-
center.com

Encuentros Comunicación y Cultura

Apartado Postal 2-71
Calle Morelos 36
Colonia Acapantzingo
62440 Cuernavaca, Morelos
Phone: (73) 12 50 88
e-mail: encuent@infosel.net.mx or
encuent@microweb.com.mx
Web site: http://cuernavaca.infosel
.com.mx/encuentros/spanish
.htm

Escuela Azteca

Rio Usumacinta 710
Colonia Vista Hermosa
Cuernavaca, Morelos
Phone: (73) 1524-69

Experiencia-Centro de Inter-cambio Bilingue y Cultural

Apdo. Postal C-96
Cuernavaca, Morelos
Phone: (73) 12-65-79 or, in U.S.,
(512) 331-5925
Fax: (73) 18-52-09 or, in U.S.,
(512) 257-7237
e-mail: experiencia@weblane.com
Web site: http://www.weblane.com
/experiencia/
Contact: Sherry Howell Williams

OAXACA

Amigos del Sol Language School

Libres #109
Oaxaca, Mexico
Phone: (951) 5-31-04
e-mail: amisol@antequera.com
Web site: http://www.mexonline
.com/amisol.htm

Becari Escuela de Español y Ingles

M. Bravo 210
Oaxaca 68000, Oaxaca
Phone/Fax: (951) 46076

Centro de Idiomas

Universidad Autonoma Benito
Juarez de Oaxaca
Apdo. 523
Oaxaca 68000, Oaxaca
Phone/Fax: (951) 65922

Instituto Bilingue y Cultural de Puerto Escondido

Calle Primera Sur 506
71980 Puerto Escondido, Oaxaca
Phone/Fax: (958) 21-996

Instituto de Comunicación y Cultura

M. Alcala #307-12
Colonia Centro
68000 Oaxaca, Oaxaca
Phone/Fax: (951) 634-43
Contacts: Yolanda Garcia
Caballero and Warren Lyle
e-mail: info@iccoax.com
Web site: http://www.iccoax.com

YUCATÁN

Centro de Idiomas Sureste (CIS)
Calle 66 #535x57
Edificio Alejandra, upstairs
Mérida, Yucatán
Phone: (99) 23-09-54
Fax: (99) 23-37-36
Contact: Chloe Pacheco

Instituto de Español Moderno
Av. 21 No. 195 x 12 Col. Mexico
  Oriente
Merida, Yucatán
Phone: (99) 25-95-28
Fax: (99) 26-94-17

U.S. LANGUAGE SCHOOL CONTACTS

Interamerican University Studies Institute
P.O. Box 10958
Eugene, OR 97440
Phone: (541) 344-8940 or (800)
  345-IUSI
Fax: (541) 686-5947

e-mail: iusi2oregon@efn.org
Web site: http://www.efn.org/~iusi

Language Study Abroad
1301 N. Maryland Ave.
Glendale CA 91207
Phone: (818) 242-5263
Fax: (818) 548-3667
e-mail: cd002380@mindspring
  .com
Web site: http://www.
  languagestudy.com
Contact: Richard Simmons

Language Studies Abroad
249 S. Hwy. 101, Suite 226
Solana Beach, CA 92075
Phone: (619) 943-0204
Fax: (619) 943-1201
Contact: Charlene Biddulph

Lingua Service Worldwide, Ltd.
211 E. 43rd St., Suite 1303
New York, NY 10017
Phone: (212) 867-1225 or (800)
394-LEARN
Fax: (212) 983-2590

DIRECTORY OF MEXICAN CYBERCAFES

Where to access your Internet e-mail, surf the Web, and down a hot cup of Latin American java? "Cybercafes" are popping up all over Latin America. Mexican cybercafes are becoming hot spots for travelers and locals alike. Many of the café owners are using their establishments to promote regional travel and local culture. Want to see Tarahumara art? Go to Arroba Cafe-Internet in Hermosillo. Want to check out local Michoacán artists? Visit the Shareweb café in Morelia.

The following information is updated regularly online at Americas' Cybercafes Web page, http://www2.planeta.com/mader/ecotravel

/coffeeag/cybercafe.html.
Arroba Cafe-Internet
Blvd. Rodriguez No. 96 esq. con
  Garmendia
Hermosillo, Sonora
e-mail: cafe@acnet.net
Web site: http://www.cafe-arrobba
  .com.mx
Contact: Gabriel Haro

Biblioteca
San Miguel de Allende
Guanajuato

Cafe Internet
Av. Juarez 1449 #100 and 11
Centro Commercial EME
Ensenada, Baja California
Phone: (61) 76-1331
Web site: http://www.compunet
  .com.mx/cafe/cafe2e.htm

Ciberpuerto
Alfonso Reyes No. 238, Col.
  Condesa
Mexico City
Phone: (5) 286-4744 or 286-0868
e-mail: cafe@ciberpuerto.com
Web site: http://www.ciberpuerto
  .com/cafe

Coffee Net
Av. Nuevo Leon 104-B, Col.
  Condesa
06170 Mexico City
Phone: (5) 286-7104
e-mail: coffeenet@nova.net.mx
Web site: http://www.nova.net.mx
  /coffeenet

CyberBase Saltillo
Periferico Luis Echeverria 438

Col. Republica
25290 Saltillo, Coahuila
Phone/Fax: (84)-16-1894
e-mail: cyberbase@metro.com.mx
Web site: http://www.cyberbase
  .com.mx

Cybercafe de ATX
Automatizaciones
5 de Mayo No. 911
90300 Apizaco, Tlaxcala
Phone: (241) 76-600
e-mail: cafe@apizaco.podernet
  .com.mx
Web site: http://atx.com.mx

CyberNet Cafe
Av. Juarez No. 240 Pte.
27000 Torreón Coahuila
e-mail: joel@teleinfo.com.mx
Web site: http://www.cybernetcafe
  .com.mx

Cyberspace Cafe
Mazatlan 148, Col. Condesa
Mexico City
Phone: (5) 211-6877
e-mail: corp@mpsnet.com.mx
Web site: http://www.spacecafe
  .com.mx

CyberStudio
Blvd. Garcia de Leon 256
Col. Nueva Chapultepec
Morelia, Michoacán
Phone: (43) 24 44 44
e-mail: zcom@morelia.podernet
  .com.mx

Estacion Internet
Recreo St. #11, upstairs
San Miguel de Allende,

Guanajuato
Web site: http://www.m3w3.com
.mx/estacion-internet

Inter Cafe
Av. Lazaro Cardenas 2996
Col. Chapultepec Sur
Morelia, Michoacán
Phone: (43) 15 74 16 or 15 76 75

Shareweb Cybercafe
Av. Madero Ote. 573-C
Col. Centro
Morelia, Michoacán
Phone: (43) 12-68-80 or 12-24-46
e-mail: shareweb@morelia.teesa
.com
Web site: http://morelia.teesa.com
/~shareweb

The Net House Cyber Cafe
Ignacio L. Vallarta #232
Col. Emiliano Zapata
Puerto Vallarta, Jalisco, 48380
Phone: (322) 2-57-64
e-mail: cafe@the-net-house.com
Web site: http://www.the-net-
house.com

WebChat—Cafe & Internet
Blvd. Luis Encinas y Reforma
Hermosillo, Sonora, 83190
Phone: (62) 14-1155
Web site: http://www.webchat-cafe
.com.mx/

MEXICO'S ART MUSEUMS AND GALLERIES

Some people travel to Mexico just for the museums. Favorites include the Templo Mayor in Mexico City and the Museum of Mexican History in Monterrey. Public museums and galleries are generally free on Sundays and closed on Mondays. Discounts are available for students attending Mexican universities.

CHIHUAHUA

**The Museum of Northern
Mexico Cultures**
Casas Grandes, Chihuahua

GUADALAJARA

Instituto Cultural Cabanas
Plaza Tapatia

Museo de las Artes
Universidad de Guadalajara

**Museo Regional
de Guadalajara**
Liceo 60/Sector Hidalgo

**Museo-Taller Jose
Clemente Orozco**
Aurelio Aceves 27/Sector Juárez

MEXICO CITY

**Centro Cultural/Arte
Contemporaneo**
Campos Elisos and Jorge Eliot
Centro Cultural San Angel
Av. Revolución and Francisco
Madero

Centro de la Imagen
Plaza de la Ciudadela

Galeria de Arte Mexicano
Gob. Rafael Rebollar 43
San Miguel Chapultepec

**Museo de Arte Contemporaneo
Internacional Rufino Tamayo**
Paseo de la Reforma and Gandhi

Museo Franz Mayer
Av. Hidalgo 45/Plaza de la
Santa Veracruz

**Museo Nacional de las
Culturas**
Moneda 13
Centro Histórico

**National Anthropology
Museum**
Paseo de la Reforma and Gandhi

Palacio de Bellas Artes
Av. Juárez at Lázaro Cárdenas
(Eje Central)
Templo Mayor Museum
Seminario 8/Centro Histórico

MONTERREY

Centro Cultural Alfa
Av. Roberto Garza Sada 1000

**Museum de Arte
Contemporaneo**
Zuazua and Ocampo

Museum of Mexican History
Dr. Coss 445 Sur

OAXACA

**Museo de Arte
Contemporaneo de Oaxaca-**
Macedonio Alcala 202

**Museo de Arte Prehispanico de
Mexico Rufino Tamayo**
Av. Morelos 503

APPENDIX B
TRAVEL & ENVIRONMENTAL CONTACTS

Note: The international country code for Mexico is 52.

TRAVEL CONTACTS

Mexico is developing both government offices and private industry groups to promote ecotourism. Operations are in a nascent stage, so be patient if you want to access information or book tours at the national level.

NATIONAL OFFICES

Mexican Association of Adventure Travel and Ecotourism (AMTAVE)
Av. Insurgentes Sur 1971
Nivel Paseo, loc. 251
Col. Guadalupe Inn
01020 Mexico, D.F.
Phone: (5) 661-9121
Fax: (5) 662-7354
e-mail: 74174.2424
  @compuserve.com
This group of about 40 travel providers supporting various interpretations of the word "ecotourism" was formed in 1994. Request a copy of their latest catalogue.

National Association of Ecotourism and Adventure Guides
Nicolás Bravo y Marcel Rubio

23000 La Paz, Baja California Sur
Phone: (112) 5-22-77 or 1-15-60
Fax: 1-15-15.
Excellent source for local guides and nature tourism guides in Baja California.

BAJA/SEA OF CORTEZ

Ecotourism Kuyima
San Ignacio, on Plaza San Ignacio
Phone: (115) 4-00-26
Fax: (115) 4-00-70
Well-respected travel agency run by the local *ejido* and a fishing cooperative. While these people are not long-term locals, they have a good reputation in the community.

Expediciones Ecotur
Kilometer 16 on the highway to Ensenada
Phone: (66) 36-11-83
Fax: (619) 662-1720 in U.S.
This reputable Tijuana-based company works very closely with the guides at **Ecotourism Kuyima** and offers numerous travel packages. Five-day hiking trip to the Sierra de San Francisco costs $295 and can be combined with whale-watching.

Malarrimo Eco-Tours
1.4 kilometers (1 mile) west of
  Highway 1 on the edge of
  Guerrero Negro
Phone: (115) 70-1-00
Offers two trips daily to Laguna Ojo
de Liebre, leaving at 8 a.m. and
noon. Trips cost about $40 and
include a box lunch and beverage.

Pueblito Mexico
Matamoros Poniente 314
90500 Huamantla, Tlaxcala
Toll free from the U.S.:
  (888) 313-7252
Fax: 011-52-247-21999
e-mail: pueblito@df1.telmex.net.mx
Web site: http://www
  .eco-travel-mexico.com
Customizes environmental trips in
Veracruz, Puebla, and Tlaxcala.

CENTRAL MEXICO

Al Aire Libre
Centro Comercial Interlomas
Local 2122 Lomas Anahuac
52760 Huixquilucan, Edo de Mexico
Phone: (5) 291-9217
e-mail: RCHRISTY
  @compuserve.com
Offers hiking, mountain climbing,
and adventure sports.

Bike Mex
Calle Guerrero #361, Col. Centro
48300 Puerto Vallarta, Jalisco
Phone/Fax: 011-523-223-1680
e-mail: bikemex@vallarta
  .zonavirtual.com.mx
Web site: http://www
  .vivamexico.com
Offers bike trips along the
Pacific coast.

Campamento Jamapa
Cotaxtla Sur No. 16
Col. Petrolera
Bocca del Rio
91889 Veracruz
Offers river trips down the Jamapa
River to the Pescados, Filo-Bobos,
and Actopan Rivers.

COSCATL
Zacatecas 114
Cuernavaca, Morelos
Phone: (73) 132-146
Contact: Meliton Cross
e-mail: meliton@mail.giga.com
Web site: http://www.giga
  .com~meliton.mx
Operates an eco-friendly lodge (Villa
Calmecac) in Cuernavaca and offers
river trips and caving.

EcoGrupos de Mexico
Centro Comercial Plaza Inn
Av. Insurgentes Sur 1971
Nivel Paseo, loc. 251
Col. Guadalupe Inn
01020 Mexico, D.F.
Phone: (5) 661-9121
Fax: (5) 662-7354
e-mail: ecomexico
  @compuserve.com.mx
Web site: http://www.ecogrupos
  .com.mx
Offers group tours.

EcoGrupos Vallarta
Canario 212 Fracc. Aralias
48328 Puerto Vallarta, Jalisco
Phone: (322) 2-66-06
e-mail: 74174.2424
  @compuserve.com
Contacts: Astrid Frisch and
  Karel Beets
Offers whale-watching and hikes.

Grupo Ecologico Sierra Gorda
Juarez #9
76340 Jalpan de Serra, Queretaro
Phone/Fax: (429) 6-02-42
Contact: Martha Isabel Ruiz Corzo
Offers bird-watching trips in the
Sierra Gorda.

Iguana Expediciones
Cotaxtla Sur 16
Col. Petrolera
94299 Boca del Rio, Veracruz
e-mail: iguanaexp@hotmail.com
Contact: Olga Diaz Ordaz
Offers community-based social
ecotourism and side trips to
archaeology sites.

Mexico Verde
Jose Maria Vigil No. 2406
Col. Italia Providencia
44620 Guadalajara, Jalisco
Phone: (3) 641-5598
Fax: (3) 641-1005
Offers river trips throughout Mexico.

Open Air Expeditions
Guerrero #339, Col. Centro
Apdo. Postal 105-B
48300 Puerto Vallarta, Jalisco
Phone/Fax: (322) 2-3310
e-mail: openair@vallarta
   .zonavirtual.com.mx
Web site: http://www.vivamexico.com
Offers whale-watching tours.

Parque Ecologico de Xochimilco
Periferico Oriente No. 1
Col. Cienega Grande
16070 Xochimilco, D.F.
Phone: (5) 673-8061, 673-7890
Fax: (5) 673-7653
Museum and cultural center in
southern Mexico City featuring
raised gardens, or chinampas.

Rebozo
Apartado Postal 1038
62001 Cuernavaca, Morelos
Phone: (73) 130285
Tailors individual environmental
tours.

Rio y Montaña
Prado Norte 450-T
Lomas de Chapultepec
11000 Mexico, D.F.
Phone: (5) 520-2041 or 520-5018
Fax: (5) 540-7870
e-mail: rioymontana
   @compuserve.com.mx
Offers river trips throughout Mexico.

Terra Noble
Miramar 276
Puerto Vallarta, Jalisco
48300 Mexico
Phone: (322) 3-0308
Fax: 2-4058
e-mail: terra@vallarta.zonavirtual
   .com.mx
Web site: http://www.terranoble
   .com.mx
Spa offering meditation and nature
walks.

Trek Mexico
Havre N. 67-605
Col. Juarez
06600 Mexico, D.F.
Phone: (5) 525-6813 or 525-5213
Fax: (5) 525-5093
Offers adventure tourism trips.

Veraventuras
Santos Degollado No. 81, Int. 8
91000 Xalapa, Veracruz
Phone: (28) 18-9579 or 18-9779
Fax: (28) 18-9680
Offers river trips in Veracruz.

NORTHERN MEXICO

Biodiversidad Mexicana
Antonio Narro #70
Quinta Trinidad
25000 Saltillo, Coahuila
Phone/Fax: (84) 14-96-90
    or 12-84-90
Tours visit cacti in their
native habitats.

Contraste Laguna-Desertica
Av. Victoria No. 826 Sur
Gomez Palacio, Durango
e-mail: canaco@halcon.laguna
    .ual.mx
Web site: http://www.ual.mx/canaco
    /ecoturismo.htm
Offers tours of the Chihuahua
Desert.

Desarrollo Sostenible Para el Valle de Cuatro Cienegas, A.C.
Casa de la Cultura
Cuatro Cienegas, Coahuila
Has list of bed-and-breakfasts and
tourism services in the beautiful town
of Cuatro Cienegas. Offers tours of
the area's white gypsum dunes and
desert lagoons.

LOBO, S.A.
Turismo de Aventura
Av. Francisco Villa No. 3700-10A
Col. Lomas del Sol
31200 Chihuahua, Chihuahua
Phone: (14)-21-56-26
Contact: Fernando Dominguez
Arvizo, Director General
Specializes in Corredor Turistico
Basaseachi-Uruachi.

Pantera Excursions
Apdo 670
Durango, Durango

Phone: (18) 25-06-82
e-mail: pantera@omanet.com.mx.
One of Mexico's ecotourism pio-
neers, this company offers several
four-day cycling trips ($60 per per-
son per day) to Copper Canyon,
and regional waterfalls and hiking
trips in the Zone of Silence (Mapimí
Biosphere Reserve).

Renacer de la Sierra
Ave. Nogalar Sur #321
Monterrey, Nuevo León
Phone: (8) 353-90-23
Rents cabins in the spectacular Sierra
Santa Marta. Visits help fund refor-
estation efforts.

SOUTHERN MEXICO

Agencia de Viajes Chincultic
Real de Guadalupe No. 34
29200 San Cristóbal de las Casas,
    Chiapas
Phone/Fax: (967) 8-09-57
Promotes travel throughout Chiapas.

ATC Tour Operadores
16 de Septiembre #16, Box 226
San Cristóbal de las Casas
29200 Chiapas
Phone: (967) 8-2550
Fax: (967) 8-3145
e-mail: atc@sancristobal.podernet
    .com.mx
General-purpose travel agency in
Chiapas.

Chiapas' El Triunfo Biosphere Reserve
Apartado Postal 391
29000 Tuxtla Gutiérrez, Chiapas
Phone: (961) 139-04
Fax: (961) 236-63
e-mail: inhreservas@laneta.apc.org

Contact: Claudia Virgen
Run by the Natural History Institute.

Escudo Jaguar
Las Guacamayas, Chiapas
For reservations contact the
office of STAACH
Tuxtla Gutiérrez,
Chiapas
Phone: (961) 1-14-10
e-mail: staach@laneta.apc.org
Web site: http://www.laneta.apc
    .org/staach
Promotes rural ecotourism
in Chiapas.

**Laguna Miramar:
Ecoturismo Comunitario**
Association Dana
Dr. Navarro 10
Barrio El Cerrillo
San Cristobal de las Casas,
Chiapas
Phone: (967) 8-04-68
e-mail: danamex@mail.internet
    .com.mx
Contact: Fernando Ochoa
    or Ron Nigh
Promotes organic agriculture and
ecotourism in Chiapas.

**SEDETUR, Secretaría
de Desarrollo Turistico**
Gobierno del Estado de Oaxaca
Av. Independencia esq. Garcia Vigil
68000 Ciudad de Oaxaca, Oaxaca
Phone: (951) 61500
e-mail: turinfo@oaxaca.gob.mx
Web site: http://oaxaca.gob
    .mx/sedetur
Provides ecological lodging in
the Tourist Yu'u hostels near
Oaxaca City.

Viajes Pakal
Cuauhtemoc 6-A
San Cristóbal de las Casas,
Chiapas
Phone/Fax: (967) 8-28-19
Fax: (967) 8-28-18
Packages trips to Chiapas.

YUCATÁN

Aqua Safari
Box 41
Cozumel, Quintana Roo
Phone: (987) 20101
Fax: (987) 20661
e-mail: dive@aquasafari.com
Highly recommended diving
operation.

Ecoturismo Yucatán
Calle 3 #235, between 32-A and 34
Colonia Pensiones
Mérida, Yucatán
Phone: (99) 25-21-87
or 20-27-72
e-mail: ecoyuc@minter.cieamer
    .conacyt.mx
Web site: http://www.imagenet.com
    .mx/EcoYuc/
Contacts: Alfonso Escobedo
and Roberta Graham de Escobedo
Offers specialized tours for
bird-watchers and nature lovers.
Destinations include Celestún
Biosphere Reserve and Ría
Lagartos. Offers week-long lodging
at Xixim, a luxury hotel north
of Celestún.

El Eden Ecological Reserve
Apdo. Postal 770
Cancún, Quintana Roo, 77500
Phone/Fax: (98) 80-50-32
e-mail: mlazcano@cancun.rce
    .com.mx

Web site: http://www.ucr.edu/pril
/peten/images/el_eden/Home.html
Private nature reserve and
local NGO committed to
conservation.

U.S. TRAVEL CONTACTS

Baja Discovery
P.O. Box 152527
San Diego, CA 92195
Phone: (800) 829-2252
e-mail: BajaDis@aol.com
Web site: http://www
.bajadiscovery.com/
Offers whale-watching trips.

Baja Expeditions
2625 Garnet Ave.
San Diego, CA 92109
Phone: (800) 843-6967
Fax: (619) 581-6542
e-mail: travel@bajaex.com
Web site: http://www.bajaex.com/
Offers whale-watching trips.

Ceiba Adventures
P.O. Box 2274
Flagstaff, AZ 86003
Phone: (520) 527-0171
Fax: (520) 527-8127
Contact: Scott Davis
Offers kayak and paddle-boat trips on
the rivers of southern Mexico, as well
as cave trips and treks to Maya ruins.

Earthwatch
680 Mt. Auburn St.
P.O. Box 9104
Watertown, MA 02272-9104
Phone: (800) 776-0188
Fax: (617) 926-8532
Natural-history trips and volunteer
opportunities.

Far Flung Adventures
P.O. Box 377
Terlingua, TX 79852
Phone: (915) 371-2489
    or (800) 359-4138
Offers river trips in Veracruz and
Chiapas as well as in the Big
Bend/Maderas del Carmen area on
the border.

Far Horizons
P.O. Box 91900
Albuquerque, NM 87199-1900
Phone: (800) 552-4575
Offers cultural and archaeological
tours.

Forum Travel International
91 Gregory Ln., #21
Pleasant Hill, CA 94523
Phone: (510) 671-2900
Fax: (510) 671-2993
Offers environmental tours.

International Expeditions
One Environs Park
Helena, AL 35080
Phone: (800) 633-4734
Offers natural-history tours.

Mountain Travel Sobek
6420 Fairmount Ave.
El Cerrito, CA 94530
Phone: (800) 227-2384
Offers natural-history tours.

Sierra Club Outings Department
730 Polk St.
San Fransisco, CA 94109
Phone: (415) 923-5522
Offers natural-history tours.

Victor Emmanuel Tours
P.O. Box 33008
Austin, Texas 78764

Phone: (512) 328-5221 or
(800) 328-8368
Offers birding and natural-history
tours, as well as trips to El Triunfo
Biosphere Reserve in Chiapas.

MEXICO'S ENVIRONMENTAL CONTACTS

BINATIONAL INSTITUTIONS

**Border Environment
Cooperation Commission
(BECC)**
Apartado Postal 3114-J
Ciudad Juárez, Chihuahua.
P.O. Box 221648
El Paso, TX 79913
Phone: (16) 29-23-95, 96, or 98
Fax: (16) 29-23-97
e-mail: becc1@ITSNET.COM

**International Boundary and
Water Commission (IBWC)/**
La Comision Internacional de
Limites y Aguas (CILA)
4171 N. Mesa, Suite 312
El Paso, TX 79902
Phone: (915) 534-6699
Fax: (915) 534-6680

**North American Development
Bank (NADBank)**
425 Soledad, Suite 610
San Antonio, TX 78205-1506
Phone: (210) 231-8000
Fax: (210) 231-6232
e-mail: anniea@ONR.COM

MEXICAN GOVERNMENT AGENCIES

**Comisión Metropolitano para
el Control y Prevención de la**

Contaminación Ambiental
Plaza de la Constitución No. 1
Piso 3
Col. Centro Histórico
06000 Mexico, D.F.
Phone: (5) 542-9311
Fax: (5) 522-6289
Instituto Nacional de Ecologia
Av. Revolución 1425
Col. Tlacopac del Avaro Obregón
01040 Mexico, D.F.
Web site: http://www.ine.gob.mx/

**La Comisión Nacional para el
Conocimiento y Uso de la
Biodiversidad (CONABIO)**
Fernandez Leal # 43 Barrio de la
Concepción Coyoacan
04020 Mexico, D.F.
Phone/Fax: (5) 554-4332
or 554-7472
e-mail: dirproy@xolo.conabio
.gob.mx
Web site: http://www.conabio
.gob.mx/
Contact: Jorge Soberon

**Secretariat of Environment,
Natural Resources, and Fisheries
(SEMARNAP)**
Phone/Fax: (5) 516-9144
Web site: http://semarnap.conabio
.gob.mx/

NONGOVERNMENTAL ORGANIZATIONS (NGOs)

Central Mexico

**Centro Ecologico
los Cuartos, A.C.**
Camino a Valladolid s/n
Ex- Hacienda Los Cuartos
Jesus Maria, Aguascalientes
Phone: (496) 5-0012 and 5-0138
e-mail: cecac@laneta.apc.org

Contact: Martin Barberena-Cruz
Works on reforestation projects in
Central Mexico.

**Centro Mexicano de Derecho
Ambiental (CEMDA)**
Atlixo 138
Col. Condesa
06148 Mexico, D.F.
Phone: (5) 211-2457
Fax: (5) 211-2593
e-mail: cemda@laneta.apc.org
Contact: Gustavo Alanis Ortega
Environmental law group which has
prepared a number of reports, in-
cluding one on the decentralization
of environmental laws and another
on the Cozamel Pier issue.

**Comite Nacional para la Defensa
de los Chimalapas**
Av. Division del Norte #1238-1
Col. Letran Valle
03650 Mexico, D.F.
Phone: (5) 605-5242
Fax: (5) 605-5281
e-mail: pacto@laneta.apc.org
Works on community issues in the
Chimalapas, Oaxaca.

**ECOH-Ecodesarrollo
Humano, A.C.**
Dr. Barragan # 631-5, Col. Narvarte
03020 Mexico, D.F.
Fax: (5) 590 6191
e-mail: arcoredes@laneta.apc.org
Contact: Carlos E. Pacheco Ochoa
Focuses on environmental education
and spirituality.

Ecosolar
Av. Eugenia No. 1510
Col. Narvarte
03020 Mexico, D.F.
Phone: (5) 543-4431 or 543-7398
Contact: Hector Marcelli

e-mail: ecosolar@laneta.apc.org
Promotes environmental
technologies.

**Environmental Education and
Training Institute of North
America (EETINA)**
Campos Eliseos 400, Planta Baja
Col. Lomas de Chapultepec
11000 Mexico D.F.
Phone: (5) 281-1516
Fax: (5) 280-2851
e-mail: eetina@mail.internet.com.mx
Respected environmental group spe-
cializing in environmental education.

**Fondo Mexicano para la
Conservacion de la Naturaleza
(FMCN)**
Fondo Mexicano
Calle Damas 49
San Jose Insurgentes
03900 Mexico, D.F.
Phone/Fax: (5) 611-9779
e-mail: fmcndher@datasys.com.mx
Contacts: Lorenzo de Rosenzweig
Pasquel (director), Diane Herman-
son (communications)
This new organization funds conser-
vation efforts in Mexico.

**Fundacion Ecologica
de Guanajuato**
Apdo. Postal 454
Guanajuato 36000, Gto.
Phone: (47) 17-20-98 or 17-01-11
Fax: (47) 17-13-70
Contact: Robert Avino
Protects the Santa Rosa Forest
Watershed which feeds the city of
Guanajuato.

**Grupo de Estudios
Ambientales (GEA)**
Allende No. 7
Apdo. Postal 76-089

Col. Santa Ursula Coapa
04650 Mexico, D.F.
Contacts: Alfonso Gonzalez and
Margot Aguilar
Phone: (5) 617-9027 or 617-1657
e-mail: gea@laneta.apc.org
Produces practical environmental
studies.

**Grupo de Los Cien
Internacional, A.C.**
Sierra Jiutepec 155-B
Col. Lomas Barrilaco
11010 Mexico, D.F.
Phone: (5) 540-7379
Fax (5) 520-3577
e-mail: grupo100@laneta.apc.org
This respected environmental group
has pushed for the conservation of
sea turtles, monarch butterflies, and
gray whales.

Grupo Ecologico Sierra Gorda
Juarez #9
76340 Jalpan de Serra, Queretaro
Phone/Fax: (429) 6 02 42
e-mail (Jalpan): sierrago@ciateq.mx
e-mail (Queretaro): sierrago
@mpsnet.com.mx
Contacts: Martha Isabel Ruiz Corzo
and Roberto Pedraza
Promotes environmental education
in the Sierra Gorda.

**Instituto Mexicano
de Recursos Renovables**
Dr. Vertiz 724
Mexico, D.F.
Phone: (5) 519-1633 or 519-4505
e-mail: imernar@laneta.apc.org
Contact: Enrique Beltran Gutierrez
This is one of Mexico's pioneering
environmental institutes. Their
library is open to the public.

**Mexican Action Network
on Free Trade (RMALC)**
Godard No. 20
Col. Guadalupe Victoria
07790 Mexico, D.F.
Phone: (5) 355-1177
e-mail: rmalc@laneta.apc.org
Web site (Español): http://www
.laneta.apc.org/rmalc/rmalcesp.htm
Web site (English): http://www
.laneta.apc.org/rmalc/rmalcing.htm
Contact: Berta Lujan
Links environmental and trade
issues.

Naturalia, A.C.
Auriga No. 9,
Col. Prado Churubusco
09480 Mexico, D.F.
Phone: (5) 674-6678
Fax: (5) 674-3876
e-mail: nturalia@servidor.unam.mx
Contact: Oscar Moctezuma
Publishes the bimonthly *Naturalia*
magazine on Mexican biodiversity
and supports a number of conserva-
tion efforts throughout Mexico.

**Programa de Accion Forestal
Tropical (PROAFT)**
Avenida Progresso 5
Col. Coyoacan
04110 Mexico, D.F.
Phone: (5) 568-2905 or 568-3318
e-mail: proaft@laneta.apc.org
Contact: Marcela Alvarez Perez-
Duarte
Protects tropical forests by working
with local communities.

Pronatura
Aspergulas No. 22
Col. San Clemente
01740 Mexico, D.F.
Phone: (5) 635 5054

e-mail: 74052.2137@CompuServe
.com; Contact: Hans Hermann
e-mail: 74052.2130@compuserve
.com; Contact: Teresa Chavez
One of Mexico's larger
environmental groups.

Pronatura Veracruz
Av. Murillio Vidal
Museo de Ciencia y Tecnologia
91000 Xalapa, Veracruz
Phone: (28) 128-844
e-mail: verpronatura@laneta.apc.org
Promotes conservation in the state of
Veracruz.

Red de Desarollo Sostenible
Av. San Jeronimo 458, 1er piso
Col. Jardines del Pedregal
01900 Mexico, D.F.
Phone: (5) 668 2064
e-mail: xochram@laneta.apc.org
Web site: http://www.laneta.org/rds/
Contact: Xochitl Ramirez Reivich
U.N.- and Mexican government–
funded organization promoting sus-
tainable development.

**Red Mexicana de Accion
Ecologica y Pacifista (Red
ECO-PAZ)**
Prol. Ote. Av. Moctezuma No. 50
Col. Romero de Terreros Del.
Coyoacan
04310 Mexico, D.F.
Phone: (5) 659-3074
Fax: (5) 658-9471
e-mail: afa0804@aries.fi-b.unam.mx
Contact: Ruben Trevino
Friederichsen
This activist organization links grass-
roots environmentalists.

Unidos Para La Conservacion
Sierra Madre
Prado Norte 324

Lomas de Chapultepec
11000 Mexico, D.F.
Phone: (5) 520-4500
e-mail: asmupc@infosel.net.mx
Contact: Patrico Robles Gil
Environmental conservation group.

Northern Mexico

**Alliance of the Sierra Madre
(CASMAC)**
Divison del Norte 2300,
Suite CH44-0119
Colonia Altavista, Chihuahua
Phone/Fax: (14) 15-5912
U.S. mailing address: 3815 Buckner
"E", Suite CH44-119,
El Paso, TX 79925
e-mail: sierrarg@igc.apc.org
Contact: Edwin Bustillos or
Randy Gingrich
Promotes conservation of the Sierra
Madre Occidental.

Bioconservación
Apartado Postal 504
San Nicolas, NL 66450
Phone: (8) 376-2231
Fax: (8) 376-2231
Contact: Salvador Contreras
Focuses on biodiversity in Nuevo
Leon.

Bosques de las Californias
Ensenada, Baja California
e-mail: cuevas@cicese.mx
Promotes binational cooperation in
the protection of the Sierra San
Pedro Mártir.

Club Ecologico Novaterra
Morelos 870 Ote.
Monterrey, NL 64000
Phone: (8) 342-1330
Fax: 344-9714
Contact: Alfredo Perez Salinas

Environmental education and recreation group.

Comite de Divulgación Ecologica

Mexicali, Baja California
Phone: (65) 52-20-80
Contact: Fernando Medina Robles
This activist organization is known for its environmental research and information distribution.

Ducks Unlimited

Monterrey, NL
Phone: (8) 378-6648
Web site: http://www.infosel.com.mx /mercado/dumac/
This group of hunters protects duck habitat throughout North America.

Eco-Sol Educacion y Cultura Ecologica

Rio Colorado No. 836
Col. Revolución
22400 Tijuana, BC
Phone: (66) 86-3687
Contact: Jose Luis Morales
This group's focus is on environmental education.

Federacion Mexicana de Asociaciones Privadas de Salud y Desarrollo Comunitario (FEMAP)

Plutarco E. Calles 744 Nte.
Col. Progresista
32310 Ciudad Juárez, Chihuahua
Phone: (16) 16-0833 or 13-6035
Fax: (16) 16-6535
e-mail: femap@infolnk.net
Created the Ecotechnological Research Institute in 1993. Projects include the training of brickmakers, development of a safe water program, and recycling industrial solid waste.

Guardianes del Valle

Direcion de Ecologia
Cuatro Ciénegas, Coahuila
Phone: (869) 600-24
Fax: (869) 600-51
Contact: Gonzalo Zamora and Javier Gonzalez

Holistic Resource Management

Guerrero 103 Poniente
26340 Muzquiz, Coahuila
Phone: (861) 606-80
Contact: Gullermo Osuna
Promotes sustainable management of Mexican range land.

La Red Fronteriza de Salud y Ambiente

Apartado Postal 712
Hermosillo, Sonora 83000
Phone: (62) 60-2250
Fax: (62) 60-2250
Contact: Rosa Delia Caudillo
Environmental network.

Pacto Ecologico

Pino Suárez #1123
Monterrey, NL 64000
Phone: (8) 74-07-31
Fax: (8) 74-07-48
Contact: Maria de Jesus Huerta Rea
Promotes industrial views of how well business complies with environmental norms in Nuevo León.

Profauna

Universidad Autonoma Agraria
Apartado Postal #486
25000 Saltillo, Coahuila
Phone: (841) 7-30-22
Fax: (841) 4-49-97
Contact: Eglantina Canales, Cecilia Ochoa Blackaller, or Rocio Trevino
Environmental research and education in the state of Coahuila.

Pronatura Baja California
e-mail: pnbaja@el-vigia
.microsol.com.mx
Promotes conservation in Baja
California.

Terra Nostra
19 Mendez y Doblado #220-A
Cd. Victoria, Tamps. 87000
Phone: (131) 6-83-52
Contact: Sergio Medellin, Jose Luis
Duran Montenegro
Promotes sustainable development in
several communities, including the
El Cielo Biosphere Reserve.

Southern Mexico

Amigos de Sian Ka'an
Ave. Coba No. 5, Desp. 48-50
Apdo 770
77500 Cancún, Quintana Roo
Phone: (98) 84-9583
Fax: 97-3088
e-mail: sian@cancun.rce.com.mx
Contact: Juan Bezaury
Works within the Sian Ka'an
Biosphere Reserve.

**Centro de Investigación
y Desarrollo Binniza**
Simbolos Patrios S/N
Juchitan, Oaxaca
Phone: (971) 10829
e-mail: guenda@antequera.com
Contact:Vicente Marcial or
Lilia Cruz Altamirano
Works with community organizations
and specializes in the sustainable har-
vest of natural dyes such as indigo.

Centro Mexicano de la Tortuga
Apdo, Postal, 16
70902 Puerto Angel, Oaxaca
Mazunte, Tonameca, Oaxaca

Phone: (958) 43-055
Fax: 43-063

**Comisión Oaxaquena
de Defensa Ecologica**
M. Bravo 210, segundo patio altos
68000 Ciudad de Oaxaca, Oaxaca
Phone/Fax: (951) 60-097
e-mail: codeinso@laneta.apc.org

**Estudios Rurales y Asesoria,
A.C.**
A.P. 24 Colonia Reforma
68050, Oaxaca, Oaxaca
Phone/Fax: (951) 356-71
e-mail: era@antequera.com
Web site: http://www.antequera
.com/personales/era.html
Contact: Francisco Chapela
Conducts environmental research in
Oaxaca.

Instituto de Historia Natural
Calzada Cerro Hueco S/N
Miguel Alvarez del Toro
Apartado 970
Tuxla Gutiérrez, Chiapas 29000
Phone: (961) 237-54
Promotes conservation in Chiapas.

Luum Kanaab
Puerto Morelos, Quintana Roo
Phone: (987) 10126
Contact: Sandra Dayton
   or Dina Drago
e-mail: starseed@cancun.rce.com.mx
Environmental education group; promotes and builds composting
toilets.

Maya Ik'
Turismo Ecologico y Cultural del
Pueblo Maya
San Cristóbal de las Casas Chiapas
Phone: (967) 8-69-98

e-mail: mayaik@sancristobal
.podernet.com.mx
Contact: Margarito Ruiz
Promotes sustainable tourism in
indigenous communities throughout
Mexico.

Mi Amigo el Arbol
Tinoco y Palacios 411
068000 Ciudad de Oaxaca, Oaxaca
Contact: Jorge Augusto Velasco
Committee formed to protect tule
trees.

OCEAN
22 de Diciembre, No. 1,
Col. Manuel Avila Camacho,
53910 Naucalpan, State of Mexico
Phone: (5) 293-1322, 294-1710, or
294-1032
e-mail: Andrew@bciencias.ucol.mx
Web site: http://www.ucol.mx/ocean/
Focuses on environmental studies
and conservation, particularly in the
state of Colima.

Planeta Limpio
Blvd. Kukulcan, Kilometer 13
Zona Hostelera
Cancún, Quintana Roo
Phone: (98) 85-22-00
NGO formed in February 1995 "by
a group of young entrepreneurs
interested in protecting the environ-
ment." Works with the Center for
Marine Conservation (CMC) based
in Washington, DC.

Pronatura Chiapas
Av. Benito Juárez 9
29200 San Cristóbal de las Casas,
Chiapas
Phone/Fax: (967) 8-5000
e-mail: pronaturach@laneta.apc.org
Conservation group in Chiapas.

Pronatura Yucatán
Calle 1-D No. 254-A x 36
Col. Campestre
97120 Mérida, Yucatán
Phone: (99) 44-22-90 or 44-35-80
e-mail: ppy@pibil.finred.com.mx
Contacts: Susana Rojas, Rodrigo
Migoya, or Sonya Macys
This environmental group works
closely with the Calakmul, Celestún,
and Rio Lagartos Biosphere
Reserves.

Yaxche, Arbol de la Vida
Calle 68 x 51 S/N
Apdo. Postal 7
Altos SM 4
Cancún, Quintana Roo
Phone/Fax: (98) 844-312 or 847-987
e-mail: ecab@cancun.rce.com.mx
Contacts: Carlos Meade or Victor
Sumohano
Links conservation and indigenous
issues in Southern Mexico.

RESEARCH CENTERS AND UNIVERSITIES

Central Mexico

**Centro de Ecologia y
Desarollo (Cecodes)**
Chiapas 208, Dept. 7
Colonia del Valle
03810 Mexico, D.F.
Phone: (5) 264-8758 or 264-2138
e-mail: cecodes@laneta.apc.org
Contact: Ivan Restrepo
Formerly known as the Centro de
Ecodesarollo, this respected research
institution produces numerous reports
and studies on Mexican environmen-
tal issues, including the monthly
Ecologia supplement that appears in
La Jornada newspaper.

Coffee Producers Confederation

(Coordinadora Nacional de Organi-
zaciones Cafetaleras or CNOC)
Tabasco 262-301
Colonia Roma
01400 Mexico, D.F.
Phone: (5) 207-0508 and 514-0205
e-mail: cnoc@laneta.apc.org
Web site: http://www.laneta.apc
  .org/cnoc/
Contact: Fernando Celis
Autonomous network of 125
campesino organizations that work
with more than 75,000 small-scale
Mexican coffee producers. CNOC has
established a company, Promotora
Comercial de Cafes Suaves Mexicanos, to promote coffee exports.

Fundacion Dana, A.C., Consultores en Agricultura Organica

Parque Ecologico Loreto y
  Peña Pobre
Avenida San Fernando 765
14210 Tlalpan, D.F.
Phone/Fax: (5) 666-7366
e-mail: danamex@mail.internet
  .com.mx
Contact: Ron Nigh
Promotes grassroots development,
particularly in the state of Chiapas.

Instituto Autonomo de Investigaciones Ecologicas (INAINE)

Gladiolas 56
Col. Jardin
04370 Mexico City, D.F.
Phone: (5) 689-6885
Fax: (5) 689-5972
An established environmental
research group. Director Guerra is a
respected radio commentator who
promotes environmental awareness
in Mexico City.

Programa Universitario de Medio Ambiente

Edificio de la Coordinación de la
Investigación Cientifica
Planta Baja
Ciudad Universitaria
04510 Mexico, D.F.
Phone: (5) 622-4186 or 622-4170
Fax: (5) 550-88-34
Web site: http://tzetzal.dcaa.unam
  .mx/puma/puma.html
The National Autonomous Univer-
sity's environmental program.

Northern Mexico

Centro de Calidad Ambiental (Cedes)

Monterey Tech
Ave. Eugenio Garza Sada 2501 Sur
Monterrey, N.L.
Phone: (83) 358-2000, ext. 5019
Fax: (83) 359-6280
Environmental studies and
technology.

El Colegio de la Frontera Norte (COLEF)

Blvd. Abelardo L. Rodriguez, #2925
Zona del Rio
22320 Tijuana, Baja California
Phone: (66) 30-04-11
Fax: (66) 84-87-95
Contact: Oscar Romo
Environmental studies and research;
focuses on the borderlands.

El Colegio de Mexico

Avenida Obregon #54
83000 Hermosillo Sonora
Phone: (62) 120015
Fax: (62) 125021
Contact: Catalina Denman
Environmental studies and research;
focuses on the borderlands.

Instituto del Medio Ambiente y Desarrollo Sustentable del Estado de Sonora (IMADES)
Col. San Benito
83190 Hermosillo, Sonora
Phone: (62) 14-32-01, 10-3662
Fax: (62) 14-6508
e-mail: arias@cideson.mx
Contacts: Juan Carlos Barrera, Ivan Parra, or Hector Arias Rojo
A new institution which merges CIDESON (Centro de Investigación Desarrollo de los Recursos Naturales de Sonora) and CES (Centro Ecologico de Sonora).

Universidad Autonoma de Ciudad Juárez
Centro de Estudios del Medio Ambiente
Av. del Charro 610
Cd. Juarez, Chihuahua.
Phone: (521) 617-5758
Fax: (521) 611-2114
e-mail: fvazquez@infolnk.net;
   Contact: Adrian Vazquez
e-mail: garzavic@infolnk.net;
   Contact: Victoriano Garza
Web site: http:\\www.uacj.mx
Develops low-cost mitigation technologies and collects and studies information on the status of the environment along the border.

Universidad Autonoma de Nuevo León
Facultad de Ciencias Biologicas
Apartado Postal 134-F
Cd. Universitaria
66450 San Nicolas de los Garza, NL
Phone: (8) 352-4783 or 352-2139
Contact: Glafiro Alanis Flores
Conducts environmental research in Nuevo León.

Universidad Autonoma de Nuevo León
Facultad de Ciencias Biologicas
Unid. B.
Cd. Universitaria, Apdo. 2970
64000 Monterrey, NL
Phone: (83) 76-22-31
e-mail: scontrer@ccr.dsi.uanl.mx
Contact: Salvador Contreras Balderas
Offers environmental programs and conducts research with a focus on Northeastern Mexico.

Universidad Autonoma de Tamaulipas
Instituto de Ecologia y Alimentos
Blvd. Adolfo Lopez Mateos No. 928
87040 Ciudad Victoria, Tamaulipas
Contact: Carlos Gutierrez Nunez
Environmental research in Tamaulipas.

Southern Mexico

Bosque Modelo Calakmul (Calakmul Model Forest)
Zoh Laguna, Campeche
Fax: (983) 23304
Contact: Esteban Martinez, general manager
Operates within southeastern Campeche, and borders on Guatemala, Belize, the Calakmul Biosphere Reserve, and the state of Quintana Roo.

Centro de Investigación y de Estudios Avanzados del Instituto Politecnico Nacional (CINVESTAV)
A.P. 73, o Km 6 Antigua Carretera a Progreso
97310 Merida, Yucatán

Phone: (99) 81-29-60 or 81-29-73,
ext. 73
Fax: (99) 81 46 70
Conducts academic research on environmental conservation in the Yucatán.

Estudios Rurales y Asesoria, A.C.
A.P. 24 Colonia Reforma
68050, Oaxaca, Oaxaca
Phone/Fax: (951) 356 71
e-mail: era@antequera.com
Web site: http://antequera
.com/esturura.html
Contact: Francisco Chapela
This well-respected group focuses on environmental conservation and rural development in Oaxaca.

INTERNATIONAL FOUNDATIONS AND ENVIRONMENTAL FRANCHISES

Centro Mexicano para la Filantropia (CEMEFI)
Mazatlan No. 96
Col. Condesa
06140 Mexico, D.F.
Phone: (5) 256-3739
Fax: (5) 256-3190
e-mail: cemefi@laneta.apc.org
Philanthropic group.

Conservation International, Chiapas
Rancho el Arenal
Carretera al Club Campestre
Terran, Kilometer 2.2
Tuxtla, Gutierrez 29050, Chiapas
Phone/Fax: 96151951
e-mail: CI-Chiapas
@conservation.org
Focuses on environmental research and conservation.

Conservation International, Guaymas
Miramar #63 Altos
Colonia Miramar
85450 Guaymas, Sonora
Phone: (622) 10194
Fax: (622) 12030
e-mail: CI-Guaymas
@conservation.org
Focuses on environmental research and conservation, particularly in the Sea of Cortez.

Conservation International, Mexico, A.C
Camino al Ajusco No. 124, 1o piso
Fracc. Jardines de la Montana
14210 Tlalpan, D.F.
Phone/Fax: (5) 6301407
e-mail: CI-Mexico@conservation.org
Contact: Alejandro Robles
This is the U.S. environmental group's main Mexico office.

Ford Foundation
Alejandro Dumas No. 42
Col. Polanco
11560 Mexico, D.F.
Phone: (5) 280-3047
This foundation sponsors meetings of academics, environmental groups, and government officials which are usually held behind closed doors.

Friederich Ebert Foundation
Ejercito Nacional 539
5 Piso
11520 Mexico
Phone: (5) 250-0533 or 250-0050
Produces numerous grassroots publications and workshops, and has done exceptional work in Veracruz.

Greenpeace
Av. Cuauhtemoc 946
Col. Narvarte
03020 Mexico, D.F.
e-mail: greenpeace.mexico
@green2.greenpeace.org
Stages popular environmental theater.

Sociedad Audubon de Mexico
Sierra Gorda #12
37720 San Miguel de Allende,
Guanajuato
Phone/Fax: (415) 2-3337
e-mail: LaJudyA@aol.com
Environmental education and refor-
estation, focusing on the states of
Guanajuato and Queretaro.

World Wildlife Fund
Avenida Mexico #51
Colonia Hipodromo
Mexico, D.F.
Phone: (5) 286-5631 or 286-5634
e-mail: gcastiwwfmex
@compuserve.com
Uses international monies to funds
several programs throughout the
country.

INTERNATIONAL CONTACTS

Friends of PRONATURA
240 East Limberlost Drive
Tucson, AZ 85705
Phone: 602-887-1188
e-mail: closfree@aol.com
Assists programs of various
Pronatura chapters in Mexico. The
group has a strong presence in the
Sonoran Desert.

**Mesoamerican Environmental
Law Project**
Center for Governmental
Responsibility

University of Florida College of Law
230 Bruton-Geer
Gainesville, FL 32611
Phone: (352) 392-2237
e-mail: Ankersen@LAW.UFL.EDU
Contact: Tom Ankerson
Environmental law research and
activism; focuses on Mexico and
Central America.

EMBASSIES IN MEXICO CITY

Argentinian Embassy
Plaza Inverlat
Blvd. Manuel Avila Camacho No. 1,
seventh and eighth floors
Col. Lomas de Chapultepec
11000 Mexico, D.F.
Phone: (5) 520-9431
Fax: (5) 540-5011

Australian Embassy
Plaza Polanco
Jaime Balmes No. 11
B-Tower, tenth floor
Col. Polanco
11510 Mexico, D.F.
Phone: (5) 395-9988
Fax: (5) 395-7870

Austrian Embassy
Sierra Tarahumara No. 420
Col. Lomas de Chapultepec
11000, Mexico, D.F.
Phone: (5) 251-9792 or 251-1606
Fax: (5) 245-0198

Belgian Embassy
Musset No. 41
Col. Polanco
11550 Mexico, D.F.
Phone: (5) 280-0758 or 280-1008
Fax: (5) 280-0208

Belizean Embassy
Bernardo de Gálvez No. 215
Col. Lomas Virreyes
11000 Mexico, D.F.
Phone: (5) 520-1274 or 520-1346
Fax: (5) 520-6089

Brazilian Embassy
Lope de Armendáriz No. 130
Col. Lomas Virreyes
11000 Mexico, D.F.
Phone: (5) 202-8737 or 202-7500

British Embassy
Río Lerman No. 71
Col. Cuauhtémoc
06500 Mexico, D.F.
Phone: (5) 207-2089 or 207-2186
Fax: (5) 207-7672

Canadian Embassy
Schiller No. 529
Col. Chapultepec Polanco
11560 Mexico, D.F.
Phone: (5) 724-7900

Chilean Embassy
Andres Bello 10
Col. Polanco, 11560
11000 Mexico, D.F.
Phone: (5) 280-9681

Chinese Republic Embassy
Río Magdalena No. 172
Col. Tizapan San Angel
0109TK Mexico, D.F.
Phone: (5) 616-0609 550-0823
Fax: (5) 616-0460

Colombian Embassy
Paseo de la Reforma No. 1620
Col. Lomas de Chapultepec
11000 Mexico, D.F.
Phone: (5) 202-7299
Fax: (5) 520-9669

Costa Rican Embassy
Río Poo No. 113
Col. Cuauhtémoc
06500 Mexico, D.F.
Phone: (5)525-7764 or 525-7765
Fax: (5) 207-6444

Cuban Embassy
Presidente Mazaryk No. 554
Col. Chapultepec Polanco
11560 Mexico, D.F.
Phone: (5) 280-8039

Danish Embassy
Calle 3 Picos No. 43
Col. Polanco Chapultepec
11580 Mexico, D.F.
Phone: (5) 255-3339 or 255-3405
Fax: (5) 245-5797

Dominican Republic Embassy
Insurgentes Sur No. 216-300
Col. Roma Sur
06170 Mexico, D.F.
Phone: (5) 533-5784

Ecuadorian Embassy
Tennyson No. 217
Col. Chapultepec Polanco
11560 Mexico, D.F.
Phone: (5) 545-9504

Egyptian Republic Embassy
Alejandro Dumas No. 131
Col. Polanco
11560 Mexico, D.F.
Phone: (5) 281-0698

Ethiopian Embassy
Miguel de Cervantes No. 465-602
Col. Irrigación
11500 Mexico, D.F.
Phone: (5) 557-2238 557-0772

Finnish Embassy
Monte Pelvoux No. 111, fourth floor
Col. Lomas de Chapultepec
11000 Mexico, D.F.

French Embassy
Campos Elíseos No. 339
Col. Chapultepec Polanco
11560 Mexico, D.F.
Phone: (5) 282-9700

German Embassy
Lord Byron No. 737
Col. Chapultepec Polanco
11560 Mexico, D.F.
Phone: (5) 280-5409 280-5534
Fax: (5) 281-2588

Greek Embassy
Paseo de las Palmas No. 2060
Col. Lomas Reforma
11020 Mexico, D.F.
Phone: (5) 596-6333 or 596-6038
Fax: (5) 251-3001

Guatemalan Embassy
Explanada No. 1025
Col. Lomas de Chapultepec
11000 Mexico, D.F.
Phone: (5) 540-7520 or 520-9249
Fax: (5) 202-1142

Honduran Embassy
Alfonso Reyes No. 220
Col. Condesa
06140 Mexico, D.F.
Phone: (5) 5515-6689 or 211-5250
Fax: (5) 211-5425

Israeli Embassy
Sierra Madre No. 215
Col. Lomas de Chapultepec
11000 Mexico, D.F.
Phone: (5) 540-6340 or 282-4825

Italian Embassy
Paseo de las Palmas No. 1994
Col. Lomas de Chapultepec
11000 Mexico, D.F.
Phone: (5) 596-3655 or 554-6662

Jamaican Embassy
Monte Líbano No. 885
Col. Lomas de Chapultepec
11000 Mexico, D.F.
Phone: (5) 520-1421 or 520-1814

Japanese Embassy
Paseo de la Reforma No. 395
Col. Cuauhtémoc
06500 Mexico, D.F.
Phone: (5) 211-0028

Korean Republic Embassy
Lope de Armendáriz No. 110
Col. Lomas Virreyes
11000 Mexico, D.F.
Phone: (5) 202-9866 or 202-7866
Fax: (5) 540-7446

Netherlands Embassy
Montes Urales Sur No. 635,
Second floor
Col. Lomas de Chapultepec
11000 Mexico, D.F.
Phone: (5) 202-8267 or 202-8346

New Zealand Embassy
J.L. Lagrange No. 103, tenth floor
Col. Los Morales Polanco
11510 Mexico, D.F.
Phone: (5) 281-5486
Fax: (5) 281-5212

Nicaraguan Embassy
Valle de Rivera No. 120
Col. Lomas de Chapultepec
11000 Mexico, D.F.
Phone: (5) 520-4421 or 540-5625
Fax: (5) 520-6960

Norwegian Embassy
Virreyes No. 1460
Col. Lomas Virreyes
11000 Mexico, D.F.
Phone: (5) 540-3486 or 540-5220
Fax: (5) 202-3019

Pakistani Embassy
Hegel No. 512
Col. Chapultepec Morales
11570 Mexico, D.F.
Phone: (5) 203-3636 or 203-1242

Panamanian Embassy
Schiller No. 326
Col. Chapultepec Morales
11570 Mexico, D.F.
Phone: (5) 250-4045
Fax: (5) 250-4174

Paraguayan Embassy
Homero No. 5415, second floor
Col. Chapultepec Polanco
11560 Mexico, D.F.
Phone: (5) 545-9285 or 545-0405
Fax: (5) 531-9905

Peruvian Embassy
Paseo de la Reforma No. 2601
Col. Lomas Reforma
11020 Mexico, D.F.
Phone: (5) 570-2443 or 570-5509

Russian Embassy
José Vasconcelos No. 204
Col. Hipódromo Condesa
06140 Mexico, D.F.
Phone: (5) 273-1305
Fax: (5) 173-1545

Salvadoran Republic Embassy
Paseo de las Palmas No. 1930
Col. Lomas Chapultepec
11000 Mexico, D.F.
Phone: (5) 596-7366 or 596-3339
Fax: (5) 596-7512

Saudi Arabia Embassy
Paseo de la Reforma No. 607
Col. Lomas Reforma
11020 Mexico, D.F.
Phone: (5) 540-3179 or 520-1531

Spanish Embassy
Galileo No. 114
Col. Polanco
11550 Mexico, D.F.
Phone: (5) 282-2974 or 282-2982

Swedish Embassy
Paseo de las Palmas No. 1375
Col. Lomas de Chapultepec
11000 Mexico, D.F.
Phone: (5) 540-6393 or 540-6394
Fax: (5) 540-3253

Swiss Embassy
Torre Optima
Av. De las Palmas No. 405
Col. Lomas de Chapultepec
11000 Mexico, D.F.
Phone: (5) 520-8535 or 520-8685

Uruguayan Embassy
Hegel No. 149, first floor
Col. Chapultepec Polanco
15560 Mexico, D.F.
Phone: (5) 531-0880 or 254-1163
Fax: (5) 531-4029

U.S. Embassy
Paseo de la Reforma No. 305
Col. Cuauhtémoc
06500 Mexico, D.F.
Phone: (5) 211-0042 or 202-6303

Venezuelan Embassy
Schiller No. 326
Col. Chapultepec Morales
11570 Mexico, D.F.
Phone: (5) 203-4233 or 203-4232
Fax: (5) 203-8614

RECOMMENDED READING AND ONLINE RESOURCES

RECOMMENDED READING

CONSERVATION

Defending the Land of the Jaguar: A History of Conservation in Mexico, by Lane Simonian. Austin: University of Texas Press, 1995. Top-notch history of Mexico's environmental consciousness. It will soon be translated into Spanish and made available in Mexico.

Endangered Mexico, by Joel Simon. San Francisco: Sierra Club Books, 1997. Well-crafted overview of Mexico's environmental problems and the citizens who are working to put things back into balance.

Reservas de la Biosfera y Otras Areas Naturales Protegidas de Mexico, by Arturo Gomez Pompa and Rodolfo Dirzo. Mexico City: INE and CONABIO, 1996. Coffee-table book with maps and biological information about all of Mexico's biosphere reserves. It's a terrific resource if you read Spanish.

Two Eagles/Dos Aguilas: The Natural World of the United States-Mexico Borderlands, by Tupper Ansel Blake and Peter Steinhart. Berkeley: University of California Press, 1994. Wonderful coffee-table book, but it's disappointing the sponsoring Nature Conservancy group hasn't made borderland information more widely available.

TRAVEL

Backpacking in Mexico, by Tim Burford. London: Bradt Publications, 1997. Good review of hiking routes in Mexico.

Bicycling Mexico, by Ericka Weisbroth and Eric Ellman. Edison, NJ: Hunter Publishing, Inc., 1990. Slightly out of date, this is an excellent view of Mexico from the cyclist's seat.

Mexico: Travel Survival Kit, by John Noble, Wayne Bernhardson, Tom Brosnahan, Susan Forsyth, Nancy Keller and James Lyon Berkeley: Lonely Planet, 1995. My favorite guide to hotels, bus schedules, and artesenia. Due to be updated in the near future.

Mexico and Central American Handbook, by Ben Box. Chicago: Passport Books, 1995. If you're looking for one-star to five-star hotels and restaurants, this classic guidebook can't be beat.

Mexico's Colonial Heart, by "Mexico" Mike Nelson. McAllen, Texas:

Wanderlust Publications, 1995. Sampling of Mexico's choice colonial cities, complete with a driving guide.

Mexico's Copper Canyon, by Richard D. Fisher. Tucson: Sunracer, 1992. Beautiful photos and an eclectic text.

The New Key to Cancún and the Yucatán, by Richard Harris. Berkeley: Ulysses Press, 1995. Fine review of environmental concerns and travel in the Yucatán.

Northern Mexico Handbook, by Joe Cummings. Chico, Calif.: Moon Publications, 1994. Covers the region from coast to coast. Great resource for border aficionados.

The People's Guide to Mexico, by Carl Franz, edited by Lorena Havens and Steve Rogers. Santa Fe, N.M.: John Muir Publications, 1998. This is the book that brought me to Mexico and Guatemala ten years ago. Now in its 25th year of publication, this book earns its reputation as a classic.

Rethinking Tourism and Ecotravel: The Paving of Paradise and What You Can Do to Stop it, by Deborah McLaren. West Hartford, Conn.: Kumarian Press, 1997. Not a guidebook in the traditional sense, but it provides a good review of what tourism is and can be in developing countries. This is one of my favorite books.

The Road to Mexico, by Lawrence Taylor and Maeve Hickey. Tucson: University of Arizona Press, 1997. Descriptive narrative and evocative photos on the road stretching from Tucson, Arizona, to Magdalena de Kino, Sonora.

Sonora: An Intimate Geography, by David Yetman. Albuquerque: University of New Mexico Press, 1996. A beautiful and personal testimony of changes in Mexico's northwestern border state by a writer who has spent the past 30 years touring the region.

ENVIRONMENT

Biological Diversity of Mexico: Origins and Distribution, edited by T.P. Ramamoorthy, Robert Bye, and Antonio Lot. Oxford and New York: Oxford University Press, 1993. First major review of biodiversity in Mexico. Excellent!

Desert Legends: Re-storying the Sonoran Borderlands, by Gary Paul Nabhan and Mark Klett. New York: Henry Holt and Company, 1994. Mosaic of text and photos from the authors' backyard.

Estadisticas del Medio Ambiente: Mexico 1994, Mexico City: INEGI, 1995 Comprehensive collection of environment-related statistics.

Green Guerrillas: Environmental Conflicts and Initiatives in Latin America and the Caribbean, edited by Helen Collinson. London: Latin American Bureau, 1996. A fine balance of writings by journalists and scholars who have been tracking environmental issues throughout the hemisphere.

Losing Ground: American Environmentalism at the Close of the Twentieth Century, by Mark Dowie. Cambridge: MIT Press, 1995. Demonstrates how national and international environmental groups have lost touch with local environmentalists. A good review of NAFTA and politics in the U.S.-Mexico borderlands.

Monarcas y Campesinos, by Gonzalo Chapela and David Barkin. Centro de Ecologia y Desarrollo, 1995. Links environmental conservation in the Monarch Sanctuary with the lives of nearby farmers. Also proposes interesting ecotourism solutions.

Medio Ambiente y Desarrollo en Mexico, by Enrique Leff. Two vols., Mexico City: Centro de Investigaciones Interdisciplinarias en Humanidades and Miguel Angel Porrua, 1990. Spanish-language review of environmental policies.

Mountain Islands and Desert Seas: A Natural History of the U.S.-Mexican Borderlands, by Frederick R. Gehlbach. College Station: Texas A&M University Press, 1993. Engaging review of the borderlands.

Naturalist's Mexico, by Roland H. Wauer. College Station: Texas A&M University Press, 1992.

Parques Nacionales de Mexico, by Fernando Vargas Marquez. Mexico City: Instituto de Investigaciones Economicas, 1984. Outdated, but the best review of the development of Mexico's national parks.

Programa de Areas Naturales Protegidas de Mexico 1995–2000. Mexico City: SEMARNAP, 1996. Overview of environmental protection and priorities. A conceptual work, this book is very light on specific recommendations.

World as Lover, World as Self, by Joanna Macy. Berkeley: Parallax Press, 1991. A collection of talks and essays connecting Buddhism and environmentalism. Macy encourages her readers to treat the world as a lover and as an extension of ourselves.

FIELD GUIDES

A Guide to the Birds of Mexico and Northern Central America, by Steve Howell and Sophie Webb. Oxford: Oxford University Press, 1995. Incredible field guide used by birders throughout Mesoamerica.

Healing with Plants in the American and Mexican West, by Margarita Artschwager Kay. Tucson: University of Arizona Press, 1996. A fine guidebook in any sense of the word. Artschwager asks and answers the right questions: Which plants are dangerous? Where do they come from? What should we know about borderland biodiversity?

A Neotropical Companion: An Introduction to the Animals, Plants and Ecosystems of the New World Tropics, by John Kricher. Princeton: Princeton University Press, 1989. Illustrated and highly useful guide.

INDIGENOUS PEOPLES

The Ancient Maya, by Sylvanius Morley and George Brainerd; revised by Robert Sharer. Stanford: Stanford University Press, 1983. A classic.

Breath on the Mirror: Mythic Voices of the Living Maya, by Dennis Tedlock. San Francisco: Harper Collins, 1993. History and current affairs of the Maya.

Maya Cosmos: Three Thousand Years on the Shaman's Path, by David Friedel, Linda Schele, and Joy Parker. New York: William Morrow, 1993. A wonderful book and must-read for anyone heading to the Yucatán or Chiapas.

Mexico, by Michael Coe. New York: Thames and Hudson, 1982. A beautiful book! Teaches the difference between Zapotec and Olmec cultures, art, and symbolism.

Popul Vuh, by Dennis Tedlock. New York: Simon and Schuster, 1985. The original history of the Maya.

So Sings the Blue Deer, by Charmayne McGee. New York: Athenaeum, 1994. Wonderful children's novel that provides a colorful picture of rural Nayarit and the Huichol Indians.

ONLINE RESOURCES

There are hundreds of great Web sites with information on Mexico. Perhaps one of the most encouraging signs of the information age is that many are created by Mexican students who combine a love of their country with a passion for explaining it to the rest of us.

I have included a number of sites with information in Spanish. Consider this an opportune time to practice your Español. These are all top-notch, content-rich archives; the best are given a star (✮). Updates to this list and other resources are maintained on the **Eco Travels in Latin America** Web site at http://www.planeta.com.

GENERAL INTEREST

Border Encyclopedia
http://www.utep.edu/border/

GlobalNet (SPANISH)
http://www.dirglobal.net

Mexican Yellow Pages
http://www.yellow.com.mx

Mexico Amigo ✮
http://amigo.mexonline.com/

Mexico Connect
http://www.mexconnect.com/

Mexico Online, Inc.
http://www.mexicool.com/

Mexico Web Guide ✮
(SPANISH)
http://mexico.web.com.mx/mexicot
.shtml

Mexmaster (SPANISH)
http://www.mexmaster.com/

South Mex
http://www.southmex.com/index.html

Trace ✮ (SPANISH)
http://www.trace-sc.com/

University of Texas Latin American Information Network Center
http://lanic.utexas.edu/la/Mexico/

Virtual Mexico
http://VirtualMex.com

ENVIRONMENTAL INFORMATION

Centro Ecológico de Sonora
(SPANISH)
http://yaqui.cideson.mx/operacio/

Ducks Unlimited of Mexico
(SPANISH)
http://www.infosel.com.mx:80
/mercado/dumac/

Mexico's National Parks and Protected Areas ✿
http://www2.planeta.com/mader
/ecotravel/mexico/mexparks.html

Na Bolom (SPANISH)
http://www.mexred.net.mx/

National Commission on Biodiversity CONABIO ✿ (SPANISH)
http://www.conabio.gob.mx/textos
/conabio.htm

Natural History Bibliography of Mexico—Roger Steeb ✿
gopher://csf.Colorado.EDU:70/00
/environment/orgs/El_Planeta
_Platica/Mexico/RS_Natural
_History_Bibliography

Rivers of Mexico—INEGI
(SPANISH)
http://www.inegi.gob.mx/homeing
/geografia/climhidr/trio.html

Sea of Cortez: The Dying Sea ✿
http://www.sacbee.com/news
/projects/dyingsea/index.html

SEMARNAP Mexican Environmental Secretariat ✿ (SPANISH)
http://semarnap.conabio.gob.mx/

Specialty Guides

Azteca Empire in Cyberspace
http://www.qvo.com/azteca.html

Baja Information Pages ✿
http://math.ucr.edu/~ftm/baja.html

BBS Laguna ✿ (SPANISH)
http://www.bbslaguna.com.mx/index
.html

Borderlands Environmenal Archives ✿
http://www2.planeta.com/mader
/ecotravel/border/borderlands.html

Ciudad de México—Guia Roji
(SPANISH)
http://www.guiaroji.com.mx/

Fobia (SPANISH)
http://www.fobia.com.mx

Immigration Issues—Daniel Hernandez Joseph
http://spin.com.mx./~dhjoseph/

Internet Providers in Mexico—Daniel Germán ✿
http://www.reidgroup.com/~dmg
/mexico/internet/mexico.html

Internet Resources for Latin America—Molly Molloy ✿
http://lib.nmsu.edu/subject/bord
/laguia/

Letters from Oaxaca—Stan Gottlieb
http://www.mexconnect.com
/letters_from_mexico/lettersindex
.html

Maná (SPANISH)
http://www.mana.com.mx
/f-ecologia.html

Mesoamerican Archaeology ✿
http://copan.bioz.unibas.ch
/meso.html

Mexican Heritage Almanac ✿
http://www.ironhorse.com/~nagual
/alma.html

**Ministry of Tourism
of Mexico**
http://mexico-travel.com/

Mountain Biking in Mexico
http://www.sdm.net.mx/mtybike/

**The Pacific Coast of Oaxaca,
Mexico** ✿
http://www.eden.com/~tomzap
/index.html

Rock 'N' Road Mexico
http://www.rocknroad.com/mex
/mexico.html

**Sanborns Automobile
Insurance**
http://www.hiline.net/sanborns/

Walkabout Travel Gear
http://www.walkabouttravelgear.com/

**Xtreme—La Página de la
Aventura en México**
(SPANISH)
http://xtreme.planet.com.mx/

Newspapers and Magazines

Cronica (SPANISH)
http://www.cronica.com.mx

El Imparcial (SPANISH)
http://www.imparcial.com.mx
/imparenglish.html

El Nacional (SPANISH)
http://serpiente.dgsca.unam.mx
/serv_hem/nacional/home.html

El Norte (SPANISH)
http://www.infosel.com.mx/elnorte/

Guadalajara Reporter
http://www.guadalajara reporter
.com/

La Jornada (SPANISH)
http://www.sccs.swarthmore
.edu/~justin/jornada/index.html

Mexico Business
http://www.MexicoBusiness.com

Mexico Desconocido ✿
(SPANISH)
http://www.mexicodesconocido
.com.mx/

The News ✿
http://www.novedades.com.mx
/environm.htm

INTERNET LISTSERVS

The following services are free and
available to anyone with e-mail.

BECCNET
BECCNET addresses the border
institutions, the Border Environmen-
tal Cooperation Commission
(BECC), and the North American
Development Bank (NADBank).
To subscribe, send the message,
"Subscribe beccnet Your Name"
to listserv@LISTSERV
.ARIZONA.EDU.

CHIAPAS-L:
This is an open, unmoderated discussion list concerning the conflict in
the state of Chiapas and its ongoing
status. This is a very active service.
To subscribe, send the message,
"Subscribe Chiapas-L Email

@Address" in the body of an
e-mail to Majordomo@profmexis
.dgsca.unam.mx.

ELAN

ELAN (Environment and Latin
America) studies ecosystems and
environmental protection throughout
Latin America. To subscribe, send
the message, "Subscribe elan Your
Name" to listserv@csf.colorado.edu.

LATCO

The best means of accessing and
querying business information in
Latin America is found on this list-
server, run by the Latin American
Trade Organization of Oregon. The
Web site is http://www.latco.org.
Subscribe by sending the message,
"Subscribe latco email@address" to
LSERV@psg.com.

Mexico2000

Provides a daily collection of news
articles and reactions. To subscribe,
send the message, "Subscribe Mex-
ico2000 Your Name" in the subject
line to majordomo@mep-d.org.

US_MEXBORDER

The EPA usess this site to host a
focused discussion on the border
environment. To subscribe, send the
message, "Subscribe us_mexborder
Your Name" to listserv@unixmail
.rtpnc.epa.gov.

COMMERCIAL INTERNET SOURCES

Letters from Oaxaca is available as
an e-mail subscription prepared by
Stan Gottlieb. The cost is $25 per
year. A sample newsletter is available
online at http://www.mexconnect
.com/letters_from_mexico
/lettersindex.html. For more details,
contact Stan at stan@infosel.net.mx.

SOURCEMEX is an electronic
weekly offering an insightful synthe-
sis of national news. It's published by
New Mexico's Latin American Data
Base (LADB), and subscriptions are
$50 per year.

The Mexico Internet Report is a
weekly compilation of government,
economic, business, and national
news. Subscriptions cost $25 per
month. Request a trial subscription
from Roy Segovia at rsegovia
@adnc.com. The Web site is
http://www.adnc.com/web/rsegovia/
mexrep.html.

315

INDEX

ABOUT THE AUTHOR

Ron Mader is an environmental writer and journalist—and he *knows* Mexico. Ron is an expert on Latin American ecotravel and environmental business. His articles have appeared in *Transitions Abroad, Forbes, The News* (Mexico's English language daily newspaper), and many other publications in the United States and Mexico. He also publishes a newsletter on environmental issues, *El Planeta Plática*, and hosts his own web site, *Eco Travels in Latin America* (http://www.planeta.com)

Ron grew up in America's heartland: Fort Wayne, Indiana. He began his career writing screenplays but soon discovered a passion for Latin America and vowed to learn as much as he could about the region.

"In the United States," says Ron, "Latin America appears on the news only when there is a crisis—what journalists call 'coups and earthquakes' coverage. That's a lousy way to treat a neighbor! Plus it does not guide readers in understanding critical issues in those countries."

Ron spends much of the year living in Mexico City. He travels extensively and is happy to bring readers his secrets about the best places to visit and the most interesting things to do, from snorkeling the Great Maya Reef to swimming in the lagoons of Cuatro Ciénegas.

Ron is the co-author (with James D. Gollin) of *Honduras: Adventures in Nature* (also from John Muir Publications). When not writing, Ron enjoys painting and photography.

Cater to Your Interests on Your Next Vacation

**The 100 Best Small Art Towns in America
3rd edition**
Discover Creative Communities, Fresh Air, and
Affordable Living
U.S. $16.95, Canada $24.95

**The Big Book of Adventure Travel
2nd edition**
Profiles more than 400 great escapes to all corners
of the world
U.S. $17.95, Canada $25.50

Cross-Country Ski Vacations
A Guide to the Best Resorts, Lodges, and Groomed
Trails in North America
U.S. $15.95, Canada $22.50

Gene Kilgore's Ranch Vacations, 4th edition
The Complete Guide to Guest Resorts, Fly-Fishing,
and Cross-Country Skiing Ranches
U.S. $22.95, Canada $32.50

Indian America, 4th edition
A traveler's companion to more than 300 Indian
tribes in the United States
U.S. $18.95, Canada $26.75

Saddle Up!
A Guide to Planning the Perfect Horseback Vacation
U.S. $14.95, Canada $20.95

Watch It Made in the U.S.A., 2nd edition
A Visitor's Guide to the Companies That Make Your
Favorite Products
U.S. $17.95, Canada $25.50

The World Awaits
A Comprehensive Guide to Extended Backpack
Travel
U.S. $16.95, Canada $23.95

**JMP travel guides are available
at your favorite bookstores.
For a FREE catalog or to place a
mail order, call: 800-888-7504.**

John Muir Publications ◆ P.O. Box 613 ◆ Santa Fe, NM 87504